HEAVY WEATHER SAILING

Frontispiece. *Cohoe III* at the start of the Fastnet Race 1957. *Photo: Gabor Denes*

HEAVY WEATHER
SAILING

by

K. ADLARD COLES

JOHN DE GRAFF, INC.
Clinton Corners, N.Y.

First published in Great Britain 1967
First published in U.S.A. 1968
©K. Adlard Coles 1967, 1975
Library of Congress Card Number: 68-26061
ISBN: 8286-0067-8
Reprinted 1969
Reprinted 1970
Reprinted 1971
Reprinted 1972
Revised and Enlarged Edition, 1975
Reprinted 1976

Printed in U.S.A.

John de Graff, Inc.
Clinton Corners, N.Y. 12514

To my wife and to the crews who have shared these experiences

ACKNOWLEDGEMENTS

This book could not have been completed properly without the help of many other yachtsmen. For particulars of the Channel Storm of 1956 I am indebted to the Committee of the Royal Ocean Racing Club and to the Editor of *Yachting World*, who sent out the questionnaire on which the report is partly based. I also thank Mr. F. Cartwright for the information he gave me, and I am most grateful to Mrs. O'Sullivan for particulars of the loss of *Dancing Ledge*, sent to me so that the information may be of service to others. I thank Sir Ernest Harston and the Editor of *The Yachtsman* for the extract from an article which appears under *Thunderstorm in the Bay* in Chapter 4. For the painful task of reading and commenting on the typescript (untidy and almost illegible through corrections in my own handwriting), I am grateful to Mr. Paul Spens and Mr. Alasdair Garrett, who was also kind enough to write the Foreword.

To yachtsmen on the other side of the Atlantic I am indebted for contributions on great storms and other experiences which widen the scope of this book. Mr. Warren Brown has contributed *September Hurricane*, besides giving me considerable help on the subject of heavy weather generally. I am indebted to Mr. Joe C. Byars for *Twice Rolled Over*; to Mr. William H. Mathers for his account of *Pendragon* in Hurricane *Carol*; to Mr. Edward R. Greeff for *Mediterranean Mistral* and other American yachtsmen who have helped. Much of my knowledge of the other side of the pond comes from reading *Yachting* and I must add my thanks to Mr. Critchell Rimington, Mr. William W. Robinson and the late Mr. Alfred F. Loomis, whom I first met in 1950 and after many Fastnet Races later. All of these kind helpers have been most generous.

Turning to the technical side of this book, I must explain that I am not a meteorologist nor am I an oceanographer. Captain C. Stewart, who is an extra master and is engaged on hydraulic and wave research, has contributed the appendix on *Wave Theory and Facts*. In addition to this he has given patient research into the storm north of Bermuda and the synoptic charts and maps have been drawn by his wife under his supervision. Mr. L. Draper, of the Institute of Oceanographic Sciences has written the appendix on *Freak Waves*, which are the principal cause of knockdowns, pitch poling and damage to yachts. Mr. Alan Watts has contributed the *Meteorology of Depressions* which links with the experiences described in this book and has added information on my analyses of gales. The synoptic charts have been prepared from information provided by the Meteorological Office and are based on Crown Copyright. They are reproduced by permission of H.M. Stationery Office, except those in chapters 7, 15, 18, and 19 for which I am indebted to the Climatic Information Section, National Weather Records Center, Asheville, North Carolina, U.S.A. I thank both authorities for their help.

I also wish to thank the Editors of the British yachting magazines: *Yachting World* and Mr. J. A. N. Tanner for the synoptic charts covering the Santander Storm of 1949 and the Fastnet Race of 1957, *Yachting Monthly* in which Mr. F. Cartwright's account of the Channel Storm of 1956 first appeared, and *The Yachtsman* and *Motor Boat and Yachting* in which many of my own logs have been published. The photographs other than my own are separately acknowledged to Messrs. Beken & Son of Cowes, Mr. Morris Rosenfeld, Capt. Th. D. A. de Lange and Mr. Jan Hahn, editor of *Oceanus*, who has also advised me on other matters. The picture of the schooner *Curlew* in the Atlantic Storm was taken from U.S.S. *Compass Island*, and the account of *Curlew*'s experiences appeared in *Yachting*.

Bibliography

Alone through the Roaring Forties, Vito Dumas. Adlard Coles Ltd.
Deep Sea Sailing, by Erroll Bruce. Stanley Paul Ltd.
Heavy Weather Guide, by Captains Ewin T. Harding and S. Kotsch, U.S. Navy United States Naval Institute.
Once is Enough, by Miles Smeeton. Rupert Hart-Davis Ltd.
Royal Cruising Club Journal 1961. Royal Cruising Club.
Royal Cruising Club Journal 1966. Royal Cruising Club.
To the Great Southern Sea, by W. A. Robinson. Peter Davies Ltd.
Vertue XXXV, by Humphrey Barton. Adlard Coles Ltd.
Yacht and Sea, by Gustav Plym. Adlard Coles Ltd.

CONTENTS

CONTENTS

LIST OF PLATES

LIST OF PLATES

MAPS AND DIAGRAMS

ALASDAIR GARRETT
Editor of the Journal of the Royal Cruising Club

FOREWORD

'Any fool can carry sail on a ship—" burst out the master, indignant at the officer of the watch failing to order sail to be shortened. But the words were spoken a century ago in the Golden Age of seafaring before mechanical propulsion drove sail from the face of the great oceans. Indeed, the shipmaster often found himself between the devil and the deep blue sea. On the one hand, his owners expected as fast a passage as the ship was capable of; on the other, a voyage account which included a long list of items of heavy weather damage—spars, sails and cordage carried away—was likely to incur the owners' displeasure and they were often not slow to make the master aware of it. Yet one cannot fail to draw inspiration from their achievements in an age when radio, weather forecasts and all the other aids to the safe conduct of a vessel of today were unknown. Of course, the sea exacted its toll and there were casualties. Ships were posted overdue and later, after weeks of anxiety, as lost without trace. All too often the reason for their being overwhelmed remained a matter for conjecture.

The middle decades of the present century have seen the regeneration of sail and its reappearance on the oceans is now commonplace. The great square-rigger of yesterday with its towering masts and spread of canvas and a ship's company of two score men or more has given way to tiny vessels, some with less canvas than would make a belltent and manned by only four or five souls and often fewer. Although for the most part they are amateur sailors, they are the living heirs to a noble tradition of sail, and it therefore behoves them to acquire the skills of a seaman in order to be worthy of their inheritance. It is true that science and the ingenuity of man have made great advances. Our knowledge of the behaviour patterns of wind and sea has increased immeasurably and with it the means of placing this knowledge at the disposal of the seafarer a thousand miles or more from the land. But still the might of wind and sea remains unsubdued, ready to exact a toll of those who treat them lightly.

Indeed, the sea demands definite qualities in the seafarer—certain attitudes of mind and character. Humility, prudence and a recognition that there is no end to learning and to the acquisition of experience. Humility I put first, for who would dare be other than humble in the presence of two great elements—of sea and sky and all the uncertainties which they hold for us? Prudence comes second—it is the ingrained characteristic of the professional seaman—and I would define it as the ability to distinguish between the risk which can reasonably be accepted having regard to prevailing conditions and the risk which must be rejected as unacceptable. Lastly, learn by your own experience and by the experience of others, for there is never an end to your learning. When some months ago my friend, Adlard Coles, disclosed to me that he was engaged upon a book about heavy weather sailing, my interest was immediately aroused, for few sailing men today have had as much experience as he of the handling of small sailing vessels in heavy weather. The book is proof of an excellent pudding and I would go further and say that it is a valuable contribution to sailing lore. It should be studied by everyone who puts to sea in a small sailing boat. Indeed, the book offers a splendid opportunity to increase your knowledge and experience and so to equip yourself to face the onset of your first gale at sea with some measure of confidence. And even if you count yourself a man of experience in these conditions, consider your own experiences in the light of those related in this book. In making the comparison, it is likely that you will be the gainer.

Last autumn I had some correspondence with Bernard Moitessier, who earlier in the year had completed a voyage from Moorea to Alicante by way of Cape Horn—a voyage of 14,216 miles in 126 days without any intermediate port of call. This was a most remarkable achievement. Moitessier explained to me the reasons which led him to select this route, but what really impressed me was the very thorough researches which he made into all the literature available about high latitudes in the South Pacific and the handling of boats in the conditions to be anticipated in those waters. Here, then, was a seaman of considerable experience demonstrating the attitude to which reference has been made—a willingness to learn from the experience of others even though these were only available through the medium of the written word. Later he described running before a severe gale which lasted six days with hurricane force gusts. Warps had been streamed astern and Moitessier found the vessel somewhat sluggish on the helm. He felt great anxiety that he might be pitch-poled by one of the enormous greybeards which carried the boat forward at great speed, the rush of water completely engulfing the hull so that only the masts were visible. Of a sudden, he wrote, he appreciated the wisdom of Dumas's technique of running free and taking the following seas at a slight angle. Immediately he cut his warps adrift and the vessel, becoming responsive to her helm, could be handled with safety. Moitessier makes it clear that he owed the survival of his wife, himself and the yacht to this decision—*to knowledge gained by reading*.

The narrative chapters in this book are fascinating and the author's conclusions are put forward boldly and clearly. Few will venture to disagree with them, but in shades of emphasis I like to think that they will be the subject of discussion and comparison among sailing men. Let me quote the words of an uncommonly articulate and experienced seaman of yesterday:

"Like all true art, the general conduct of a ship and her handling in particular cases had a technique which could be discussed with delight and pleasure by men who found in their work, not bread alone, but an outlet for the peculiarities of their temperament. To get the best and truest effect from the infinitely varying moods of sky and sea, not pictorially, but in the spirit of their calling, was their vocation, one and all; and they recognized this with as much sincerity, and drew as much inspiration from this reality, as any man who ever put brush to canvas. The diversity of temperaments was immense amongst those masters of the fine art."

These words were written of the shipmasters of the Golden Age—they are still true today and apply as well to the professional masters of the enormous mechanical monsters of our day and age as they do to the yachtmasters of sea-going small craft. And here let me, as a sailing man, pay brief tribute to our professional brethren—they have a fund of knowledge and experience which only a fool would disdain. For years I was engaged in the management of merchant shipping and became closely associated with many shipmasters. It always gave me the liveliest pleasure to listen to their discussions of the problems of ship-handling—there was so much to be learned from them and from the professional seaman's attitude of mind—the coveted quality of prudence, as I have defined it, which is the hall-mark of the true mariner.

For myself, although I have been at sea on several occasions in a hard blow, I am no collector of gales. I have experienced moments of anxiety—of being laid over on my beam ends, of seeing a topmast go by the board and a headsail burst with a crack like a cannon-shot and reduced in a second to a few wisps of tattered canvas—but all this is nothing to the rich harvest of experience contained between the covers of this book, and I believe that if one can absorb this fund of knowledge and learn to apply it, one may at length be able to say, like Conrad: 'Well, I have loved, lived with, and left the sea without ever seeing a ship's tall fabric of sticks, cobwebs, and gossamer go by the board.' And for many of us that, too, may be sheer luck.

The Royal Cruising Club
April 1967

© Alasdair Garrett, April 1967

PREFACE

By heavy weather I refer in this book to fresh winds of 17–21 knots (Force 5), strong winds of 22–33 knots (Force 6 and 7) and gales of 34–40 knots (Force 8) and sometimes over.

It is the gales that provide the big-game shooting of cruising and ocean racing in yachts. They provide a bit of line-shooting, too, for they add to sailing the element of risk that marks the difference between a pastime and a sport.

Gales are rarely pleasant experiences, except for the sense of exhilaration in their early stages, and of elation when they have passed. The intermediate part is often one of anxiety and tiredness, but, whether one likes it or not, heavy weather at some time or another is the lot of most of us, whether cruising or ocean racing.

I suppose that I can claim to have experienced a fair ration of hard weather, as I made my first long-distance cruise as far back as 1923. Since then, mostly with my wife or family, we have cruised along a large part of the coast of Europe from Spain in the south, Ireland in the west and north-eastward to Finland and Russia in the far Baltic. After the Second World War I started ocean racing, which took me on Bay of Biscay and Fastnet Races and farther afield in the Bermuda and Transatlantic events, and I was involved in most of the heavy weather R.O.R.C. races over a period of 20 years.

From these experiences I have made a selection of gales, or near gales, from which something useful was learnt. The early ones make more colourful reading because they occurred in my apprenticeship to heavy weather sailing. It would be wrong to leave them out, because they illustrate the fact that gales appear more serious when one is not so accustomed to them, especially if the boat is sailed short-handed, as is normally the case when family cruising.

My later experiences were gained in ocean racing. This provides a good school in which to acquire knowledge of heavy weather sailing, as the races are started and continued regardless of weather conditions. Hence one gets "caught out" more often than would otherwise be the case, and one also learns how much punishment a yacht and her crew can stand up to. Where a number of yachts are involved in gales it is possible to compare experiences with one's fellow-competitors which, together with anemometer readings and meteorological reports, enable fair assessments of the weather to be arrived at.

With some exceptions, the heavy weather experiences which I record are limited to the "common or garden" varieties of gales, associated with the normal depressions or troughs passing through, which are the occasional lot of the ordinary amateur sailor. In order to broaden the picture I have added major gales met with by other yachtsmen. In Chapter 11, for example, I record the experiences gained when the ocean-racing fleet was caught out in a Force 10 storm in the English Channel. Many valuable lessons were learnt from the report prepared on this by a special committee appointed by the Royal Ocean Racing Club. For a similar gale in ocean racing on the other side of the Atlantic, I refer in Chapter 14 to the experiences of the American yachts in a Bermuda Race gale. From gales I lead up to survival storms and hurricanes of a severity exceeding my own experiences, but which have to be reckoned with as possibilities on the western side of the Atlantic and elsewhere.

The method which I have adopted is to give a description of each gale, followed by observations and conclusions drawn from it. These express my own views, but Mr. Alan Watts (who is both a meteorologist and a yachtman and is the author of *Wind and Sailing Boats*) has contributed a chapter on the Meteorology of Depressions. In this he reviews some of the principal gales and the meteorological conditions causing them. In particular his analysis of the Channel Storm of 1956 will be found most informative. The interesting appendices on *Wave Theory and Fact* by Captain C. Stewart, Extra Master, and *Freak Waves* by Mr. L. Draper, M.Sc., throw a more scientific light on many occurrences described earlier in the book.

Most of the photographs are my own. They were taken in following winds of about 30 to 35 knots, Force 7 to 8 on the Beaufort Scale, gusting perhaps 40 to 50 knots. I have found it impossible to obtain pictures of the sea when going to windward in rough weather because of the spray, and, as it chanced, most of the major gales I have experienced occurred at night or in appalling visibility, so no photography was possible. Nevertheless, although unimpressive, the pictures are at least practical in illustrating the kind of seas to be expected in ordinary gales or near gales. To these I have added photographs from other sources of seas which are not ordinary, and of which you and I would prefer to have no experience.

An unexpected sidelight thrown by this book reveals the remarkable developments in the efficiency of the modern small yacht in her equipment and in her sea-going ability. More and more circumnavigations and long voyages are being accomplished by smaller and smaller yachts. Passages across the Atlantic have become almost a commonplace. Even the extremes of heavy weather of the Roaring Forties and Cape Horn have been sought by adventurous single-handlers such as the late Sir Francis Chichester, Sir Alec Rose and others.

Parallel with the development in small yacht voyaging, historic changes have occurred during the period covered by this book and in the attitude towards small yachts in ocean racing. It was in 1949 that for the first time a small Class III yacht carried on beating to windward throughout a severe gale without heaving-to. In 1950 small yachts were admitted for the first time in a trans-atlantic race organized by the Royal Ocean Racing Club, but it was not until 1954 that they were accepted, albeit rather reluctantly, in the Fastnet Race.

Six years later the Royal Western Yacht Club sponsored the start of the first east to west single-handed transatlantic race. In 1963 the windward perform-ance of three small yachts during a short spell of heavy weather in the Fastnet Race confirmed the R.O.R.C. in its conclusion that in the last quarter of a century the small yacht had improved her efficiency more than the big one. The time allowances in the handicapping system were altered to help the larger yachts, marking the first change in the time scale since its introduction in 1926. The alteration may be said to have been rather a back-handed compliment, but it marked an epoch in the evolution of the small yacht, hitherto regarded as inferior to larger in heavy weather.

SECOND EDITION 1975

Since this book was first published the most important innovation has been the introduction of the IOR (International Offshore Rule) so that yachts of dif-ferent countries can race under the same system of rating and regulations. This has greatly widened the scope and interest in international ocean racing and has had a profound effect on offshore yacht design and performance, incorporating features which had been developing over previous years. The rule has also had a considerable influence on cruising yacht design.

In this new edition I have made a number of modifications to bring the book up to date and to meet what may be termed the scientific age of sailing. Laurence Draper has revised Appendix 2 on *Freak Waves* in the light of recent research into the maximum height of waves and two chapters have been added: *Multihulls in Heavy Weather* by Michael Henderson, and *Motor Craft in Heavy Weather* by Peter Haward, both experts in their subjects. The disaster of *Morning Cloud* has been added as a late appendix as it occurred in home waters and much is to be learned from it. However, on the general principles of heavy weather sailing I have found little that I wish to alter.

WIND AND WAVE

Opinions on wind strengths vary greatly according to the experience of the observer. Judgement is also influenced by psychological reasons. For example, bad weather and heavy seas appear much worse when viewed from the deck of a 4-tonner than they do from a larger yacht. A man and his wife cruising alone will find a gale more impressive than it is for a tough crew of five or six men in an ocean racer—for apart from anything else, a light crew will tire more easily. Finally, everybody is influenced by the particular weather conditions. If the wind is Force 6, 7 or 8, but the weather is clear and sunny, its strength is often underestimated, especially when running downwind. On the other hand, if the gale is in its early stages with driving rain, bad visibility and ragged clouds chasing across the sombre sky, there will be a tendency to exaggerate the wind force, particularly if the crew is exhausted or seasick or if the yacht has been allowed to get out of order, with ropes adrift on deck and the disorder of mis-placed articles and unwashed dishes below.

Even experienced owners make errors of judgement, because it is impossible to estimate with any exactitude how high is the force of the wind. A skipper may be able to assess Force 5, Force 6, and even Force 7 from experience, and in relation to the amount of sail his boat can carry, but sustained winds of a genuine Force 8 and over are so rare that he may have to think back several years to find anything as a yardstick for comparison. To put it bluntly, dogmatic statements of high wind forces are pure guesswork, unless confirmed by a masthead anemometer, with the appropriate adjustments between apparent and true wind or by the Meteorological Office.

A number of gales recorded in this book were major gales which made headlines in the newspapers at the time, but I am afraid the reader looking for big game in the way of wind forces will be disappointed at the low figures which I give. The reason why yachtsmen and yachting authors often overstate wind forces is that they are impressed by the gusts more than the lulls which result in a lower average velocity. Alan Watts tells me there is a scientific reason for this, because a lull (a transitory and sudden lack of wind speed) where the wind drops, say, to 10 knots for 1 second will travel some 32 ft. (the same length as many small yachts) when the mean wind is 36 knots. Thus a lull will be felt only for a brief instant and not last long enough appreciably to reduce the yacht's angle of heel before the wind rises again. A lull may thus not be noticed at all, because it passes too quickly.

On the other hand, as the air pressure varies as the square of the velocity a 40-knot gust of the same duration as the lull cannot fail to be observed as it delivers sixteen times more heeling punch. Thus it is natural for the yachtsman to be most influenced by the gusts and squalls. It is these that make the impacts on the boat and which masts and sails have to stand up to. A gust of 64 knots or over can dismast a yacht or knock her down flat on her beam ends as effectively in a few seconds as in a prolonged blow. In fact, a wind of mean Force 6 accompanied by violent gusts and squalls is more dangerous to yachts and dinghies than a relatively steady Force 7. Gusty winds create far worse seas than steady gale-force winds do, and often are the cause of abnormal seas, particularly when accompanied by a shift of wind as a cold front goes through. It is thus sensible to describe a bout of heavy weather as say, "a gale gusting up to 50 knots", but it may be entirely misleading to call it a "Force 10 gale", because the force on the Beaufort notation is lower, as it is the *mean* and not the *maximum* force. In a genuine storm of Force 10 on the Beaufort notation the gusts might well be up to the 64 knots which, if sustained, would be hurricane force.

However, Alan Watts in his book *Wind and Sailing Boats*, considers that a fairer estimate of the strength of the wind as experienced by a yacht is what he terms "the yachts' mean wind", which is the average of the mean speed on the Beaufort notation and the mean velocity of the gusts. He tells me that in his opinion, because of the relatively small size of yachts compared with ships, a "yachtsman's gale" could be defined as wind of mean speed of 25–30 knots gusting regularly (i.e. every few minutes) up to 40 knots.

Nevertheless, in this book I prefer to express the wind forces at their *mean* velocities on the Beaufort notation. This scale is the official one which is used by the Meteorological Office, both for its weather forecasts and by shipping generally. And it must be remembered that ocean-racing and ocean-voyaging yachts experience precisely the same winds as larger ships. My estimates are based on long experience coupled with considerable research, aided by the Meteorological Office in digging out records as far back as 1925.

One difficulty which I found in the assessment of wind force is that gales are rarely uniform in character and are often very localized. For this reason, a yacht can meet exceptional local weather conditions and severe storms that are missed by other yachts in her vicinity, perhaps only 30 or fewer miles distant. This was particularly evident in the Channel Storm of 1956 in which the boats involved experienced widely different conditions of wind and sea. The reasons for this are explained in Alan Watts's analysis of the storm in Chapter 21.

The height of waves is another thing which is often overstated by yachtsmen and indeed sometimes by professionals. Yachtsmen usually measure the height of big seas in relation to the known height of the mast, maybe half, two-thirds, or masthead. This can be checked independently by the crew, and the average will give an honest expression of opinion. However, when the estimate is compared with the sea disturbance scale, taking into account wind force, duration, and fetch, it will be found that the height of the waves cannot possibly be what they appear. I take the real height of a wave to be three-fifths the measured height, but I have reluctantly come to the conclusion that this estimate is on the high side and that the real height is probably only about half the apparent height. I cannot explain why this is so, but oceanographers state that it is impossible to judge the height of waves just by eye. It is a matter of optics.

While I can to a great extent prove or disprove wind forces with the aid of Meteorological Office statistics, or of recent years by masthead anemometer, I cannot provide any evidence on the height of waves. I have therefore, with few exceptions, omitted estimates of height, as it is as upsetting to the yachtsman to question his big wave as it is to question a fisherman's big fish. I have sometimes seen waves in a Force 7 or 8 gale reported at 40 ft. Waves of 35 to 40 ft. may be encountered in a West Indian hurricane, but not as a rule, I am thankful to say, in an ordinary gale.

On the other hand, there are occasional abnormal waves which attain a height far in excess of the normal run of the seas. Such waves can attain heights as much as 100 ft. in violent ocean storms, and, as I shall show, the same phenomena can occur on a lesser scale even in near gales as low as Force 6 and Force 7. In this book I call such seas "freak" waves. The pedantic will say that they are not "freak" waves, because there is a scientific explanation for them—see Appendices 1 and 2. However, in the absence of a better term I use the word "freak" and I would point out that Mr. Draper does the same in the appendix he has contributed. What is good enough for an oceanographer is good enough for an amateur like me. I describe waves as freaks when they are abnormal in height, size or shape, whether caused by synchronization or crossing of different wave trains, or by wind shifts, frontal squalls, tidal streams, currents, shoals or several of these factors combined.

While on the subject of waves, I should add that to the oceanographer a wave is a wave, but to the seaman, a wave is a sea. As I am neither fish nor fowl, I use the word which seems most appropriate in the context of what I am writing.

Finally, the following definitions may be useful:

Observations at Shore Stations. The mean wind force as recorded by a station ashore is taken at the average *over the past hour*, during which a higher force may have been attained for part of the time. The wind as recorded by a station ashore is not necessarily representative of conditions over the open sea. The wind over the sea is generally stronger than on the coast, where the speed is likely to be diminished by friction and turbulence. This is explained by Alan Watts in Chapter 21 on the Meteorology of Depressions.

Gusts. A gust is a brief increase in wind speed, in contrast to a squall, which may last ten minutes or more. The wind speeds of gusts quoted in newspapers are issued by the Meteorological Office in statute miles per hour. For maritime purposes, the velocity of gusts is expressed in knots. A gust should not be graded as a Force of the mean wind on the Beaufort notation, because it is only momentary, but for purposes of comparison in this book gusts are sometimes described as at the equivalent wind force. For example, if it is gusting at 60 knots it is sometimes convenient to describe it as gusting Force 11 to afford comparison with the mean speed force of say, Force 8 or 9. The gustiness factor over the land may range from 25 per cent to 100 per cent above the Beaufort force. Gustiness (but not squalliness,) over the sea is far less than over the land.

Squalls. A squall has been defined as a sudden increase of wind speed by at least 16 knots, the speed rising to 22 knots or more and lasting for at least one minute. When the Beaufort notation is used, squalls would be reported as a sudden increase in wind speed by at least three stages of the Beaufort notation, the speed rising to Force 6 or more, and lasting for not less than one minute. The difference between a gust and a squall is therefore a matter of duration. A squall lasts much longer and may include many gusts.

Gales. A gale is a sustained mean wind of 34–40 knots, which is Force 8 on the Beaufort notation. Gale warnings are issued only when winds of Force 8 or gusts reaching 43 knots (momentarily equivalent to Force 9) are expected. They are issued if there is a possibility of winds rising to gale force, even for only *ten minutes.* On the other hand, warnings are not circulated where the gusts are likely to occur only locally, with thunderstorms or with squalls in cold front as temporary phenomena. The gales do not always mature and it does not follow that because a yacht has sailed in a sea area for which a warning has been issued she will have encountered Force 8 winds. On the contrary gale warnings are a commonplace, but gales in the sense used in this book, with a mean of Force 8 sustained for an hour or more, are rare. The term "severe gale" implies winds of Force 9 or above, and "storm" means Force 10 or above. The term "imminent" implies arrival of the gale within six hours of the time of issue: "soon" implies between six and twelve hours; "later" implies arrival in more than twelve hours.

Terminology for gales is as follows:

	British	American
28–33 knots	Near gale	Moderate gale
34–40 knots	gale	Fresh gale
41–47 knots	Strong gale	Strong gale
48–55 knots	Storm	Whole gale

Extratropical cyclones (extratropical low, extratropical storm) Any cyclonic-scale storm that is not a tropical cyclone, usually referred to the migratory frontal cyclones of middle and high latitudes.

Tropical cyclone. A cyclone that originates over the tropical oceans. At maturity winds exceeding 175 knots (200 m.p.h.) have been measured and rains are torrential.

m.p.h. and knots. Wind velocities are usually expressed in m.p.h. over the land and in newspaper reports, or in knots at sea. Many of the figures I have received have been given in m.p.h., which means statute miles per hour. In order to be consistent I have converted these throughout this book to knots, nautical miles per hour.

Barometric pressures. Likewise, for the sake of consistency, I have given barometer readings in millibars, though inches are still commonly used and my own barometers were graduated in inches up to about 1960.

Time. In the accounts of gales occuring in the North Sea, English Channel and the Bay of Biscay I have used summer time where appropriate, but the synoptic charts reproduced are at Greenwich mean time. An hour should be added to G.M.T. to reconcile them with the summer time as logged. In the Atlantic Bermuda time is given in Chapter 7 both for text and the chart; in Chapter 8 ship's time in text, G.M.T. on chart; in Chapters 15, 18 and 19 Eastern Standard time.

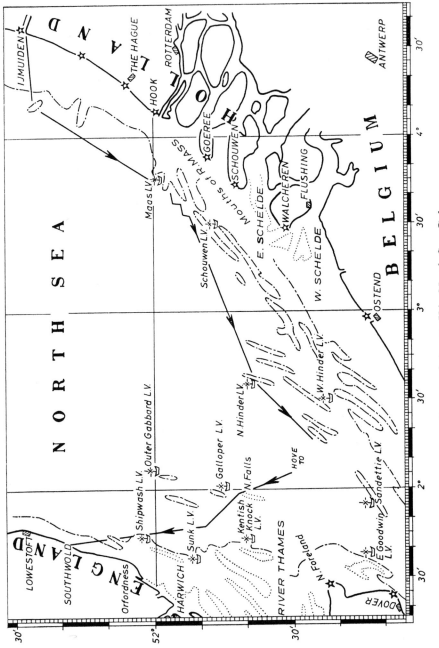

1 Course of *Annette II* in North Sea Gale.

NORTH SEA GALE

The first occasions on which I got properly "caught out" in gales occurred in 1925. That is not to say that I had no previous experience of gales, for in 1923 I had made a long cruise with two undergraduate friends in my 7-tonner *Annette* to the Baltic. It happened to be a year of particularly bad weather, and as a result we experienced a number of gales in which we broke the boom, parted a shroud, pulled out the bobstay, sprang the mast and suffered much minor damage. But all this occurred near coastal waters and we were never caught in the open sea beyond reach of harbour.

In 1925 my wife and I bought a 12-ton gaff ketch at Riga, which we renamed *Annette II*. She was a heavy double-ender of Scandinavian design measuring 29 ft. 7 in. overall and no less than 11 ft. 4 in. in beam. The draft was 3 ft. 9 in., or 7 ft. 9 in. with the centreboard down, and the sail area was 430 sq. ft. She was fitted with a hot-bulb semi-diesel engine, which I could rarely get to work. Everything about this yacht was heavy and solid. She seemed huge after the first *Annette*, which was of light displacement and only 19 ft. on the waterline.

My wife and I had a wonderful cruise in *Annette II*, sailing from the strange historic port of Riga to Gotland and Öland, and then to Sweden and Denmark, before passing through the Kiel Canal to the North Sea, and westwards past the Frisian islands to Ymuiden in Holland.

We had a fair amount of bad weather during the cruise and were hove-to west of Öland Rev lightvessel in a gale, but it only lasted about six hours. The real gale was reserved for the last lap of the voyage, when at dawn on 18 September 1925 *Annette II* sailed out of Ymuiden on the sandy coast of Holland bound for Dover. Her staysail, mainsail and mizzen were set close-hauled to a light southerly breeze and she could just lay a little south of west. The yacht sailed steadily seawards over the grey waves, the Dutch coast gradually fading to a pencilled line, until it was finally lost as the distance increased and the hands of the cabin clock marked the passing hours.

During the morning the wind backed and freshened. Occasionally spray whipped across the deck and tumbled along the lee scuppers before running back into the sea. The backing wind, an ominous sign, had the merit of enabling the course to be altered to the south towards the Maas lightvessel, and progress was good.

At sunset *Annette II* passed the lightvessel, some fifteen miles WSW. of the

29

Hook of Holland, leaving her a few miles to the eastward. The evening meal was prepared and eaten, and by the time the crockery had been washed and stowed away night was upon us. The wind moderated and headed and the tide was foul for six hours, so, although the yacht sailed well throughout the night, she failed to bring the Schouwen lightship abeam by morning.

Despite the light wind and sea it had been by no means an idle night, for we had to keep a vigilant watch as we sailed through a fleet of fishing boats and from time to time ships crossed our course; so for much of the night both of us were on deck. The yacht's navigation lights were inefficient, but I had bought two hurricane lamps at Ymuiden, one with red glass and the other green, which were kept in the cockpit and shown as required.

At dawn (19 September) my wife was at the helm and it was my turn on watch. I have never shared a poet's love of the dawn at sea. It is then that the long sleepless hours make themselves felt. The dawn is grey, the sea is grey. It is cold and it is damp and one gets hungry.

Annette II was just ploughing over a waste of empty sea, for the low Dutch islands were far below the horizon. The glass was falling steadily and the wind was freshening again. We had no wireless and, therefore, no weather forecasts, but the conditions were a warning in themselves. The only cheerful prospect was that the wind had backed so we could lay the course and were making fine progress with a fair tide.

Throughout the morning *Annette II* sailed in a welter of foam on her course for the North Hinder lightvessel. After lunch I began to feel anxious, as we had failed to sight the lightship, when happily a spidery red form was vaguely discerned in the distance ahead. I had made the common mistake of overestimating the distance made good. We passed close to the lightship just before 1500, and her crew turned out to greet us. I had no time to respond to their friendly hails, for a squall struck us and I was busy reefing the mainsail and setting the storm jib.

By then it was blowing half a gale and the barometer had fallen no less than 20 millibars since early morning. From the yacht's position the Sandettie lightship lay about 30 miles to the south. The distance from the Sandettie to Dover is only a matter of another 20, so we determined to carry on and get to Dover or another port on the English side of the North Sea.

On we sailed, the wind continued to harden all the time. The wind had backed to a little east of south, and with shoals off the coast of Belgium little over 20 miles to windward the seas, although rough, were not high. The hours slipped by as *Annette II* held on her course, and the glass continued to fall. It dropped another 7 millibars, making a total fall of 27 millibars.

Towards sunset *Annette II* was more than half-way from the North Hinder to the Sandettie lightship. The sun was low and fiercely yellow, and gradually a great bank of purple cloud spread across the sky, covering the whole horizon to the southward. The sun became hidden behind the cloud as it advanced, but a wan light lit up the white-capped sea.

Then it arrived. The first squall was on us. The seas were obscured in the whiteness of pelting rain, and there was a sizzling noise. The yacht heeled far over, the wind whistled in the rigging with every sail, every stay and sheet hardened under the strain. The seas leapt short, steep and breaking. One came aboard heavily and broke over the cabin top and cascaded off to leeward. The yacht was hard pressed with her lee rail under in spite of her tremendous beam, and I let the mainsheet fly. That eased her, and I sheeted the storm jib to weather and belayed it. I sheeted in the reefed main and mizzen hard and with the helm lashed slightly down the yacht lay hove-to on the port tack.

For a while I sat in the steering well. The force of the wind was stunning. The rain was torrential, ironing out the breaking seas with its pelting drops, leaving only the deep furrows. The squall was accompanied by thunder and lightning.

Annette II lay hove-to very well. The heavy oak hatch to the companionway was closed, and the dinghy was well secured on the foredeck by four lashings. The yacht seemed safe enough, but she might have been better without the mainsail, though I did not lower it. With the onslaught of the gale the wind veered to the south-west, at once dispelling any hope of fetching to Dover. The yacht was slowly drifting towards the middle of the North Sea. There was no danger in that direction for many hours to come, but if the wind veered to west or north-west the Belgian shoals and coast would be under the lee.

There was nothing to be done. Seizing my chance between the seas, I opened the hatch and slipped into the warm interior of the cabin. In the meantime my wife had been busy with the lamps, filling and trimming them: white, red and green. She jammed them between the cabin table and a bunk, where they were ready for use. She had also prepared malted milk, and this, together with some dry biscuits, formed our evening meal.

Night was soon upon us. There was nothing to do but lie as best we could in our bunks. We took watches in turn to open the hatch and look out for the lights of approaching ships and to see that all was well. Down below in the cabin it was wretched. The atmosphere was close and damp, for leaks had developed in the deck and round the coachroof and there was condensation everywhere. The ceaseless hammering and shaking as the seas struck the boat were wearying, and as the sea rose we had to use continual effort to prevent ourselves being thrown out of our bunks. We were both very wet, as the violent rain and spray had penetrated our oilskins, so that when we went below the wet clothes gave a feeling of clammy dampness. Neither of us slept, but we dozed a little from time to time.

When one or other of us went on deck we occasionally saw the lights of steamers sufficiently close to warrant exhibiting one or other of the flickering hurricane lamps. On deck the scene was impressive in the extreme. The seas were black, but their formation was outlined by the gleam of the breaking crests. They came in sinister procession. The bows of the boat would rise to meet one, then down it would fall on the sloping mass of water into the trough, before rising again in time to climb the next. Sometimes the top of a sea would break aboard green and fall with a thud on the top of the cabin roof to stream aft in a cascade of water over the closed companion doors into the cockpit.

There was tremendous noise: the wind in the mast and rigging, the hiss of advancing breakers and the splash of running water. Above all raged a non-stop thrumming and vibration in the rigging. I believe the sea steadily increased, for the motion became worse and worse. Two of the lamps got smashed, but it did not matter much, as they flickered so much when exposed to the wind that there was little chance of them being seen. Moreover, we grew lethargic and our visits to the deck became less and less frequent; we were quite game to accept the chance of one in a thousand of being run down.

The position was wild in the extreme: we were hove-to in the night of a severe gale, surrounded at a distance of about 20 miles, except to the north, by a broken circle of shoals, on which the seas would break heavily. We were absolutely in the hands of chance. At the time we were profoundly miserable. We just lay in our bunks only half asleep. The position was not imminently dangerous so long as the wind did not shift to the west.

The night went by steadily, time passing neither slowly nor quickly. The hours went by until the moment arrived when in the dark cabin one could discern the outline of the porthole against the dim light of approaching day. We had only a vague idea of our position and my wife very appropriately suggested that I should go on deck again while it was still dark to see whether the lights of any lightships were in sight. On my reckoning there was little prospect of this, and I remained as I was for a few minutes before summoning energy to do my wife's bidding. Then I climbed out and stepped up into the cockpit. It was bitterly cold on deck and a big sea was running, but the wind was less vicious. It was still dark and, to my surprise, I saw at intervals the loom of several flashing lights reflected in the sky to the west. There must have been a clearance in the visibility. My wife's intuition was right. Then, suddenly, away on the starboard beam I saw distinctly the glow of a distant red light. It disappeared. It came again. A long interval and there it was again!

I had been anxious about our position, but in a few seconds the situation was utterly changed. Unfamiliar as I was with the Thames Estuary I could not be misled by two red flashes. On the face of the whole chart it could mean only one thing, the Galloper lightship (the character of the light has since been changed).

2. The ketch *Annette II* in the Stint See, Riga, at the start of her cruise to England. The Estonian family is bidding farewell.

3. The Tumlare yacht *Zara*, showing the extremely high aspect ratio of the sail plan.

5. *Cohoe II*, 35 ft, yawl designed by C. A. Nicholson. The mast was later cut at the upper spreader to convert to masthead rig. With this reduced rig she was Class III winner of the La Coruna race, and first in all classes in the heavy weather La Rochelle—Benodet and Cork races. *Photo: Beken, Cowes.*

4. *Cohoe I*, 32 ft, light displacement, large Tumlare designed by Knud Reimers, winner of the Transatlantic Race, 1950. She is seen here with her 'false nose', the bow having been lengthened to qualify for the Bermuda Race. *Photo: Morris Rosenfeld.*

The wind, which had shifted from time to time during the night, was SSW. I unlashed the helm, sheeted the jib to leeward and bore away to the NW. As the yacht gathered way with the sheets eased she crashed over the seas, and the wind hurled the spray across the ship in massive sheets. With a roar a big sea flung itself aboard, struck the dinghy, and fell on the cabin top. A few minutes later another reared up and came crashing over the ship, breaking in a solid mass over the companion cover, and struck me a heavy blow across the chest. My wife joined me on deck. All night we had lain in our bunks damp to the skin and, now in the bitter cold before dawn, the driving water constantly penetrated our oilskins and chilled us to the bone. We were both pretty tired after the sleepless night and the effort of keeping ourselves from rolling off our bunks. We were also hungry, for under these conditions cooking had been almost impossible.

We had a few sips of whisky and Riga balsam. The latter was a potent drink which we had bought in Riga. It was rather an unpleasant bitter taste like medicine, but I fancy it has a very high alcoholic content and is warming. The edge of hunger was relieved by eating macaroons which we had bought at Ymuiden; they were wet, for a sea arrived at the exact moment that we opened the tin. It was rather an odd kind of breakfast and an odd time to have it, but basically it was alcohol, sugar and protein—a good mixture when one is tired and cold.

In a wild welter of foam-capped seas the ship sailed on. Time after time she was swept by seas. But the knowledge of the yacht's position gave us confidence. We could see the friendly red flashes of the Galloper lightship and before dawn it came abeam. The sea was then tremendous and very confused, as we were crossing shallower water in the vicinity of the North Falls.

My wife sat beside me, trying to identify the looms of the distant lights. The steering was too heavy for her, but she was cheerful and took a full share in any work to be done. An hour after we had passed the Galloper the distant lights still remained below the horizon. Before long even the looms could no longer be distinguished against the lightening sky.

Navigation posed problems, as I was totally unfamiliar with the east coast of England and I was unable to leave the deck to go below to lay proper courses. I had charts of the Continental coast, but the only ones I had of the east coast of England were a small-scale chart of the North Sea and an old Blue Back on an equally small scale. Harwich was little over 20 miles away, but the approaches would be tricky without a proper chart and the wind was likely to veer and head us. On the other hand, Lowestoft appeared to have an easy approach. It was nearly 50 miles distant, but even if the wind veered to the west it would still be free and the passage would take less than ten hours' sailing. So we eased the sheets and altered to the estimated new course.

Running before the gale with the wind on the quarter, *Annette II* was very hard on the helm. I was very cold and it was exhausting work. The hours passed slowly. My wife tried to take a spell at steering, but the effort to hold a steady course before the big following seas was beyond her physical strength.

At length the time arrived when land should be in sight, but there was nothing to be seen except sea and more sea in every direction. Nevertheless, the gale had moderated and we passed a few ships.

At last my wife (who has exceptionally good sight) declared she could see something like land on the port bow. I could see nothing of it myself, but I knew she must be right and the end of our difficulties was in sight. This cheered us immensely. My wife went below and got a primus going to heat the cabin. There was a shambles in the cabin from articles thrown adrift during the gale. The water in the bilges had risen to the cabin sole and everything was soaked. But the sea was moderating under the partial lee of the land and presently my wife appeared on deck with a tin of cold baked beans, which between us we devoured hungrily. She then took a watch, for the yacht was becoming easier on the helm, and I went below into the warmth of the cabin, peeled off my oilskins and slowly changed into dry clothes.

When I returned on deck to resume steering, with dry clothes on and a shot of whisky inside me, I felt a different man, but my wife, who was also wet through, would not change.

A low coast was abeam, and short brown seas replaced the confused mass of grey. A black buoy was passed, the sun appeared, but the minutes still seemed like hours. At last we saw a town on the port bow and after some consideration came to the conclusion that it was Southwold. It came nearer and, through the glasses, we distinguished two long low wooden piers. References to the Cruising Association Handbook gave a few notes on the shallow harbour at Walberswick which were far from encouraging, but on nearer approach we realized that we had a leading wind up the reach between the piers. The yacht was steered more inshore, the entrance came near and we could see the seas breaking on either side. I calculated that it was two hours after high water. I took two soundings with the lead before sailing on straight for the piers. *Annette* foamed up the narrow entrance between the piers and her anchor was let go in the calm of the harbour. The voyage was at an end.

It may be of interest to add that the name *Annette II* was adopted by me as a pseudonym in my early book *Close Hauled* (now long out of print) for Arthur Ransome's *Racundra*. When I sold *Annette II* the new owner installed a new engine and reverted to the original name of *Racundra*. Since the war her whereabouts had been something of a mystery until a yachtsman identified her, by means of a photograph, sailing and apparently in good condition in the Mediterranean.

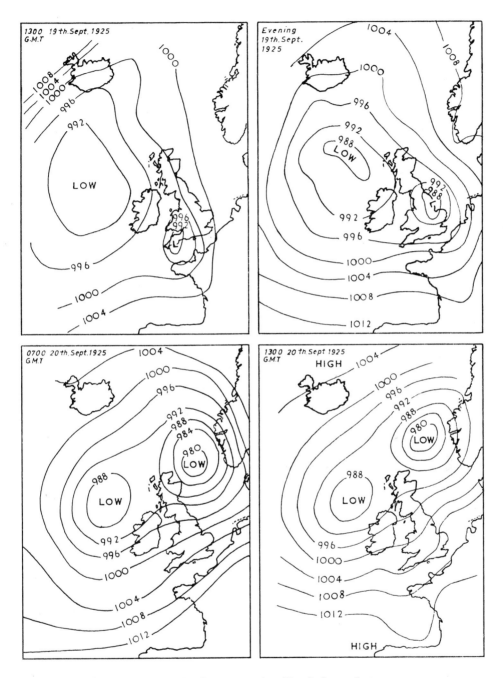

2   Synoptic charts covering North Sea gale.

Conclusions

The weather was featured in the Sunday and Monday newspapers, which described the week-end as the worst of the year, with "violent" gales and fierce rainstorms. The disturbance was reported as developing off the north coast of Spain early on Saturday morning and travelling NE. across England at a rate of 40 to 45 knots, but the accompanying synoptic charts show that the cause of the trouble was a deepening secondary. At Dungeness the wind was 35 knots (Force 8) sustained from 0900 on Saturday evening till 1700 on Sunday. At Calshot, Hants, and Spurn Head, Yorkshire, it reached about 43 knots (Force 9). Many vessels were in distress round the coasts.

From these reports, it seems reasonable to regard the gale as experienced by *Annette II* in the North Sea as mean of Force 8 for a few hours, falling on Sunday morning to Force 7, as recorded at Calais at 0700. The frontal squalls when *Annette* hove-to could have been anything up to 50 or 60 knots, possibly bringing the mean to up to Force 9 on the Beaufort scale for an hour or so.

The following lessons were learnt from our cruise in *Annette II* and the gale on the last lap.

1.   *Sail area.* A yacht with a very small sail area, such as *Annette II*, is so slow in light and moderate winds that, without auxiliary power, she is a sitting duck for gales when on long passages.

2.   *Time.* Our holiday was drawing to an end when we were caught out, otherwise we would probably have taken shelter long before the gale started. Shortage of time and the need to get a yacht to her home port in a hurry are the most common causes of the cruising man getting caught out.

3.   *Heaving-to.* The yacht hove-to well without coming up into the wind or forereaching too much. No doubt the long, straight keel and the sail plan distributed over three low sails helped her performance. Leeway, however, must have been considerable.

4.   *Rain.* From later experience I can confirm that torrential rain, so violent that the surface of the sea smokes with it, has the temporary effect of taking some of the viciousness out of the seas.

5.   *Tiredness.* On arrival in port we had been fifty-three hours at sea in narrow waters, out of which we had perhaps a total of four to six hours sleep. We felt tired, but we quickly brightened up ashore in front of a blazing fire at the Bell Inn. It is probable that in heavy weather, when sleep is difficult to get because of the din, the lack of it is not exhausting providing that the crew can get a reasonable amount of rest in their bunks. People suffering from insomnia carry on with relatively little sleep.

The passing hardship made no apparent impression on my wife, who had taken it all calmly and uncomplainingly, but years later she told me that for weeks afterwards she suffered from nightmares of huge seas.

36

2

POOPED FOR THE FIRST TIME

The first boat I owned after the war afforded a complete contrast to the heavy *Annette II*. She was a Tumlare yacht named *Zara*. The Tumlare class boats were built to the design of Knud Reimers of Stockholm, and were a kind of 20 sq. metre Skerry Cruiser. They were comparable in size and speed to the Dragons, but had a much larger cabin, where, as I once put it, "one person can be accommodated in comfort, two in tolerance, three in tenseness and four in bitter enmity". *Zara* had a long low narrow hull with the typical Scandinavian pointed stern, with outhung rudder. She was 27.2 ft. overall length, 21.8 ft. on the waterline, 6.5 ft. beam, and 4.2 ft. draught. The total sail area was 215 sq. ft., and the sail plan was of very high aspect ratio.

A light-displacement yacht of this kind is a delight to handle. Although inclined to be sluggish in light airs, in any reasonable wind *Zara* was lively and fast, well balanced and light as a feather on the helm. She was good fun for day sailing or racing and week-end cruising, though my wife never really enjoyed more extended cruising in so small a boat. The cramped size of the cabin, the lack of headroom and the absence of a proper galley, or large lockers for food and clothes, took the fun out of it for her.

However, I did put in one cruise down west to Brixham which I made single-handed very soon after the end of the war. The following incident occurred during the passage back to the Solent, and I record it as it shows that there is a limit beyond which one must not go in a very small yacht with a large open cockpit.

I had spent the night anchored in Babbacombe Bay, near Torquay. I was up at dawn the following morning, for this, I hoped, was to be the day for the home-ward passage across Lyme Bay. At least, I tried to convince myself of this reason for an early rising, for to tell the truth I had spent an exceedingly uncomfortable night in *Zara*. An unpleasant swell had been running into the bay and all night *Zara* had rolled hideously and kept me awake.

Up early as I was, I did not weigh anchor until 0900, as much had to be done before setting sail. At the start the course was set for the position of Lyme Buoy, a little over 20 miles to the eastward, though this buoy had been removed during the war and had not then been replaced.

There was little doubt that *Zara* was going to get enough wind. It was south-west and fresh; already there was plenty of it. As I sailed out of Babbacombe Bay

I brought *Zara* close to a fishing boat and hailed them for a weather report. They shook their heads and one replied: "Look at the sky. It's going to blow hard. No day for crossing the bay, sir".

I would normally have postponed my crossing of Lyme Bay, but it was already October, the days were getting short and I wanted to get back to my office before the weather broke. I looked at the sky and it seemed to me that, although a strong wind and a rough passage were to be expected, the wind was not likely to reach gale force in the immediate future. *Zara* seemed to be an able sea boat for her size, well able to hold her own within reasonable limits, her only weakness being the fine lines aft, the low freeboard, and the open cockpit. With me alone on board she would be buoyant aft, and there would be no second person to be asked to sit in the cabin to trim the ship, as is sometimes necessary in a Tumlare yacht, in order to reduce the weight in the cockpit when there is a steep following sea.

So I sailed on. At first the sea was smooth under the lee of the land, and I set the mainsail and the genoa. No sooner was the yacht clear of Babbacombe Bay than the genoa had to come down and the staysail be hoisted in its place. It was a grand day, with a sunny sky and a blue sea, but when the yacht sailed beyond the protection of Hope's Nose and opened up Torbay the seas grew larger, livelier and white crested.

Writing now, I see before me the pencil marks on the big chart showing *Zara*'s progress on an almost easterly course over the first half of the 40 miles of open sea between Babbacombe and the Bill of Portland. At 1000 I reckoned she

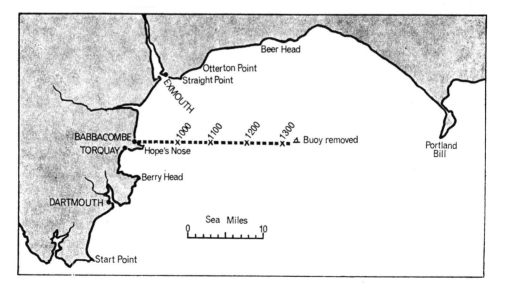

3   Course of *Zara* across Lyme Bay.

was 6 miles offshore, tearing along at great speed. I suppose that it must have been at about this time that the wind began seriously to freshen. Reefing became necessary even with the following wind and, knowing that conditions would become livelier as each mile of broken water was left astern, I brought the yacht to the wind and hove-to. I did not do the reefing by halves, for I rolled down four complete rolls, bringing the peak of the mainsail down to the upper spreaders. The sail area was reduced from 215 down to about 120 sq. ft. and, more important, the head of the sail was at the same height as the forestay and backstay, so the mast was well supported. Yet under such conditions with even this small spread of canvas (not more than is carried by a 14 ft. International racing dinghy) *Zara* was very fast. This was due to the efficient shape of the high, narrow sail, and her easily driven hull. Snugged down like this, *Zara* was a yacht that could take a lot of knocking about, yet still remain lively and close-winded.

Time passed. On the chart the positions recorded that *Zara* was 11 miles east of Babbacombe Point at 1100 and 16 miles by noon. By then she was well out of the shelter of Start Point, which lay nearly 30 miles to the south-west and the sea was coming with unimpeded fetch from the direction of the Atlantic. The Channel tide was running in the teeth of the wind, though not as yet at its maximum rate, for it is not until a yacht gets well to the east side of Lyme Bay towards Portland Bill that she meets the full strength of the tidal stream.

In an account of a rough passage in a smallish yacht one wants complete accuracy to give a true picture of the conditions and the behaviour of the yacht. Well, this was no gale. It was what the fishermen afterwards described as a "hard wind", what is often called "half a gale of wind". The seas were fairly regular, but inevitably they were large, coming in from the open ocean and meeting the westerly running spring tide. There was a gale warning in operation in the Plymouth area only 40 miles to the westward, so I heard afterwards.

At times I felt a little apprehensive, but the yacht was behaving wonderfully and made light of the following seas. A thing which pleased me was the zest and beauty in the scene. It was a most glorious day, with a blaze of sun on the water and it was really warm. The seas afforded a magnificent picture, a mass of blue and white glinting in the sun, and, on top of all, the dinghy, her wet red enamel shining brightly and spurts of spray flying off each side as she foamed along in the wake of the yacht. From time to time I saw big seas of frightening height rearing up astern, but as they never hit *Zara* I came to the conclusion that they were an optical illusion, as the weight of the wind did not seem to justify anything so vicious. I had never experienced more exhilarating conditions. They were vigorous and lively in the extreme. The seas chasing up astern, the dinghy scudding over their tops, the incessant motion of *Zara*, the hard-pressed sails and the taut sheets, and above all, the strong wind.

Land was out of sight, as there was a slight haze. At 1230 I had lunch on deck. I had heated soup before leaving Babbacombe Bay and put it in a Thermos flask ready for this occasion. It tasted grand and after that I had bread and cheese and apples.

The next position that I marked on the chart was at 1300. The yacht had covered about 20 miles and I made a pencil cross at a position 2 miles west of the normal position of Lyme buoy.

And so *Zara* raced on across the sunlit seas, the dinghy following gamely at her stern. It was, I think, about a quarter of an hour later when something caused me to look back. It must have been the sound of water.

Two enormous seas were bearing down on us. Instantly I put the helm up and ran dead before the wind to take them true on the stern. The towering top came climbing up. The stern of the dinghy lifted high. For a moment the dinghy planed and then, in a flash, I realized that I had never seen a dinghy at such an angle. Her bow was down. It was under water. I could see the water overlapping the forward transom. The stern was rearing up. But there was something higher than the dinghy. A great white crest of foaming water was above her, embracing her aft transom in its curling top. The whole thing, water and dinghy, was coming at a speed I never want to see again. I caught a glimpse of a sea that was steep as a wall, like a breaker throwing itself on a shore such as at Chale in the Isle of Wight, where the sea comes deep to sharply shelving shingle. The dinghy was in the act of making a complete somersault stern over bow.

I ducked under the cockpit coamings and held on. There was a deluge of water, followed by a resounding crash. It flashed through my mind that the mast had gone.

It is difficult to describe the supreme violence of a breaking wave when it comes cascading over the stern. There is a great noise, the shock of cold water, and an impression (whether true or not, I cannot say, for my eyes were filled with water), of seething sea, as though the cockpit is a bubbling cauldron.

When I rubbed the salt out of my eyes, I found *Zara* was still afloat, and I was astonished to see the mast was still standing. A quick survey for damage showed that there was none at all. The yacht had gybed and broached-to. The crash which I had taken to be the mast going over the side must have been the boom against the runner as the yacht gybed. There *Zara* lay, riding quietly to the big seas, her boom resting against the lee backstay and her jib sheeted loosely on the weather side. She was practically hove-to on the port tack. Her short boom and narrow sail plan had saved her from what, in some yachts, might have resulted in the breakage of the mast or boom, or both.

I hurriedly set up the weather runner and cast off the lee one. I sheeted in the mainsail and the weather jib sheet, and *Zara* responded, heading up into the wind and lying quietly hove-to, facing the turmoil of breaking seas.

The painter of the dinghy had parted, and I spotted the dinghy away to leeward, floating bottom upwards on the waves. There was no possibility of salvaging her. To have tried to come alongside the boat in the sea which was running would have been highly dangerous and useless, too, for it would have been impossible to have righted the boat and bailed her out single-handed. My first attention had to be given to *Zara*, and that urgently, so the last I saw of this faithful companion of many months' cruising was the waves breaking over her white upturned bottom as she bobbed up and down after her abandonment. I heard later that she went ashore near Otterton Point (Budleigh Salterton) and was salvaged on 16 October with, in the words of the Receiver of Wreck, "five planks shattered, one keel cracked, six ribs broken, and a shattered nose". It read more like a medical report. I wonder what part of her was left whole!

In *Zara*'s cabin I found trouble. The bilges were full and water was running over the cabin sole and over the lee planks, as she heeled to the gusts. This was not quite such a serious matter as it may sound, for it must be remembered that *Zara* is a yacht of light displacement, with narrow floors, so that the amount of sea required to make the water in the bilges rise above the floorboards is not so great as in a larger yacht. Still, it was more water than I had ever seen in her before.

Before the wave struck her *Zara* had been a thing of life, riding confidently over the following seas. From a buoyant yacht she became in an instant an irresponsive, partially waterlogged object that could sink under the next wave. I realized that she was like the gaily-coloured metal boats that I played with as a child and which sink in the bath if too much water gets into them.

How my friends would have laughed to have seen me manning the pump. I hate exertion, but I set to work with greater enthusiasm than I had ever shown before to get the water out of her before the next big sea came along. It took quite a long time, but once the hull was clear of water there was no immediate danger. *Zara* was lying hove-to like a duck, her tiller locked in the steering contrivance with which I had fitted her.

She was heading up to the seas and they broke over her bows and forward deck and not into the vulnerable open cockpit.

Although there was no longer any immediate danger, I was averse to running the yacht off again before the wind on her course, because I did not want to be pooped again, and I thought the wind might continue to harden and the seas get worse until the tide turned to the eastward. Even then, with a fair tide, Portland Bill is not a place I would choose for so small a boat. Disturbed water extends a long way beyond the confines of the race itself. At the right state of tide the inner passage offers a safer route, but the overfalls are not entirely avoided.

The alternative was to beat all the way back to the shelter of the Devonshire

41

coast. It was quite a tough prospect, for it meant beating against a strong wind and heavy breaking seas, but there was no doubt that this was the right course of action.

I was drenched to the skin despite my canvas smock, and I now began to feel cold, whipped as I was by the stinging wind and spray. Happily I had some soup left in the Thermos, and this hot drink greatly revived me.

Then I set *Zara* to her task. I let the sails draw and she went off at a great pace, taking the seas magnificently. The seas were so big that she did not slam at all as she had inside Portland Race on the outward passage, or as she usually did in the Solent when beating in the short wind-over-tide seas there. From time to time I would luff to a "big 'un"; she would lift over the top and slither down the steep slope on the other side. Forward she was like a half-tide rock, with the stem cutting through the tops of the waves which would come streaming over her long foredeck in deluges and run off over the lee side in continuous waterfalls. But aft in the cockpit it was comparatively dry. Nevertheless, for a time sailing was not without anxiety. The seas were undoubtedly severe for the size of the ship, but as I sailed westward her wonderful performance gave me added confidence in her windward ability. Close-sheeted, *Zara* could lay almost due west, but it was better to ease the sheets a fraction and keep her travelling fast heading WNW.

After an hour I sighted land again. A misty white smudge appeared against the sky to the northward. It must have been Beer Head, about 10 miles distant. Then I hove-to again, for the water in *Zara*'s hull was once more rising above the cabin sole. With water flowing in a constant stream over her foredeck it was continually leaking through the hawse pipe and the forehatch. I locked the tiller in position so that the helm could be left while I pumped her out. The seas were already easier. There were fewer really big waves, but it remained a lively scene of endless white horses in every direction as far as the eye could see. The yacht was happy enough, bobbing up and down in the seas, so, as I was feeling cold despite the sun, I took the opportunity to change from my wet clothes, and get a rub down with a towel. The cabin was in a dreadful mess, but I found a pair of dry pyjamas in a sail bag, a pair of flannel trousers which I pulled over them and a tolerably dry reefer jacket. With oilskins over the lot I was well protected and it was wonderful to feel dry again after the unpleasantness of the clammy cold garments. I blessed the sun, for in grey and cold weather it would have been grim indeed.

Then I put the yacht back on her course. The seas became progressively smaller as we got farther west, and in the late afternoon I berthed *Zara* alongside a big yacht moored off the Morgan Giles yard at Teignmouth. Close-reefed she had made good 20 miles in four hours including two tacks which is fast for so small a boat sailing hard on the wind in rough water.

Conclusions

The nearest record of wind forces was from the shore station at Pendennis Castle, Falmouth, but it is pointed out in a letter from the Meteorological Office that according to the synoptic charts there is not likely to have been much difference between the wind forces at Pendennis and Lyme Bay.

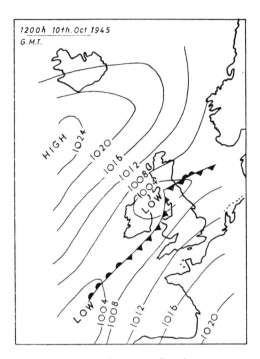

1200h 10th Oct 1945
G.M.T.

4   Synoptic chart, 10 October 1945.

The mean wind speeds were west Force 7 (28-33 knots) at 1130 G.M.T. Force 6 (22-27 knots) at 1230 and 1330, Force 5 (17-21 knots) W. by S. at 1430. The wind must have been fairly steady, the highest gust recorded being 33 knots (almost Force 8) at 1115. The times are G.M.T., to which an hour must be added to coincide with my own report, assuming summer time was in operation. The strength of the wind in Lyme Bay would be higher than recorded by a shore station, but I think a considered estimate might put it somewhere about 25–30 knots, Force 6 to 7. The strong winds were caused by a relatively high "high" to the NW. of a "low".

There were several useful lessons to be learnt from this experience.

1. *Pooping*. Ansted's *Dictionary of Sea Terms* states "when a sea comes over the stern of a vessel it is said to poop her". If this is so (and many yachtsmen agree with the definition) ocean-racing yachts are frequently pooped when running downwind above Force 7, for the heads of waves often break over the stern and half fill the cockpit. To my mind, however, pooping means something much more severe. It means being overwhelmed aft by a breaking following sea. It may result in a broach-to which throws the yacht on her beam ends as she rounds to the wind. This can be a dangerous thing if it leads to dismasting or structural damage to the yacht. Genuine pooping is a very rare thing indeed and I have experienced it only twice in a lifetime.

2. *Danger Downwind*. *Zara* started in sheltered waters under the lee of the land and running downhill, so to speak, the strengthening of the wind and the increase in the sea was gradual as the fetch increased. With a following wind the temptation is to carry on, whereas with a strong headwind the going is so rough that

43

the temptation is to turn back. Once, when my wife and I were at Keyhaven in a westerly gale, three canoeists set out for Lymington. The water was smooth when they started, as they had a weather shore, but gradually the seas increased and somewhere off Lymington two of the canoes capsized and their occupants were drowned. Running downwind is the cause of many accidents in open boats and dinghies, since the increase in wind and sea is so gradual as to be almost imperceptible until it is too late.

3. *Freak Waves*. In rough weather there are occasional waves, larger and more unstable than the others. The exceptional wave which may be called a "freak" wave can be caused by the synchronization or form of wave trains or by tidal overfalls or by shoals or obstructions on the bottom. In this particular case, I think *Zara* had passed over one of the wrecks just west of the normal position of Lyme Bay. The depth in the vicinity is about 23 fathoms, but it is only 16 fathoms over the wreck a mile WSW. of the buoy. One can easily see that the westerly-running stream meeting these big obstructions on the bottom would cause turbulence on the surface which might cause a big sea to break. It is a useful point to remember that such things as big underwater rocks and wrecks, even if deep down, can cause overfalls on the surface if the tidal stream is strong and the sea rough.

4. *Buoyancy Aft*. The Norwegian pilot cutters had pointed sterns and were noted for their ability in heavy weather. *Annette II*, which I described in the previous chapter, ran through the North Sea gale without giving any trouble. *Zara*, however, was too narrow in beam and too fine aft to give sufficient buoyancy for her to rise to an exceptional breaking sea. It is said that an advantage of a sharp-ended stern is that it divides following seas as they run harmlessly past. But the dangerous waves are the ones that do not divide but rear up over the stern like a breaker on the beach. Such seas are rare, but for a boat to rise quickly enough to avoid pooping it must have great buoyancy aft. Certainly the combination of lack of buoyancy aft and a large open cockpit is dangerous.

5. *Time*. The incident demonstrated again that the most frequent reason for getting "caught out" is shortage of time towards the end of a holiday.

3

THE GALE OFF THE CASQUETS

We only kept *Zara* for one season, as she was too small for our family. In her place I bought *Mary Aidan*, a new 7½-ton sloop designed by Fred Parker and built at the Dorset Yacht Company's yard at Hamworthy, near Poole. She was a cruising yacht with a good turn of speed, somewhat the ocean-racing type, although too short on the waterline to be eligible, even for Class III. Her dimensions were 34 ft. overall length, 23 ft. waterline, 8 ft. 1 in. beam and 5.2 ft. draught. *Mary Aidan* was sloop rigged with a total area of 444 sq. ft., consisting of 286 sq. ft. in the mainsail and 158 sq. ft. in the staysail. She was fitted with an 8 h.p. Stuart Turner engine, and was thus the first yacht which I owned which had a practical auxiliary.

We had a good season of cruising and handicap racing in *Mary Aidan* during 1946, in the course of which we experienced one gale. I was cruising with my daughter Arnaud, and a friend named George. We had sailed down west in mixed weather to Brixham. From there we took a departure from Berry Head at 1115 on Saturday, 28 July, bound for Guernsey. The weather forecast was good except for "general rain spreading from the west tonight".

This was my first cruise to the Channel Islands and French side of the English Channel. Although I have sailed on the French coast nearly every year since and visited practically every harbour and anchorage between Barfleur and La Rochelle, I was at that time a stranger to it. I regarded it as a rather hazardous cruising ground, with its innumerable rocks and strong tides.

After eight hours of fast reaching with a sunny sky above and a blue sparkling sea around us, we made a landfall on a gaunt, craggy little islet above which rose two lighthouses, and in the distance beyond was a bigger island. We were lucky to make this landfall, because even as a stranger I soon identified it as the Casquets, which I still think have a somewhat sinister appearance. Arnaud and George were in high spirits, but my own feelings were tempered by a slight uneasiness about the weather. During the morning we could not have asked for better conditions, but some ominous signs had developed: there was a halo round the sun, the swell was higher than the wind justified, though this had slowly but steadily increased. At the start of the passage *Mary Aidan* had logged little over 5 knots; in mid-Channel she was doing 6½ and for the last two or three hours she had reeled off a steady 7. The glass was falling slowly.

At about 2000 the bad omens took more definite shape. A great bank of dark

45

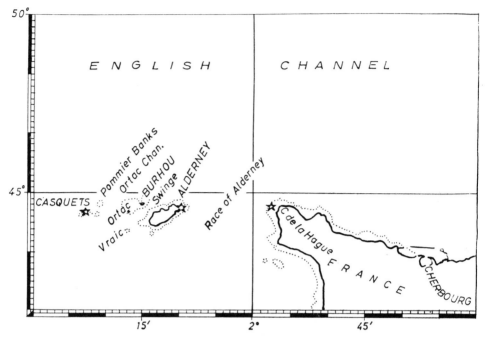

5   Casquets to Cherbourg.

cloud was gathering to the westward, the sea was getting lumpier, and the wind
began to pipe up in earnest. It was time to lower the genoa and replace it with
the staysail. George went forward to do this, but as he was grappling with the
big sail he slipped and, with his foot caught in a loop of the sheet, he made a
spectacular dive overboard, complete with oilskins and his Army oilskin cap.

The leaden, tide-troubled swell off the Casquets, the gloom of the advancing
clouds and approaching night provided a grim background for an accident
such as this, but by the mercy of Providence George had grabbed a rope as he
fell. He reappeared by the shrouds and was quickly back on deck, where he
stood like a great glistening fish, as the water poured off his yellow oilskins. I
was glad to note that Arnaud, who was steering, was so quick with a lifebuoy
that she had it out ready to cast before George would have been swept past. In
Mary Aidan the lifebuoys are carried loosely, standing vertically between brass
strips and the sides of the cockpit coamings, so they can be thrown in an instant.
This is a better practice than having a buoy on the counter, so often recklessly
lashed down. Seconds lost cutting a lashing or freeing a slip-knot may make the
difference between life and death with a man overboard in heavy garments.

George went forward again to complete his job, and soon the staysail was
set and the genoa stowed below out of the way. He came aft cheerfully, declaring

46

he was warm, and I had to be very firm before he would consent to go below to change into dry clothes and have a glass of rum.

When the Casquets lighthouse lay about 2 miles ahead the wind was rising so rapidly and the general conditions were so threatening that I decided that more reefing was desirable as a precaution, though not yet strictly necessary. We hove-to and tied down two reefs. This took some little time, for we had no tackle on the cringle and the weight of the wind made it difficult to haul it in hard enough. When all was done and the *Mary Aidan* nicely snugged down, we sailed on towards the Casquets.

If the weather had been reasonably settled, I would have let the yacht sail herself temporarily to the westward close-hauled, or hove-to on the port tack with the yacht slowly jogging ahead until the tide turned and we could sail to St. Peter Port. But the wind was backing and conditions looked so ominous that it appeared wiser to run for shelter to leeward. I did not fancy piloting *Mary Aidan* into Alderney harbour (with which I was then unfamiliar), owing to the submerged breakwater marked on the chart, and the strong tidal streams which would make the approach difficult in the dark. Cherbourg, 30 miles to the eastward, seemed the best bet, with a fair wind and fair tide.

So *Mary Aidan* squared away and ran to the eastward into the gathering night. We gybed her to get a good offing from the Pommier Banks and the dangers WNW. of Alderney. The sea grew increasingly rough as *Mary Aidan* ran before the wind through the overfalls of the roaring tide.

By the time it was really dark the wind was blowing so hard and the seas had become so rough that, in order to take things comfortably, we lowered the mainsail and ran under staysail, but the yacht's speed was hardly lessened. I navigated by the Casquets light astern and Alderney light to starboard. We gybed again, as I had let the yacht run unnecessarily far to the northward owing to a kind of rock-shyness, and my reluctance to bring her too close to the gap between Alderney and Cap de la Hague, where Alderney Race thrusts into the English Channel.

George took the first night watch and I went below, being occupied with calculations of tidal streams and other points of navigation. The tide was due to turn just after 2300 and, as it was springs, there would be a spectacular sea when the westerly ebb stream began to run against the wind.

Gradually Alderney light changed position and we came into the track of steamers. The masthead light of one looked exactly like an occulting light, so regularly did it disappear in the troughs of the seas. George was finding it difficult to steer, for even under jib alone it needed a lot of concentration to keep the yacht running straight before the breaking seas striding up astern. Presently the patter of rain was heard and the lights of Alderney disappeared in a squall. It was blowing great guns.

47

A little later George shouted to me that the weather was getting worse. He asked what was to be done. The night was pitch black, but one could hear the breaking seas above the wind. I went forward and lowered the staysail, lashing it down hard against the forestay. *Mary Aidan* was now under bare pole. Even so she was running at great speed, but George steered her carefully, always meeting the seas stern on, judging them by sound and by the motion of the ship. I went back to the cabin, closing the companion doors after me, and opened the cocks under the bridge deck controlling the pipes of the self-draining cockpit.

The plan of running to Cherbourg had now to be abandoned, as between the yacht and her port of shelter lay a piece of water marked on the chart "7-knot springs, strongest part of the tide". This note on the chart, which worried me at the time, is not repeated on recent charts. The rate is probably lower, about 5 knots at spring tides. With a wind then estimated at over Force 7 I did not fancy experiments, even with wind and tide together. Moreover, owing to our detour to the northward it was clear by then that there was no chance of the yacht arriving at Cherbourg before the tide turned, when a wicked sea would be running.

At some time after 2300 there was a heavy crash, followed by a strange sound of rushing water. In the cabin Arnaud and I were thrown across the ship. I opened the cabin doors and looked out. The head of a sea had broken on board. It had thrown George from the tiller across the bridgedeck and half filled the cockpit. The unfamiliar sound was that of the streaming water as it gushed through the outlet drains of the self-emptying cockpit. On deck I found there was pandemonium with the howling wind and the din of the seas and rain.

It seemed to me that some water might have got into the bilges as well as into the cockpit. I tried the pump, but it was no use, for the motion was so violent that the water, of which there cannot have been very much, was sluicing across the bilges first to one and then to the other side of the hull, and the pump only worked intermittently as the flood rushed across the strum box.

In the cockpit the exit pipes had dealt with the flood of water at first quickly, but later at reducing speed. Some minutes after the influx there were still some inches of water over the gratings, and it would have been nasty if a second sea had broken aboard before the yacht had rid herself of the first.

Mary Aidan was running too fast even under bare pole. George reckoned she was doing a good 5 knots. I hurried below again, carefully closing the cabin doors after me. Crawling forward into the peak, I extracted a 25-fathom length of warp. Then, pushing it through the cabin door again, I got out into the cockpit and made fast one end of the rope to a great big cleat that has often been laughed at on account of its massiveness. I paid the other end over the starboard quarter, fathom by fathom. That steadied her immediately. Then I took the tiller from George and lashed it down slightly to starboard and the yacht headed north with the seas on her port quarter.

"All right," I said to George, "it's time to turn in now", and we went below to the cabin, switched on the electric navigation lights (hitherto only used when in proximity to ships) and shut the companionway doors firmly after us against the gale.

Down below in the cabin it was difficult to realize what a wild scene had been left behind on deck. The electric cabin light lit up the interior and added a touch of domestic bliss which contrasted oddly with the grimness of the conditions outside. The motion was not so severe as might have been expected. The wind in the mast steadied the boat, and although she rose and fell great distances she did so less violently than before. Certainly one had to hold on to steady oneself, but here is the advantage of a small boat, for it is possible to put one hand against the cabin top, and there is never the risk of being thrown across a big open space. It was possible to lie down on the berths with the canvas leeboards tied up to hold one in. Probably the worst thing was the din—things breaking loose, cooking utensils clanking, and the mess as things broke adrift. A packet of cleaning powder appeared from nowhere and spread itself in a slippery mess at the foot of the companion steps. A tin of blackcurrant purée overturned, followed soon afterwards by a tin of condensed milk.

Above the hubbub came the sibilant sound of rushing water as the seas bore down on the yacht out of the night. At intervals there would be a plonk as heavy spray broke into the cockpit, followed by the gurgle as it trickled down the outlets to the sea.

George was soaked to the skin (although I had not realized it at the time), but kept tolerably warm in blankets. Arnaud asked: "When shall we get into Cherbourg, Daddy?"

There was some point in this question, for a little while earlier she had been lifted bodily in the air and flung from her bunk against the cabin table. But she took the news that the night was to be spent at sea with cheerfulness, and even managed to get some sleep towards morning.

A major objection to the cabin was the smell of sodden clothes and another very strange smell. Thinking that the latter must have been a leak of Calor gas, I went forward to the fo'c'sle to investigate, but I found the cock there was turned off. As I was returning to my bunk I saw a saucepan which had got adrift and contained three fine chops bought the previous day, which were now chasing each other along the cabin floor. They were the most handsome chops we had seen for a long time, and we had wondered at the butcher's preference in parting with them to strangers at a time when meat was still in short supply after the war. We now realized the reason why. They were high.

At midnight I marked *Mary Aidan*'s approximate position on the chart. I

49

must confess I was apprehensive. Although a good 7-tonner should be able to live through any gale, there is the proviso that she must be in deep water, clear of shoals and tide races. Here, although we were north-east of Alderney, the tidal stream runs very strong at springs. The stream had already turned and would soon be ebbing at full strength directly in the teeth of a WSW. gale. *Mary Aidan* was in for a dusting.

None of us felt sea-sick. It was fortunate that such was the case, for with the fore-hatch closed, the portholes screwed down tightly, and the cabin doors shut in case a big sea should break aboard, sea-sickness would have created a fetid atmosphere.

From time to time I went on deck, pushing open the companion doors against the wind and shining my torch on the compass. Then I would take a look round for the lights of steamers. Close at hand there was nothing to be seen except for the phosphorescent white of breaking crests. In the squalls the sea seemed to be boiling and the lisp and hissing of the seas was uncanny.

So passed the night, a night of violence and racket, the roar of the wind, the noise of the breaking seas, and the regular gurgle of the water trickling out of the cockpit outfalls. I switched off the cabin lights. At about 0400 the sky lightened. The portholes admitted a grey light and the outline of the mast and table could be seen. When dawn came it lit up a wet little ship with a tired crew. At about this time I noticed that the wind had moderated. There was less noise in the rigging, but the sea was higher and more irregular, and spray seemed to be breaking aboard as much as ever. A big sea was still running, but by 0600 the tide had eased, the waves had lengthened, and were no longer breaking. I turned in again until 0730 and then got the yacht under way.

Conclusions

In the first place one must consider whether there was a gale at all. Here you have all the ingredients which contribute to exaggeration. First, the landfall on an unfamiliar coast. Next a man overboard off the Casquets. Then the run before an increasing wind at night during spring tides in an unfamiliar area, notorious for the strength of the tidal streams.

It would be all too easy to paint too colourful a picture. Yet when I reread the words which I wrote many years ago there were certain facts which stand out: "Doing a good 5 knots." You do not get such a speed under bare pole with a wind of less than Force 7. Then again you do not normally under Force 8 experience heads of seas which "half fill the cockpit", especially when running under bare pole.

I must, however, plead guilty to one element of exaggeration which appeared in an earlier account of the gale. When, twenty years ago, I obtained the wind speed at Thorney by telephone, I took it to be the mean speed in knots, but it must have been the velocity of the highest gust expressed in statute miles per hour and not in knots, because, now that I have received figures from the Meteorological Office, I see that the mean hourly value of the wind at Thorney was only Force 5, though gusts of 36 knots and 32 knots were recorded at 2350 and 0020 G.M.T., which indicates that the wind was exceptionally turbulent. As explained in Chapter 21, Thorney is a sheltered coastal station and Portland, where the hourly value to midnight was Force 7, is a better guide. I think this is a fair assessment, but the wind, funnelling through the Alderney Race gap between Cap de la Hague and Alderney, might well have attained Force 8 locally, accompanied by violent squalls and gusts, while the front (which moved from the Scillies to Spurn Head) was going through. I make the following comments:

1. *Tidal disturbances.* When sailing in strong tidal streams these will appreciably add to or reduce the strength of the apparent wind. If the true wind is say 31 knots (Force 7), a contrary stream of 4 knots running against it will give an apparent wind of 35 knots (Force 8) on the surface of the water. If it is a lee-going stream, it will have the effect of reducing it to 27 knots (Force 6). This is an exaggerated example, but often there is one whole grade in the Beaufort Scale between the strength of the apparent wind when the stream is weather-going and when it is lee-going.

There is more in it than this. As Captain Stewart explains in Appendix I, a tidal stream or current causes an increase in the wave height and steepness when the stream is running against the waves or the wind and a decrease when it is running in the other direction. The height may be increased by 50 to 100 per cent, and breaking seas may occur even without much local wind.

This explains why the navigator in coastal waters or in currents such as the Gulf Stream meets seas which may be out of all proportion to the strength of the wind.

2. *Harbours of refuge.* Alderney is a good harbour, but we were right in not attempting it at night for the first time in rough weather. My instinct in a gale to get away from the land was a sound one. It is better to lie a-hull and go to bed in the relative safety of deep water than to attempt to reach an unfamiliar harbour.

4. *Bare poles. Mary Aidan* lay well under bare pole. We discovered the technique of lying a-hull by experiment, found it to be good and adopted it later in stronger gales. But it should be noted that, although the exit pipes of the self-emptying cockpit coped with the heads of seas, they would need to be of greater diameter to be effective if bigger seas had broken aboard. Cockpit drains in yachts are nearly always too small.

5. *Morale.* The morale of the crew was high. Granted that the gale was a short-lived one, no more than Force 7 or 8 possibly, we thought at the time that it was

blowing harder. It makes a great difference in heavy weather if everybody keeps cheerful.

6. *Stowage*. In a gale anything loose, such as cooking utensils, provisions, etc., will take to flight. Everything should be secured on the approach of bad weather and not left until it arrives.

4

STARTING OCEAN RACING

In prewar years I always took an armchair interest in ocean racing. It seemed to me the most genuine form of sport, for the races, if not all on the ocean, were at least offshore over open water, to the Bay of Biscay, Spain and the Baltic, not to mention the 635-mile Fastnet Race, the Grand National of ocean racing. Racing such as this in any weather, gales, calm or fog, impressed me as the ultimate in sailing, providing a test of boats, crews, navigation and racing skill.

After the war I thought I would like to have a shot at it myself, before it was too late to start. The minimum length of yacht eligible for ocean races was then 25 ft. in waterline length. *Mary Aidan* was only 23 ft. L.W.L., so I sold her in 1946 and bought instead a yacht named *Cohoe*, which had just been built by A. H. Moody & Son Ltd., at Bursledon, and was virtually new, as she had only been sailed for two week-ends in the Solent. *Cohoe* (the name is that of a species of small fast Canadian salmon) was an enlarged version of a Tumlare, designed by Knud Reimers, with a 30 sq. metre sail plan instead of the 20 sq. metre of *Zest* and *Zara*. The shape of the hull was very similar, with moderate overhang forward, wine-glass sections and a Scandinavian stern with outhung rudder, but the stern was much fuller than in the smaller design, giving greater buoyancy aft, and she was thus less liable to be pooped.

Her design dimensions were 32.1 ft. length overall, 25 ft. 4 in. length waterline, 7 ft. 4 in. beam and 5 ft. 2 in. draught. She worked out at 7 tons Thames measurement, but she was only $3\frac{1}{2}$ tons designed displacement, and in reality a considerably smaller boat than *Mary Aidan*.

I stress the word "designed" displacement, because modifications had been made to the design of her former owner which added considerably to her actual displacement. The height of the topsides had been increased and a long coach-roof and a doghouse had been added. This greatly improved the space below. There was a full-length cabin with a berth on each side, and aft under the doghouse there was a galley with a primus stove to port and a quarter berth with chart table over it to starboard. Forward of the saloon was a compartment with cupboards and storage space separated by doors from the forecastle, in which there was a pipe cot, sail and anchor stowage and a Baby Blake W.C. Although *Cohoe* was narrow (Humphrey Barton described her accommodation as "like living in a tunnel"), the arrangements below were comfortable, and there was

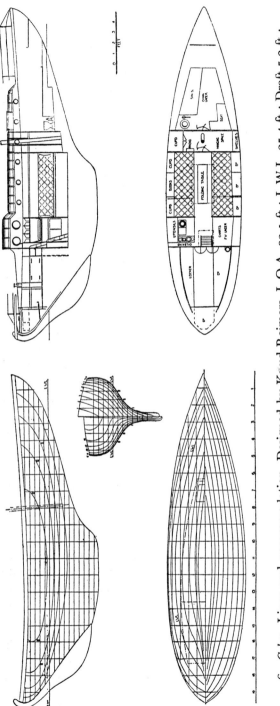

6 *Cohoe.* Lines and accommodation. Designed by Knud Reimers. L.O.A. 32.1 ft.; L.W.L. 25.4 ft.; Draft 5.2 ft.; Displacement 3.5 tons; Sail area 362 sq. ft.

fair headroom with over 6 ft. under the doghouse and over 5 ft. at the forward end of the saloon.

The cockpit was a comfortable size and self-emptying, and situated below it was an 8 h.p. Stuart Turner engine driving a three-bladed propellor. To compensate for this extra weight aft, 5 cwt. of lead had been added to the forward end of the keel. Many of our friends, especially cruising men of the older school, were very critical of *Cohoe*, saying that a yacht of such light displacement was unfit to go outside the Solent. I even overheard her described contemptuously as "a toy yacht". Nevertheless, she was a well-built boat and a thoroughbred, and I still look back on her with affection.

We bought *Cohoe* in August 1946, and my wife and I managed to get away in September for our first cruise, which was a delightful one in the Channel Isles and on the coast of Brittany. During the winter I prepared *Cohoe* for ocean racing the following season. The trouble was that the extra weight resulting from the alterations to the basic design and the addition of an auxiliary engine had spoilt her racing performance. She was not nearly so fast as her sister ship *Josephine*, owned by a friend of ours, Mr. C. Smallpeice, who had kept to the original design. Light displacement is all right as long as it is kept light, but *Cohoe* floated inches below her designed L.W.L. This made her longer on the waterline, which in theory provided a higher theoretical maximum speed, but, as all racing men know, superfluous weight in the wrong place makes a yacht tender and slower under all conditions except when running in strong winds. At a guess her real displacement in final racing trim may have been as much as $4\frac{1}{2}$ tons, but the ballast keel even with the additional 5 cwt. was only $1\frac{3}{4}$ tons, giving a ballast ratio of under 40 per cent, which is low for a boat lacking beam and hull shape stability. When she was measured in 1950 in America for the C.C.A. rules the official measurer remarked that the only thing about her which surprised him was "how she floated upright".

The only way I could reduce weight was by having the engine removed. I had this done, much to my wife's annoyance, as it was a good one, and substituted a light 6 h.p. engine with a feathering propellor. Another alteration I made was to cut down the foot of the genoa, which was too long for the R.O.R.C. rule and attracted a penalty. I also shortened the foot of the mainsail. The reduction in sail area reduced *Cohoe*'s rating, but made her sluggish in light airs, for to compensate for extra weight a yacht needs more sail area, not less. There is no advantage in a low rating if it is achieved only at a corresponding loss of speed. This lesson I learnt many seasons later.

In our first year of ocean racing we had a good introduction to heavy weather sailing, with wind forces of 6 and 7 and occasionally higher, such as are experienced in most seasons, but we encountered none of the major gales of the kind I refer to in later chapters.

FORCE SEVEN

Our first ocean race was the Southsea to Brixham Race, over a course of about 200 miles from Southsea to Le Havre lightvessel and thence to Brixham. We raced with a total of three, our complement consisting of Roger Heron (at that time a partner in the yacht designers, Laurent Giles and Partners) and Jim Hackforth Jones, the son of Commander Gilbert Hackforth Jones, the well-known author. Our routine was for each man to take two hours at the helm, then to take two hours stand-by below (available instantly at call) and two hours off. A boat of *Cohoe*'s size needed only two men to handle her, except when setting or lowering the spinnaker. I did the navigation as well, while cooking was divided between us. It was a good system, as all had full responsibility in watches and the result of the racing depended upon teamwork, which makes for a happy ship. It was a system we followed in all our early offshore races.

There were twenty-eight entries in the Brixham Race, of which eight were in Class III, which is the small yacht class which included *Cohoe*, the smallest of all. The race started on Friday, 27 June, at 1845 and the first leg of the course to Havre L.V. was eventless, as there was a light free wind, though it was foggy during the night.

After rounding Le Havre lightship on Saturday forenoon, the next leg was diagonally across the English Channel, WNW. to Brixham, a distance of 120 miles, which provided genuine offshore sailing which would normally take about twenty four hours. It was on this leg that we were to meet our first gale or near gale when racing.

The wind had been easterly during the night and after rounding the lightship in the morning the course provided a broad reach, but the barometer was falling and during the Saturday evening the wind quickly veered to dead ahead. It freshened steadily and by midnight, when *Cohoe* was in the middle of the English Channel, all yachts were reefed. At dawn on Sunday morning it was blowing harder still and conditions were dismal, as they always are in a small yacht turning to windward in rough water.

In *Cohoe* the angle of heel was extreme. She was a tender yacht, heeling readily, but once heeled to a certain point the leverage of her keel stiffened her and she went over no farther. However, it is tiring work when a yacht is sailing on her ear. The motion was lively and on deck sheets of spray were flying aft into the helmsman's eyes. We were close-reefed and I thought the wind was about Force 6 to 7. *Cohoe* lay on the port tack. Several sails were in sight but these were not our immediate competitors. The best course she could lay would take here into the middle of Bournemough Bay. The sun came out when we made our landfall, sighting the cliffs of the Isle of Wight to starboard. I remem-

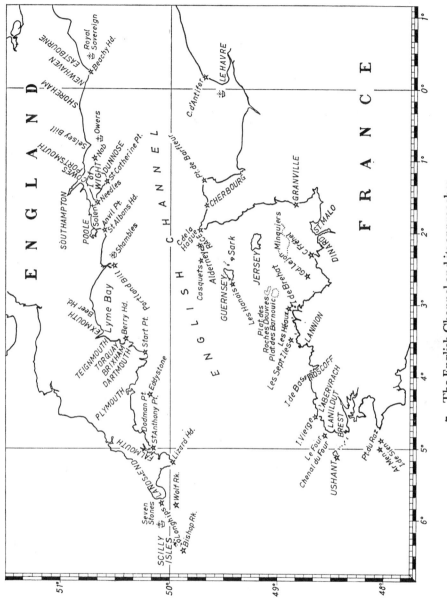

7   The English Channel and its approaches.

57

ber that the strong westerly wind against the tide caused a big sea to run and it was rough going.

By the time we reached Swanage Bay we were pretty tired of beating and the tide was due to turn against us. I realized then that if we were to tack in a strong wind against a foul tide off St. Alban's Head we should make little progress, so we decided to anchor in Swanage Bay.

There we had the luxury of changing into dry clothes and eating a hot meal. We pumped the bilges dry, kept the primus going, which helped to dry out the cabin, for everything below was wet. We mended a torn sail and carried out a number of minor repairs. Then we turned in for a couple of hours' rest before getting under way to catch the early inshore stream at St. Alban's Head.

We had felt a little ashamed of ourselves for sheltering, as when we anchored in Swanage Bay we had seen the R.O.R.C. club yacht *Griffin* standing out to sea on the starboard tack. *Griffin* was a boat of which we were to see a lot in our future racing. She was a Class II yacht, measuring 24 tons T.M. However, when we had tacked from Swanage up to St. Alban's we sighted *Griffin* again, and to our surprise we saw that the tide had set her back some 2 or 3 miles. Our self-indulgence inshore had been rewarded. If we had kept at sea, not only would we have made no progress but we would actually have been carried eastward by the tide. It was a useful lesson from which we profited in the future.

The wind by then had moderated and the rest of the race provided another night at sea, but plain sailing. The finish, however, was interesting. We were tired and despondent when we arrived and could see a forest of masts rising above the long breakwater of the Brixham harbour, suggesting all our competitors were ahead of us. We anchored off the yacht club and Roger Heron rowed off in the dinghy to learn the worst.

When he returned he was smiling. "*Cohoe*'s won," he announced; "no other Class III boat finished." "And," he added, "we've also beaten all Class II on corrected time."

Thus ended our first ocean race. Sixteen yachts had retired. Some had given up because owner or crew had to be back on Monday morning and others because they had been damaged in the strong winds, among them the Class I yawl *Eostra* of 44 tons which had been dismasted. *Bloodhound* was winner in Class I and *Phemie* in Class II.

Conclusions

I have received data from the Meteorological Office. At the Lizard the wind records showed 27 knots and 26 knots (top of Force 6) for two hours to 0030 Sunday morning. For the next hour it rose to 28 knots, which put it at the bottom of Force 7, after which it fell to 26 knots. The highest gust was 35 knots at 0100.

A front would have arrived later in the Wight area and the strength of the wind at sea might have been a little higher.

1. *Sheltering*. The relative performance of *Griffin* soldiering on at sea and *Cohoe* temporarily sheltering in Swanage Bay shows that, if the sea is really rough, the average small yacht cannot make progress beating to windward against a strong foul spring tide off a headland. It is better to shelter, make such repairs as are necessary and feed and rest the crew. *Griffin* was gaff rigged and *Cohoe* was small, so both were handicapped in windward performance in rough weather. Modern yachts, designed for ocean racing, would not nowadays shelter in winds under 40 knots (Force 8) in the absence of special reasons for it.

2. *Historical*. As the modern development of the small ocean racer is indirectly traced in this book, it is interesting to read a cutting from *Yachts and Yachting* on this race. "Conditions . . . again throw some doubts on the suitability of a long course for the very small boats that are now admitted to R.O.R.C. events." *Yachts and Yachting* has always been closely associated with ocean racing, so the comments may be taken as a fair expression of the general opinion at the time.

THUNDERSTORM IN THE BAY

We experienced heavy weather in two other races in our first year of ocean racing. In the Channel Race there was a strong easterly blow which John Illingworth described as attaining "over Force 7". It was a hard sail for the three of us on the 70-mile beat to windward, but after rounding the Royal Sovereign lightvessel the wind moderated and with full sail set *Cohoe* headed across Channel towards Le Havre.

We were all feeling happy and Gerald Harding, the mate, got the primus going and hotted up a large saucepan of soup. Then followed a nasty accident, for the swell was still running and the saucepan was flung off the gimbals and Gerald got badly scalded by splashes of soup. I gave first aid, according to the directions for burns in *Reed's Almanac*, but he was in severe pain for two hours. We sailed back to the English coast, and anchored for the night off Eastbourne, where an aunt of his was living. He was out of pain and slept well until the following morning, when a shore boat landed him on the beach and a diligent Customs officer conducted him to his aunt's, but the burns proved worse than I had realized at the time.

I mentioned this race because two things can be learnt from it. The possibility of burns or scalds is a real risk in heavy weather, owing to the violent motion of a yacht. When the gale was over tension was relaxed and it was then that the accident happened. A considerable swell was still running. A sea cook should never wear shorts, because there is always a risk of things being thrown off a stove. Trousers afford some degree of protection. The second point is more important.

An amateur with no medical knowledge may be inclined to judge the serious-
ness of burns by the condition of the patient and think once the pain is over and
he appears cheerful there is nothing to cause anxiety. On the contrary, as I
have learned since, only a doctor can judge how serious a burn may be. It is the
shock following it that matters, and in the event of an accident of this kind the
patient should be got ashore for medical attention as quickly as possible. In the
meantime he may be given hot tea and sugar, but no alcohol.

The final race of 1947 was the Plymouth to La Rochelle, and it was in this
race we experienced a thunderstorm which at the time we thought was the
beginning of a heavy gale. The Rochelle Race was an exciting event for us, as
it was *Cohoe's* first venture into the Bay of Biscay. The distance was 355 miles,
and at the conclusion of the race the yachts sailed through the battlemented
entrance between the towers into the basin of the medieval port.

The thunderstorm occurred in the Bay of Biscay about 20 miles south of
Belle Ile and about the same distance off St. Nazaire, and I cannot do better
than to quote the description of it which appeared in the *Yachtsman*, Spring 1948,
by Sir Ernest Harston, who then owned *Amokura*, the beautiful Class II yawl
later owned by George Millar, and described in his books:

"At six I was awakened by hearing Roger at the chart table and asked him
what was happening. He said he was just marking up the D.R. because there
was the most awful sunrise he had ever seen, a dipsomanic's dream of hell,
red, green, purple, yellow and black. As Roger is not conspicuously addicted
to hyperbole, I knew I had to get up, so I groaned out of bed and went on
deck, where covers were being lashed on the hatches and skylight and the
genoa changed for the No. 1 foresail, a doughty piece of stuff that has stood
some hard blows in its time. The reefing handle was brought out, but I was
watching the approaching squall and called out, 'To hell with reefing—
down with the mainsail!' It was about half-way down when the blast hit us
and what a draught it was! It was a tough job getting the rest of the sail down
and lashed to the boom, but the crew did splendidly,

How glad I was for our permanent gallows; I kept heading up into the
wind as close as I dared to see how she took it. We were heading in the wrong
direction, but no one worried about that. The wind freshened and the rain
came down in sheets, but the sea was flat as glass. I spun her round and ran
before it for awhile; she handled perfectly under jib and mizzen. Finally, as I
got more used to things I came back on to the course with the wind abeam
and watched the speed variation indicator creep steadily round until it registered 9½ knots. The boat felt like a flying armchair and I wished I had kept to
our course from the start. However, we've all got to learn. The thunder and
lightning was most impressive. By 0745 hours, however, we had the full

mainsail on again— the squall had lasted an hour and a quarter. There have been various estimates of its strength ranging up to Force 10 or Hurricane— but at any rate Force 8 is not far out either way. We had been lucky and nothing carried away, but other yachts reported burst jibs, parted halliards and other troubles of that kind."

Conclusion

Alan Watts has kindly contributed the following meteorological comments:

Thundery troughs—this was probably a cold front—are usually narrow and stretch across the wind. They may be sometimes referred to as line squalls. One would be most unlucky if a troughful of thunder lasted two hours, providing one did not foolishly run before it, so making the time of its passing slower. Theoretically the best course would seem to be the one chosen—a broad fast reach with apparent wind beam.

It should not be difficult to distinguish between a gale due to a depression and a gale-force wind from a thundery trough, because, although both are preceded by a falling barometer, the former has a long build-up of cloud, while the latter normally has not. The same sort of sky as described preceded the Channel gale referred to in Chapter 11, but in this case it was a sunset and not a sunrise which was the portent of hell.

THE LADIES' RACE

To the end of this chapter I am adding a description of a gale which occurred in the Dinard Race the following year (1948) and it rounds off my account of the different sorts of ordinary heavy weather sailing experienced in our first year of offshore racing, in which *Cohoe* won the class R.O.R.C. Points Championship.

The Dinard Race is popularly known as a Ladies' Race, as it is the only R.O.R.C. event of under 200 miles in length, but it is a misnomer in these days, when women are often as able at sea as their menfolk, and sometimes better. However, there are more wives, sweethearts and daughters taking part in this race than in any other R.O.R.C. event. The course (See p. 57) is a very interesting one, starting from Cowes and taking the fleet past the Casquets to Les Hanois lighthouse on the SW. corner of Guernsey, and thence into the Gulf of St. Malo, skirting the Minquiers group of rocks, and so to the finish at the fairway buoy off the entrance to the River Rance and Dinard. Although shorter than other R.O.R.C. races, the course is a tricky one, for in bad weather there are heavy overfalls off the Casquets and along the coast of Guernsey. In fog the combination of strong tides and rocks provide a navigator's nightmare. Once across the English Channel one is sailing in narrow waters the whole time. As always in this race, there was strong international competition and in our class alone there were eighteen competitors from England, the Channel Isles, France, Belgium and Canada. Of recent years entries have increased to well over a hundred.

For this race I had as crew my son Ross and Gerald Harding, who, after he had recovered from his accident in the Channel Race, had become a "regular" crew member of *Cohoe* and a much-valued one, owing to his determination and cheerfulness under all conditions of weather.

The race started during the morning of Friday, 16 July, in light airs and easy conditions which held while the fleet was crossing the Channel close-hauled during the afternoon and night. Landfalls were made at various points on the Cherbourg peninsula, depending on the windward ability of the individual boats. Here the wind freshened and there was a forecast of strong winds backing to the SW., accompanied by heavy rain and moderate to poor visibility. Bad visibility is the one thing above all others that is not wanted in the rock-strewn Channel Island waters.

At the Casquets the following morning, Saturday, we had to reef the mainsail and set a staysail in place of the genoa. The sea was beginning to build up, as it always does very quickly in those waters. Conditions were soon gloomy in the extreme. There was dense rain which cut down visibility, and when we were beating off the Guernsey coast it was barely possible to sight land on the inshore tack before entering the danger area of the outlying submerged rocks.

It was not until late in the evening that *Cohoe* fetched Les Hanois lighthouse off the SW. of Guernsey and it took a long time to work round the lighthouse against a foul tide.

At about 2200 the wind strengthened rapidly. The official forecast was of strong winds (indicating Force 6 and 7 in the Beaufort notation), and I logged the wind in the lower region of Force 7. Three reefs were taken in the mainsail and the storm jib was set. The rain was fierce, the night was black and the visibility was so poor that no lights could be seen. There was then a weather-going tide and a wild sea, so I decided to heave-to for three hours, between Les Hanois and the dangerous group of rocks known as the Roches Douvres, before entering narrow waters in the vicinity of the Minquiers plateau of rocks.

With the storm jib backed, *Cohoe* lay quietly rising and falling on the seas. All the tumult was over, the slamming, the noise, the spray and the motion. I took the quarter berth, as I always do on these occasions, for a skipper has to be handy to go on deck, and in the quarter berth he can hear what is going on, put his head on deck from time to time and be ready for instant action if occasion demands it. But in rough conditions it is an uncomfortable position, as so much water descends upon the occupant; its sole merit is that there is little risk of falling asleep.

It was ironical to be wasting a fair tide and to be waiting a foul one, but in

Channel Island waters there is an exceptionally steep breaking sea when wind is over the tide. Then it is like sailing in overfalls.

About three hours later (between 0100 and 0200 on Sunday) the tide turned and became lee-going, so the apparent wind and seas moderated as a result. The seas were higher, but they broke less and the viciousness was taken out of them. The visibility must have still been poor, as no lights were in sight. We let draw and sailed on, still seeing nothing, though we must have passed very close to the Roches Douvres without sighting the light. We gave a wide berth to the Minquiers, setting a course between this plateau of rocks and the French mainland to the west. Here the deep water is 17 miles wide, which should provide easy navigation, but for the strong tidal sets. When dawn turned into day the weather gradually improved and the sun came out, but we sighted no land until we came off Cap Frehel and altered course for the remaining few miles to Dinard. We had sailed 50 miles and rounded the Minquiers blindfold.

Oddly enough the end of the race followed the precedent of the Brixham Race. After crossing the finish line we sailed up the river, feeling tired and depressed. Then as we approached Dinard Roads we saw yachts at anchor. As we passed the nearest we hailed her, inquiring what other Class III boats were in. The answer came clearly: "None". *Cohoe* had won boat for boat without calling on the handicap allowance due to her small size and despite her loss of time when hove-to. The only other boat in her class to complete the course was *Alethea III*, a 9-ton cruising yacht owned by Vernon Sainsbury, who later made a great reputation as Commodore of the R.O.R.C. The winners in Class I and Class II were *Latifa* and *Golden Dragon*.

Conclusions

Only thirteen out of the forty-two starters in the three classes completed the course. *Seafalke* had a man swept out of the cockpit and *Seahorse* was reported to have had two overboard. Happily, all were recovered. Many of the twenty-nine yachts which retired suffered damage to sails (which in 1948 were often of pre-war vintage), parting of stays and other breakages. Other retirements were due to the dirty weather, involving a plug to windward in the very rough tidal seas peculiar to the Channel Islands and Gulf of St. Malo, and having to round the Minquiers rocks in bad visibility, which was recorded at Guernsey meteorological station at 0600 on Sunday morning (18th July) as "thick fog". Nevertheless, the weather conditions were spoken of at the time as a gale or near gale, with general agreement that the wind attained Force 7 (28–33 knots).

I was therefore astonished when, nearly twenty years later, I received reports from the Meteorological Office, and found that only the top Force 5 (21 knots had been recorded at the shore station Guernsey (only about 10 miles to leeward of *Cohoe*) and from the met. station at the Lizard. From this cruising men may infer that ocean racing is very sloppy, but I would point out that among skippers of the twenty-nine yachts which retired were cruising men, including some distinguished ocean voyagers. There was something more to it than this.

Referring to the synoptic charts, it will be seen that there was a slow-moving shallow depression to the north-west of Ireland, and that the Channel Islands were under the stable winds of a warm sector. This is amply confirmed by the poor visibility, which is a trademark of maritime air originally from the tropics. The isobar spacing over the area at 1800 on Sunday suggests winds of 20 to 30 knots (Force 5 to 7) at the surface under these stable conditions. The tightness of the isobars over the Channel Islands as the cold front moved over Guernsey around 0600 on Sunday, 18 July, is consistent with perhaps Force 7 (28–33 knots) sustained temporarily. Taking the recorded wind velocity at Guernsey and adjusting for height of anemometer and multiplying by the factor for increase at sea compared with a shore station (as explained in Chapter 21), we again arrive at Force 7. This in turn agrees with my log and I think is a true assessment and has since been confirmed by other evidence.

1. *Wind forces.* That wind force tends to be overestimated in rough going if accompanied by dismal weather, driving rain and bad visibility. It is under such conditions (though most had retired to St. Peter Port before the fog) that retirements attain their maximum. Given the same strength of wind after a cold front, with sun and good visibility, retirements would be fewer.

2. *Tidal waters.* That a small yacht will have a rougher time in strong tidal waters at Force 7 with a weather-going tide or current (such as the Gulf Stream) than in a genuine gale.

3. *Light displacement.* These early ocean races proved that a small light-displacement yacht is safe at sea in the sort of heavy weather conditions she may occasionally have to face when cruising or ocean racing. It showed that a small modern Bermuda-rigged yacht can stand up to and beat the traditional powerful yachts such as Bristol pilot cutters and Brixham trawlers of many times her size, boat for boat without handicap, provided the wind is strong enough and right on the nose, where the gaff rig is at a disadvantage when reefed. *Cohoe* was not the first light-displacement yacht to prove her sea-going ability, as H. G. Hasler had won the class championship the previous year in *Tre-sang*, a 30 sq. metre even lighter than *Cohoe*. Neither *Tre-Sang* nor *Cohoe* ever won an ocean race except in heavy going.

4. *Heaving-to.* The experience also proved that short-keel yachts could heave-to. It had been thought at the time that this was a tactic available only to long straight-keeled yachts, but the fact is that the ability to heave-to depends on hull and sail balance, though a yacht with a long straight keel still retains an advantage in this respect.

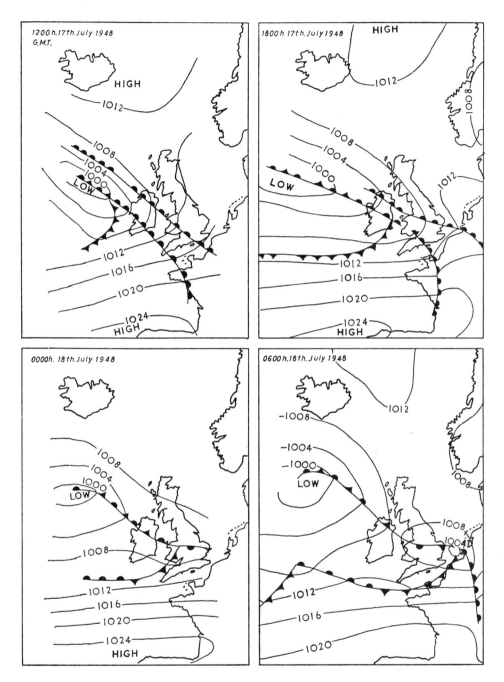

8   Synoptic charts covering Dinard Race, 1948.

5. *Despondency*. Beginners in ocean racing may feel despondent towards the end of a race. It is a condition of mind to which even experienced crews are prone, particularly if no other yachts have been sighted. It is induced by tiredness, but as the results of the Brixham and Dinard Races showed, a race is never lost before it is over. Time after time we have done well when we thought we had fared badly. One sees one's own mistakes, but forgets that competitors make mistakes too.

5

SANTANDER RACE STORM

Our first experience of being "caught out" in *Cohoe* in open water in a severe gale occurred in the famous Santander Race gale of 1948. The last time I had been properly caught out was as far back as 1925, which goes to show that a real gale is a rare bird indeed.

When I first entered *Cohoe* in this long race, I must admit that I did not know the precise position of Santander. I knew, of course, that it was on the coast of Spain, but only when I turned out the charts did I learn that it lies about midway on the south coast of the Bay of Biscay, approximately 440 miles on a direct course from the starting-point at Brixham. Of British ocean races, the Santander is one of the most genuine. Only once does one approach land, and that is when rounding Ushant, the most westerly point of France and an island of ill repute because of its strong tidal streams and off-lying reefs and rocks and the frequency of fog. For the rest, some 300 miles across the Bay, if the wind is westerly, one is for all intents and purposes racing in the Atlantic, in soundings of well over 2,000 fathoms.

As usual, *Cohoe* had a crew of three in total. Geoff Budden, a schoolmaster, came as astro-navigator, having learnt his craft as an instructor during the war. He was then new to offshore racing yachts, but settled down quickly, as he was an experienced dinghy sailor. As mate and cook I had my son, Ross, also a dinghy sailor, who had sailed with me in several previous ocean races. Watches were arranged in the usual manner, but in practice, with so small a crew, the duties and responsibilities overlap and we raced as a team, each ready to take over anything needed. There was precious little sleep for any of us.

In the three days before the race we were kept pretty busy. *Cohoe* was not in good racing trim, for in the Dinard Race she had bent the fitting at the foot of the forestay, and we had also found that the bolt through the mast at the head of the forestay had cut its way like a blunt knife downwards through the wood, so that the forestays were slack. The rigging screws of the forestays had been taken up as far as they would go, which was not enough to compensate for the distance which the bolt had been drawn down the mast. In the intervals between the races there had been no time to have the mast out for complete repairs, but thanks to Moody's Yard a temporary fitting for a new forestay had been provided, together with a new mast-band, since most of the cleats had been broken or torn off. I also had a temporary preventer stay set to the mast above the lower

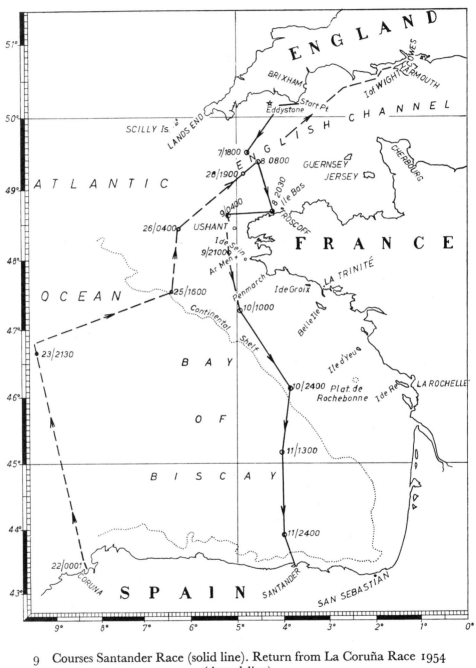

9   Courses Santander Race (solid line). Return from La Coruña Race 1954
(dotted line).

spreader, which, when required, could be set up by a tackle to any convenient cleat.

There were many other things to see to, including provisioning. A small yacht may not make good more than an average of 100 miles a day, and less if she meets prolonged calms or gales. I reckoned we needed rations which could be stretched out to cover ten days in the event of the yacht being disabled or dismasted. Allowing half a gallon of water a day per man, we required about 15 gallons. The main tank held 11 gallons and we had a $3\frac{1}{2}$-gallon portable tank made to fit under the cabin sole.

The race was to start from the line of the Brixham Yacht Club at 1530 on Friday, 6 August. Thirty-one yachts were entered, including many of the well-known ocean racers. The morning's weather report was not good. A depression was moving in from the west and there was a southerly gale in the Bay of Biscay. Strong winds were probable, so nobody was under any illusions as to what might be expected.

The wind was light at the start, but soon freshened. For the first twenty-four hours the racing fleet beat westwards off the English coast. The night was thundery and squally. Several yachts retired, reporting "Friday's gale", but if it was a gale it must have been very local, as we experienced nothing over Force 6, but at 0300 on Saturday morning 7 August it was blowing hard. *Cohoe* was going like a train under genoa only, surprisingly carrying weather helm under this single sail. However, by 0730 the wind had moderated temporarily and we were once more under full sail. Later in the morning the wind backed and I noted the barometer had fallen two-tenths of an inch (7 millibars) since the start of the race. We stood close-hauled on the port tack and the best course we could lay was about SW., which would take us some 30 miles west of Ushant.

During the Saturday afternoon the wind freshened again. In view of the forecast and the long swell which was building up, I set about reefing again. At 1500 I double-reefed the main and at 1600 set the brown staysail in place of the genoa. A little later the small white jib was hoisted in place of the staysail and the storm jib hanked on the spare forestay and halyard. At 1730 we lowered the mainsail, ran it off its groove and lashed it down, and set the storm trysail and storm jib. At this time the wind was about Force 6 and a fairly rough sea was running. The reefing and shifting of sails had been precautionary and in anticipation of events to come.

It is of interest here to look at the barograph readings of *Golden Dragon* (Page 70), which are reproduced by courtesy of her owner, the late Mr. H. J. Rouse. *Cohoe* was far astern of the Class II *Golden Dragon*, so the depression would have reached *Cohoe* an hour or two later. It will be seen that the slope steepens rapidly, falling three-tenths (10 millibars) in three hours, followed by an almost vertical half an inch (17 millibars) within 2 hours. A secondary depression had formed NE. of Spain in the morning and had deepened and moved rapidly across the Bay of Biscay, though we were not to know it at the time.

It was shortly before 1800 that the wind increased to well above Force 6, and this, coupled with the falling glass, the driving rain and the menacing conditions, decided me on reefing the trysail and bringing *Cohoe* down to storm canvas. At

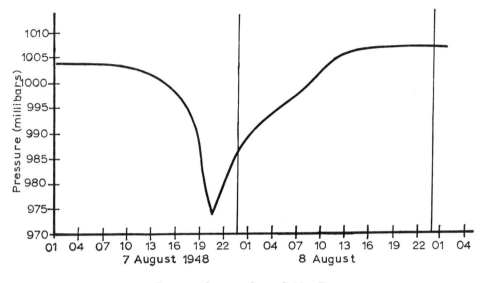

10　Barograph trace from *Golden Dragon*.

this time Geoff was at the helm, while Ross was below off watch. I was stand-by, and I pulled down the forward earring of the trysail and made fast. Then in order to take the strain off the clew pendant I checked off the main sheet. Then I returned to the cabin top to swig in the after reefing tackle.

The next moment I found myself overboard. Fortunately as I fell I held on to the reefing tackle. I suddenly realized that Geoff was overboard, too, for I saw him floating aft, but hanging on to something. Meanwhile the yacht was well balanced between her storm jib and the mainsail, which was checked right off. She was sailing herself on a 5-knot reach to the west.

At that instant, it being the 1800 change of watch, Ross had put his head on deck. His appearance was providential, for he was in time to haul aboard Geoff —whose position was precarious, as he had fallen in head first, and his head was towed under water by the speed of the yacht. In some miraculous way he retained his grip on a lifeline which with the stanchions had gone over the side and was trailing in the water.

My circumstances were less pressing. I had managed to get a foot aboard and wedged it into some wire rope, presumably the runner. But, suspended between the reefing tackle at the outer end of the boom, which was checked off, and my foot at the other, my body was in the water and I was unable to extricate myself. Instead of putting my foot aboard I ought to have pulled myself forward along the tackle to the inboard end of the boom, but one does not think of these niceties at the time—so I was glad when I was pulled on deck again.

It had been a narrow shave, for both Geoff and I were wearing heavy oilskins. If we had lost our hold, there would have been but a slim chance of survival, as with the trysail half-reefed it is doubtful whether Ross could have manoeuvred single-handed in such a sea to find and pick up survivors (not wearing life-jackets). It is easy to make light of such incidents after all is over, but it was something little short of a miracle that there was no casualty. The incident resulted from an extra large sea catapulting both Geoff and me against the lifelines simultaneously. These collapsed under the impact of our combined weight as the after securing eye was torn from the deck, and one stanchion rooted out, taking with it part of the toerail.

All in all the damage was light. Geoff had lost his glasses and for some while he feared he had broken a bone in his hand. I had some nasty-looking scratches on my skin and ankle, which bled a bit. Ross probably came off worst, as it must have been a shock to come on deck and find he was alone with not a single man left on board, and a second shock when he saw us both in the water.

Once aboard I finished reefing the trysail (apart from the reef points which were not urgent) and then went below with Geoff to change into dry things, and to bandage my foot, leaving Ross at the helm, for it was now his watch. It is easy enough to talk of dry clothes, but after racing for twenty-four hours to windward there is often precious little left that is dry. Geoff had run out of clothes, but fortunately I had a reserve kitbag forward and Ross had a few spare dry garments. I donned winter pyjamas (what warm, comfortable things these are at sea), sailing clothes on top and oilskins over that. I felt like the well-known Mr. Michelin of the inflated tyres.

Meanwhile the barometer was starting on its spectacular plunge and the wind increasing all the time. I decided to prepare for the worst and went back to join Ross on deck. We lowered the reefed trysail and storm jib and secured them.

For this race I had brought a sea anchor. To be of real value at sea one wants a sea anchor of very large dimensions, too cumbersome for stowage, but *Cohoe*'s was a small one. It was sufficient only to satisfy the qualms of those who thought that *Cohoe* was too small to look after herself. However, I decided to experiment with it. To the sea anchor we bent 30 fathoms of nylon, and at the inboard end we parcelled the rope with cloth where it would lead through the fairlead before belaying it to a cleat and also to the mast for extra security.

First we experimented with the anchor in the conventional position forward. Here it did no good. The yacht continued to lie broadside to the seas and the anchor lay away on the windward quarter. So we passed the nylon warp aft and made it fast. At the stern it had much the same result as is achieved by towing warps. It seemed to have a steadying effect, and the yacht lay with the seas broad on her quarter. She was perfectly happy, just like a cork, though, of course, the motion without steadying sails was wild in the extreme. At this time there was violent rain and hail. Then we went below, for there was nothing more we could do but reserve our energy for the race, when the gale had blown itself out.

Not long afterwards a Blue Funnel liner approached us closely, evidently desiring to offer assistance. Boats such as *Cohoe* are small from the point of view of a liner, and when lying under bare poles are often the object of investigation. During *Cohoe*'s first two seasons ships stood by on four different occasions, and, although their assistance was not required, the courtesy of the sea was appreciated.

The liner steamed off, and soon *Cohoe* was alone again on the wind-swept seas. I looked at the barometer. It was falling faster than ever.

At nightfall I was confronted by the problem of lights. My big fisherman's oil light had been smashed in the Dinard Race, and it had not been returned from repair by the makers in time for the Santander Race. In any case I doubt whether it would have kept alight under such conditions. The same reasoning applied to the small anchor light I had brought as a reserve. It might not blow out, but, as I have pointed out before, oil lights rarely stand up to the shaking of a gale; it is the vibration rather than the wind which extinguishes them. Besides this I had a small electric all-round light. This I put up, but in the dense rain and spray I felt it was not enough, so I switched on the navigation lights as well, and exhibited a Powerlite electric lamp over the stern. The chances of being run down were small, for the English Channel approaches comprise a large area and ships tend to keep to the north or south.

I have often been asked what it is like in the cabin of a small yacht in a gale. I say unhesitatingly that it is beastly. It is an experience nobody desires, but from time to time is unavoidable. To some extent it is frightening, for a severe gale is such a very violent thing that there is an instinctive apprehension. On the other hand, a yacht's cabin is an extraordinary haven of peace in hard weather compared with what it is like in the cockpit. The cabin lights swing in their gimbals, flooding the little compartment with light and warmth. One has companions to talk to.

When Geoff came off watch he expected to be stand-by for two hours and had taken the quarter berth so as to be within call from the cockpit. Quarter berths are the wettest in the ship, so Ross and I were lucky to have the cabin berths, one on each side of the saloon. The canvas leeboards were lashed up, so we could not be thrown out. Our principal discomfort was damp. Geoff had got wet again in the quarter berth when the companion door was opened and I went on deck to deal with the lamps. Ross and I got soaked when lowering the sails, and no more dry clothes were available. The cabin was wet, too, not from leaks, but from the water carried below by our clothes when Geoff and I changed after being thrown overboard, and from general condensation. Forward there was an occasional deluge of spray through the forehatch, despite its canvas storm cover. Our cumbersome clothes added to the discomfort, especially the oilskins which we had to wear in case we should suddenly be needed on deck. Ventilation was not good either, as both ventilator cowls had been caught, lifted off the Dorade boxes, and flung overboard by the flogging jib sheets when tacking. We were, however, able to keep a lee porthole open, while the companion hatch was also kept ajar until the head of another sea descended upon the protesting Geoff.

The glass was still falling. It had fallen an inch (34 millibars) since we left Brixham, and the barograph record, which I was shown after the race was over, indicated a fall of over ⅓ inch (22 millibars) in 3 hours. At midnight the greatest fury of the gale fell on us. The wind and rain flattened the sea. The yacht heeled as though under full sail. On the deck above our heads blasts of rain hammered fiercely. I think then the wind shifted. How heavy the sea was I do not know, for the sea cannot be seen at night except for the flashing white phosphorescent crests. It was certainly violent and large. One exceptional wave woke us up later as it threw the yacht almost on her beam ends. Some said afterwards that the seas ran "mountains high". But as for the wind; it was the highest I had known up to then. If the reader examines the barograph readings he can judge for himself. With a gradient so steep as this, winds far exceeding Gale Force 8 are inevitable and the gusts may be anything.

In all this *Cohoe* behaved very well. The yacht was lifted bodily great heights in the air and then down she would go. Down, down and one tensed oneself for crash, but at the bottom she never slammed, but gently came to rest before rising once more to the next. No seas broke over the coachroof or came aboard solid, but Ross said the self-emptying cockpit was often a foot or two under water from heads of seas and driving spray.

By dawn on Sunday (8 August) the wind had moderated, but in *Cohoe*'s cabin conditions did not seem much quieter. For a while after a gale the sea is often more truculent than during its height. The yacht is no longer steadied by the wind and the motion is worse in consequence. At 0700 I got up. I felt amazingly well and refreshed, for I had had a good deal of sleep—more than we got at any other time in the race. I went forward through the cabin and tried the radio, as we wanted a weather report. It would not work. I tried various ways, but the only thing to do was to take it into the cabin for drying out and testing. I unscrewed it and carried it aft. At that moment I suddenly began to feel sea-sick.

I handed the radio to Ross and lay down, feeling fit again at once. Ross played with its innards and inserted a new valve, but after sitting up he, too, suddenly felt ill. All of us were fit when lying down, but each felt seedy the moment he sat up and tried to do anything. Ross, however, dealt with the radio, alternately working on it and lying down when he felt sick. I decided not to make sail again until we got the 0800 weather report. The glass was rising, with a jump which might presage more bad weather. By 0800 Ross got the report, though feebly, having to press his ears to the instrument. The report was fair, but the past twenty-four hours was described as a "vigorous depression with severe local gales in Biscay and the West Channel". A severe gale is Force 9, with a mean wind velocity from 41 to 44 knots.

Once the weather report had been received we immediately made sail. Geoff and Ross got *Cohoe* under way. The two of them heaved on the long warp leading to the sea anchor. Aware of the great strain imposed by a sea anchor without a tripping line, they heaved hard, and with remarkable success, for they got the nylon rope in hand-over-hand as if nothing were at its end. With the final heave they discovered the truth: there *was* nothing at its end. The sea anchor had gone in the night, and none noticed any difference.

Before we had been long under way we sighted a sail. At one moment it would appear high in the sky and at the next it would be lost in a trough. The sea had gone down, but a lumpy swell was still running. As *Cohoe* drew near we fetched cameras and as we passed close under the yacht's stern we exchanged photographs. She was *Mehalah*, a Class III rival, and the picture reproduced of her (Plate 6) is one of the few authentic photographs of a yacht hove-to, though taken after and not during the gale. Unfortunately, our arrival on the scene was the sign for feverish sail-making in *Mehalah* and she was quickly after us. We responded by setting more sail. As the morning drew on the wind softened and eventually *Cohoe* was under full sail again.

During the afternoon I took the opportunity afforded by the light weather to check the water position. I was shocked to find only about 3 gallons left in the tank, and that water had been leaking from the cap when the yacht was severely heeled. At first I took a poor view of this, but investigation proved it was not the fault of the crew, for although the cap appeared screwed down tight, the screw thread was broken and when the yacht heeled the water leaked out into the bilges. It must have leaked a lot during the gale. So here we were with 3 gallons left of the main supply and a reserve of only $3\frac{1}{2}$ gallons in the portable tank. Over 300 miles of the course still lay ahead, with possibility of calms or gales. The crew took the news more happily than I did. Geoff calculated we could survive for some days if need be on the juice out of tins of soup and other provisions. In the end we compromised by rationing water to $1\frac{1}{2}$ pints a day per man, which compares with the normal usage of 4 pints per man per day. If this could be maintained, we had enough for ten days. To encourage thrift, tea and all hot drinks and orangeade were cut out. Ross drew a little diagram which he pinned to the bulkhead showing three half-pints per man per day. When one of us had a drink out of a half-pint mug he put a stroke through one of his rations on the communal card. For the benefit of others who may run short of water at sea it can be recorded that we not merely kept to our ration but we saved on it. When we arrived at Santander we had the reserve $3\frac{1}{2}$ gallons untouched.

We had been about mid-Channel when we hove-to and as the wind did not veer as forecast we made a landfall on the French coast some 50 miles east of Ushant, which we did not round until Monday afternoon (9 August) as the wind was light. It was not until nightfall that we entered the Bay of Biscay, leaving to port the Ar Men buoy which marks the end of the Saints', the finger of reefs and ledges which extend from France nearly 10 miles into the Atlantic.

Tuesday (10 August) was a day of moderate winds in which the ship's company settled down to the routine of deep-water sailing as the yacht drew out far away from land into the Bay of Biscay. The only incident occurred when I was below off watch and heard a bang. *Cohoe* had struck a glancing blow on a floating log. There were numbers of these floating about and for a while the helmsman was kept busy avoiding them. We heard afterwards that a timber ship had lost her deck cargo of timber during the gale; it brought a rich harvest to French fishing vessels.

Early in the afternoon there was a sharp fall of rain, and we were able to collect fresh water for washing from the pools in the corner of the lee cockpit seats.

In the early hours of Wednesday morning (11 August) *Cohoe* had left the Continental shelf with its soundings of 100 fathoms or so, and passed into the 2,000-fathom depths of the Atlantic. By 0200 it was blowing Force 4 and there was quite a vicious sea and by 0300 we took a double reef in the mainsail, and the wind settled down to a good hard steady blow.

Shortly before 0500 we heard a sharp "ping". Geoff and I rushed on deck, but could find no breakage. As soon as it became light we discovered that the bolts of the track for the weather runner had sheared. I made temporary repairs by putting a long wire seizing on the runner and set it up again farther aft on an undamaged part of the track.

At 0700 the wind moderated so we shook out the reefs, but an hour later we had to pull them down again. At 1100 we lowered the genoa and set the intermediate jib. The runner threatened to lift the remaining track off the deck. This was a serious worry, and an unanticipated one, as I had had the track through-bolted during the previous winter, after the same trouble in La Rochelle Race.

At 1400 we lowered the working staysail and set the small white 6-metre jib, but two hours later this had to be lowered and the tiny storm jib was set in its place. With the runner in such doubtful condition we could not afford to risk the loss of the mast, which was subject to great strains as the ship plunged. *Cohoe*'s speed fell to 6½ knots, a very serious loss of time in a race such as this. Meanwhile the sea was steadily increasing.

Geoff had managed to get a noon latitude by lashing himself to the mast while he took the sight, but in the afternoon the sky was overcast and we sailed through a series of squalls, so no further sights were possible. At 1800 we passed a floating gin bottle, which gave us a clue to our longitude, as we guessed some other yacht ahead of us had passed that way.

During the evening the sea was very rough indeed and the weather stormy. We heard later that even the Class I *Latifa* was at this time down to storm canvas. The wind had veered and freed; under double-reefed mainsail and storm jib we were soon logging 7 knots again, despite the weak runner. When Ross was on watch he made frequent remarks about planing, which as a dinghy sailer he should know something about. Besides being large, the seas had very steep breaking tops. It seemed amazing that none broke aboard. *Cohoe* was lifted up and surfed forwards as each breaking, foaming pyramid came up to her stern. Then she would subside down its back before lifting again to the next sea. It became necessary to lash the helmsman in the cockpit, and at nightfall I shortened the watches to hourly spells. It was quite enough, for the boat needed concentration to steer, and the helmsman was constantly blinded by spray.

At midnight we knew our distance off the Spanish coast, under 30 miles, by dead reckoning and from a noon sight, but apart from the gin-bottle clue we did not know our exact longitude.

Early on Thursday morning (12 August), at 0130, Ross identified the loom of the double flash of Cabo Major light at the entrance to Santander, less than 20 miles distant. Course was altered and with a quartering wind *Cohoe* sailed very fast, so before long the blaze of lights of the town of Santander could be seen. At 0355 we let off two white flares as we crossed the finishing line. The eventful race was over and, with the dawn, the sun rose above the mountains of Spain, 440 miles and five and a half days from our departure in England.

Eilun proved to be the all-over and Class I winner. Hers was a well-merited victory, as she was an old Fife boat adapted for ocean racing and the smallest in her class. Pat Hall, her experienced owner, told me before the race started that his tactics would be to make as much westing as possible when the wind backed early in the gale and southing when the wind veered, and he proved right. *Erivale* won Class II and *Mindy* Class III. *Cohoe* was second in her class with *Mehalah* third. The ocean racing fleet survived the gale well. Out of the thirty-two starters only eleven retired owing to damage of one kind or another, and the only serious accident occurred in *Benbow*, one of whose crew broke his arm, but the same night that Geoff and I went over the side from *Cohoe* a man went overboard from *Erivale*. This happened when it began to blow. It was very dark and raining hard. The headsail was being changed down and Peter Padwick, then a medical student and one of her crew, was winching in the sheet whilst her owner, Dr. Greville, was "tailing on". A sea seemed to catch the ship on her wrong foot, so that Padwick was catapulted over the lifelines, but fortunately, lying on his back, he managed to get his arm round a stanchion. The owner grabbed his ankle and, coinciding with the reverse lurch of the ship, got him back on board, when he continued to winch as though nothing had happened. The stanchion, of stainless steel, was bent over 45 degrees from the vertical.

Conclusions

Let us now assess the gale. A depression was moving west towards Ireland and a vigorous secondary established itself in the early hours of Saturday morning NW. of Spain and crossed the Bay of Biscay, arriving off Brest at 1800, and continued across the English Channel approaches towards Plymouth. The centre of the low (which had deepened to 976 millibars) thus passed a little to the northward of the leaders of the ocean-racing fleet and directly across those in mid Channel, which included *Cohoe*, *Mehalah* and others hove-to near by.

In the Bay of Biscay a number of fishing vessels were lost when running for shelter and there were casualties along the coast of Brittany. The gale was reported as one of the worst known in the Channel Islands. The *Isle of Sark*, with 750 passengers, took shelter at St. Peter Port, where even in the harbour six pleasure vessels broke from their moorings and were sunk. On the English coast many yachts and other vessels were in distress. Cross-Channel steamers reported their worst crossing of the year. As I have remarked, a severe gale is always recorded in the newspapers, but this particular gale featured as the leader on the front page of the *Daily Telegraph*, which devoted three columns to it, so great was the damage and loss.

The gale was reported in the newspapers as a 70 m.p.h. (61 knot) gale. Mr. J. S. A. Rendell (a former officer in the Clan Line), in a letter to *Yachting Monthly* in September 1966, stated that he had passed the yachts during the gale in M.V. *Stirlingshire* when homeward bound from Australia. If he remembered correctly, it was logged at Force 11 (56–63 knots) at one stage.

I thought perhaps there might be an error in the recollection of the *Stirlingshire*'s log or that the entry related to gusts, but Alan Watts, as a meteorologist, comments in Chapter 21 that "it seems inevitable that the report of Force 11 from the Clan liner was correct, even though . . . such wind strength could not have been sustained for long", and he gives barometric graphs in support of his opinion. The only evidence in the ocean-racing fleet came from *Theodora*, who recorded gusts of 6o knots on her anemometer, which were not necessarily the the highest and were probably taken at deck-level, which gives a lower reading than 33 ft. aloft, which is the correct position for judging the wind on the Beaufort Notation.

The only records that I have received from the Meteorological Office show hourly values of Force 8 at Portland Bill and Force 9 at Guernsey. These are coastal stations where winds are usually lower than at sea, and what is more, they were not in the direct track of the centre of the low.

Looking at the tight isobars on the synoptic charts, I think a fair assessment of the gale when it passed over the yachts was possibly Force 10 (48–55 knots) or even Force 11 during squalls. If this is true, the gusts might have been about hurricane force. I write with caution, because I frankly admit that I cannot judge wind strengths over Force 8 or 9, as they are so few and far between, and in the general hubbub it is difficult to guess the mean speed on the Beaufort Scale or to distinguish between gusts of 65, 60 or 55 knots. The latter is quite enough for me.

1. *Severe gales*. A severe gale or storm is a very rare bird in summer months. Eight years elapsed before ocean racers were caught out again in home waters in a storm to match it. This was the Channel gale of 1956, described in Chapter II. Force 10 is so rare (except on weather forecasts) that it need hardly be reckoned with when cruising, though it remains a remote possibility.

Loss of life occurred in fishing vessels running for shelter, and coastal vessels and yachts in narrow waters were in distress, but all the ocean racers in deep water in the West Channel, including the small *Cohoe* and *Persephone*, came through the storm safely, apart from loss of sails and minor damage.

This rubs in the old lesson that in a severe gale or storm the safest place is out at sea, as far from land as possible.

2. *Secondaries*. A secondary depression is sometimes more intense than its parent. It is something a yachtsman should look out for, especially when a major depression is passing to the northward. The development and course of secondaries are not so easily predictable as those of their parents, and hence there may be shorter warning of them on the forecasts. They are of comparatively short duration (the gale referred to lasted under twelve hours) and although the wind forces are high the seas may not attain their maximum height in relation to the wind strength, as the gale may not last long enough for them to develop fully.

3. *Sea anchors*. The experiment with the sea anchor was inconclusive, as it was too small. Nevertheless, it confirmed the experiences of other sailing men that a short-keeled yacht will not readily lie head to wind to a sea anchor without a riding sail aft. The important fact emerges that *Cohoe*, a very small yacht, was reasonably safe lying a-hull and left to herself under bare pole.

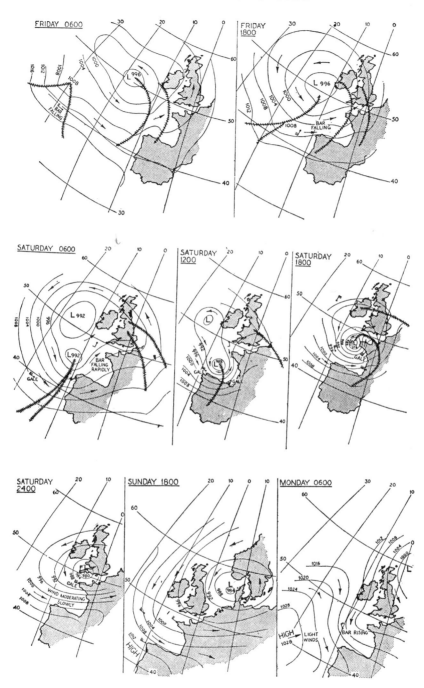

11   Synoptic charts covering Santander Race, 1948.

79

4.   *Drift downwind.* When lying a-hull under bare pole the yacht's drift to lee-ward appeared to have been not less than $1\frac{1}{2}$ knots.

5.   *Height of waves.* The owner of an 18–ton cruising yacht whose crew were rescued reported "seas that must have been 40 ft. high". As stated in the Intro-duction, yachtsmen are inclined to measure a wave by its apparent height compared with the mast, but in my opinion it is an optical illusion and the true height is only about three-fifths or perhaps half of the apparent height. After all, a 24 ft. wave ($\frac{3}{5}$ × 40 ft.) is immense for the West Channel.

6.   *Stanchions.* Stanchions and lifelines must be very strong. In *Cohoe* the stan-chions were screwed to the deck and bolted to the toerail, but the combined weight of Geoff and myself not only uprooted the stanchions but tore the toerail out. The R.O.R.C. has brought in strict regulations about securing stanchions, but I think it unwise to rely entirely upon these safety measures unless the fittings are immensely strong, which is not the case in many yachts. Stanchions seem liable to bend or break, as is confirmed by other incidents recorded later in this book.

7.   *Life-jackets and safety harness.* Because of their bulk we never wore life-jackets before 1950. If this is criticized, I may add that the Brixham trawler crews with whom I sailed after the 1914-18 war did not either, even in gales. Nor could they swim.

The thing to avoid is going overboard at all, and it is here that personal lifelines and harness are useful, but they did not come into general use before the 1950 Transatlantic Race to which I refer later. Personal safety harness (if strong enough) would have provided a link with the ship when Geoff and I went overboard. Nevertheless, I still think safety at sea depends primarily upon self-reliance, and that a safety harness is only a secondary aid which should not be overdone.

8.   *Water.* Where there is only one water tank, a reserve of water should always be carried in separate containers during a long-distance race or cruise.

9.   *Sea-sickness.* Sea-sickness is the greatest handicap in a gale. Many sailing men will experience nausea if they do work below which involves bending down, such as looking for the right tin lost among a mass of provisions in a locker, or, as occurred in this race, bending down trying to repair a wireless. Sea-sickness can sometimes be avoided by keeping on deck or lying down when below. Nowadays, sea-sick pills may give immunity against nausea, but do not neces-sarily against extreme sea-sickness.

10.   *Anxiety ashore.* Anxiety to relatives was caused by the late arrival of several yachts, which were reported as unaccounted for, including *Cohoe*. A small yacht averages only about 100 miles a day. In a gale she may be long delayed when hove-to or sheltering, possibly where there is no means of communication with the shore. A gale is often followed by a calm which slows her passage. Minor

damage such as loss of sails may cause further delay, and serious damage such as a rudder breakage or even dismasting may make arrival several days late. This applies whether racing or cruising, so anxiety ashore is fortunately often premature.

11. *Confidence*. The most valuable part of our experience in the Santander Race gale was that, following on successes in lesser gales, it gave us complete confidence in the hitherto much-disputed sea-keeping qualities of a small light-displacement yacht such as *Cohoe*.

6

THREE MORE GALES

From the last chapters it may be thought that *Cohoe* was used entirely for ocean racing. This was far from the case, as apart from racing we cruised 1,000 to 1,500 miles or more each season, and in her first three seasons she made the crossing of the English Channel nearly forty times. Many offshore races finish in a foreign port, which affords a good start for cruising, and we did a great deal of sailing besides this. Sometimes *Cohoe* was manned by crews who had holiday time remaining after the races, but mostly I cruised with my wife or family.

Constantly on the move as we were, we had plenty of heavy weather sailing, but we never really got caught out in the open water in the same way as we did when ocean racing. Thus, I hope the reader will forgive me if I continue what seems to be a catalogue of ocean racing, for it was from these experiences that I acquired most of the knowledge I possess of gales.

HOVE-TO OFF BELLE ÎLE

It was a strange coincidence that *Cohoe* should be involved in another depression in the very next race after the Santander, and have the dubious honour of having it all to herself.

The race from Santander to Belle Île was started on the afternoon of 15 August. The course was a little east of north, 235 miles direct across the south-east of the Bay of Biscay (see p. 68, fig. 9). In the meantime Geoff's leave had run out and he had returned to England. His place in *Cohoe* was taken by Dick Trafford, a Cambridge friend of Ross.

We had been royally entertained in Spain during our three days' visit and few of us had had much sleep. We were sorry when the time arrived to exchange the sun and the warmth of the hospitality for the cruel sea and tinned provisions.

However, we started on a brilliant Sunday afternoon with a fine fresh breeze to shake us down. The wind headed in the early hours of Monday morning and by 0830 it had freshened so much that we had to take in a reef. We kept the genoa standing, but the bolt holding the runner plate sheared under the strain and repairs had to be effected. At 1000 the mainsail tore right across under the headboard. The sail came down with a run and the headboard and halyard went aloft to the masthead.

82

Cohoe's mast was solid, high and thin, and above the jumpers it was little more than the thickness of a big walking stick. A considerable swell was running and a fairly rough sea, so there was no prospect of swarming up the mast to retrieve the halyard. The burgee sheave was a strong one, so we tried to lead a wire rope through it by means of the burgee halyard, but the attempts were unsuccessful and finally the burgee halyard broke.

We then shackled the bosun's chair to the fore halyard and hoisted Dick Trafford, the lightest of the three of us, up to the forestay block. But the motion was so wild aloft and he was thrown about so much that he could not reach the peak and retrieve the main halyard. When he was lowered to the deck he was violently sick.

Deprived of her mainsail, the yacht was rolling tremendously in the seas. It was difficult to retain one's foothold even on deck, and aloft, even when secured to the mast, it was like being at the end of a pendulum, as it swung first one side and then the other over the sea. It was enough to make anybody sea-sick.

We abandoned the attempts to retrieve the main halyard and lashed the mainsail to the boom. Next we tried setting the trysail by means of the spinnaker halyard, but this failed because we could not get the lead right.

Only one thing was left that could be done and that was to reeve a new halyard through a block and lash the block to the mast above the upper spreader. When the block and halyard were ready Ross volunteered to go aloft with them, but Dick and I did not relish the idea of pulling over 13 stone in weight up the mast by means of the fore halyard; nor would it have been fair on the small mast winch. Accordingly, I, as the next lightest, went up in the bosun's chair. This was quickly done with the aid of Ross's and Dick's beef at the winch. Like Dick, I found the motion aloft made things difficult. I really needed both hands to hold on by, but I got a temporary grip with my knees round the mast when lashing the block in position. The repair was a strong one and I was soon on deck again, when I, too, was promptly sick. All three of us had now been sick, which after all was a compliment to the tremendous parties we had enjoyed in Spain.

As the burgee halyard had broken and hence our racing flag was down, I got a sail needle and cotton and sewed the racing flag to the peak of the trysail before setting it. It was an act of bravado, but it made us feel better.

This attempt to retrieve the halyard and the other activities which take only a few lines to describe wasted no less than four hours. Happily the wind was about Force 6, so, despite the loss of the use of the mainsail, reasonable progress was made under genoa and trysail.

However, the wind moderated early on Tuesday (17 August) and remained light. Under reduced sail *Cohoe* was very slow. The loss of the mainsail had already put us out of the race so far as winning a place was concerned.

83

It was not until 0400 in the morning of the Wednesday, 18 August, that we sighted the loom in the sky of the powerful Goulphar light on Belle Île bearing N.15°E., distant 22 miles by dead reckoning. The barometer was falling and the wind had backed and freshened, so we were making over 5 knots.

At 0700 there was dense rain and the visibility closed down to about three-quarters of a mile and often less.

Cohoe sailed on in a grey world of her own. Belle Île is not difficult of approach when one knows it, as most of the outlying dangers are off the Goulphar lighthouse and at the northern end. The tidal streams, however, are fairly strong and rather unpredictable close in to the island, and less than 5 miles to the eastward lies a particularly dangerous area of submerged rocks between the Cardinals and Quiberon.

At 0900, having sighted nothing and being then totally unfamiliar with Belle Île, I decided it was best to alter course and stand out into deep water to the north-west of the island. Visibility was very bad owing to the heavy rain, and it

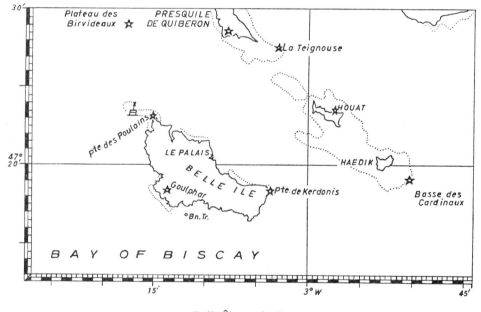

12   Belle Île to Quiberon.

was blowing so hard that we had to set the storm jib, which meant that, with the trysail already set, we were down to storm canvas. We found ourselves in company with a big tunnyman. For a short time we followed. We could hold but not overhaul her and she kept eluding us in the rain squalls, so we came back to our course to keep clear of the land.

At 1030 we hove-to. We had been doing 6½ knots under storm canvas, but now the wind was near to gale force and a big sea was making. The yacht lay heading WSW. on the port tack and we lay-to under trysail only, with helm up instead of down, as the storm jib was rather much for her. It was an experiment, but it worked perfectly and left to herself *Cohoe* lay steady, riding the waves and forereaching slightly.

Our position was to the NW. of Belle Île, but as I had seen no land since leaving Spain, except for the loom of the Goulphar lighthouse, a deck watch had to be kept all the time just in case there was any error in navigation. A motor trawler appeared out of the dense rain, and ranged up close alongside to inquire whether assistance was needed and, when satisfied that it was not, disappeared in the murk. At about 1400 we refreshed ourselves with a bottle of champagne we had bought in Spain. A little later, in better spirits, we tacked under trysail, set the storm jib, and reached back towards Belle Île, keeping a sharp look-out.

Between 1700 and 1800 the visibility was worse than ever and there was no sight of Belle Île. Although casts of the lead showed we were in deep water, the bottom shelves rapidly off the rocky NW. coast of Belle Île and there are offlying rocks, so we did not like to stand on any longer. It was blowing harder than ever, so we tacked and hove-to again on the offshore tack. I decided not to attempt to get nearer the land until after dark, when we ought to be able to see Goulphar lighthouse, which has a range of 23 miles in clear weather. We decided to get some rest, as we should have to sail through the night, but at 1930 we were roused by shouting. It was another French tunnyman that was offering assistance.

None of her crew spoke English, but I remembered the words which a governess or schoolmaster used to apply: "Allez vous en"—and we were able to wave them away with the empty champagne bottle. The tunnyman bore away quickly and disappeared in the rain. We remained hove-to, had dinner and washed up.

By 2100 it was dark and we sighted Pointe des Poulains light, which is at the extreme north of Belle Île, so we were not far out in estimated position. The light was to the south of us and the harbour of Le Palais was only 5 miles SE. of the lighthouse and the wind was free as it had veered. It would have taken little over an hour to gain shelter and get a good night's sleep, but the rules of the race provided that the Pointe de Kerdonis on the SE. of Belle Île had to be left to port. This meant we had almost to circle Belle Île, which involved a long beat to windward and a distance of 25 miles to cross the finishing line off Le Palais from the correct direction. It says a lot for Ross and Dick that the thought of giving up never crossed their minds. Perhaps it was because the racing flag was sewn to the sail, but this attitude was common to all my crews in *Cohoe*.

It was a slow passage. First we had to beat round the north end of Belle Île. The wind had moderated and we set the genoa. No sooner was it set than the wind freshened and it had to be replaced by the staysail. Then it came on hard again and we had to set the storm jib.

Meanwhile the sky had cleared and the moon shone. Under the lee of the land the big swell had subsided. At midnight there was a violent squall and it blew so fiercely that the boat was almost knocked down by it. We lowered the storm jib quickly and carried on under trysail only. It was very slow work, but fortunately the tide was fair. The barometer was rising sharply and presently the wind moderated, enabling first the storm jib and later the staysail to be set. At dawn next morning the Goulphar lighthouse and Belle Île were in sight.

At 0900 we set the genoa. It was a lovely sunny day, but the wind was dying away and under trysail, instead of a mainsail, progress was desperately slow. It was not until 1320 on Thursday that we crossed the finishing line off Le Palais under trysail on a windless summer day. We were the last in the race, but *Cohoe* received a cheer from the ocean-racing fleet as she limped into the harbour, some thirty-six hours overdue. The R.O.R.C. is not given to sentiment, and in twenty years of racing this was the only occasion I have known such a warm welcome accorded to any yacht. We appreciated it more than any prize.

Conclusions

There is nothing to corroborate this gale, as we received no weather reports and saw no French newspapers. The British meteorological stations were too far away to be much help, but the synoptic charts suggest about Force 6. Yet the wind must have been stronger.

I have chanced to come across a cutting from *Yachting World* reporting the race. Referring to Monday night (long before the gale) it reads: "freshened to about Force 6 with occasional heavy squalls and a very awkward sea . . ." "Nearly everybody agreed that it was one of the most unpleasant nights they had ever experienced at sea." "*Myth* . . . hard on the wind at an average speed of over 6 knots, some of it in the vilest conditions."

What, then, was the force of the wind in the gale on Wednesday when the storm jib was set at 0900 and in the squall at night when even the storm jib had to be lowered? Link this with the fact that a number of large ships sought shelter in Belle Île roads, and the yachts in harbour were so uncomfortable that many of them went through the locks to find security in the inner basin.

This evidence suggests Force 8, but remember that *Cohoe* was an exceptionally tender boat. With the hindsight conferred by long experience I should say the wind was probably Force 7, and the squall on Wednesday night probably 50 knots or so, as this is not uncommon when a cold front is going through.

The experience added to my apprenticeship in heavy weather sailing and may be of interest to owners of small yachts of 3 to 4 tons displacement, but the performance would now be outclassed owing to the improvements in the design of small ocean racers. My present boat, *Cohoe III*, for example, has about three times the stability of the first *Cohoe*, and with the aid of electronic instruments the handling is more scientific At Force 7 by anemometer she would carry a small genoa and a mainsail two rolls reefed. A minimum speed of 6 knots to windward, or over 7 knots downwind, would be maintained as measured by

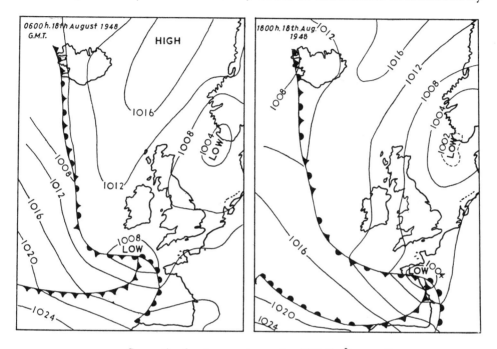

13   Synoptic charts covering gale off Belle Île, 1948.

Harrier speedometer. D.F. bearings would render approach to Belle Île easy. Likewise with a crew of five instead of three much of the wear and tear of ocean racing would be eliminated.

1.   *Damage aloft.* The loss of the main halyard was the primary cause of the trouble, as otherwise *Cohoe* would have been in harbour long before the gale, in company with her competitors. Going aloft in a rough sea proved a very different task from doing it in harbour. Maybe we made too much of it, as wonderful repair jobs have been done at sea in other yachts.

2.   *Errors.* When, after the race was over, I checked the course on the chart I found I had made an error of 10 miles in pricking off the distance run. The loom of Goulphar light had been sighted at a distance of 32 miles and not 22 miles. Hence it was not surprising that we failed to sight Belle Île five hours later, for we still were some miles south of the island when we altered course away from the land.

This stupid mistake was no doubt due to being rather tired. A racing skipper in a small yacht crewed by a total of three has to do navigation as well as his full share of watch-keeping and seamanship, and I had been short of sleep for the whole of the twelve days (allowing for festivities in Spain) between Brixham and Belle Île.

The moral is to be particularly careful when tired and to double check every-thing, for it is then all too easy to make a silly slip such as I did. Better still is the independent check by a member of the crew.

3. *Heaving-to*. The method of heaving-to under trysail only was original and worked well. The helm was lashed up instead of down, just sufficiently to prevent the yacht from luffing head to wind and getting in irons. The best position was found by trial and error.

4. *Halyards*. A spare halyard is desirable. A masthead topping lift can be used if there is one, or the burgee sheave can be made large enough and strong enough to accept a halyard.

5. *Visibility*. When cruising it is good seamanship to stand out to sea rather than approach an unfamiliar coast in bad visibility, unless one is certain of position. This is a principle I still maintain, where the coast is rock-strewn, as in North Brittany, and one can get into trouble before land is even sighted. Belle Île, however, is not a bad landfall and maybe I was rather overcautious by racing standards.

GUSTING OVER 60 KNOTS

The first occasion on which I have ever been able to get precise confirmation of wind strength in the precise position of the yacht was in the Solent in 1947 or 1948. *Cohoe* was lying at Cowes and there was one of those exceptional gales which occur only once every few years. We made the trip back to Bursledon under storm jib only and after our return I telephoned to Calshot, who told me that it was gusting 70 m.p.h. (61 knots, equivalent to the top of Force 11) at the precise time *Cohoe* was off Calshot. This was useful, for although *Cohoe* had been at sea under such conditions she had been lying a-hull in open water, whereas on this occasion she was under sail, though in the sheltered water of the Solent.

The feature of this wind force when under sail is the vibration in the rigging if the stays and shrouds are not set up hard. We had to gybe off the West Bramble buoy. The jib was tiny, but to avoid damage we had to sheet it across using both winches and even so when it gybed the shock was so great that it shook the mast from truck to deck.

Although there is only a relatively short fetch in the Solent, there were real seas in the vicinity of Calshot lightship, and I closed the cabin doors in case one should board us. Even off Hamble Spit buoy it was rough, but the seas were more regular, wind and tide being in the same direction. We ran up the river at tremendous speed, passing dinghies sunk at their moorings and yachts which had broken adrift and gone ashore. As we approached Moody's yard I got the engine going, because we had to alter course under the lee of Land's End marshes. Here the wind is always fluky. I did not want to risk getting out of control with only the storm jib set, so the sail was lowered and we proceeded up the reach under power. Under the lee of the high land by the Jolly Sailor I brought *Cohoe* round, motored back downriver and, with two men forward with the boathook ready, I luffed for the mooring.

Did she luff, though? With no protection except the low marshes, the gale was too strong for her. She lost way, her rudder became useless, and a gust took charge. With the bodies of the crew acting as a sail the bows were blown off by the wind. In a matter of seconds down she went to leeward straight on to the putty to join the other yachts which had broken away from their moorings.

So, when I read advice to beginners, recommending that if caught out in a gale they should use the auxiliary engine, I wonder to myself what sort of gale and what sort of engine? I cannot imagine any 6 h.p. or even 10 h.p. engine in a small auxiliary yacht would have been the least use getting to windward in *open water* in any of the major gales I have described. Windage and seas would be too much, but in Chapter 20 I give an example of where an engine was used by a yacht caught out in a hurricane.

THE WOLF ROCK RACE

(See p. 57, Fig. 7)

Few new yachts were constructed immediately after the war expressly designed for ocean racing. Of the few, Captain John Illingworth's *Myth of Malham*, built 1947, was the most outstanding and remained one of the best ocean racers for a record number of years. In 1949 the R.N.S.A. (Royal Naval Sailing Association) 24 ft. waterline class was introduced. These boats were designed by Laurent Giles and Partners in collaboration with John Illingworth, and were commonly known as the R.N.S.A. 24's. These were short-ended boats with high freeboard and transom sterns. Compared with *Cohoe*, the R.N.S.A. 24 was 1¼ ft. shorter in overall length, but not having such fine sections as *Cohoe* was of rather higher displacement. In addition, the R.N.S.A. 24 set almost 100 sq. ft. more canvas and therefore carried a higher rating.

The R.N.S.A.s proved the most successful class designed up to then and swept the board during 1949 and remained near the top of Class III ocean racing for several years. The principal boats in the class were *Minx of Malham* owned by John Illingworth, *Blue Disa* owned by Colonel Dick Schofield, and *Samuel Pepys*, which was the R.N.S.A. club boat, later to become one of the most famous small ocean racers.

At that time Class III yachts were not allowed to enter in the Fastnet Race, as they were considered too small. The Wolf Rock event, which was run at the same time as the Fastnet, was a kind of consolation race for Class III. The course was a good one, starting from Cowes to C.H. 1 buoy off Cherbourg, thence round the Wolf Rock off Land's End and back to finish at Plymouth, a distance of 305 miles with plenty of windward work.

I do not propose to describe this race, as it was much like many others and I will limit myself to the gale which occurred.

The race started on a Saturday (6 August) at 1000 in summery conditions and it was not until 0800 on Sunday morning, when we were off the Casquets, that we received a gale warning. At noon this was repeated. A deep depression was moving in a NE. direction which would give rise to "severe" gales in the West Channel and Irish Sea. The wind backed to SE. and the barometer fell slowly. It was not until the Sunday afternoon (7 August) that the sky darkened and the wind began to rise. The yachts raced on over a dismal sea through a belt of heavy rain, and sail was reduced by stages.

The wind reached gale force SSW. in the early evening, when we were south of Plymouth. We adopted our usual tactics of lowering all sail and lying a-hull. The seas seemed to be running as high as they did in the Santander Race gale, but perhaps this was because it was daylight and we could see them, whereas the worst of the gale in the former race occurred during the night, when we were below either sleeping or trying to do so. On the other hand, the wind was not so strong, at least where we were lying. *Cohoe* lay comfortably, but she heeled at a greater angle than she had the previous year. She had been fitted with a stronger mast, which was similar to those in the R.N.S.A. class. It was of considerably greater section and both mast and rigging were designed to be strong enough to withstand a gust that would lay the yacht flat on her beam ends. The spar was hollow and supposed to be lighter than the old one, but when it was built I think it must have been made with thicker walls than specified. As a result, the extra windage and weight (remember that the yacht's ballast keel was only $1\frac{3}{4}$ tons) made the yacht more tender than ever.

Gale force conditions lasted little more than six hours. Among the competitors in the Wolf Rock Race and the Fastnet Race there were altogether twenty-five retirements. Two yachts were dismasted, one broke her rudder and many suffered minor damage.

The wind force recorded at the Lizard on Sunday, 7 August, was SW. by S. Force 8 in the morning, rising to Force 9 SW. at 1330 and 1430. The highest gust (58 knots) occurred at 1340. The gale then moderated to Force 8 WSW. at 1530, Force 7 W. by N. at 1730, and Force 6 NW. by W. at 1930.

The competitors in the Fastnet Race bore the full brunt of this gale, as they encountered it between the Lizard and Land's End. *Myth of Malham* was the only yacht to beat right through it without heaving-to and was the winner of what I think was the best of John Illingworth's many ocean racing victories.

In the Wolf Rock Race the R.N.S.A. 24's put up an equally notable perform-ance. *Blue Disa* was driven right through the gale, under close-reefed mainsail and storm jib, never logging less than 3 knots, and deservedly won the Wolf Rock Bowl. *Samuel Pepys* and *Minx of Malham* (skippered by Commander Erroll Bruce) in second and third place did almost equally well, and if they hove-to in the gale at all it must have been for only a short while.

Mindy, *Cohoe* and *Mehalah*, the Class III leaders in the Santander Race, all either hove-to or lay a-hull and none of them was even placed.

Conclusions

1. *Plugging through gales*. The Wolf Rock Race of 1949 was one of the most important in the annals of ocean racing. Hitherto, small ocean racers hove-to in gales and victory went to the ones which were quickest to make sail again, after the worst was over. In this race three of the smallest boats (under 5 tons displace-ment) carried on through all or most of the gale. Their tactics introduced a new technique as far as ocean racing in Class III was concerned, and the days of heaving to, lying a-hull or to a sea anchor were over, at any rate in the ordinary gale, unless special circumstances warranted it.

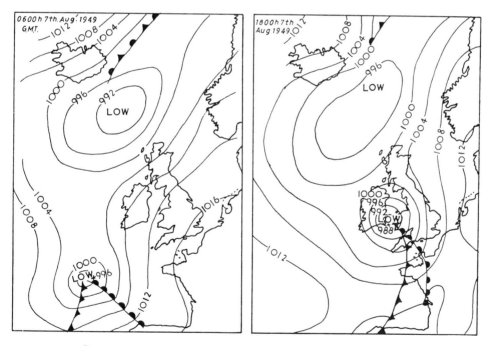

14   Synoptic charts of gale in Fastnet and Wolf Rock Races in 1949.

2. *Wind at shore stations*. The strange thing was that the highest hourly value of the wind recorded at Plymouth was only Force 5 as compared with Force 9 at the Lizard, less than 50 miles to the NE. From the synoptic charts it is clear that the gale must have attained at least Force 8 at sea south of Plymouth. Indeed, it is said that a gust of Force 11 (56–63 knots) was recorded at the Eddystone lighthouse only about 10 miles to the south.

This confirms that the records of some shore stations cannot always be relied upon to afford an indication of the wind force at sea, as they are subject to local influences and turbulence depending upon the direction of the wind in relation to the position of the anemometer (see Chapter 21).

7

GULF STREAM STORM

In 1950 the Royal Ocean Racing Club planned a Transatlantic Race from Bermuda to Plymouth to follow after the Bermuda Race organized by the Cruising Club of America. The Class III ocean racers, hitherto excluded as being too small for the Fastnet Race, were to be admitted to the Transatlantic event, as the sea-going ability of very small yachts had been proved over the previous three seasons. The Transatlantic Race was largely inspired by John Illingworth, then Commodore of both the R.O.R.C. and the Royal Naval Sailing Association. The challenge appealed to me enormously, so I entered *Cohoe* immediately both for the Bermuda and Transatlantic Races.

The yachts were to be shipped to Bermuda and would then sail to Newport, Rhode Island, from where they would race back to Bermuda and thence 3,000 miles to Plymouth. I will not go into details of the long preparations, or of the Bermuda Race itself, beyond mentioning two alterations which were made to the yacht. In order to improve stability that had been so poor the previous year (owing to the new mast) I arranged during the winter for a 6-in. false keel to be inserted between the existing wood keel and the lead-ballast keel. This would have little effect on initial stability, but once the yacht began to heel the extra leverage would take effect. The other alteration was the now famous false nose which was added to the bow to lengthen the yacht up to the minimum 35 ft. overall length required for eligibility under the rules of the Cruising Club of America. This was constructed of aluminium sheeting over a honeycomb of timber laths and it was a miraculous operation performed by the builders, A. H. Moody & Sons Ltd., in twenty-four hours.

The false bow proved a success. It had a distinctly steadying effect on the helm and gave *Cohoe* the feel of a longer, faster and bigger boat, more like an 8-metre to steer. I was not entirely easy in my mind about it, because an extension added to the bow is not the same thing as a long forward overhang structurally designed for the job in the first place, with suitable stem and frames. However, it was to be tested sooner than I had anticipated.

After arrival at Bermuda as deck cargo on the 5,000-ton freighter *Araby*, the three small English yachts, *Samuel Pepys*, *Cohoe* and the rather larger *Mokoia* were unloaded. After a refit and provisioning they set out under sail on their 630-mile passage to Newport, R.I., from where the Bermuda Race was to start.

On this passage I had with me Lieutenant-Commander Basil Smith as navigator and Group Captain Jack Keary, who was to be mate in the Bermuda and Transatlantic Races. Basil Smith was on short leave from H.M.S. *Glasgow*, the mother ship for the three small yachts at Bermuda, and before he joined the Royal Navy had served in the Merchant Service. *Mokoia* was skippered by her owner, the late Major James Murray, with Wing Commander Marwood Elton as navigator and Major Murray's daughter Jean as crew. *Samuel Pepys* had her full racing crew and was skippered by Commander (then Lieutenant-Commander) Erroll Bruce, R.N., who was Captain of the R.N.S.A. team in the Bermuda Race.

The three yachts set sail from St. George's, Bermuda, on Wednesday, 24 May, in fine settled weather and with a good weather report. We had the prospect of a pleasant, easy passage of 630 miles, with perhaps a little rough going when passing through the Gulf Stream, as the strong current often creates a steep, tumultuous sea.

All went according to plan at first, and we hove-to the first night while Jack cooked dinner, and *Mokoia* likewise took it easily. *Samuel Pepys* was ahead and none of the three yachts regained contact until arrival at Newport, R.I.

At noon on Thursday, the following day, the wind backed to the ESE. and freshened to Force 4. By 1630 the wind had backed farther to due east and freshened to Force 5. The sea had got up and half an hour later we close-reefed the mainsail and set the small jib, as the wind was hardening. Conditions steadily worsened. The barometer was falling and there was heavy rain. By 2000 the wind had reached gale force and the sea was really rough. We lowered all sail and lay a-hull under bare pole. I remember that when I went forward to lower the storm jib, I crawled on hands and knees, so the wind must have been very strong, as I had never had to do this before.

Before nightfall I went on deck to measure the force of wind by the cup-anemometer. It was extremely difficult to get a proper reading, because the waves were already so high that the yacht was under their lee in the troughs most of the time. It was only on the crests that the full force of the wind could be felt. The anemometer readings varied between 33 and 38 knots and accordingly Basil Smith logged it as Force 7 to Force 8 easterly.

Wind speeds of 33 to 38 knots give an average of 35 knots. I did not know then that a third had to be added to arrive at the *gradient* wind, 33 ft. above surface-level, which is correct for the Beaufort notation. The height of the seas accounted for a good part of the 33 ft., but if you add only a fifth instead of a third to the readings that makes a mean of 42 knots, which is Force 9. Gusts of 50 to 60 knots might occur at this wind force, so the reports of all the yachts tallied approximately for the first night of the gale.

The tactics adopted by *Cohoe* were by now almost routine. With helm down she lay a-hull almost broadside to the sea. The wind was so strong that she heeled over as if under sail, which steadied her and also increased her freeboard on the windward side, so that she presented her greatest buoyancy to the seas. Her keel prevented excessive leeway, but being tender she gave way and heeled over enough to avoid opposition to the seas. Her moderate drift to leeward may have created an eddy to windward to take some of the vice out of the breaking seas. Hers was the strength of the sapling bowing to the storm.

On deck it was difficult to distinguish between air and water, on account of the spindrift and torrential rain. I have little recollection of the sea except that it was steep and white, for, I must confess, it was very wet on deck and I got below just as quickly as I could.

Later it was a black night outside and an almost tropical downpour rattled on deck like hail. Nevertheless, down below things were comparatively peaceful. Jack and Basil were tucked in their berths, held in by canvas lee boards. I slept in the quarter berth in oilskins, as I had to be ready for any emergency and occasionally put my head on deck to ensure that all was well. Beyond that there was nothing to do. I had warps ready if needed and proper oil bags and two tins of heavy oil in the cockpit locker.

I say that the cabin was *comparatively* peaceful, and so it was in contrast with conditions on deck. But there was tremendous noise all the time: the violent rain beating down on deck, the howl of the wind in the rigging and the seas breaking on the windward side, rushing over the cabin top and running away to leeward. Occasionally a sea would deal the yacht a pretty hard smack, and one sometimes wondered whether the hull and cabin top would stand up to a harder one, but apart from mild apprehension the night passed tolerably. The worst feature was the wet below. The cockpit was constantly being half filled by breaking seas and the whole boat was virtually covered by flying spray. Under such conditions a yacht is pretty well under solid water, which penetrates any weaknesses of deck or joinery and seems to come from nowhere. All my boats, even when new, have required regular pumping in gales. A lot used to get below through the cockpit lockers, though this defect was partially cured in later years.

Cohoe lay under bare pole all night. I think the wind strengthened in the night, for I recorded it in my book *North Atlantic* (describing the expedition and the races) as a fresh gale, by which I meant 34–40 knots mean, a fair Force 8. Nevertheless, we managed to get a good deal of rest.

Friday, 26 May, dawned as a beastly day, with a dark stormy sky heavy with driving rain. By 0730 the wind had veered to SE. and moderated sufficiently to allow the storm jib to be set. The barometer was 993 millibars and still recording its slow fall. The weather was so ominous that Basil as navigator decided to treat it as a tropical storm and we ran off with the wind on the starboard quarter.

During the morning the wind continued to moderate and by the afternoon (1545) we were able to set the full mainsail to a southerly wind, temporarily only Force 3. However, the barometer had dropped another 3 millibars.

That evening Jack made one of his splendid stews (he cooked in any weather) and that put new life into us. However, the lull in the gale was short-lived. By 2030 the wind was increasing again and under reefed mainsail and small jib I logged a speed of 8 knots, almost certainly an exaggeration, as it was above *Cohoe*'s maximum theoretical speed. Anyway it was faster than she had ever run before.

Unknown to us, Humphrey Barton's *Vertue XXXV* was away to the NE. of *Cohoe* when at 1930 she was struck by an immense sea and nearly foundered. We noticed a deterioration of the weather and at 2140 *Cohoe* was once more down to storm jib. It was about midnight that she entered a very confused sea which I described in *North Atlantic* as "a huge swell from two directions, and the seas heaped in complete confusion".

On Saturday (27 May) the gale continued at varying force. In the morning at 0600 the double-reefed mainsail was set. By 0930 the barometer was rising very rapidly, but the wind had backed to ENE., Force 6 to 7. At 1100 the barometer had risen to 998 millibars and the wind had increased so much that the mainsail had to be lowered. Half an hour later the jib had to be lowered and replaced by the storm jib. Basil logged a speed of 6 knots under 30 sq. ft. of canvas, which was as fast as she ran in the gale gusting over 60 knots off Calshot. At 1230 she was under bare poles doing 3 to 4 knots and the entry in the log reads "gale". Five minutes later she was hove-to once more under bare pole.

It was not until 1955 on Saturday that the gale moderated sufficiently to allow the small jib to be set and the voyage continued in gradually improving conditions, finally ending in dense fog off the American coast. On arrival at Newport it was found that *Cohoe*'s false nose was still intact, but much of the paint had been washed off it by the seas during the storm.

So far I have written of the gales as we saw them from *Cohoe*, but other yachts were involved and their experiences contribute to form the picture of the gale as a whole.

Mokoia appears to have been the nearest to *Cohoe* and she hove-to in the gale at 1630 on Thursday evening, 25 May. Her experiences were much the same as *Cohoe*'s, but, close as she must have been, her barometer did not fall to the same extent and on 26 May she had different winds: 0915 light airs S., 1800 W. Force 1 to 3, 2000 new winds from S.

Samuel Pepys was about 60 miles to the northward on Thursday, 25 May. She had been reaching under spinnaker. She lowered this at tea-time and continued under genoa only, the wind freshening to Force 6. The gale did not reach her until just before midnight (nearly four hours later than *Cohoe*). The genoa was lowered when, to quote from Erroll Bruce's book *Deep Sea Sailing*, "before any other sail could be set the sky was black all round, rain torrential and wind gusting at whole gale Force 10 from the east. Ran under bare pole. In view of the sudden increase of wind and ominous conditions, decided to treat this as a tropical revolving storm . . ."

At 0530 on Friday morning, 26 May, gusts were of 60 m.p.h. (about 54 knots) and the seas were breaking down their whole slope. Shortly afterwards the wind suddenly fell dead, the rain stopped and a spot of blue sky appeared. *Samuel Pepys* may then have been in the eye of the storm, but the lull lasted only seven minutes before the wind pounced again at full blast from the east (the same direction as before) and the barometer, instead of rising, continued its slow fall. Except for a brief respite in the afternoon at 1600, when the wind backed NE. and moderated to a fresh gale, the storm continued unabated until early the following morning and was logged at Force 10. The seas steadily built up with nearly thirty hours of easterly or NE. winds. The height of the biggest waves was estimated at 35 ft.

On Saturday *Samuel Pepys* appeared to have met much the same weather as *Cohoe*. She reported Force 6 at 0530; Force 7 at 0930 and an hour later heavy squalls required the mainsail to be replaced by the trysail and she was once more down to storm canvas. Later she proceeded on her passage and reached Newport R.I., a day or two ahead of us.

Our first intimation that *Vertue XXXV* was in the vicinity of the three yachts was early on the following Monday morning (28 May), when we were hailed by the U.S. Coastguard cutter *Castlerock*, who was searching for her. We were astonished, for, although we knew that *Vertue XXXV* had started on her famous east to west crossing of the Atlantic on 15 April, it had never occurred to us that she might be near to us. It was a shock to learn that she was storm damaged.

Thursday, 25 May, was the fortieth day out from Falmouth for Humphrey Barton and Kevin O'Riordan. *Vertue XXXV* was running due west and early in the morning the wind backed and freshened. At noon her position was about 180 miles NNE. of Bermuda, and about the same distance to the NE. of *Cohoe*, on whom she was converging quickly, as both yachts were sailing fast. She reported she entered the Gulf Stream on that day.

The wind was SE. and the glass continued to fall slowly. Obeying Buys Ballot's Law, as Humphrey Barton puts it in his book *Vertue XXXV*, "Face the wind and the centre of the depression is approximately 100° [90° to 135°] on your right—I find that puts the centre at about SW. by W."

This was in the direction of *Cohoe*. At 2200 the wind freshened: "it is a simply foul night with blinding rain". "The yacht was tearing along at a frightening speed." Humphrey Barton is a hard driver, as I know, for I have sailed with

97

him, and he kept *Vertue* going all the Thursday night, gradually shortening canvas until at midnight the mainsail was down to trysail size. The rain was torrential.

At 0400 on Friday morning, 26 May. Humphrey Barton handed over to Kevin O'Riordan. He reports the wind as "blowing hard now—Force 8 or 9 I would guess. I have no intention of heaving-to."

At 0605 *Vertue* was reduced to bare pole, and typically of Humphrey, he still kept the yacht running at 3 to 4 knots. "It is blowing 65 m.p.h. (56 knots) now, quite one of the hardest blows I have ever been out in . . . the sea is all white. The crests are fairly being torn off. Barometer dropped nearly one-tenth (3 millibars) in the last hour." At 1300 conditions were described as absolutely shocking: "A wind that has reached a state of senseless fury." "It became difficult to make out where the surface of the sea began or ended."

In the afternoon at about 1600 it became no longer possible to steer downwind. "For one thing we were 45° off our course and for another the mental and physical strain were pretty severe." Humphrey Barton is a master of understatement.

A 21 in. diameter Admiralty pattern sea anchor was let go over the starboard quarter. It was considered that the yacht lay better thus than wallowing broadside in the trough, but at 1500 a sea fell on *Vertue XXXV* which Humphrey Barton reported as far and away the worst he had seen yet. The barometer was down to 29.26 (994 millibars) and still falling slowly.

It was about 1930 on that grim Friday evening that the accident occurred. I quote Humphrey Barton's words, because they convey in a single paragraph the sudden contrast between security and danger.

"It happened just as we were finishing our supper, about 1930 I suppose, on the 26th. We had had fried sardines and potatoes, tinned peaches and I had just poured the hot water over the Nescafé. The gale was blowing as hard as ever but there we were in our snug, dry little cabin with an oil lamp burning as it was dusk, almost dark, in fact. It came with devastating suddenness; a great fiend of a sea that picked the yacht up, threw her over on her port side and then burst over her. There was an awful splintering of wood, a crash of broken glass and in came a roaring cataract of water."

Note the contrast. At one moment Humphrey Barton making coffee in the security af the cabin and the next facing disaster and the elements raging on deck during that fearful night.

What had happened was that an immense sea had struck *Vertue XXXV*, throwing her on her beam ends so hard that on the lee side the coaming was split at deck-level for nearly the whole length of the cabin, the doghouse window was smashed and the water was cascading into the cabin at every sea.

The yacht was saved by a narrow margin by running her off dead before the seas, and through the fine seamanship and tremendous energy of her crew in manning the pump and effecting repairs in time. Had she broached and been struck by a second sea she would undoubtedly have been lost.

The log is incomplete during the hours when the crew were at their work and when the exhausted men were resting, but it was not until late on Saturday morning the gale had moderated sufficiently to allow the head of the mainsail to be set. The whole dramatic story of the near disaster appears in Humphrey Barton's book *Vertue XXXV*.

Conclusions

This Atlantic storm has always been a puzzle, because of the different experiences of the yachts involved in it. The first theory was that the depression had two centres and the second that it was one intense depression which became almost stationary over the yachts.

It was not until over fifteen years later that I received from the U.S. Weather Bureau a track of the storm which proved to be an extra-tropical cyclone which made an anti-clockwise loop north-west of Bermuda, with the yachts near the centre of its coil.

At my request Captain C. Stewart, who is an extra master engaged in hydraulic and wave research, kindly studied the problem, with the aid of all the relative data available from the British Meteorological Office.

He points out that while the broad pattern of any pressure distribution is correct on synoptic charts no more can be done where information is lacking (particularly if it is lacking in the centre of a storm) than to draw in the lowest isobar for which there is definite evidence. The area thus enclosed may be as much as 300 miles or more in diameter, in which a deeper centre may exist. It was in such an "area of uncertainty" that the yachts met their severe storm, but it is impossible to determine its exact track in the absence of regular barometer readings together with wind directions and forces from all the yachts. There were reports from many ships to the westward between Bermuda and Cape Hatteras and elsewhere, but no ships' reports from the area in which the cyclone made its loop.

Captain Stewart arrives at the conclusion that the centre of the low moved rapidly from the north-west from off the Chesapeake towards Bermuda, but the track shown by the American authorities shows it moving in from a south-westerly direction. It is impossible to reconcile the two opinions without the data on which the U.S. track is based, but it is immaterial, as the track from 0200, 26 May, Bermuda time, more or less coincides in the anti-clockwise loop in the area over which the yachts were sailing. This U.S. track is shown on the diagram (p. 100), together with the alternative approach from the north-west which is shown in dotted line. Captain Stewart has also plotted the positions of

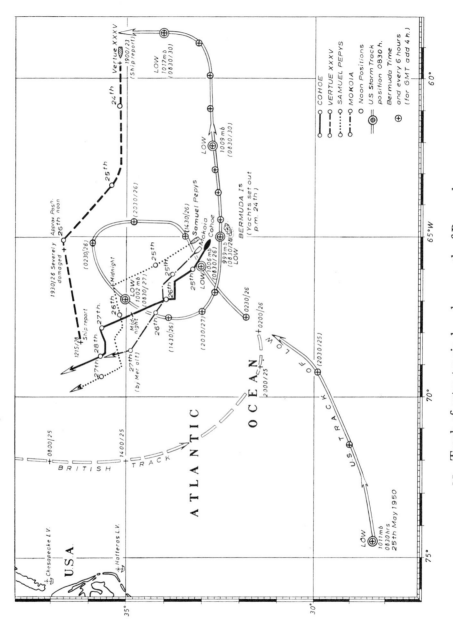

15 Track of extra-tropical cyclone north of Bermuda, 1950.

the yachts from such information as was made available to him and altered all times, including the U.S. track, to Bermuda.

On the first day of the gale (Thursday, 25 May) no problem is presented. Whether the low came in from NW. or SW., the centre passed first to the southwest and close to *Cohoe* and *Mokoia*, and the following day and night moved round towards *Samuel Pepys* and *Vertue XXXV*.

My report of the gale proved to be rather an understatement, as my opinion was influenced by several factors. I had no idea that a third has to be added to the wind speed recorded by an anemometer used in the cockpit, and hence the gale was probably one grade or more higher on the Beaufort Notation. Secondly there was no spectacular fall in the barometer as occurred in the Santander Race, so I did not anticipate such strong winds. It is only recently that I have learnt that a fall in barometric pressure in lower latitudes has a much greater effect on the strength of wind than in higher. For example, a pressure gradient which at the Scillies, about 50°N., would produce 30-knot winds would produce about 40 knots in latitude 35°N., to the north of Bermuda.

It is on the second day of the gale (26 May) that the experiences of the yachts differ so much.

At 0730 the wind had moderated to Force 5, S.E., and by 1545 *Cohoe* was running under full sail before a Force 3 southerly wind. It was not until 2130 that the wind increased again and it was just after midnight that she entered an area of very confused swell and sea. She had a respite from the gale of about fourteen hours and *Mokoia* to the NW. experienced lighter conditions, and had a respite which lasted about thirty-six hours, for she was gaining distance from the centre and did not heave-to again until 1730 on Saturday.

This was the puzzle, because, while *Cohoe* had a respite from the gale until shortly after midnight, *Samuel Pepys* and *Vertue XXXV* to the north were fighting a battle for survival in winds gusting up to hurricane force.

From this I arrived at the conclusion that the first theory was right, and that while *Cohoe* was running before increasing southerly winds a vigorous secondary had developed in which *Samuel Pepys* and *Vertue XXXV* were involved to the northward. However, Captain Stewart does not think that there were two distinct centres of the low, although he does not discount the possibility. He thinks that it followed the loop as shown, although possibly the curve may have been flatter at the top and the loop more lozenge-shaped, with the centre wandering or oscillating and at the same time intensifying, probably due to "backbending" of the fronts that had already occluded near the centre. It seems fairly clear that the centre rounded and passed between the yachts, somewhere to the north of *Cohoe* on 26 May and to the south of *Samuel Pepys* and *Vertue XXXV*.

From the approximate track it will be seen that after the first night the centre moved round to NE, north and SW in such a way that *Samuel Pepys* and *Vertue XXXV* were involved in it continuously for a much longer time, while the centre of the disturbance circled round south of them, which gave longer for ocean seas to build up. As previously mentioned, Captain Stewart believes the depression intensified as it moved and its isobars were much tighter on the north side of the centre, which would account for storm to hurricane gusts for *Samuel Pepys* and *Vertue XXXV*. In the second place I attach significance to the dramatic change in the character of the seas encountered by *Cohoe* at midnight on 26 May. This could have been due to the seas left in the wake of the centre of the low after it had passed, but it could have been that *Cohoe* had entered the edge of the Gulf Stream and that *Vertue XXXV* and *Samuel Pepys* could have been in a meander of the Gulf Stream during the whole of the storm. This would cause more dangerous seas, and the sharply warmer temperature of the Stream could account for an intensification of the storm and squalls of hurricane force.

It was certainly a survival storm for *Vertue XXXV* and *Samuel Pepys* and a near miss for *Cohoe* and *Mokoia*. The only positive certainty is that the disturbance was a very complex one of near-hurricane violence.

1. *Sea anchors.* The sea anchor used in *Cohoe* during the Santander Race gale and in *Vertue XXXV* in the Atlantic appear to have been of identical type. *Cohoe* lost hers because the ring broke, whereas the failure in *Vertue XXXV* was due to a 2-in. manilla warp chafing through at the taffrail.

The loss of the sea anchors confirm the experience of other deep-sea sailing men that tremendous strains are imposed on a sea anchor and its gear, which should be very strong.

The question remains whether the sea anchors did any good? I doubt it, and Humphrey Barton goes further in believing that the trouble was due to *Vertue XXXV* being tethered to a sea anchor. But it must be noted that neither yacht set a riding sail.

2. *Running before the gale streaming warps.* This tactic was adopted by *Samuel Pepys* with complete success. In exceptionally heavy weather this throws a strain on a small crew, as steering dead before the wind requires concentration and the cockpit is often filled with water. Nevertheless, the tactic seems to have been the best one.

3. *Lying a-hull.* This method of dealing with gales was almost routine in *Cohoe*, but it must be remembered she had hitherto only encountered Force 9 or possibly Force 10 (with gusts of over 60 knots) in the Santander Storm. Gales in the English Channel of short duration are different from prolonged gales with the longer fetch of the Atlantic which produce more formidable seas.

My opinion is that *Cohoe*'s tactics of lying a-hull in the Bermuda gale were adequate for a yacht with less buoyancy aft than is afforded by a transom stern.

I attributed her immunity partly to her light displacement and the considerable angle of heel at which she lay, giving way rather than resisting the seas. Humphrey Barton, on the other hand, thinks lying a-hull is safe only up to about Force 9. Above that he recommends running off, streaming warps as *Samuel Pepys* did, because of the risk when lying a-hull of being knocked down by a sea, or even rolled over, as sometimes occurs with yachts in exceptional storms.

4. *Freak waves.* It appears that *Vertue XXXV* was struck by one of the freak waves which ride high in most gales. I describe a parallel experience, in Chapter 16, where a yacht was nearly sunk, though only in a Force 7 to 8 Biscay gale. Turbulence of wind has much to do with sea formation and in both cases the wind must have been gusting far above the mean speed of the Beaufort Scale.

5. *Doghouse and superstructure.* Note that *Vertue XXXV* was not damaged by the weight of the invading wave, but was thrown on her beam ends so violently that she was split open on the lee side as though she had fallen on a pavement. As will be confirmed later, when damage is suffered it is usually on the lee side.

6. *Barometer.* During gales there is a tendency to take barometer readings only occasionally, such as first thing in the morning, at noon, and at 1800 in the evening. This makes is impossible to assemble a true picture of a depression, especially if the lowest reading is not recorded. For many years now I have carried a barograph in my boats. The graph produced on this instrument shows the relative steepness of the gradients and provides the only really complete permanent record.

8

POOPED IN THE ATLANTIC

For our next gale we jump to the second week in the Transatlantic Race. In this event the three small yachts *Mokoia*, *Samuel Pepys* and *Cohoe* were entered together with two larger yachts, Mr. Jack Rawlings's new Class I *Gulvain* and Lieutenant-Commander G. C. L. Payne's Scandinavian double-ender *Karin III*. Before the start of this Transatlantic Race I had *Cohoe*'s false bow removed. It had given no trouble, but I thought the boat would be better without it. I need not have worried, for it proved so strong that it took us a tremendous time to dismantle it, even with the aid of two shipwrights from the dockyard. There were hundreds of screws to undo and we were thankful when at last the task was done and it lay by the roadside in pieces. It would have survived a hurricane.

With me in *Cohoe* I had Jack Keary as mate, Tom Tothill as navigator and John Halstead, a young American ex-marine who wanted to work his passage to take up a vacation job in France. They were a tough crew and I needed them, for the race was to prove something of an endurance test. With a total of four, watch-keeping arrangements were altered. In day-time, watches of three hours were kept and at night six hours, in order that the watch below could in theory get six hours' continuous sleep, though in practice they rarely did. There were always two on watch at a time, although the one not steering was free to go below if he was not needed for spinnaker handling or other duties.

The race started on Sunday, 2 July, in an almost complete calm, and it was not until the fourth day, with *Cohoe* tailing (as she always did in light airs) over 100 miles behind the fleet, that the wind freshened, bringing with it almost trade wind conditions, with a smart following breeze, a big blue sea under a sunny sky and zest and movement in hull, spars and sails. These conditions gradually gave place to grey skies and rough sailing in the second week as the yachts entered the mid-Atlantic stage of the race, where a series of depressions were moving across.

On Tuesday, 11 July, *Samuel Pepys* and *Cohoe* were very close, had we known it, and *Cohoe* for the first time had temporarily taken the lead. Both yachts reported Force 5 to Force 6 winds, both crews were beginning to feel fatigue following on ceaseless driving and spinnaker work. On Wednesday, 12 July, conditions were much the same, but the wind backed to the west and the barometer fell 7 millibars to 1,009 millibars.

6. *Mehalah* hove-to after the Santander Race storm. The blow is over but the swell remains.

7. The stanchion of *Cohoe* uprooted in the Santander storm, and the jury runner.

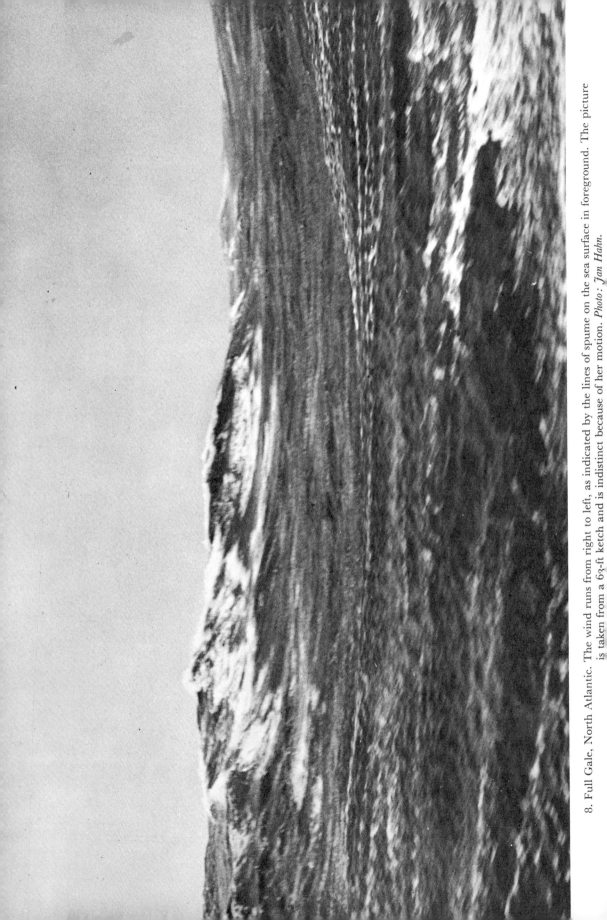

8. Full Gale, North Atlantic. The wind runs from right to left, as indicated by the lines of spume on the sea surface in foreground. The picture is taken from a 6¾-ft ketch and is indistinct because of her motion. *Photo: Jan Hahn.*

9. Full Gale, North Atlantic. Conditions appear to be much the same as when the British yachts were encircled by the anti-clockwise loop of an extra-tropical cyclone north of Bermuda. *Photo: Jan Hahn.*

10. Mid-Atlantic, the morning before *Cohoe* was pooped. Sea Disturbance Scale No. 6, 'very rough' but wind only Force 6-7. Note the strain on the tiller, indicated by curvature, probably through being under-canvassed.

The night had been very tiring for the crews, owing to the size of the seas, and spinnakers had been handed in both yachts.

In the early morning the wind was only Force 4, and *Cohoe* was logging 6 knots, but by 0730 it had freshened and the following seas seemed so high that we lowered the mainsail and ran under genoa. This brought the speed down to 4 knots, the reduction in sail having been made on account of the seas rather that the weight of the wind.

During the morning the seas continued to build up and the wind freshened, but it was sunny and warm and I took photographs of the steepening seas. By 1500 *Cohoe*'s motion was so uncontrollable that the genoa had to be replaced by the storm jib, the 30 sq. ft. pocket handkerchief.

The following extracts from my diary carry the story a stage further:

"Half an hour later we lowered even the storm jib and ran under bare pole. The wind is well *under* Force 8, but the Atlantic seas are so big that they throw the yacht about and punish her severely, making steering difficult.

"Under bare pole we only make about 2 knots in the troughs of the waves, but on the crests she runs at 4 knots and seems to skid on the breaking crests.

"At about 1630 I was called on deck to see the Italian liner *Saturnia* which was tearing close past on a reciprocal course to the westward. She made no sign of seeing us. In fact, in the seas our helmsman only saw the liner when she came close by.

"I returned below, leaving Jack and Tom on deck. Then all of a sudden there was a roar of breaking water. The yacht lurched violently, then went right over. The cabin went dark, water spurted through the tightly screwed port lights. There was a tremendous noise of rushing water, and a loud report as though the hull was cracked in. *Cohoe* had been pooped by a big sea and broached to.

"The yacht rose again and came to even keel. John and I tried to open the hatch to see that all on deck were safe, but it took a minute or two (which seemed hours) to get it opened, as somebody was sitting on it.

"Jack and Tom were safe and told us what had happened. A large sea (but not much larger than the others) with an immense breaking crest had struck the yacht on the quarter. This caused her partly to broach-to, threw her over on her side and half filled the cockpit.

"While the yacht was staggering under this blow a second sea, larger than the first, came roaring down. It was this second sea which gave her such a tremendous crack. It completely filled the cockpit, ran as high as Tom's arm where he was clinging to the runner, and knocked the yacht on her beam ends right down over the cabin top.

"The yacht recovered and Jack, at the helm, straightened her out before the seas. No serious damage was done and the pump quickly dealt with the inrush of water.

"Shortly afterwards it was observed that the *Saturnia* was turning. It was probably her wash that had caused the big wave to break.

"Round she came in a great circle. Well handled, she passed slowly by. She seemed crowded with passengers. We signalled MIK 'Please report me to Lloyds, London' and exhibited a strip of canvas with the name of the yacht *Cohoe* painted on it.

"We hoisted our ensign and the liner, acknowledging our signal, made a complete circle around us to satisfy herself that no help was needed."

The sea puzzled me. The wind was strong, but not Force 8, and yet the seas were big enough to make the yacht almost unmanageable. On the tops of the "big-uns" she would simply be picked up bodily and thrown forward, planing on the crest.

Three times she nearly broached-to and at 2000 at the end of my dog-watch I agreed to the mate's suggestion that we should heave-to.

Waiting for a "smooth", we put down the helm and she came gently up into the wind and fell off broadside to the seas. As usual, she was happy in this position, riding the seas like a duck.

Nevertheless, as a result of this delay *Cohoe*'s noon to noon next day was only 65 miles against *Samuel Pepys*'s run of 158 miles, which was her third best in the whole race.

If I seem unduly severe, I will add that we made good our shortcomings later. We set the spinnaker at Force 6 the following evening and carrying it through a ramping tearing night *Cohoe* achieved a noon to noon run of 177 miles. The yacht surfed on the tops of the big seas, the bow wave each side abreast the mast, a great wedge of foaming water shooting out like a fan 3 ft. above the level of the guard rail, and at the stern a high wave, boiling almost to the top of the rudder. Her speed was anybody's guess, possibly 10 to 12 knots for perceptible moments until she slowed as the crests passed. The speed was higher than I have ever experienced before or since, even with a speedometer jammed at the 10-knot maximum. It was followed by another record of 174 miles. Hour by hour, day by day and night by night in ceaseless din, like the roar of a weir or waterfall, *Cohoe* gradually whittled down *Samuel Pepys*'s lead until five days later the pair were almost level. Then *Samuel Pepys* began to draw ahead again and on the final day crossed the finish line at Plymouth in 21 days 9 hours.

Cohoe saved her time by two hours on handicap and won the Transatlantic Race, but *Samuel Pepys* was first home and had the honour of making the fastest elapsed time ever accomplished by so small a vessel, a record which remains unbeaten.

Conclusions

There is nothing to suggest a gale on the synoptic chart for 12 July at 1200 G.M.T.

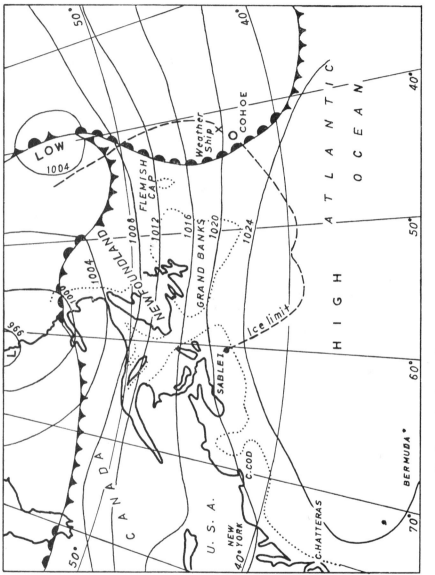

16 Synoptic chart, Western Atlantic, 1200 G.M.T. 12 July, 1950.

107

(about 0900 by ship's time), some six hours before she came down to storm jib. The warm front might give rise to strong winds and squalls, but the isobars are widely spaced and suggest a geostrophic wind force of only 20 knots (Force 4 to 5) at the weather ship about 100 miles to the NNE. On another chart a conspicuous wave low with a sharp kink in the isobars is indicated and the front is shown as occluded, but there is no notable difference in barometric pressures, and according to Captain Stewart's investigations *Cohoe*'s barometer was registering low.

The only suggestions of strong winds come from the synoptic charts covering the whole of the Atlantic Ocean. A deep low giving Force 10 winds had crossed the Atlantic and was situated SW. of Iceland on 12 July. This would leave moderate to fresh westerly winds for *Cohoe* and her immediate competitors. These winds would be augmented on the north side of the high to the SW. and by the low NE. of Newfoundland. Yet another low (996 millibars east of Hudson Bay) with an occlusion between the centres of the two. With a family of depressions some forming and some filling, the weather situation can rapidly change hour by hour, and can vary locally even in mid-ocean.

Let us look for other evidence. *Mokoia* about 90 miles to the NE of *Cohoe* logged Force 8 and hove-to. *Samuel Pepys* about an equal distance to the SW reported Force 6 and ran under twin headsails. Both yachts had experienced skippers and crews and, as *Cohoe*'s position was about half-way between her competitors, it seems reasonable to put the wind at Force 7, as I logged at the time.

However, the most authorative evidence comes from the captain of the Italian liner *Saturnia*, who logged the conditions as "Sea Disturbance No. 6 Beaufort Wind Force 6". Sea Disturbance No. 6 is usually associated with wind Force 7, so I think a reasonable guess at the strength of the wind gives a mean of about 25 to 30 knots (Force 6 to 7), gusting perhaps up to 40 knots, which is in Alan Watts's terms a "yachtsman's gale".

I have gone into these assessments of wind force with particular care, because they illustrate the point that the state of the sea, even in the open ocean, cannot be judged entirely by the mean force of the wind on Beaufort Notation, and that a small yacht may occasionally run into trouble in winds of under gale force in which in the ordinary way she would only be moderately reefed. In another chapter I shall give a converse example where in a vigorous secondary, giving verified winds of Force 9-10, the seas never rose high enough to warrant attention.

There is no doubt that the seas on 12 July were out of all proportion to the wind, which had backed from NNW. to west in the early morning. The height of the seas during the afternoon was independently judged by each of us at 30 ft. in relation to the known height of the mast. Such estimates by eye from the deck are inaccurate, however carefully and coolly judged, and usually should be halved. This gives 15 ft., but as this seemed too conservative at the time I logged 18 ft., being three-fifths of the estimate by eye. This, as it happens, was confirmed by the *Saturnia*, for sea Disturbance No. 6 is "very rough" and gives a mean height of the waves as 19 ft. Tom Tothill, our navigator, estimated the length of the waves as 250 ft., but this was probably on the low side, since oceanographers state that while height is usually exaggerated the length is often underestimated. The size of the seas could be accounted for by the long duration and unlimited fetch along the straight isobars to the north of the huge high to the south-west, but the feature was their confused pattern, which must have been due to the shift of wind, frontal gusts and the combination of wave trains caused by the movements of the depressions.

1. *Pooping and speed*. I think the pooping was due to the wash of the liner (passing fairly close at high speed) superimposed on the already high and confused seas. The wash probably combined to form two pyramidical, high, breaking seas which struck *Cohoe* on the quarter and did the damage. Freak waves can be caused by any interference with the normal run of the seas.

This, however, does not account for the difficulty which was experienced by all the helmsmen in *Cohoe* when steering that day. It may well be asked why *Samuel Pepys* was able to carry on efficiently under twin staysails at a time when *Cohoe* was running under bare pole? Why did *Cohoe* make so much better weather of it running before the gale north of Bermuda when the gale was incomparably stronger?

According to the synoptic chart and her log, *Samuel Pepys* possibly experienced less severe wind and sea conditions, but I think her immunity was due to carrying more sail. She averaged $6\frac{1}{2}$ knots. Likewise, when running under storm jib in the Bermuda gale, *Cohoe* was averaging about $6\frac{1}{2}$ knots, and at the end of the Transatlantc Race she effortlessly maintained the same speed in a depression for which a gale warning had been received.

I think that on the day *Cohoe* was pooped she was not carrying sufficient sail. As the seas got worse sail was progressively reduced in the traditional manner until she was down to bare pole. If the seas were running 18 ft. high she would be partially under their lee in the troughs except for the upper part of the mast. Her speed would thus fall in the trough and when the next crest rode up it would be inadequate to give the quick response to the tiller, which is necessary in high confused seas. She ought to have carried more sail, not less, because under heavy ocean conditions speed is needed so that a boat is quickly responsive and can be steered with a flick of the helm to take a "big-un" stern on.

To maintain quick control I suggest a speed of about 5 knots is desirable, but the right speed will only be found by trial and error, as so much depends upon the characteristics and size of the individual yacht in relation to the pattern (or absence of pattern) of the seas. There may, however, come a time when speed becomes dangerous. It is still necessary to keep the stern to the seas and this is accomplished by towing warps to steady the yacht and the use of the helm as well. In other words, if a yacht runs in heavy weather in the ocean she must *either* maintain sufficient speed to keep her lively and responsive (but see Chapters 19, 20 and 22 for running in storms or a hurricane) or, on the contrary, she must adopt gale tactics and tow warps.

2. *Shape of stern.* Only on two occasions in my life have I had the experience of being in a yacht when she has been well and truly pooped by a following sea. In each case, the wind was below gale force and the yacht was a double-ended one with a Scandinavian pointed stern and outhung rudder. The Norwegian pilot cutters and the Colin Archer designs with their pointed sterns are noted for their ability to run well before gales, and Vito Dumas demonstrated the efficiency of the type when he ran round the world in the Roaring Forties in *Lehg II*. But in these vessels the pointed stern was associated with wide beam, which enables the buoyancy to be carried aft. This cannot be done so effectively in narrow light-displacement boats such as *Zara* and *Cohoe*. There was little to complain about in *Cohoe*, as the pooping was probably just a coincidence due to the wash of the liner, but I think that a transom or a well-designed counter stern is better, as it provides greater buoyancy aft.

3. *Damage.* In my book *North Atlantic* I referred to a "loud report as though the hull was cracked in" when the sea struck *Cohoe*. Long after the book was written and published *Cohoe*'s builders, A. H. Moody & Sons Ltd., made a survey of the yacht and found two oak timbers fractured on the port quarter inside the stern locker in the position exactly where the sea struck.

When a yacht offers resistance to a big breaking sea damage nearly always follows.

4. *Safety harness.* In the Bermuda and Transatlantic Races we used personal lifelines in *Cohoe* for the first time, having on previous occasions merely used the end of a sheet or a short length of rope in the cockpit when steering in exceptionally bad weather.

Commander Erroll Bruce devoted much time to the subject of considering lifelines and safety precautions and later Peter Haward designed and marketed a very efficient type of safety harness which came into general use. The R.O.R.C. added safety harness to the compulsory equipment under the Club's regulations and today almost all sea-going yachts, whether racing or cruising, are equipped with it.

9

RETURN FROM LA CORUÑA

In 1952 I had a new yacht built for me, partly because my wife wanted a more comfortable boat and partly because *Cohoe* was becoming rather outdated for racing in home waters.

Cohoe II, as we named her out of affection for the former boat, was a yawl designed by Charles A. Nicholson and built at Cowes by A. W. Souter. In case I should want to enter her for the Bermuda Race without repeating the facial operation of adding a false bow, she was built to comply with the minimum rule length of 35 ft. overall, and her length on the waterline was 26 ft. With a beam of 8 ft. 6 ins. the Thames measurement worked out at $8\frac{1}{4}$ tons. She had a fuller-bodied hull than *Cohoe* and displaced $6\frac{2}{3}$ tons. In common with most of Charles A. Nicholson's designs at the time, she had broad shoulders and a fine run aft, in the cod's head and mackerel tail tradition. But her bilges were slacker than is commonly found in this designer's work, and the lines were experimental, producing something in the nature of a cruising version of the former International 8-metre class.

The accommodation below in *Cohoe II* was conventional and consisted of a forecastle with one root berth, sail locker, stowage room and the "heads". A large locker and wardrobe were arranged between the forecastle and the saloon, which had a settee berth on either side and a folding table in the centre. The mast was stepped on deck, which was reinforced by steel beams and further strengthened under the mast by a steel tube which carried through to the keel. Abaft the saloon, but divided from it by a curtain running on slides in a track, was the galley on the port side and a dresser and cupboards opposite. Right aft there were two quarter berths. The arrangement was simple but effective, except in very heavy weather, when, despite canvas protective curtains, the quarter berths were always wet. A portable chart table fitted over the starboard quarter berth, and a light, horizontally opposed piston petrol engine was situated under the companionway. The interior was spacious and airy.

When we came to race *Cohoe II* in 1952, which was a season of fresh and strong winds, we found her fast in light or moderate breezes, but she proved to be overmasted and overcanvassed in strong winds, and the world's champion rhythmic roller. This was partly due to her being designed to carry a lead keel, but having had an iron one substituted, as lead reached a peak price in the year that she was built.

Accordingly, in consultation with her designer, I had the sail plan reduced the following winter, by cutting the mast at the jumpers and cutting the mainsail. The reduction in sail area was drastic, being equivalent to two reefs. As it chanced the two following Fastnet years of 1953 and 1955 (in which through a change in the rules the small class of ocean racers were admitted) happened to be light seasons in which *Cohoe II* would have fared better under her original rig. Nevertheless, the alteration greatly improved the yacht. From being a tender boat she became a stiff one, not only because of the reduction in sail area, but because of the reduction in weight and windage aloft. Gone was the rhythmic rolling, gone was the excessive leeway. And what a good rig for cruising is the masthead yawl! There are no runners to bother about, which is a great advantage when short-handed, and the foot of the mainsail is short, so that there are no terrors in gybing, however hard the conditions may be. *Cohoe II* handled admirably under a small genoa and mizzen alone, even in light winds. In strong winds my wife and I never reefed. We merely lowered the mainsail. Although perhaps more suited to a longer boat, the yawl rig lends character in these days when almost every yacht is a sloop. For sea-going it is safe rig, because the sail area is split into smaller units, and the mizzen staysail is a practical sail which can be set or lowered quickly. Besides which I prefer two masts (independently stayed) to one, because in the event of losing one there is a sporting chance of being able to make a reasonably efficient jury if the other remains. This argument may be contentious, but the fact remains that I like yawls and would still have one if they were not virtually penalized under the ocean-racing rules.

The experience I now describe occurred in 1954, not in a race but when cruising home afterwards.

We had raced from Cowes to La Coruña, a slow event involving a 200-mile beat to Ushant mostly under rough conditions with rain and poor visibility, which were followed by calms over an immense area of the Bay of Biscay and finally by dense fog when we arrived off the Spanish coast. My crew consisted of Alan Mansley, Jim Kentish, Mike Awty and Barrie Kendall, and after the race, which we won in our class, we relaxed in La Coruña, a sunny, breezy town where we were most hospitably entertained by the Real Club Nautico. We remained in these happy surroundings three days, when peace was disturbed by one of my crew. He had sent a cable to the head of his department asking for an extension of his sailing holiday on account of inclement weather. The reply was prompt and to the point: "Leave granted. Divorce pending."

This carefully worded missive seemed to have a more atomic effect than if the reply had merely read, "Sacked on the spot", and the whole of my crew evinced a sudden enthusiasm to return to work. As I have remarked before, time running short at the end of a holiday is the most frequent cause of the cruising man getting caught out in bad weather, and our homeward passage was to prove no exception.

Our last evening in Spain was spent at the club having dinner at a table on the balcony overlooking the yachts anchored immediately below. The meal was a pleasant one, and we lingered so long over our coffee and brandy that the hour was already late when we paid our bill and jumped into the dinghy to row off to the yacht.

Once aboard we changed from shore-going clothes and donned our sea-going rig for the night's sail. Five men in a tiny cabin—clothes everywhere, everything anywhere. It was not until nearly midnight that all was ready, order had been restored, and the anchor weighed. So it may be said that our passage started at 0001 on Thursday, 22 July (see chart, Fig. 9, page 68).

When the yacht was 10 miles out, and beyond the sheltering arm of Cabo Priorino we began to feel we were really at sea again. It had been blowing fresh for some days from the north-east, and the midnight weather forecast gave promise of strong winds in the Bay of Biscay and rain. The night was very dark, and to the eastwards over the land the sky was blacker still. Ominous clouds were approaching and soon the rain came in torrents, and the wind hardened. We lowered the mainsail (one of the advantages of the yawl rig) and continued under genoa and mizzen alone, doing a good 6 knots. All turned in, except the man on watch, for we were cruising now, and only one was needed on deck. With five of us it meant two hours on and eight off, apart from sail shifting, cooking and navigation.

What never fails to surprise me, even after many years of sailing, is the sharpness of the contrast between life ashore and life at sea. Only a few hours before we had been part of the land world. The table at which we were seated was steady, the wine and food were excellent and well served, and the brightly lighted club was gay. It was a well-ordered and comfortable existence. But once at sea again, the yacht became a compact little world unto herself in which all our activities were centred. Life ashore was as remote to us as life on another planet. On deck the helmsman is alone. As he looks seaward nothing breaks the impenetrable darkness of the night except for the phosphorescent top of a breaking wave and perhaps the flash of a lighthouse. The yacht plunges forward on her course, throwing aft sheets of spray which patter over the cabin roof and drive into the helmsman's face.

Throughout the night the wind hardened. A strong onshore wind nearly always means rough conditions until one gets into deep water. I went on watch at 0200. We were 3 miles west of Cabo Prior and now exposed to the full force of wind. It was blowing about Force 7 and raining hard. Watches had been reduced to an hour at a time. It was long enough, for the incessant spray driving in the helmsman's face is quickly tiring. By the end of my watch the salt was burning my eyes, and I was delighted to be relieved and return to the cabin for breakfast.

Although the wind remained strong the seas became more regular as we got into the deep water of the Atlantic. Conditions were not so severe during the second night and at 0400 on the next morning (Friday 23rd July) the wind moderated, so that we were able to set the mainsail again. The day developed into a pleasant one. The sun broke through the clouds in time for a noon sight to be taken and in the afternoon we got our longitude. The sight placed us nearly 30 miles west of our dead reckoning, so we assumed that the strong north-east winds had produced a west-going current off the Spanish coast.

In the afternoon the wind petered out and *Cohoe II* lay becalmed in a long ocean swell. The course combined with the current had taken the yacht out of the Bay of Biscay and well into the Atlantic. At 2100 our position was 46° 40′ N., 9° 20′ W.—over 300 miles from the shores of the Bay, and almost equidistant, at 200 miles, from La Coruña and Ushant, with over 2,000 fathoms of water under the keel. The sea remained calm all night, but next morning (Saturday, 24 July) the weather forecast gave south-west winds in the north of the Bay of Biscay. Sure enough to the north the sky was overcast. At 0400 we went on the other tack and an hour later a light breeze got up from west of north, and we were sailing once more, but this time in the direction we wanted to go, to Ushant instead of out into the Atlantic.

On Sunday morning (25 July) the wind freshened. An overcast sky still lay to the north, but we were getting much closer to it. The barometer at 1,016 millibars showed a tendency to fall. During the morning the wind steadily increased and we lowered the mainsail. At noon I was just in time to get a sight of the sun through the gathering clouds, and in the early afternoon the spinnaker was handed, as the yacht was rolling heavily, and a small genoa was set in its place. The midday weather forecast was bad. There was a gale warning for the Sole area just north of us, and a forecast of strong winds, gale force locally, coastal fog and otherwise poor visibility, for the north of the Bay of Biscay and Plymouth to the east of us.

The 1800 forecast was even more ominous. A depression was deepening off Ireland and there was a deep depression off Iceland. The yacht was then running fast, doing nearly 8 knots under small genoa and mizzen only. Before nightfall both sails were handed and the storm jib was set. It did not set well, as we found the strain on the genoa halyard had nearly drawn the winch off the mast, so that the storm jib halyard had to be set on a cleat, which also worked loose. The speed under only 50 sq. ft. of canvas dropped to about 4½ or 5 knots, but the yacht was incomparably easier to steer, and if the moderate gale matured into something serious she would be under the right canvas for it, without the need for sail shifting at night.

Ushant, the most westerly point in France, is a bad corner to round at night in severe weather. The navigator has to anticipate the possibility of the lights being obscured by fog and rain, and owing to the strong tidal streams in the vicinity, the seas in a south-west gale from the Atlantic can be formidable. For these reasons, although I wanted to fix the yacht's position by the lights on the French coast if they could be seen, I decided to give Ushant a wide berth. The yacht was gybed and stood away to the north.

As anticipated, it proved a dirty night. It was exceptionally dark owing to driving rain, with not a glimpse of moon or stars. The only light was from the phosphorescent tops of the waves now breaking in every direction, and the fiery wake. The distant breaking crests were so luminous that they could easily be mistaken for the loom of a distant lighthouse. The barometer was still falling smartly; it fell 24 millibars in twenty-four hours. The boat was behaving beautifully. The long smooth run left a clean, though phosphorescent, wake. She answered the lightest touch of the helm and no heavy water came aboard. Nevertheless, steering was responsible work, and once again the helmsmen were relieved hourly. As the visibility was so bad and we were approaching steamer routes, a radar reflector was hoisted in the rigging, and a white flare was placed in the waterproof bag for the helmsman in case of need.

It was a turbulent scene on deck, and below decks there was the usual discomfort of four men penned up in a small space—wet oilskins, cigarette ends and spent matches. The motion made sleep almost impossible. There was also a slight uncertainty about our position, for we had sailed over 300 miles since leaving sight of land.

However, the night although rough proved uneventful. Even the glutinous spaghetti-au-gratin which we had for dinner was shaken down. At dawn (Monday, 26 July) we reckoned *Cohoe II* was a good 30 miles west of Ushant. Although visibility was still thick, we had plenty of sea room to enter the English Channel, and a course was set for Portland Bill, still 200 miles distant. Now that it was light we could see the seas and judge their potential. For the weight of the wind and the long fetch they were not excessive. They were, of course, breaking heavily and occasionally forming into white-topped pinnacles of water, rearing against the sombre sky, but they were not unmanageable, so we set the mizzen, as we wanted to get well round the corner into the English Channel as quickly as possible in case the weather should worsen further.

The visibility did not improve in the morning, but we sighted a small tanker making heavy weather of it as she passed close to us, and at noon the sun showed through the clouds conveniently in time to give us a sun sight. We also got a fix from radio beacons which put us well in the English Channel off the French coast some 40 miles north by east of Île Vierge lighthouse.

However, the glass was still falling. By then it had dropped from 1,016 millibars to 989 millibars. The weather forecast that evening was greeted by the crew with hilarity. By the time the announcer had finished his gale warnings there was hardly an area left where the weather was normal. A deep depression was moving east across Scotland, and, if my memory serves correctly, gale warnings were given for Rockall, Malin, Shannon, Fastnet, Lundy, Sole, North Biscay, Plymouth, Portland, Wight and some of the North Sea. We were in the Plymouth area and approaching Portland and Wight, so there was no escaping a blow which covered such a vast sea area.

So we prepared for another night of discomfort, though we were becoming acclimatized to it by then. The yacht was again proving herself an able sea boat and we had a strong crew. One hour on watch and four below is light work, even if sleep is difficult. The night passed much as had the previous one, but we were lucky next morning (Tuesday, 27 July), for the sun came out. True, it was an unhealthy sort of sun and there was a haze over the sea (which if anything was running higher than before), but it was sufficient to give us a sight. The yacht was sailing quite fast enough for normal cruising, but divorce by their bosses once again became a topic of conversation among the crew. To hurry things up we reefed the mainsail, and set it. Immediately the yacht picked up to her maximum speed, and although steering became more difficult she still remained under perfect control. It was blowing a moderate gale and no more. We passed a trawler, a tanker and a coaster, so we concluded we were crossing the steamer track off the south coast of England.

It was our sixth day at sea and, allowing for the headwind in the Bay of Biscay, the yacht had sailed nearly 600 miles through the water, the last part of in thick weather, so it was an exciting moment when land was sighted on the port bow at 1030. England showed as distant hills, and then a ray of sun passed over a yellow headland, none other than Golden Cap in Lyme Bay. Not long afterwards Portland could be identified. It had not been far distant, but obscured by low cloud, so our landfall was precise and a credit to Barrie, who did most of the navigation.

The tide was foul, so we gybed to get an offing of 5 miles when passing the Bill. The notorious Race of Portland only extends a couple of miles, but in bad weather the sea is disturbed even 10 miles out and it should be given a wide berth, except when racing. It was a good day for taking photographs of the sea, as the sun was out, and Alan and I seized the opportunity.

The sea as the yacht drew south of the Bill became heavier. Alan took a trick at the helm and enjoyed the experience of surf riding, with the speed indicator reading 9 knots, no doubt overregistering, but none the less an exhilarating performance. We were lucky again with our tide, for it was fair when we arrived off the Bill. There would have been a really dangerous sea if the tide had been weather-going. As it was the seas were building up formidably.

It is always difficult to assess the strength of the wind when running before it. Under such conditions it is often underestimated, just as it may be exaggerated when beating into it. The observer's judgement is affected by such things as the height and severity of the sea, and especially by the conditions, whether sunny or overcast, with rain to add to the gloom. The variations are subtle, and it was not until the next watch, with Barrie at the helm, that I guessed the wind had touched at least gale force. We were then off St. Alban's and crossing the tail of the bank, when Barrie called for relief. The boat was getting unmanageable. It had been blowing hard from the Atlantic for some days, and the waves by then were pretty big. The sea was indeed a mass of foam. It was time to slow down, so I lowered the mainsail instantly. That relieved the boat, and she was happy once more.

After passing Anvil Point the seas grew smaller, and we crossed Bournemouth Bay and safely entered the Solent through the North Channel, which is partially sheltered by the Dolphin Bank and the Shingles Bank.

As we approached Yarmouth in the Isle of Wight we saw the Roads were dotted with coasters at anchor sheltering from the weather, which confirmed that we had not overestimated the strength of the wind when running before it. We tied up in the harbour before 2000 and the Customs came alongside immediately on arrival and cleared us, in time for three of my crew to hurry ashore to return to their jobs. Before they left, the Customs officers gave us a bit of news. Another gale warning!

Conclusions

The synoptic charts are reproduced and it will be seen a fairly deep depression to the south of Iceland moved rapidly across the north of Scotland, where it slowed down and deepened to 980 millibars. It was accompanied by minor troughs of low pressure which moved across England and the English Channel. The weather affords a typical example of that experienced in the English Channel when a depression is passing to the northward, giving rise to Force 6 and Force 7 winds and Force 8 gales locally. This particular depression caused a longer period of bad weather than usual, as it became almost stationary over Scotland and lasted long enough to allow the seas to build up to maturity.

The nearest shore station of which I have records is at the Lizard. The wind forces recorded there on Monday, 26 July, were a consistent Force 6 pretty well all day, rising to Force 7 for the two hours to 1230 G.M.T. and Force 8 for the hour ending 1530 G.M.T. On Tuesday, 27 July, the wind was maintained near the top of Force 6, but rose to Force 7 in the early morning from 0230 to 0530. The notable feature on both days was the squalliness of the wind. On Monday a gust of 43 knots (Force 9) was recorded at 2025 G.M.T., nearly double the mean wind speed for the hour of Force 6 (22–27 knots); on Tuesday a similar 43–knot gust was recorded at 0335 G.M.T. when the wind was mean Force 7. At sea the strength of the wind would have been higher, and undoubtedly there were considerable periods when it attained the 34–40 knots of Force 8.

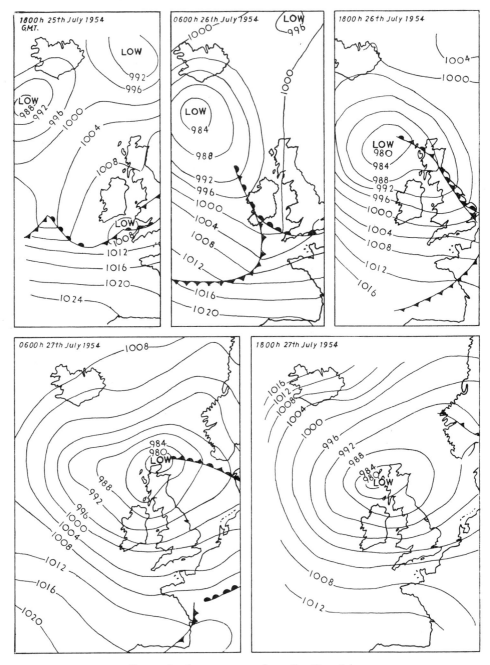

17 Synoptic charts, return from La Coruña, 1954.

1. *Shoaling water*. High seas were experienced off Portland Bill. I have noticed before and since during gales in this vicinity that the waves take the form of a very high steep swell, literally towering much as they do approaching a steep-to shore. With a lee-going tide they are toppling rather than breaking, although white-crested. Such seas are impressive, but harmless provided nothing causes them to break heavily. It would be dangerous if one of them actually did so. With a weather-going spring tide against a south-westerly gale they would break and the whole locality is dangerous. It is safer to keep 10 miles south of Portland Bill.

The roughest seas were found SE. of St. Alban's Head, where there is an irregular bottom with only 9 fathoms as much as 5 miles seawards, coupled with strong tidal streams. After passing St. Alban's the seas gradually lessened. When approaching the Solent by the North Channel the seas grew steeper and whiter, but they were much smaller than out at sea, probably due to being under the lee of the Dolphin Bank, which, although it has 6 to 9 fathoms over it, acts as a brake on size. As a matter of purely local interest, the North Channel is said to be safer than the Needles Channel in a south-westerly gale.

2. *Running in gales*. As I have remarked before, it is remarkably difficult to judge the force of a following wind. When a yacht is running at 6 knots or more this alone reduces the apparent wind by about one grade in the Beaufort Scale. A Force 8 gale will only feel Force 7 on the face, when looking astern. A lee-going tide, so that the yacht may really be doing 10 knots over the bottom, even further reduces the apparent wind.

The interesting thing is to compare the performance of *Cohoe I* in the Atlantic near gale (described in the last chapter) with that of *Cohoe II* in stronger winds though not such confused seas.

As *Cohoe I* became more unmanageable I reduced sail, eventually coming down to bare pole, doing perhaps 4 knots on the crests of the seas and only 2 knots in the troughs. The speed of *Cohoe II*, on the contrary, under mainsail, mizzen and storm jib was 7½ knots, and when racing it would not be allowed to fall lower, even if the yacht became difficult to steer. Under mizzen and storm jib from Portland to St. Albans (when the wind was probably Force 8 locally) it was reduced to 6 knots and she was docile and much easier on the helm. Heads of seas often came aboard and there was continual spray flying across the cockpit, but at no time was there any threat of real pooping. It seems to me that when cruising in strong winds and ordinary gales each yacht has a natural speed at which she is easy to steer and responsive. It is undesirable when cruising to exceed or fall much below the natural speed unless wind or seas dictate resorting to gale tactics, such as streaming warps. This point might be arrived at somewhere about a genuine Force 9, according to the ability of the individual boat and other factors such as turbulence, tidal streams and shoal water.

10

A RACE TO CORK

When *Cohoe II* was back on her moorings at Bursledon there remained little over a week in which to turn her round, refit and provision for the Cowes to Cork Race due to start on Saturday, 7 August (see chart, Fig. 21, page 46).

For this event I had two of my Coruña crew, Alan Mansley and Jim Kentish, but Mike Awty and Barrie Kendall had no leave left and their places were taken by Dr. A. Hudson, who had sailed with me on the previous Fastnet Race, and John Webster, then a Lieutenant R.N., making a total complement of five. The course was direct from Cowes through the Needles Channel and thence to Cork, a distance of 330 miles. Only ten yachts entered, three in Class I, six in Class II and *Cohoe II*, which raced with Class II in the absence of any other small-boat entries. There was a south-westerly gale on the Saturday, so the start of the race was postponed until Sunday (8 August), owing to the risks involved in beating through the Needles Channel under such conditions. The weather had improved on Sunday and after crossing the starting line the boats turned to windward against a light SW. wind. Good conditions continued throughout the day, until on the evening weather forecast there was mention of another depression coming in from the Atlantic.

By 2200 the wind had freshened and the ocean racers were in rough water off Portland Bill, but the wind backed to the SE., so that they were able to lay across Lyme Bay.

On Monday (9 August) the wind continued to freshen, and at 0700 there was heavy rain, but the wind veered later and it was a pleasant day, though rough going. At 1800 there was a gale warning owing to "a vigorous depression centred over sea area Thames" and another off the Hebrides. Two Class II yachts with whom we had been cross-tacking all day retired to Plymouth.

At 1930 we brought the Eddystone lighthouse abeam. The sky was sunny, but the wind had hardened, and there was a very steep rough sea, although it had only a 20-mile fetch.

The gale came in then with a violent squall which hove the yacht down until her decks were awash. The mainsail was lowered at once and *Cohoe II* carried on under mizzen and small genoa. Cooking dinner, consisting merely of soup and eggs, was a grim job which Alan tackled with his customary determination. The yacht was sailing at a considerable angle of heel, crashing to windward in a cloud of spray.

Down below it was stuffy, as the Dorade ventilators had to be closed, for the seas breaking forward sometimes filled the boxes and sent occasional spouts of water, solid as from a hose pipe, through the apertures into the cabin. The scuttles were screwed down and the only air admitted below came from the companionway, accompanied by dollops of water. Two crew members were sea-sick though neither was incapacitated.

The night was cold and unpleasant, during which we made a long tack shorewards towards Fowey and another seawards. There was a note of disappointment at dawn (10 August) when we found the Lizard still some 10 miles to the west of us. Beating to windward in a gale is punishing to all. The yacht had to be sailed rather free to maintain speed and momentum to smash her way against the weight of the seas, and under such conditions the leeway was considerable. Tedious and slow as it seemed, *Cohoe II* made good 30 miles dead to windward in twelve hours; few small yachts of her size are able to do much better than 6 knots through the water and 2½ to 3 knots made good when beating against a gale.

When we drew clear of the land into the English Channel the height of the seas increased considerably. Although high cut, the genoa began to take heavy water as the boat plunged through the seas. There was a risk not only of bursting the sail but to the mast, rigging and gear, for there is immense weight and power behind a big sea. It was blowing gale force, and on the morning forecast there was another gale warning, so it was time to alter the sail plan. Alan and I tied down a reef in the mainsail and set it, and the genoa was replaced by the storm jib. There was no reduction in sail area, but the storm jib was small and set high, so it did not take the seas forward as the genoa did, and the mainsail was a safe sail. Cut down as it was, it was equivalent to double reefed before we started and the extra reef brought it down to storm trysail size.

Sailing now under storm jib, reefed mainsail and mizzen, the yacht was snugly rigged and well balanced. The tiny storm jib took no seas in it, and all strains were distributed between three sails with a low sail plan. The storm jib was, however, of the conventional pattern, roped all round and immensely strong, but cut full, and hence it was no racing sail and the yacht was not so close-winded as she had been under genoa and mizzen.

Under gale conditions the seas near the land, especially in the fast tidal streams off the Lizard Race, are very high. They run higher than they do farther east towards Portland Bill, so we continued on the starboard tack well into the deep water of the English Channel. The wind was very boisterous, with tremendous squalls followed by comparative lulls. Aubrey Hudson prepared porridge and eggs for breakfast, but part of the porridge was lost in a particularly violent lurch and spattered all over the galley and cooking utensils. Conditions below were scarcely jolly: porridge on the cabin sole near the galley, cigarette-ends, spent matches and fluff off the blankets in every corner, water oozing up from the bilges over the cabin sole as the ship heeled, and damp throughout. Wet clothes, wet blankets, wet everything! The smell was unpleasant, too, as among us was a rather heavy smoker, and stale tobacco leaves a nasty aroma in a confined wet space.

After sailing some 20 miles south of the Lizard we tacked and were delighted to find we could lay Newlyn.

At 1900 we were off Newlyn and the yacht was in partial shelter of the land, for the wind had veered. We tacked again and lay close under the cliffs with a fair tide. The evening weather report had been comparatively good, a forecast of strong winds instead of gales. While under the lee of the land Alan got busy with the cooking and we enjoyed hot soup and eggs. Then we lowered the storm jib and set the staysail in its place, which enabled us to sail a point closer to the wind.

By 2300 we had cleared Land's End and were close to the Wolf Rock lighthouse. The beam of the light lit up the sails and we wondered whether any other yachts were in the vicinity, for we had seen none that day. I had expected a heavy sea off the Wolf, as it had been blowing from the west for so long and was still fresh to strong, but the seas proved much easier. They were longer and the boat was able to ride the big seas far better than the shorter ones off the Lizard. At the Wolf we tacked and headed for Ireland, though we could only lay to the east of Cork. It was a clear night. The Longships light was on the starboard bow, the Seven Stones lightship and Round Island lighthouse to port.

That was the end of the heavy weather part of the race and by 1100 the following morning (Wednesday, 11 August) the wind was moderate and the sun had broken through. It is remarkable how quickly spirits rise on a bright morning. In no time wet blankets and wet cushions appeared on deck and wet clothes hung in the rigging. Everybody was hilarious, but in this extraordinary race the weather still had a card to play. By 1730 it started to rain and by midnight it turned to dense fog. With it the wind had backed and freed. Throughout the night we ran fast and at dawn (Thursday, 12 August) we picked up the Daunt radio beacon on which John Webster homed by D. F. so exactly that when the lightship loomed up like a dark shadow we had to alter course promptly to avoid collision with her. As we approached the land the fog cleared and at 0924 we crossed the finishing line at the entrance to Cork Harbour, second boat home. Only two other yachts (*Jocasta* and *Marabu*, both Class I) completed the course, and *Cohoe II* had put up the best corrected time. It marked the first occasion when a Class III yacht beat Class I in gales, for small yachts had hitherto won mostly in light weather.

If I may digress for a moment, I will add that my wife joined *Cohoe II* at Cork and Ross and my daughter-in-law joined at Dingle. We cruised to the Blasket

Islands before sailing home, and I can recommend south-west Ireland as one of the best cruising grounds in Europe. It was one of our happiest family cruises.

Conclusions

The period of heavy weather was a prolonged one. As on the return from La Coruña it was caused by a depression slowing up over the north of Scotland. The fundamental difference between the experiences in the return from La Coruña and those in the Cork Race were that in the former we had a joy ride running before the gale, whereas in the latter we were beating against it, which provides the real test of ship and crew.

On 10 August, Force 7 was recorded at the Lizard until 0530, followed by a consistent Force 6 for the rest of the day, but it would have been blowing harder at sea, probably Force 8 for part of the time. As on the return from La Coruña, the feature was the gustiness of the wind. The highest gust occurred at 0355, when *Cohoe II* was still east of the Lizard. Oddly enough this was precisely the same velocity as in the previous blow—43 knots (Force 9). *Cohoe II* was kept going at between 5 and 6 knots, which was an improvement over the speeds achieved by the small yachts in the Wolf Race, but *Cohoe II* was a bigger and more powerful boat than the R.N.S.A. 24's

1. *The yawl rig*. This is a good one when beating to windward in a gale. It enables the sail area to be distributed between storm jib, reefed mainsail (or trysail) and mizzen, all low-setting sails, but high enough in the foot not to be filled by any but a freak wave. The alternative sail plan of mizzen and a heavy genoa is effective up to Force 7, but, once the wind rises to Force 8 and the seas have had time to build up, any low-cut sail like a genoa becomes dangerous. The head of a big breaking sea may strike it with irresistible force, so that something is bound to go.

2. *Storm jib*. The old-fashioned storm jib of heavy canvas roped all round is adequate for cruising and for heaving-to, but the rope tends to shrink and the sail becomes too baggy for racing. Of recent years I have used terylene and sheeted it hard, so that it is as effective in a gale as a staysail in a strong wind. Terylene is so strong and the sail area is so small that storm jibs no longer need be very heavy. What is most likely to wear is the stitching.

3. *Rounding headlands*. Progress round headlands when beating to windward in a gale often seems slow. This is most disheartening to a tired crew, when after hours of tacking, soaked and half blinded by spray, the objective seems no nearer. A small yacht even if hard driven at 5 or 6 knots will only make good about 3 miles in an hour. Tacking against a strong foul tide she will make hardly any progress and when the tide comes fair, but contrary to the wind, she will be beating in very rough water in which she has to be sailed rather free.

In the English Channel, it is the headlands, Portland Bill, the Lizard and

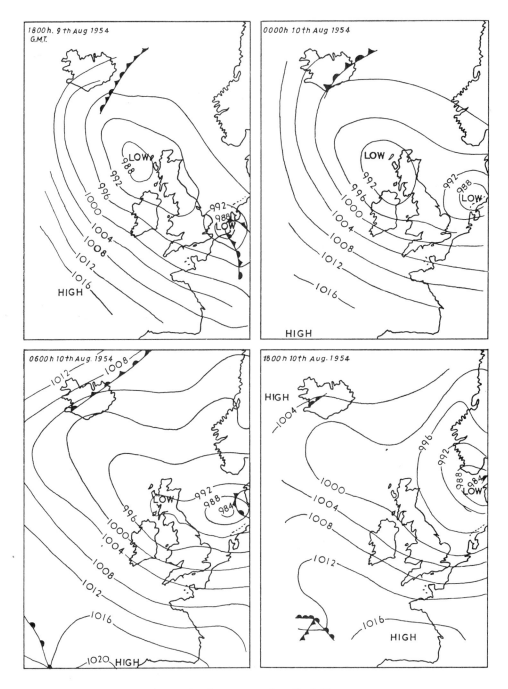

18   Synoptic charts covering Cork Race, 1954.

others that provide the endurance tests. Nevertheless, progress is made even if it does not appear to be. Ten hours' gruelling work means a gain of 20 or 30 miles and gales don't last for ever. In some circumstances it may pay in a small yacht to shelter during the period of foul tide, of which I shall have more to say in Chapter 12.

STORM IN THE ENGLISH CHANNEL

The Channel Storm of 1956 is the most important gale described in this book. The wind attained Force 11 (violent storm) at the Lizard, and it was the first occasion when an overall picture was obtained of all the yachts involved and how they fared in positions ranging from the open sea to a dangerous lee shore. The Editor of *Yachting World* sent a questionnaire to owners, and a subcommittee of the R.O.R.C. was appointed to examine their reports. Many lessons were learnt and the findings of the committee provide a valuable contribution to the knowledge of handling of yachts in heavy weather and the necessary preparations for it.

I cannot give a first-hand report of the gale, as I was not racing that year, but the R.O.R.C. has kindly given me access to all the records, from which I have been able to prepare the following account, aided by information from other sources and my personal acquaintance with the yachts involved and with their owners. In the first part of the chapter I will confine my comments to the yachts which were caught in the worst of the storm on a lee shore, and in the second I shall refer to the experiences of the remaining boats and general points arising from the gale.

Twenty-three yachts divided into the usual three classes started in the Channel Race of 1956, on the 220-mile course from Southsea to the Royal Sovereign lightvessel off Eastbourne, thence to Le Havre lightvessel (for which a buoy had been substituted) and back across the English Channel to finish between the forts at Spithead (see chart, Fig. 7, page 57).

The race started gently on the Friday evening of 27 July and except for two sharp squalls nothing of interest was reported on the passage to the Royal Sovereign lightvessel, which was rounded in the early hours of Saturday morning. The wind had freshened by then from the south-west and the next leg of the course to Le Havre buoy at first provided a beat dead to windward, but by the evening the wind had backed to the south.

It was late during Saturday night (28 July) when the wind started to increase. By this time it appears that the big yachts had rounded Le Havre buoy, but the smaller ones were still on the wrong side, and many of them did not round it until 0900 or later on Sunday morning, 29 July.

The midnight forecast had given SW. gales for Portland and Plymouth, veering NW. For Dover and Wight it gave no more than strong southerly winds,

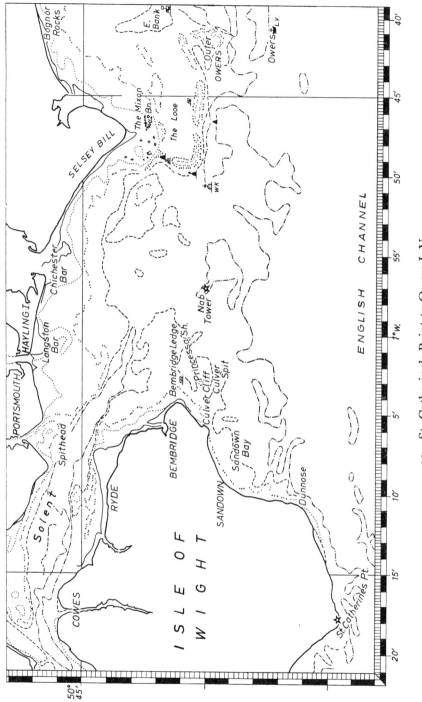

19 St. Catherine's Point to Owers L.V.

SELSEY BILL

Bognor Rocks

E. Bank

Outer OWERS

Owers L.V.

The Mixon
Bn.
The Looe

wk

ENGLISH CHANNEL

1°W.

Chichester Bar

HAYLING I.

PORTSMOUTH

Langston Bar

Spithead

Solent

Nab Tower

Bembridge Ledge
Princessa Sh.
Culver Cliff
Culver Spit

COWES

RYDE

BEMBRIDGE

SANDOWN

Sandown Bay

I S L E   O F
W I G H T

Dunnose

St. Catherine's Pt.

50°
45'

40'

45'

50'

55'

5'

10'

15'

20'

127

increasing to Force 7 and veering SW. However, a depression was moving into the English Channel and a front of cool air was moving in towards the NW. of its centre, which was rapidly deepening to 976 millibars. The low was centred over Wales on the morning of Sunday, 29 July. When the fronts had passed through they were followed by a phenomenally fast rise in the barometer and with the veer the winds on the English side of the Channel increased to storm force or over.

Gusts of 100 m.p.h. (86 knots) were reported, possibly from ships, as I cannot ascertain the source, and the following are the figures which I have obtained from the Meteorological Office.

Station	Wind force	Duration Force 8 and over	Highest gust
The Scillies	45 knots (Force 9)	7 hours	68 knots
The Lizard	57 knots (Force 11)	10 hours	81 knots
Dungeness	42 knots (Force 9)	2 hours	70 knots

The principal characteristic of this storm was its extreme turbulence, with gusts well over hurricane force. At the less-exposed shore station of Thorney Island, where the wind was only 37 knots on the Beaufort Notation, a gust of 67 knots was experienced, nearly double the mean force. These were the weather conditions with which the leading yachts had to contend, but farther away to the south of the depression the winds were progressively less. Common to both sides of the English Channel was the long duration of severe weather (nearly four days) as the depression slowed down and became almost stationary over the North Sea on Monday, 30 July, without filling in much.

Let us now see what occurred to the leading yachts when they approached the lee shore of the English coast between St. Catherine's Point and the Owers lightvessel.

THE LEADING YACHTS

Lloyd's Yacht Club's big 70 ft. yawl *Lutine* was the first to arrive. She had a very experienced skipper and a non-seasick crew. She reported Force 4–5 at 0600 on Sunday, 29 July, which steadily increased to Force 8 before 0900, with squalls of 44 to 52 knots. She made her landfall downwind of the Nab Tower, where she set a trysail for the last leg and got under the lee of the Isle of Wight before the worst of the storm and finished the race at 1100.

Bloodhound, likewise a large yacht, was about 10 miles astern of *Lutine* and to the eastward. She reported about the same forces of wind until approximately 1000, when it increased suddenly with squalls of hurricane force. A veer of the wind must have occurred when she arrived east of the Nab Tower for she was beating up westward under working staysail and mizzen when the wind increased. The visibility was reported as nil to windward and only 50 yards to leeward, owing to rain and spray. *Bloodhound* was then making 3½ to 4 knots, 5 points off the wind. At 1030 the track of the mizzen boom started to lift, so

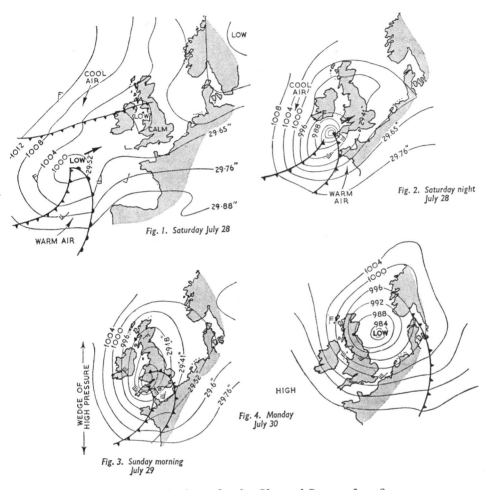

Fig. 1. Saturday July 28

Fig. 2. Saturday night July 28

Fig. 3. Sunday morning July 29

Fig. 4. Monday July 30

20 Synoptic charts for the Channel Storm of 1956.

she was left under staysail only, lying 7 points off the wind and making little headway. At 1100 the staysail split and the storm jib was set in its place. This lasted only half an hour before the luff hanks broke.

Bereft of all sail, she drifted to leeward towards the Owers Rocks. She let go her 120 lb. anchor as a last resort and this ultimately brought her up short of the breakers off Selsey Bill. She was in a position of extreme danger, but her crew were taken off in good order by the Selsey lifeboat, which returned when the weather had moderated next morning to take the yacht herself in tow. Afterwards it was discovered that both flukes of the anchor had broken. By a miracle something held, possibly the stub of one fluke jammed in a rock and held her until the lifeboat arrived to tow her off, or perhaps the flukes may have broken when the anchor was being recovered by means of the lifeboat's powerful winch.

The Class II cutter *Uomie* broke a runner fitting, and next her forestay fitting pulled out of the deck. She ran off under bare pole, but a rigging screw of one of her shrouds then parted. It was a lee one and the damage was due to its flicking, but it must have been blowing great guns for this to happen with the boat under bare pole. Further evidence of the tremendous violence of this storm was that mud and pebbles were thrown on *Uomie*'s deck by the seas when she drifted to leeward of the Owers. A frigate arrived, and as there was a risk that the yacht might drive on the lee shore she had to be abandoned. Her crew were taken off by the frigate, which was manoeuvred to bring the low afterdeck of the ship alongside *Uomie* so that the crew could clamber up the scrambling nets. The frigate must have been very well handled. Happily the yacht drifted clear of Selsey Bill and was eventually picked up by a French fishing vessel and towed into Dieppe.

The most remarkable experience in this storm was that of *Tilly Twin*, a Laurent Giles-designed 10-ton T.M. light-displacement yacht measuring 32 ft. on the waterline, with high freeboard, reverse sheer, narrow beam, and deep fin keel, owned by Mr. W. F. Cartwright. When *Tilly Twin* was about 12 miles north-east of Le Havre buoy on Saturday evening, 28 July, the forecast of strong southerly winds and of gales further westward was received. As the owner and crew had to be back on Monday morning, it was decided to retire from the race and to make the best of the southerly wind before it headed. A course was set direct for St. Catherines, and it was proposed to use the D.F. Loop to check the yacht's position. They intended on approach to the Isle of Wight to reach or to run off round the east side at the beginning of the easterly running stream which was due to start at about 0900 on Sunday morning. The decision was logical, but owing to a sharp change in the weather, it brought *Tilly Twin* into the height of the storm in company with the big class.

Tilly Twin had been carrying full sail on Saturday, but when the wind increased the yankee was lowered and at about 0700 on Sunday morning (29 July) the wind veered SW. and increased to Force 8 (34–40 knots). The yacht was running so fast and so wildly that the mainsail had to be lowered and she continued under staysail alone.

By 0800 *Tilly Twin* had crossed the English Channel at an average speed of 7 knots in a sharply rising sea and a smother of spray. Her position at this time was estimated at 7 or 8 miles south-east of St. Catherine's, but may have been less, as visibility was bad and the land above the headland was only seen for a few minutes. The weather forecast at 0740 had been worse: in Dover/Wight southerly Force 8 veering SW. and for Portland SW. up to Force 10. She altered course to the northward, intending to sail in about half-way between Bembridge Ledge buoy and the Nab Tower. By that time she was running under staysail only. Her tactics were absolutely orthodox and there appeared to be no danger, for she would arrive east of Dunnose at about slack water and soon have a fair tide.

At 0930 the yacht must have been somewhere to the eastward of the Isle of Wight, off Dunnose. Visibility was so bad that no land could be seen. The wind suddenly veered further and increased to Force 10 (48–55 knots) or over. The seas steepened equally sharply. It was decided to lower the staysail and run under bare pole.

Two men were forward lowering the sail when an immense wave struck the yacht. At the time she appeared to be running directly before the wind, but the sea struck her abeam and threw her over to starboard until her mast was pointing below the horizontal.

One man forward broke his wrist and was washed overboard. The dinghy, two lifebelts and the electric flare went over the side at the same time. One of the light alloy stanchions had snapped off like a carrot. The doghouse window framing was cracked on one side and water poured through the ventilators, which were submerged. One man in the cockpit was thrown over the mainboom in its stowed position 5 ft. above the cockpit floor and the other two were under water, but personal lifelines saved them from going overboard.

The ship righted herself. The man overboard had managed to preserve a hold on the staysail sheet despite his broken wrist. He was recovered safely, but with great difficulty, by the other foredeck hand.

The wind by then was phenomenally strong, and remained so for at least an hour, with gusts and squalls over hurricane force. The barometer had fallen to what was understood to have been the lowest ever recorded in that area, winter or summer, and, owing to the wedge of high pressure to the westward, the rise was abrupt after the front had passed. The seas were exceptionally high, very steep and breaking heavily with no great distance from crest to crest. They struck from directions varying over as much as 90 degrees, owing no doubt to a shift of wind. The fact that she was struck on her beam when running suggests that the wind may have veered as far as WSW.

Tilly Twin was in a dangerous position. A tanker of about 5,000 tons passed quite close to the yacht and appeared to have seen her, but she was herself having trouble, manoeuvring with difficulty in the high wind, and eventually she proceeded on her way. There was nothing she could have done to help, except perhaps sent down some oil. The seas were such that she was invisible every time she was in a trough.

Tilly Twin was run off before the storm and all available warps were streamed to steady her. Her C.Q.R. anchor was also let go astern and towed on 30 fathoms of nylon. This slowed her down, but she became very difficult to steer and to keep stern on to the huge breaking seas. Her adventures were not yet over.

Visibility at times was less than 50 yards, with no apparent dividing line between sea and air. In order to keep her stern to the seas, the course of the yacht varied between north and east, for the wind was still veering. Water was breaking over the entire hull as she scudded off before the seas, and the bilge pump was choked. At about 1100 *Tilly Twin* found herself over Selsey Shoals, with the Looe Channel buoy about a cable to port. The anchor had checked the yacht's progress a little as she crossed the shoals, where the water was full of sand and gravel, but it had little effect when she regained deeper water. On the lee side of the Boulder Bank the seas were shorter and very much reduced in height, though equally breaking. There was no respite from the wind.

The visibility must have improved, as soon afterwards the Mixon beacon was sighted, and later the beach at Bognor Regis. *Tilly Twin* ran on until, some 200 yards from the beach edge (at half tide) of Bognor Regis, the C.Q.R. anchor on the nylon rope got a hold on rocks, little more than a cable off the breakers.

As the yacht was riding by the stern the seas broke over the cockpit, so that it was full of water to the brim the whole time and there seemed every prospect of her ultimately filling and sinking. It might have been possible to have let go the other anchor, which was stowed in the forepeak, but it seemed dangerous to open the forward sail hatch to get it on deck. Even had this been accomplished and the yacht brought head to wind, she would have been battered to bits on the rocks when the tide fell later in the day. In the meantime it was urgently necessary to get the injured man ashore to hospital. It was learnt later that his wrist was so badly hurt that it took over a year to mend.

The owner-skipper decided to surf up on the beach. Accordingly, the anchor warp was deliberately cut. *Tilly Twin* ran on. The keel bounced on some rocks with a very severe jar, but quickly drove over them. The yacht, with her deep keel acting broadside-on as a drag, surfed gently into the shore on her beam ends, the hull itself at no time touching the ground. Her crew stepped out into about 2 or 3 ft. of water. A policeman and people on the beach gave all the help they could. The injured man was rushed to hospital and at 1630, near high water, the yacht was secured fore and aft with her topsides resting on the steep shingle bank. A few days later *Tilly Twin* was lifted by crane on to a lorry and taken to Emsworth by road.

The worst of the gale seems to have been encountered between St. Catherine's

Point and the Owers lightvessel. The 10-tonner, *Dancing Ledge*, which was not racing, but cruising, foundered off St. Catherine's. She was a boat which my wife and I had sailed and knew well, a powerful heavy-displacement yacht rather like a big *Vertue*, capable of cruising anywhere. At the time she was lost she was under charter to Lieutenant-Colonel H. Barry O'Sullivan, M.C. (an experienced sailing man and a member of the Royal Cruising Club), and crewed by his wife and two friends.

They had sailed out of Salcombe at sunset on Thursday, 26 August, and crossed to Ushant, where they altered course to the eastward for the Channel Islands because of fog. On the evening of the 28th they reefed *Dancing Ledge* at about 1730 and made for Cherbourg, as the forecast told of two shallow depressions. They arrived off the entrance of Cherbourg at approximately 2300, by which time it was blowing so hard that with the wind funnelling out of the harbour it was impossible to get in. Every combination of sail and engine was tried and tried again, but the gusts caught the bows and blew her off. At midnight it was decided to run off under storm jib.

Colonel O'Sullivan took the helm all night, with one or other of the two men helping. He sang most of the time and shouted out occasionally that it was marvellous outside. This was very reassuring to Mrs. O'Sullivan, cooped up in the dark cabin in the din of the gale, listening apprehensively to the noise of the seas streaming past close to her ear and separated from them by a mere 1-in. thick planking.

The approximate course was for Bembridge Ledge buoy, but the actual course was dictated by wind and sea, as the yacht had to be run off before the seas to avoid being pooped. This was achieved and the ship kept dry; she did not need pumping once.

At dawn on Sunday, 29 July, St. Catherine's Point was sighted in the distance, but it was already blowing Force 8 and rising. The necessity of keeping stern-on to the seas, coupled with a west-running stream, made it impossible to keep to the east of St. Catherine's Race.

The height of the storm with 80-knot gusts was near, because it was at 0930 that *Tilly Twin* (about an hour ahead of *Dancing Ledge*) reported the sudden veer and increase in the wind to Force 10 or 11 and shortly afterwards she was struck by the sea which knocked her down over her beam ends.

At 1020 *Dancing Ledge*'s storm jib blew out with a loud report, just as the overfalls of St. Catherine's Race made it more than ever necessary to have steerage way to keep to the eastward. The engine was of no real use, as the propeller was out of the water most of the time.

Quoting from a letter from Mrs. O'Sullivan, "we were pooped almost immediately (the alarm clock fell on my knees at 1030). Water broke through the starboard cabin top coaming, which burst inwards. Two or more seas heaping together spilled a few more tons of water on top of us, and *Dancing Ledge* went down very quickly. I was in the cabin, which seemed to fill from every direction. I believe that the forestay went, and the mast heel pulled out of the step. *Dancing Ledge* went forwards and downwards, the engine running for what seemed like a long time. We hit the bottom or something hard, and the engine hatch/cabin step dislodged and fell on my feet. In the cabin full of water, and dark, I got free by wriggling my feet out of my shoes and groped out. The boom was in the way, I remember. The life-jacket took charge once I got into the cockpit, and I went up fast for a long, long way.

"Once in the fresh air, we saw each other fairly soon, and also saw the dinghy, which must have broken from its chocks on the cabin top. It was upside down, but we hung on to it (aided by life-jackets) for nearly four hours and were carried inshore until we were close enough to see the window panes on the Ventnor houses. We were anxious lest we should be involved in the breakers. But the tide took us eastwards far out into Sandown Bay. There was less rough water there, just a huge swell with the crests blown off to make a thick head of spume on the sea. We knew we were invisible in this. The tide turned (we could feel) at about 1400.

"Barry insisted that we should 'bicycle' continuously with our legs to keep warm and avoid stomach cramp, which it proved successful in doing."

The youngest member of the crew had only a kapok life-jacket. This proved to be totally inadequate and as he became cold and weak his head had no support. Colonel and Mrs. O'Sullivan held on to the dinghy with one hand, and supported the crew's head with the other. The fourth member of the crew had already died.

A frigate, H.M.S. *Keppel*, approached at about this time. Colonel O'Sullivan took off his orange jacket to wave it above the spray to attract attention and this was seen as a tiny dot by the naval watch. He then attempted to put it on to the exhausted member of the crew to give him chin support, and he had therefore no jacket for himself.

When the frigate was manoeuvred alongside (no mean feat) a rope was thrown to Mrs. O'Sullivan. She let go the dinghy with one hand to grip the rope. Her hand was so cold and rigid that she could not close it round the rope. She let go the dinghy with the other hand to attempt to get a stronger grip, but it was impossible to hold the rope and it ran through her hands as a wave, deflected by the bulk of the frigate, swept her along the length of the ship and she drifted away into the clear, supported by her life-jacket, and became un-conscious. The frigate returned and Mrs. O'Sullivan was rescued by a man, secured by a lifeline, who went into the water and got her up the scrambling nets. The search was continued for the others, but there was no trace of the dinghy or the men.

The Royal Humane Society made the rare distinction of awarding post-humously the Stanhope Gold Medal to Colonel O'Sullivan. It would be presumptuous of me to say more, but Mrs. O'Sullivan has sent the following information on points to aid survival.

"(a) If caught below, or thrown under the water, take a breath of air while you can, so that you get caught with your lungs full. (b) Take in a breath before any wave looks likely to deluge down on you when you are in the water. (c) Life-jackets must be bright orange or fluorescent to be seen in the water. They must provide support for the head, and lift the chin up, if they are to be effective for more than a short time. (d) When in the water "bicycle" with your legs continuously to keep warm and avoid stomach cramp. Keep moving."

Medical opinion has altered of recent years as a result of wide research on both sides of the Atlantic into survival at sea. Doctors now recommend that if an adequate life jacket is worn and there is no place of refuge survivors should don extra clothes before entering the water if this is possible. They should stay *still* in the water, thus minimising the loss of heat from the body to the cold sea by conduction.

Conclusions

No anemometer recordings are available to me to show the exact force of the wind off St. Catherine's Point on Sunday, 29 July 1956. From the records at the Lizard and Dungeness an average is given of 50 knots, which is Force 10 on the Beaufort Scale, with gusts of 76 knots, well above hurricane force. It was reported to have been the worst depression since 1922, and was the storm in which *Moyana* was lost in the Sail Training Race.

To the south of St. Catherine's, which is a very exposed position, the wind may have been even higher. To the north-eastward the wind aggravated by the high land behind St. Catherine's and Dunnose would probably have caused gusts of greater violence when the cold front went through, possibly the 100 knots which has been said. Alan Watts has some most instructive comments to make in Chapter 21 on the meteorological peculiarities of this storm.

It is the turbulence created by the gusts striking like shots out of a gun that cause steep breaking cross seas and the rogue seas which are so dangerous. There is no doubt that the four leading racing yachts and *Dancing Ledge* met phenomenal weather and seas, which might not be encountered in the English Channel during a lifetime's sailing.

1. *Running for shelter.* In the ordinary way there would have been no great danger in running for the shelter of the Isle of Wight, for there was little warning of the sudden deepening of the depression and still less of winds attaining hurricane force in gusts. The weather conditions were unprecedented in an offshore race. The wind suddenly rose to storm force with frontal squalls coinciding with the arrival of the leading yachts on a lee shore. If this could have been anticipated the leading yachts and *Dancing Ledge* would have adopted storm tactics and remained in mid-Channel, for the experiences confirm the rule that in exceptionally severe weather it is always safer to remain at sea and keep away from

the land. But this is hindsight, as none could have forseen what lay ahead.
2. *No uniformity in gales*. When *Dancing Ledge* had to give up the attempts to gain
Cherbourg and at midnight on Saturday ran off under storm jib, only Force 7
was registered at Guernsey to the westward and by *Tilly Twin* to the eastward,
so it might be inferred that the wind at Cherbourg was the same force. On
the contrary, it was stated by French fishermen that Force 10 was recorded
locally. There is independent evidence of this, as a new 20-ton sloop, *Wawpeejay*,
was caught off Cherbourg in much the same position as *Dancing Ledge*, but an
hour later. Her experienced owner told me that it was entirely due to having a
very powerful diesel engine that he was able to make up "submarine fashion"
against the weight of the wind. The sea was flattened and had a boiling look.
It was blowing so hard that the weight of the wind funnelling down the valley
and in Cherbourg Inner Harbour against *Wawpeejay*'s bare mast heeled her
over to her gunwale in the gusts, even when she was secured to a mooring.

This illustrates the important point that gales are not uniform in strength
over a given area, and wind forces can be much higher locally. This applies
particularly when in the vicinity of land, where violent squalls and gusts can
funnel down valleys, as they did in this storm at Cherbourg with a southerly
wind and off the east side of the Isle of Wight when the wind was SW. The same
variations sometimes occur in open water, which explains the references sometimes made in weather forecasts of gales or severe gales "locally".

The tragedy of *Dancing Ledge* serves as a warning that in extreme gales, with
gusts of hurricane strength funnelling down valleys to the sea, it may prove
impossible to beat into shelter even when within a mile or two of the harbour
or inlet under the lee of the land.

3. *St. Catherine's and Dunnose Races*. When caught out in a southerly or SW. gale
in the area south of the Isle of Wight the normal course is to make for St.
Catherine's. The powerful radio beacon aids navigation, if the sea disturbance
is not so great that it interferes with reception, and at night the light has a range
of 16 miles. On approach to St. Catherine's (before reaching the race), it is in
theory only necessary to bear away to the eastward to avoid the race and to get
under the lee of the Isle of Wight and make harbour safely.

In practice this approach can be dangerous in gales because (*a*) the tidal
disturbances are more extensive than they appear on the chart and rough water
stretches in patches the whole way from SW. of St. Catherine's to the NE of
Dunnose and beyond, because the bottom is irregular, and there are underwater ledges with only from 7 to 9 fathoms over them and off Culver Cliff as
little as 5 fathoms. (*b*) In my opinion the gusts are aggravated by the high
ground of the Isle of Wight. (*c*) It may be impossible to get shelter close under
the lee of the land without entering the areas of tidal disturbances. Coming up
on Dunnose in *Cohoe III* from Le Havre in 1965, during the early part of a gale

11. Mid-Atlantic. Although on the same spool as the previous picture, this photograph was probably taken later under spinnaker, with wind Force 6, but regular seas. *Cohoe* surfed on crests at 12 knots or more, but what was gained on the crests was lost in troughs. Noon to noon run 177 miles on 25.5 ft designed L.W.L. overloaded to 26 ft.

12. Return from La Coruna. Even under storm jib many turns of the sheet are needed on the winch in *Cohoe II* when the wind is gusting 43 knots, and 9 knots is registered at times on speedometer.

13. Return from La Coruna in *Cohoe II*. The wind is Force 7 to Force 8, gusting 43 knots. The top of the following sea is well above the picture.

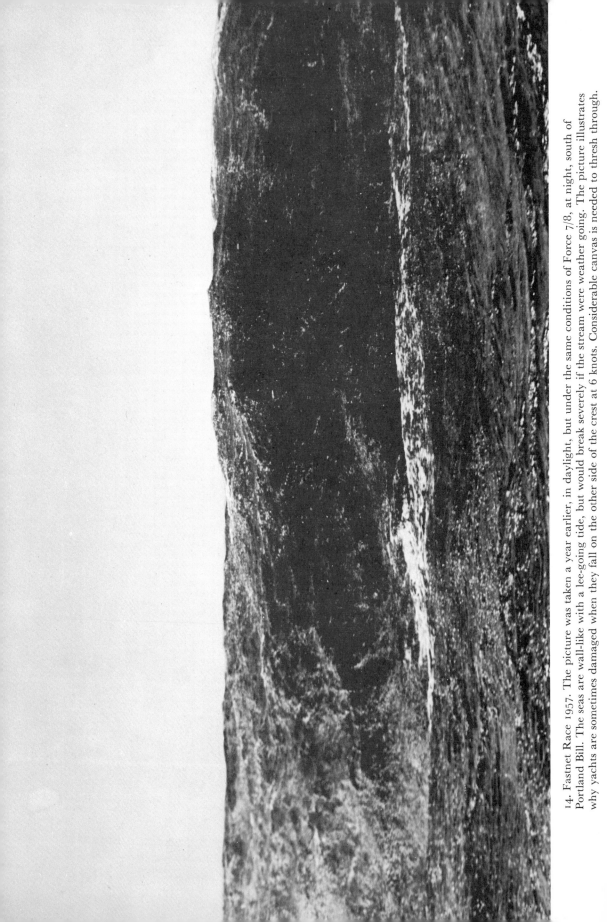

14. Fastnet Race 1957. The picture was taken a year earlier, in daylight, but under the same conditions of Force 7/8, at night, south of Portland Bill. The seas are wall-like with a lee-going tide, but would break severely if the stream were weather going. The picture illustrates why yachts are sometimes damaged when they fall on the other side of the crest at 6 knots. Considerable canvas is needed to thresh through.

which was forecast at Force 8, with thick rain and fog, we got into the overfalls before we had even sighted the land. It is better to approach nearer the Nab Tower, leaving the Princessa Shoal to port.

Much the same difficulties can be experienced at other headlands in the English Channel, where there are strong tidal streams and overfalls, such as between Anvil Point and Swanage.

4. *Pooping and speed.* In the period when *Tilly Twin* was running before the storm trailing 30 fathoms of nylon rope and warps and a C.Q.R. anchor her owner comments "it made it very difficult to steer the vessel and keep her stern-on to the huge breakers". This links with the difficulty of steering *Vertue XXXV* in the Bermuda gale when she was running at 1 knot with a sea anchor astern, and *Cohoe*'s experience when running too slowly before a near-gale in the Atlantic. It looks uncommonly as though there is a minimum speed necessary to provide adequate steering control when running before gales, and further reference to this is made in Chapters 19 and 20.

5. *Anchoring in gales.* *Bloodhound*'s experiment in letting go her anchor as a last resort shows that an anchor may hold despite seemingly impossible seas and weather conditions. The anchor in question was a 120 lb. Thomas and Nicholson type, on 45 fathoms of $\frac{1}{2}$ in. short-link galvanized steel chain, Lloyd's tested. When the anchor and chain were recovered it was found some of the links had started to collapse, and others at the top of the chain had stretched so much that they jammed each other and made the chain absolutely rigid for a short distance. It is amazing that they stood up to such a prolonged strain and it proves that to offer any chance of survival off a lee shore the anchor, chain, shackles and leads must be immensely strong. Probably 60 fathoms of nylon rope, with chain at the bottom end, would have been better, owing to the greater elasticity reducing the shocks as the yacht lifted to the crests of the seas.

Tilly Twin's experience was no less interesting. It is to be noted that her anchor held until the warp was cut. When first I heard that she had been deliberately put ashore and suffered no damage I could hardly believe it. I have seen seas breaking on open shores during gales and it seemed to me impossible that the yacht was not broken up immediately. It was amazing that her crew managed to get ashore safely through the undertow. Three points should be made, however.

If the gale was WSW. or had veered farther at the time *Tilly Twin* struck, there would be a bit of a lee to the east of Selsey Bill, although there would still be an onshore swell left over from when the wind was southerly. In the second place, I believe the skipper was familiar with the locality and knew precisely what he was doing and where he was putting the yacht. In the ordinary way I cannot believe it is feasible to run a yacht ashore in a gale on an open beach except as a last resort in at least partial shelter. Thirdly, it should be noted that

Tilly Twin is a light-displacement yacht with reverse sheer and high freeboard. Her deep fin keel would act like an anchor and lying broadside-on, tilted over on her side, the buoyancy was such that the hull would float in only 2 ft. of water. In fact, when she piled up the bilges never touched the bottom and consequently the hull (immensely strong by reason of her double diagonal multi-stringer construction) was undamaged. This tactic would only be possible, without damage to the hull, in a light-displacement yacht of exceptional strength with a very deep keel. The owner, who has wide experience of both light- and heavy-displacement hulls, considers that a normal heavy-displacement yacht would have been smashed to atoms when she went ashore.

THE OTHER YACHTS

The conditions of wind and sea experienced by the other yachts in the Channel Race varied according to their position on the Sunday morning. Storm force of wind seems to have been limited principally to a strip of water near the English coast. Yachts approaching this area, such as *Maid of Malham* and *Theta*, would probably have experienced Force 9 to Force 10 (say 40 to 50 knots) and violent gusts, but farther from the centre of the low off the French coast the strength fell to Force 8 or 9. As I have stated, at Guernsey, where records often seem to be lower than elsewhere, only Force 7 was recorded, but the wind at sea must have been higher.

The reports from the yachts themselves are factual and instructive. Inevitably estimates of the wind forces vary to some extent, as they always do in accounts of major gales, as owners tend to remember the gusts and squalls and to forget the lulls. The lowest estimates come from Commander Robin Foster, skipper of *Seehexe*, who reported Force 7 to 8, and from Mr. J. M. Tomlinson, owner of *Rondinella*, who wrote that he could not honestly put the gale over Force 8 (34–40 knots). Both are highly experienced skippers and class-winners in this race, but undoubtedly some of the boats experienced stronger winds, at any rate locally, since gales are rarely uniform in force over such a wide area.

The estimates of the height of the seas also vary. The two highest guesses are 30 ft. and 35 ft. but if these were measured by eye against the height of the mast my formula of three-fifths gives a height of 18 ft. to 21 ft. The lowest estimates come from *Seehexe* at 14 ft. to 18 ft. and *Rondinella* at 15 ft. to 18 ft. Most boats reported that near-by ships disappeared in the troughs of the waves. This is, of course, due to the line of sight from an observer in a trough to the crest of the next wave forming a wide angle with the horizontal, so that vision beyond the next crest is masked off to a considerable height. Even so, the reports show that a quite exceptionally high sea was running.

Suprisingly little real damage was sustained by the bulk of the racing fleet in this severe gale. The Royal Engineer Yacht Club's Class II sloop *Right Royal* was dismasted near Le Havre buoy at 0115 on Sunday morning, 29 July, in a southerly Force 3 to 4 wind and a moderate sea. The port preventer stay parted above the hook and the shock was such that the mast snapped 11 ft. above the deck, and went overboard together with all sails and rigging.

The sea anchor was put out over the bow and by 0300 the top of the mast and all sails and rigging were brought back on board and secured. Bolt cutters were used where necessary to free standing rigging. The sea anchor was then recovered and the yacht was run off before the wind under bare stump, which just gave her steerage way. As the stump did not provide enough windage to enable her to be steered properly, a headsail was lashed in the pulpit to afford the windage to control her. The intention was to stay the stump of the mast and to set a jury rig of staysail and trysail as soon as dawn broke and then attempt to run back to the Nab.

The wind increased and by 0500 had veered to SW. and reached gale force, so work on a jury rig was impossible. *Right Royal* ran at from 4 to 4½ knots under the mast stump and windage of hull and the headsail stowed on the pulpit, which suggests that the strength of the wind was well over Force 8, at any rate locally. All efforts were concentrated on avoiding being pooped by keeping stern-on to the seas, on pumping out and keeping the best D.R. possible in the circumstances. The cockpit was completely filled on several occasions and the gale reached its height at about noon (an hour or two later than off St. Catherine's). At this time the surface of the sea was covered by a large layer of flying spindrift.

Right Royal's danger was that the wind might veer farther to the west or to the NW., which would put her on a lee shore, but during the afternoon and throughout the night she was able to hold a course to take her through the Straits of Dover. A jury staysail had to be rigged for her to weather Cap Gris Nez as dawn broke on Monday (30 July).

Right Royal had spoken several ships which offered assistance. This had to be refused owing to the risk of collision while attempts were made to pass a towing line. At 0500 on Monday morning the tanker *Caltex Delft* was sighted and called by a pocket torch and asked to summon the Calais lifeboat. *Right Royal* was in narrow waters, but she was manoeuvred through the Straits of Dover and reached the Dyck lightvessel and made fast to her. She was later towed into Dunkerque by the Dunkerque lifeboat. *Right Royal* had run 130 miles with the stump of her mast, aided by the headsail stuffed forward. She had had a remarkable passage, but not the sort one would choose for a summer week-end, even when coupled with the fine seamanship shown by her skipper and crew.

Although a considerable number of minor breakages occurred, the only other yacht to receive structural damage was *Maid of Malham*. She was one of the larger Class II yachts and had rounded Le Havre buoy at 0325 on Sunday morning in company with *Theta*. She ran off under mainsail and staysail, logging 36 miles in four hours. When the wind increased she lowered her mainsail and ran under staysail only, but her speed was only reduced from 10 to 7 knots. At 0900 when the storm was approaching its height she was under bare pole running at $3\frac{1}{2}$ to 4 knots. She was badly pooped and about a ton of water must have got into the boat.

After being pooped she lay a-hull approximately 18 miles SSW. of the Owers lightvessel. Thirty fathoms of grass warp at the end of 30 fathoms of manilla were streamed, with a canvas bucket at the end, and she lay virtually broadside to the wind. She was less than 20 miles south of the leaders in trouble near the Owers, and the seas were reported as being spectacular.

At 1030 *Maid of Malham* was struck, when she was almost beam-on, by the only heavy sea while she was lying a-hull. It was exceptionally big and landed on the port bow and smashed about 16 ft. of the gunwale. As it happened, the damage did not endanger the yacht, but it shows what a single sea can do. If it had broken aboard aft and broken the superstructure or companion doors, matters might have been more serious. When a yacht suffers damage in a gale it is usually due to being struck by a sea and literally thrown down in the trough on her lee side, so that the doghouse or coachroof is stove in on the lee side. In the case of *Maid of Malham* the damage occurred on the weather side.

Three Class II yachts completed the course. *Seehexe* was first and finished at 1835 on Monday, having been kept sailing despite the handicap of old sails. She blew out three headsails (one three times), and for a considerable period was under close-reefed mainsail. *Seehexe* took one sea aboard severely. It was so high that the coachroof disappeared from sight, but the yacht came up straight away, without damage.

Theta, who had laid a-hull in company with *Maid of Malham* at the height of the gale, finished an hour after *Seehexe*, to take second place in her class. Third place was taken by *Joliette*. She is one of only two yachts to have reported taking anemometer readings. The maximum gusts 4 ft. above deck were 44 knots, which gives between 50 and 60 knots at masthead and suggests a mean speed of about Force 9 on the Beaufort Notation.

A remarkable performance was put up by *Rondinella*, the only Class III boat to complete the course, for she sailed throughout the gale and crossed the finishing line second to *Lutine*, beating all other competitors boat for boat without handicap. *Rondinella* is a 9–tonner, designed by Peter Brett and built by Allanson of Freckleton in 1952. She is a short-ended beamy boat with a long keel and the shallow draft of 4 ft. 6 ins., which one would have thought to be a disadvantage in really heavy weather. The design is straighforward with no frills and she is very well constructed and was meticulously kept. She had no sail or gear failures other than pulling the clew out of her working jib and stripping a number of rawhide slide ties. Her crew were very experienced and non-seasick. They consisted of Mr. J. M. Tomlinson, (her owner) and his wife, Mr. J. R. Leggate, Miss Bibbington and Dr. Hargreaves.

Rondinella rounded Le Havre buoy at 0930 on Sunday. The wind was Force 7 plus (a sensible description when one is not sure of the strength, but it is more than one likes) and her mainsail was lowered and she continued the course under storm jib, finally tacking from 2 miles west of the Owers to the finish line under this sail alone. As Tomlinson puts it, "our only tinge of worry was the size of the breakers", but as it turned out her cockpit was filled by seas only two or three times.

The 6–ton plywood *Aweigh*, one of the two smallest boats in the race, was knocked down by seas on three occasions. Her dinghy was swept off the foredeck despite strong lashings, and the motion was so violent that the Taylor paraffin stove jumped out of its gimbals and hit the deck-head above before landing on the chart table opposite. More serious was the fact she was making water nearly as fast as it could be bucketed out. Her owner traced the source to the exhaust pipe, which had sheared at its mounting in the transom, and when this had been plugged her crew felt happier.

General Conclusions. The findings of the R.O.R.C. sub-committee are printed in Appendix 3. Although they were circulated many years ago, they still hold good in principle. The most important point is made in clause 2: "In severe conditions it is far better to be caught out at sea in open water away from land influences, where, provided the vessel is well-found and not hampered by the human element, she has the best chance of coming through without serious trouble." Two of the boats which survived this storm, *Aweigh* and *Fizzlet*, were smaller even than *Cohoe*, so the experiences of both the Channel Storm of 1956 and the Santander Storm of 1948 confirm that even small yachts can look after themselves in really severe weather.

The report goes on to say that the experiences do not help to indicate "any preference for heaving-to, lying to a sea anchor from the bow or stern, lying a-hull, or streaming warps ahead or astern". This opinion, based on one of the worst summer gales, will be heartening to anybody caught out in a Channel gale for the first time, but, as I shall show in later chapters, it requires qualification when it comes to storms in the ocean, and I include the Bay of Biscay during westerly gales within the definition of ocean.

The R.O.R.C. report should be read in detail and here I only make some general comments.

1. *High freeboard*. The yachts with high freeboard and reverse sheer seem to have been the driest. *Tilly Twin* had the worst ordeal, but her owner seems to have been well satisfied with her hull design, and indeed attributes her survival to her combination of light displacement and strength of construction. *Petasus*'s

skipper reported that with her high freeboard and buoyant hull shape the yacht was very dry. *Callisto*'s skipper stated that no heavy water was taken aboard at all.

2. *Navigation*. It was found in *Tilly Twin* and *Dancing Ledge* that precise navigation was impossible at the height of the storm, because the courses were dictated by the need to take the seas stern-on to avoid pooping.

Several boats reported that visibility was reduced almost to nil to windward at cockpit level by the spray and rain driven almost horizontally by the wind. Another trouble was that the height of the waves interrupted the view of distant objects, which added to the navigator's problems even in daytime and at night made identification of the characteristics of lighthouses difficult. The skipper of *Right Royal* and several others commented on this. The seas were such that the lights could only be seen on the crests of the waves, making it impossible to count the flashes or time the periods.

Most yachts confirmed *Tilly Twin*'s difficulty in getting D.F. bearings on beacons, even on the powerful St. Catherine's beacon.

3. *Stanchions and pulpits*. One owner stated that he had two experiences of alloy stanchions breaking. The leverage when a man is thrown against a stanchion, whether of iron tube, alloy or stainless steel, is so great that I think it is a mistake to place too much reliance upon its strength.

The pulpit in *Theta* broke as the yankee was lashed to it, and the seas breaking aboard put so much drag on the sail that the pulpit carried away. It is quite common practice during heavy weather to lash down sails to the pulpit and stanchions on the foredeck, partly to avoid bringing a big wet sail below into the limited space of the fo'c'sle and partly in order to have it ready to rehoist without delay when the wind moderates. A sail thus stowed on the foredeck offers tremendous resistance to breaking seas and *Theta*'s experience suggests that headsails must be stowed below if exceptionally severe gales are expected.

4. *Cockpit lockers*. The R.O.R.C. reports that in some vessels a great deal of water got below through cockpit lockers. I believe this is the principal cause of the frequent need for pumping in heavy weather. Grooves and drains under the cockpit locker lids are usually useless in really rough going. Locker lids should be watertight, seated on rubber with fasteners that provide pressure on the rubber; or otherwise made leakproof.

5. *Trysails*. Mr. F. W. Morgan, owner of *Joliette*, gave a useful tip in suggesting that there should be eyes in the luffs of trysails so that luff lines can be laced round the mast below the lower spreaders as a safeguard against tracks and slides being carried away.

6. *Sea anchors*. In the report from *Right Royal* the skipper states as his considered opinion that "if the sea anchor had been used at the height of the gale the ship would have been overwhelmed". This is the only opinion given on the subject, but it is expressed by an experienced sailing man.

7. *Wash from ships.* Ann Speed shipped only one really heavy sea which cracked the skylight and one scuttle when the yacht was knocked down on her beam ends. Her skipper considers the exceptional sea may have been caused by the wash of a passing ship. This confirms *Cohoe*'s experience, when she was pooped, that a ship's wash crossing the big seas running in a gale confuses the pattern and causes them to break.

8. *Sail fastenings.* In the R.O.R.C. report it will be seen that attention is drawn to the weaknesses in sail fastenings. In the Channel Storm a number of yachts broke the piston hanks on the storm jibs, some of which were alleged to have been crystalline. From this experience (and confirmed by my own), it is clear that large strong hanks are essential for storm sails. Indeed, some skippers consider that all storm jibs should have shackles (at any rate at the head and foot) instead of hanks.

Seizings to slides were another common cause of failure and I personally prefer to use shackles for the mainsail slides. Damage to hanks or slides was almost always due to sails being allowed to flog, either in tacking, setting or lowering.

9. *Life-jackets and safety harness.* Mrs. O'Sullivan has stated that a kapok life-jacket was incapable of supporting the head of one of *Dancing Ledge*'s crew after a long period in the water. *Tilly Twin*'s owner goes further in stating that a kapok life-jacket was quite useless. Owing to the high velocity of the spray it acquired negative buoyancy after two or three hours.

In 1956 a life-jacket was just a life-jacket and I fancy few owners gave much thought to them. I must admit that I had kapok jackets in my own boats. Since then a great deal of research has been made into the subject of life-jackets and standards have greatly improved. They fall into two groups. In the first are buoyancy aids which can be worn without inconvenience, because they are not bulky. These serve their purpose in helping to keep a man afloat under ordinary weather conditions until he is picked up, provided this can be effected fairly quickly. For survival in rough weather or for a protracted period in the water it is necessary to have life-jackets to British Standards Institution or equivalent requirements which gives the full buoyancy required and support to the head.

Several skippers who were in this storm had a good word for the Hayward safety harness, which may well have saved some lives. It appears to me that when at sea safety harness is the first requirement, as it prevents a man overboard from being detached from the yacht, so that he can be recovered, whereas with a life-jacket only he must first be found and secondly picked up, which may take time, especially if running under spinnaker. There are many satisfactory makes of harness and life-jackets. As a result of reading the *Dancing Ledge* tragedy I have recently bought sets of a combined harness and life-jacket giving 20 lbs. permanent buoyancy and 40 lbs. when inflated. The life jacket is cased in nylon, which is more comfortable to wear, and is better then P.V.C., which sometimes gets brittle and has a tendency to crack or get punctured.

10. *Courses steered under storm canvas*. The efficiency of sails in heavy weather depends upon the type of yacht and the position of the sail or sails left standing, which varies in sloops, cutters and yawls. The following information throws light on a somewhat neglected subject.

The yawl *Lutine*, under trysail only, sailed 6 to 7 points off the wind and beat to the finish. The yawl *Bloodhound* at about Force 8 made about 3½ to 4 knots sailing 5 points off the wind under staysail and mizzen, and under staysail only at the height of the storm 3 knots, 7 points off the wind. When reduced to storm jib, after the staysail had split, she sailed to 8 points off the wind and made very little progress.

Maid of Malham made 7 knots under staysail only before coming down to bare pole, under which she made 3½ knots until she lay a-hull.

The class III sloops *Rondinella* and *Galloper*, both of recent design, sailed remarkably well under storm jib. *Galloper* rounded Le Havre buoy at 0500 on Sunday and might have saved her time on *Rondinella* had she not stripped all her mainsail slides and retired. During the height of the gale under spitfire jib she made 3 knots sailing 70 degrees off the wind. Her drift was about 20 degrees so she made good 90 degrees. *Rondinella* under storm jib steered 55 degrees off the wind and her angle of drift was 20 degrees. This is a most useful figure for leeway in a small yacht going to windward in a gale under storm jib, but the angle off the wind and leeway depends upon the individual boat. Much also depends upon the cut of the storm jib, as old-fashioned ones were too baggy for efficient windward work, compared with modern flatter-cut terylene ones.

Seehexe sailed under mainsail alone during the worst of the gale. With six to ten rolls reefed she headed 60 degrees to 70 degrees off the wind and made 1½ knots, so she was virtually hove-to. She was at a disadvantage in having old sails of odd shapes not made for the boat. Her skipper stated that in his opinion a good storm jib is far more valuable than a mainsail on getting to windward in gales. *Ann Speed*, hove-to under mainsail, reefed six rolls, and storm jib, and forereached at about 2¾ knots.

Yachts lying a-hull found they had enough steerage way to run off before the wind if desired and could then steer 25 degrees to 30 degrees each side of the wind. *Theta*, when lying a-hull estimated the leeway at 1 knot, but I think the navigator of a yacht lying a-hull in a position where a lee shore has to be considered should be prepared for the possibility of a higher rate of leeway. *Theta* forereached at ½ knot, but the owner of *Maid of Malham* told me that in his opinion his own boat when lying a-hull forereached at a higher speed than this. From this it appears that the speed may be a knot, or even more, which means that considerable distance may be covered in a long blow.

12

THE FASTNET GALES OF 1957

The Fastnet Race has a reputation for bad weather. Like the races to Spain, it starts on the last Saturday of Cowes week, early in August, and as often as not there is half a gale from the south-west blowing on that particular day.

The Fastnet is essentially a windward race along the South Coast, and when one has beaten as far as Land's End, often against a gale for part of the way, and has passed through the gap between the Longships and the Seven Stones light-vessel into St. George's Channel (which for convenience I will call the Irish Sea) the wind may suddenly veer to provide a beat of another 180 miles dead to windward to the Fastnet Rock. Once round this turning mark there is usually a lively reach, or a run, over the remaining 230 miles round the Bishop Rock off the Scilly Isles to finish at Plymouth. As the late American authority, Alfred Loomis, put it: "If the Fastnet isn't an ocean race, it has all the worst features of such a contest plus mental hazards that have to be experienced to be fully appreciated."

But the Fastnet is not always rough. It can be so calm that the betting would be on a 14-ft. International dinghy if the rules permitted one to enter. So it was in the years when I entered *Cohoe II*. With her cut-down rig she was sluggish in light airs and we were lucky to finish even in the first half of the fleet.

In 1956 (the year of the record Channel gale) I sold *Cohoe II*, and placed an order for a faster all-round boat which we named *Cohoe III*. She was built at Poole by Newman & Sons Ltd., and designed, like her predecessor, by Charles A. Nicholson. Her dimensions were 32.6 ft. overall, 26 ft. L.W.L., 9.1 ft. beam and 6 ft. draught. Like *Cohoe II*, she was an example of cod's head, mackerel tail hull with a fine run aft below water. Although 2 ft. 5 in. shorter overall than *Cohoe II*, she was much bigger, as she ended in a wide transom stern which in some respects is akin to having a larger yacht and chopping the counter off. Compared with the original *Cohoe*, of about equal length overall and on the waterline, she was more than double the size and displaced about 8 tons. She was a sloop with a sail area of 533 sq. ft. as designed, but when I later converted her to masthead rig set to a tubular stainless steel bowsprit this was increased to 615 sq. ft. The features of the new yacht were her stiffness and sail-carrying ability in hard weather and her roominess and strength. Everything about her construction, whether hull, mast or rigging, was above average strength and her coachroof was stiffened with steel. All this involved some sacrifice of speed, but I had hoped to sail her over for

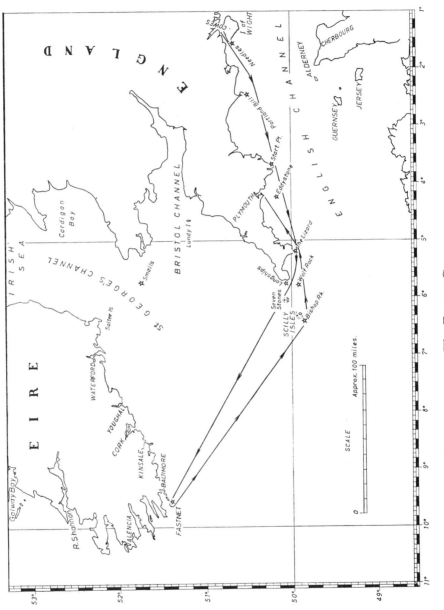

21 The Fastnet Course.

the Bermuda Race, and I remembered Humphrey Barton's advice about deck structures after his *Vertue XXXV* was nearly sunk in the Atlantic. Short-ended and sturdy-looking, *Cohoe III* was and still remains one of the most powerful and durable small sea-going yachts ever built.

The first Fastnet Race she entered was in 1957 and it ran true to form, for it was said to be one of the roughest in Fastnet history. I had with me as crew Ross, Alan Mansley, Patrick Madge and Peter Nicholson, the son of the designer and a brilliant helmsman.

Forty-one yachts crossed the starting line at Cowes on Saturday morning, 10 August, in really dirty weather. It was described as a south-westerly gale. Force 8 was reported at the Scillies and Force 6 and 7 at two neighbouring inland weather stations. *Cohoe III* started under staysail and had a few turns rolled in her mainsail, so, although it was said she was carrying relatively more sail than others, I do not think the wind force could have been more than 25 to 30 knots (Force 6 to 7), gusting perhaps 40 knots.

The conditions suited *Cohoe III*, and she quickly took the lead in her class, and by the time she had reached the Needles she had overhauled many of the Class II and Class I yachts. With the ebb stream against the SW. wind the Solent was a mass of short breaking seas and the racing fleet took a dusting. I expected a big sea off the Needles, over the Bridge where the English Channel is entered and the seas build up as the tearing ebb tide meets the full force of a south-westerly. The seas proved big and broken, but not dangerous, and as *Cohoe III* smashed her way into the open Channel the waves lengthened and speed improved. Nevertheless, it was hard going in dirty conditions with rain and flying spray adding to the poor visibility.

Tack by tack and watch by watch *Cohoe III* beat her way westwards throughout the day, with her crew half blinded by flying spray, so that the helmsmen took short spells at the tiller turn by turn.

By the late evening *Cohoe III* in a mass of spray had beaten across Bournemouth Bay, past St. Alban's Head, which was shrouded in driving rain, and had arrived off Portland, where she just missed her tide, with *Myth of Malham* and another yacht within sight ahead. The tides were springs, and with 4 knots against us our speed over the bottom slowed down, and before long night fell upon us. On deck all was dark except the friendly orange glow of the compass and the reflections of the navigation lights. The cold regular four white flashes of Portland Bill lay on our starboard bow. The watch on deck were secured by safety harness, and they needed it, for every sea broke aboard forward, and in the gusts the yacht lay far over.

Down below the aft end of the cabin was like a half-tide rock. As each sea struck the cabin top forward it came streaming aft, flooding through the aft hatch and a cabin door which had broken, as that year we had no spray hood.

Both quarter berths were flooded and the chart table unusable, so I had to spread the sodden chart on the table at the forward end of the saloon.

Navigation was a whole-time job as we were skirting Portland Race, with the spare man on deck taking hand bearings on Portland Lighthouse. It was also physically difficult, as I was thrown about so much. If the chart was left for a moment it would shoot across the cabin together with the parallel rulers and dividers on to the lee berth. Progress was desperately slow, as it always is when rounding a light, but hour by hour the bearing changed and I was able to plot each position a little west of the last one.

Regularly the yacht needed pumping. Masses of water found its way into the bilges. The seas must have been getting through the cracks edging the cockpit lockers, and spray through the cabin hatch, through the broken cabin door, and through the ventilators. It is extraordinary how much water gets below during gales and it has been the same with all my yachts, even with *Cohoe IV*, which had a fibreglass hull which cannot possibly leak. We had two pumps, but the one in use was situated in the cabin with a long hose which was led into the cockpit, so that the water returned to the sea via the self-emptying drains. I took it in turns with the spare man to man the pump. It was tiring work and a joy each time that the water subsided and the pump sucked dry.

Only one man remained on deck at a time except when taking bearings, for it is a mistake to expose two to the flying spray and the cold of the night for longer than necessary. The watches were four-hourly, but the spells at the helm off Portland were fifteen minutes only. On release from the tiller the spare man would hurry below to light a cigarette to add to the fumes of my own cigarettes as I worked on the charts. There was a record fug. As Peter was the only non-smoker, he must have suffered a lot, but he never complained.

Cohoe III did not slam when working to windward in rough water as did *Annette* and to a lesser extent *Cohoe I*. But off Portland Bill, thrashing to windward at 6 knots, she would very occasionally fall irregularly in a wave formation and come down on her stem with a most dreadful shock. The whole ship shuddered, the saucepans rattled and the teapot would be thrown off the gimballed stove. This was not a matter of ordinary, regular pounding as is found in many yachts, but it was the effect of nearly 8 tons weight of boat throwing herself at 6 knots over the head of a big sea and falling on her stem at a sharp angle on water that sounded as hard as a pavement. In the saloon one wondered how timber con-struction could stand such treatment, and after each impact I would lift the cabin floorboards to check whether there was an inrush of water resulting from damage forward, but my anxiety was uncalled for. Peter remarked that he thought for this sort of work an ocean racer should be double-diagonal planked.

As we soldiered on against both wind and tide progress seemed desperately slow, but inch by inch we edged through off the tail of the race and by the midnight change of watch we had broken through and lay about 2 miles to the SW. of Portland.

Shortly after midnight, when the new watch had taken over, I was called on deck, as the helmsman thought the yacht was carrying too much sail. When I took the tiller I found that he was right. The wind had freshened to Force 8 (34–40 knots) gusting higher in the squalls, and though the yacht was sailing grandly she was hard pressed and there was a risk of things carrying away.

It was time to shorten sail. Patrick and Peter rolled the mainsail down, bringing the peak to the upper spreaders, the staysail was lowered and the storm jib set. All this was done as smartly as if in daylight in the Solent. Alas! The yacht was now overreefed and I had forgotten that the storm jib (roped all round), inherited from *Cohoe II*, was cut too full to be of service as a racing sail. *Cohoe III* sagged badly to leeward and there are unlighted buoys to the west of Portland Bill. Under reduced sail we could no longer clear them and it was improbable that they would be spotted in the dark in time to avoid collision. Thus, we were forced to come on to starboard tack, bringing the weakening foul tide on our beam and thus losing much of the distance that had been so hard earned.

I have clear impressions in my memory of that outward tack. The moon appeared between the clouds flying overhead and at times the yacht and sea were bathed in light. The seas were high, but under reduced sail the boat was an easy match for them. A yacht passed close ahead of us, running east under bare poles, her port light shining brightly. A lifeboat also passed on the same course.

We tacked 5 miles out and I then handed over and turned in. Both quarter berths were flooded out, so I took the root berth in the fo'c'sle, which is supposed to be untenable in a gale. At each plunge of the boat I felt I was left in the air and put my hand up to prevent being struck by the deck above. Sleep was out of the question, though I managed to get a modest degree of much-needed rest.

The wind moderated in the early hours of the following morning (Sunday, 11th), falling to Force 7 and, after the change of watch, the staysail was reset and some of the turns in the mainsail were let out. It remained rough going in driving rain over forlorn grey seas the whole way across Lyme Bay, but we made better progress with more sail. To cut a long story short, the overreefing west of Portland Bill lost us a lot of time, for it caused us to miss our tide at Start Point. I put into Dartmouth for shelter during the foul tide. This gave us the opportunity to get a hot meal on a level table and with the aid of two primuses to dry the interior of the yacht somewhat and masses of wet clothes.

More important, it enabled us to carry out a number of small but useful repairs. Some of the screws in the mast track were beginning to work loose and had to be screwed up, repairs were made to the broken cabin door and I nailed canvas across the aft end of the coachroof and hatch to keep some of the water out of the quarter berths and chart table.

Once in shelter there is sometimes a reluctance to put to sea again, but on this occasion there was no delay, thanks partly to Alan, who kept us up to the mark. We left early on the tide and got past Start Point close to the rocks in the early slack. The wind had moderated and next morning (Monday, 12th) we sighted *Elseli IV*, the Swedish entry which rated at the top of the class. The race was on again and over the remaining 500 miles of the course was bitterly contested, the two yachts rarely being out of sight of each other.

West of the Lizard the wind went light and *Elseli IV*, with her big masthead rig, gained on us steadily tack by tack. She had left us far astern by the time she had rounded Land's End.

Luckily for *Cohoe III*, the wind freshened again, and we found ourselves hard on the wind for much of the 180-mile stretch across the Irish Sea. The wind was about Force 6 to Force 7 (some say Force 8), so it was a tough passage pressed under staysail and whole mainsail. Both yachts arrived off the Irish coast on Wednesday morning, 14th, almost at the same time. Meanwhile the wind had veered to the north-west and headed us, so that our landfall was some 20 miles east of the Fastnet, whereas the bigger yachts had been able to fetch the rock on one tack.

We scored a few miles off *Elseli IV* by standing in on the Irish coast and tacking inside the Stag Rocks, thus getting an earlier fair tide and smoother water under the lee of the land. Off Baltimore we all looked longingly towards the soft contours of Ireland lying so alluringly close on the starboard hand, but there was little time for such idle thoughts, for *Elseli IV* was not far astern, and by the time we had rounded the Fastnet Rock at 1340 she was snapping at *Cohoe III*'s heels.

The run of 150 miles from the Fastnet Rock to the Bishop provided closely contested racing between the two yachts. *Elseli IV* had lost her spinnaker boom, but running under mainsail and boomed-out genoa she gained on us and steered a straighter course. *Cohoe III* carried all sail with her biggest spinnaker bellying out against the light blue sky and the dark blue white-crested seas. At 1610 we gybed and with an increasing wind she became almost unmanageable at times in the big quartering seas, forcing her to tack downwind too much to the westward. But for two hours she logged over 8 knots, far in excess of the maximum theoretical speed of a short-ended boat of only 26 ft. waterline. For a while *Elseli IV* must have done better, for her log showed a steady 8 or 9 knots, and when surfing the needle was up to 11 knots. Gustav Plym describes the surfing in his book *Yacht and Sea* as "really fantastic and something that none of us had ever experienced before in such a relatively large boat . . . it was fascinating and, to tell the truth—slightly terrifying".

At nightfall *Cohoe III* lowered her spinnaker and set her genoa. It was blowing hard at a good Force 7, and higher in the gusts and the seas were building up.

The night was rough and at 0515 next morning all hands were called to gybe on to an easterly course for the Bishop Rock. This was a tricky job in the seas which Gustav Plym described as "high breaking mountains of water", because of the weight of the wind in the full mainsail and the risk of breaking something or broaching as the boom went over, but the crew managed it smartly.

When dawn came there was no sight of *Elseli IV* as we raced eastward. The wind had if anything increased, for it was blowing a good Force 7, possibly Force 8, and was reported as being Force 9. *Cohoe III*'s speed had risen again to over 8 knots. This was fortunate, because the two adversaries met again just west of the Bishop. *Elseli IV* had lost time when two hanks of her mainsail broke, and she reduced sail to avoid being pooped, but she had steered direct as compared with *Cohoe III*'s involuntary tacking downwind. There was a tremendous sea in the overfalls west of the Bishop, for here there was the full fetch of the Atlantic into a weather-going tide. The seas were positively tumultuous. *Elseli IV* was being driven through it all out. She made a spectacular sight and at times was almost lost to sight in the waves. Gustav Plym, her owner, told me afterwards that she broached-to twice, but neither yacht suffered any harm.

The seas were lower south of the Scillies and the gale gradually moderated throughout the day on the 80–mile run to Plymouth, though a gale warning was repeated at noon. Off Land's End the wind had softened sufficiently to enable *Cohoe III* to reset her spinnaker. *Elseli IV* could not respond owing to the loss of her spinnaker boom, and thus *Cohoe III* crossed the line with a lead of half an hour to win Class III by four hours on corrected time.

It had been a great battle between the British and the Swedish yacht which proved to be the only two small-class yachts left in the race. *Elseli IV*'s owner (Gustav Plym) was elected "Yachtsman of the Year" in Sweden and I received a similar honour in Great Britain.

Captain John Illingworth's *Myth of Malham* won Class II, but the first place overall in the race was won by the Class I American yawl *Carina*. It was a fine achievement on the part of her owner, Dick Nye, and his crew, for when emerging early in the race from the Solent into the Channel at the Bridge buoy, *Carina* fell off a sea and suffered considerable structural damage forward and her staysail tack parted. As *Carina* crossed the finish line at the end of the race her owner remarked: "All right boys, we're over now; let her sink." I admire his spirit.

Conclusions

Mr. J. A. N. Tanner, at that time the meteorological correspondent of *Yachting World*, says that the Fastnet Race of 1957 was sailed in variable conditions brought about by two depressions. On Friday, the day before the start, a deepening depression (982 millibars compared with 976 millibars in the Santander gale of 1947 and the Channel gale of 1956) was moving eastwards. At the start of the race on Saturday it was moving up the Western Approaches, with another trough about 300 miles astern, the winds in this phase being even stronger than those which had gone before. The boisterous conditions continued for thirty-six hours and were followed by light and variable winds during Monday and the

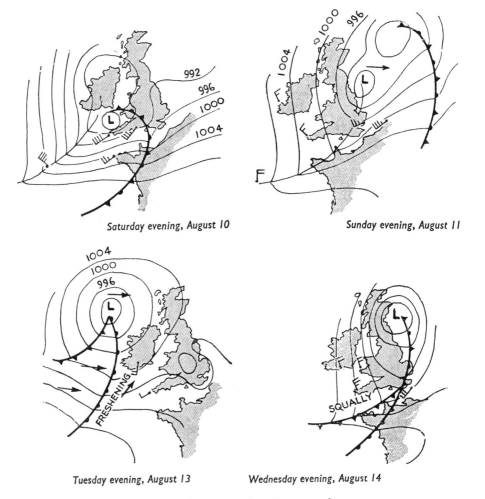

Saturday evening, August 10   Sunday evening, August 11

Tuesday evening, August 13   Wednesday evening, August 14

22   Synoptic charts covering Fastnet gales, 1957.

early part of Tuesday. The next depression (992 millibars) came in from west of Ireland and the wind set in from the north-west on Wednesday "sufficiently boisterous to say that the race which started in a gale, also ended in one, and with nothing much different in between".

Out of the forty-one starters in all classes only twelve completed the course. *Galloper* lost a man overboard. He had come on deck without a lifeline to empty

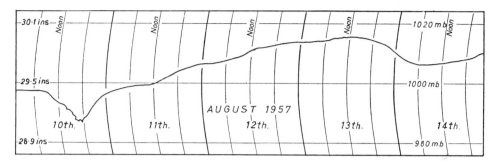

23 Barograph trace, Fastnet Race, 1957.

a gash bucket and a sudden lurch sent him over the side. The one lifebelt thrown was so light that it was blown downwind too fast for him to get it, but he was able to secure a hold on the second buoy which was a heavy, sodden one of horseshoe type. It was only by superb seamanship under such wild conditions that he was rescued.

Inschallah had her deck-house ports stove in by a sea some 2 miles off Portland Bill and after exhibiting distress signals was escorted by the lifeboat into Weymouth Harbour. Maybe this was the yacht we had passed off Portland. *Maze* had the swaged end pulled out of a lower shroud and was dismasted. *Evenlode* incurred damage to her rudder, five of *Drumbeat's* winches broke under the strain and *Santander* developed a serious leak, found later to be due to a fractured keel bolt. Broken stays and torn sails were common and accounted for some of the retirements, but no doubt the principal cause was the old seafaring malady of sea-sickness. Lessons learnt were:

1. *Man overboard.* The accident in *Galloper* illustrates that personal lifelines are needed even for temporary visits to the deck, when driving to windward against gales. A sea must have struck *Galloper* on the windward side and I suspect that her crewman was catapulted overboard just as Geoff and I were in the Santander Race. The lee side of the cockpit is particularly dangerous and crew members coming up from below to empty the gash bucket or in a rush to avoid being sick in the cabin often forget their lifelines, which are laborious to don. The experience also suggests that two kinds of lifebuoy are required, light ones for use in ordinary conditions and a heavy one for use in high winds. Alternatively a lifebuoy should be attached to a small drogue.

2. *Damage.* Long periods of beating into gales find out any weaknesses in hull, rig, sails and gear. Moderate winds prevail in most ocean races and hence some designers tend to keep everything above deck as light as possible. This lightness pays in ordinary racing, but a considerable factor of safety is required for punching to windward through gales of this kind.

3. *Pounding and falling off a wave.* In the old International metre classes the hull

form was given to pounding and they did not appear to suffer much as a result. Ocean racers with their shorter ends suffer less from this complaint, but when they do so the shock is, or appears to be much greater. John Illingworth in his book *Offshore* remarks that "one wonders that every fastening in the boat is not loosened", but he adds "the worst you are likely to do is to disturb the caulking in the forward part of the boat". John Illingworth should know, because nobody has longer experience or drives a boat harder, but his ocean racers are designed and built for the job of hard racing.

Furthermore, there is a difference between pounding and what is called "falling off a wave". That is, breaking through the crest of a big sea at 6 to 7 knots so that the yacht literally falls into the trough on her stem. It was this that caused structural damage to *Carina*. A similar mishap occurred when *Bloodhound* fell off a wave off Berry Head. The impact damaged her stem scarf and caused a leak. She hove-to until dawn, when the extent of the damage could be identified, and she was able to carry on in the race, pumping only every four hours. *Elseli IV* broke three frames off Portland and it was thought that she had broken seven planks, but the damage was later found to be limited to surface splits at the nail-heads. Other yachts suffered damage, and it was this "falling off a wave" that caused me occasional anxiety in *Cohoe III*. Much depends on the helmsman, who must luff to the crests and bear away at the top to let the boat down lightly in the trough. With a good man at the wheel the watch below will be able to relax, but with an inexperienced helmsman the impacts with waves will be terrific, enough to crack the heads in the fo'c'sle. The boat should be kept weaving in the seas, dancing all the time in the zest of it.

It used to be said that a yacht could take more punishment than her crew, but nowadays it is possible that with picked crew regularly relieved, and able to drive a yacht all out against gales, damage can result. It is no longer certain that the ship is stronger than her crew. The forward sections of an ocean racer and such matters as the scarf, frames and keel bolts certainly merit special consideration on the part of the designer.

4. *Sheltering*. No cruising man, if he is in his right senses, will continue to beat to windward for long in Force 8 if shelter is at hand. Ocean racers have to plug on, but I think it sometimes pays to shelter, as *Cohoe III* did, rather than beat round a headland against a strong foul spring tide. If one takes the strength of the foul stream as lasting four hours all one has to do is to calculate the distance it will set the yacht back according to the tidal atlas and compare it with the distance likely to be made good tacking at a wide angle to the wind on account of rough seas, surface drift and leeway. The answer depends upon the size, design and stability of the individual boat, but if little is to be gained by keeping at sea it may pay in a long race to give a respite to the crew, provided no time is lost in getting under way again when the stream weakens.

13

SWELL EAST OF USHANT

Swell is defined as being a wave outside its own original area of generation. It may confuse the pattern of the seas during a gale, but otherwise it is not associated with heavy weather sailing. On the contrary, the wind is often light when swell is at its worst.

In the ocean or in open sea there is no danger in swell. The yacht goes up and up and she then goes down and down. The boom jumps madly unless secured by a foreguy; the sails flog and flog. Wear and tear of sails and gear in a big swell during a prolonged calm may be greater than in a gale. Nothing is more sick-inducing than swell on a hot, windless day. Everybody is glad when it is over. However, swell is induced by bad weather somewhere. It occurs often as a fore-runner to a gale or is left over after a gale has passed on, so it has its place in this book.

In coastal waters swell is not entirely without its hazards. There are three. High swell finds its way into otherwise secure anchorages; it rises in height almost to point of breaking in shoal and rocky waters; it affects visibility and makes identification of a landfall difficult.

Ground swell is more pronounced on certain coasts, such as those facing the Atlantic. I have never seen a really high swell in the English Channel on the South Coast eastward of Start Point, but it is often encountered on the French side. West of the Casquets and Guernsey it is common. Off Ushant there is often a heavy swell, and in the Bay of Biscay ugly swells occur on the Atlantic coasts of Belle Île, Île d'Yeu and the other islands. On the north-west side of Belle Île there is an anchorage which we sometimes use at Ster Wenn, in a narrow fiord branching off southwards in the rocky bay of Port du Vieux Château. Here one would expect a yacht to be safe, snugly sheltered by high land from east through south to north-west, at any rate in normal weather. Nevertheless, it is said that even on a fine day swell may rise unexpectedly from some distant Atlantic storm and by refraction and diffraction enter the inlet. The swell may rise to such dimensions that is is said no anchor will hold.

Where I have found swell most pronounced is in Brittany between Ushant and Île Vierge off the harbour of l'Abervrach. I thought this might be just luck until I met a very experienced French yachtsman at Roscoff who confirmed that it was a recognized local phenomenon. He added that another locality noted for swell was in the Bay of Lannion, which lies farther eastwards between Morlaix and the Sept Îles. So I think we can accept it as a fact that swell is more commonly found in some areas than others.

I will give a brief account of the swell which can be found east of Ushant.

In September 1957 my wife and I were cruising in *Cohoe III* and the yacht was lying in the sheltered anchorage of l'Aberildut, east of Ushant, near the northern entrance of the Four Channel. It had been blowing fresh when we had arrived at midday. In the afternoon (6 September) the wind freshened to about Force 6 and during the night the wind howled in the rigging, so that we were glad to be in a safe anchorage. At 1100 the following morning (7 September) the gale was

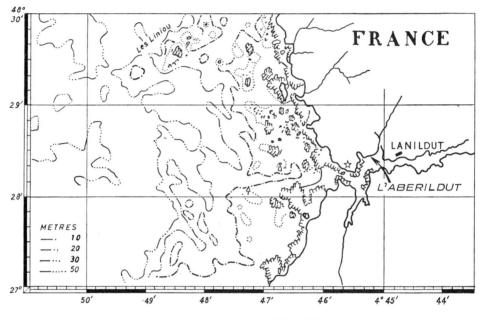

24   Approaches to l'Aberildut.

over. It was sunny and the wind light to moderate. There was a forecast of gales and severe gales in area Sole to the westward and in the Fastnet area miles to the north-west, but none for Biscay or the Plymouth area in the south of which we lay.

I did not then know l'Aberildut well, and in the morning I rowed in the dinghy to the entrance to have a look at it at low water.

There is a narrow bottle entrance between a promontory on the southern shore and a high rock (Le Crapaud) on the northern side. Here there is a stony bar which nearly dries out at low water. Westward of the bar is an approach about a mile long and varying from 1 to 3 cables wide, between reefs of rocks to the north and south. There is Le Lieu beacon tower on the north side and an iron beacon on the outer rocks on the south side. I found that the bar was completely sheltered, but from the land I could see that a spectacular swell was sweeping in from the Atlantic. Huge waves were breaking higher that the off-lying rocks.

I had secured *Cohoe III* to a mooring, but at noon the rightful owner in the shape of a gabarre (ballast boat) returned unexpectedly, so we had to vacate the mooring and temporarily tie up alongside her. She was a vessel of about 50 tons, manned by a crew of three.

Hearing that we were about to get under way, they tried to dissuade us because of the swell. "La Houle," they clamoured indicating dramatic rolls with their hands.

"Difficile, mais elle n'est pas dangereuse," I replied in my best schoolboy French.

"Mais les rochers," they argued. When my wife explained that we were sailing for l'Abervrach to collect letters they became more emphatic about "Les rochers dangereux". "Demain," they said. "Rester demain."

I have a great respect for Breton fishermen, from whom the crew of the ballast boat were probably drawn. They are as tough as nails. I often ask their opinions about the weather, but on this occasion we had a light or moderate fair wind and a fair tide and less than 20 miles to sail.

After lunch we cast off at 1400 (7 September) as planned. It detracts from this yarn, but I must confess we used the engine against the foul tide, which was a treat, as it did not always work.

We were soon at the entrance. It was narrow but quite easy and protected. Outside in the approach channel the rocks to the south at first gave protection, but swell was breaking heavily on the north side. There were fishermen on the shore and they appeared to be very agitated. *Cohoe III* must have made a picture on that sunlit summer afternoon in the narrow channel between the flashing white breakers.

The tricky part lay at the outer end of the approach channel. The swell was thundering on the rocks to port and the spray was being thrown in clouds into the sky. It was worse to starboard, for the tremendous seas were bursting high over the rocks marked by Le Lieu beacon tower.

There were spectacular seas on both sides, but my wife spotted the narrow channel left between the rough water on either hand. It was covered with great masses of foam the whole way across. I have never seen anything like it.

The yacht was safe enough because the water was not breaking in the fairway, though she was plunging in ever-increasing swell. It was not alarming, but I wanted to get clear of the proximity of rocks as quickly as possible. I set the mainsail and genoa. That speeded *Cohoe III* up. The wind was south of west and she could just lay the course against the westerly swell, so that under sail and power she was soon in the open.

Once outside we realized the full size of the swell into which we were heading. We stopped the engine and sailed on over the hills and down the valleys. All was not well, however. As we drew out we found the swell was so steep that in places it was on the point of breaking.

To starboard it was actually doing so, and away less than a mile and a half to the north-west lay the grim Les Liniou group of rocks. Here the picture was absolutely spectacular, as the swell reared up high into the air against them and the rocks in the whole area on the shoreward side. I see a note in my diary: "At Les Liniou the spray made a fine mist the whole way from the rocks to the shore two miles away, with rainbow effects from the sun." It was most remarkable.

Progress was slowed by the swell and we soon found we were being set down to leeward rapidly and unwillingly towards the "rainbow effects". The streams run very hard on this coast from the Four Channel.

I started the engine quickly again and it fired at the first press on the button. With this help the yacht cleared the dangers by an adequate margin. The swell still demanded attention, however. Hereabouts, though the water is deep the bottom is rocky and irregular. As a result the huge swell coming in straight from the Atlantic became exceptionally steep, seeming to be on the verge of toppling, though it did not in fact break.

Once well clear of Les Liniou we set a NW. course to get well out into deep water and give wide clearance to the rocks near the Four lighthouse.

This brought the wind nearer the beam and sheets were freed accordingly. The strange thing was that the mainsail then became completely useless, despite the boom being secured by the foreguy. The yacht was rolling so violently in the swell that, as she heeled to leeward to each wave this caused a draught of air against the lee side of the mainsail. The sail did no good at all and had to be lowered. The wind was then only about Force 2.

We sailed on under genoa alone, which, being lighter, did not spill so much, but we had to use the engine again.

With a fair tide we made good progress to the outer Porsal buoy, where we altered course to the eastward for the entrance of the l'Abervrach channel, only 5 miles distant. Two miles to starboard lay the Roches de Porsal, a particularly grim series of rocks extending nearly 2 miles from the shore. The swell was breaking in magnificent formation over the rocks, and as the waves struck the lighthouse the spume rose three-quarters of its 52 ft. height.

With the swell now brought aft, conditions for a while were much more comfortable, but we had a few thoughtful moments in the approach to l'Abervrach. The approach is flanked by the reef of rocks known as Le Libenter on the north side and the extensive rocks on the south extending some 2 miles offshore and marked by the spidery black and white buoy, La Petite Fourche.

The channel has leading marks and is well buoyed. It is said to be safe under all conditions, and l'Abervrach is a regular port of call for most yachts bound south for the Bay of Biscay.

Our difficulty was that the swell was running so high that it interrupted our view of the proposed landfall. It is true that there was a bird's-eye view on the crests, but it was only a short one before it became blocked out by the wave as it rolled on and left the yacht in the hollow. The binoculars were useless, because before they could be steadied on anything the view had gone. The tall Île Vierge lighthouse (249 ft.) rose high on the port bow, but ahead lay nothing except big breakers with no gap that could be distinguished between them.

The yacht ran on, with the breakers heavy on the outlying rocks to starboard, and the white plumes of the seas growing higher ahead as we drew nearer. I suppose it was not until we were half a mile off that we sighted La Petite Fourche and soon afterwards the Le Trepied buoy glinting red among the blue seas and white breakers.

Once either buoy is identified the rest becomes easy. We were soon in the channel, but the ebb tide had started, so that though the swell was lower it became remarkably steep and threw itself furiously in a confusion of flashing white breakers on the Libenter. To the west of Île de la Croix, which marks the first turning-mark in the channel, there is a big plateau of submerged rocks and over this the seas were breaking wildly. In the channel itself it became rough, and the smaller seas were breaking the whole way across between La Croix and the Petit Pot de Beurre beacon tower and to the northward right across the Malouine Channel. However, for *Cohoe III*, in the centre of the main channel, all problems were over and she sped on soon to find sheltered water and bring up in the anchorage for a pleasant warm and sunny evening.

Conclusions

This story may sound as tall as the swell. The day was sunny, the wind light and no water broke over the yacht. If we felt any anxiety it was perhaps only because we had guilty consciences after ignoring the local warnings. Nevertheless, the passage did give us a close-up view of high swell where it meets ledges of rock and shallowing water. The scene was so impressive and at times so beautiful that on no account would we have missed it.

From the synoptic charts it will be seen that an intense depression (964 millibars, which is lower than any other mentioned in this book) had moved from NW. of Ireland and was centred NE. of Scotland by 0600 G.M.T. on 7 September. The cold front would have passed over l'Aberildut an hour or two later and the wind soon moderated, for it will be seen that the isobars near Ushant became widely spaced. But the swell from the exceptionally severe storm to the NW. would remain and only subside gradually.

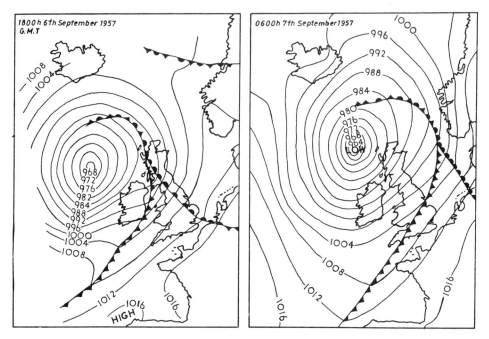

25 Synoptic charts, 964 millibar depression.

The experience illustrated two useful points:

1. In a high swell with a light wind a *sailing* yacht can become almost unmanageable and lose headway. This can be dangerous in rocky areas if the
tidal streams are strong and auxiliary power is not available.

2. High swell, even in fine weather, makes pilotage difficult owing to the
interruption of vision.

14

OTHER FASTNET GALES

A remarkable kind of gale occurred in the Fastnet Race of 1961 (see chart, p. 146). It caught most of the ocean-racing fleet between Mount's Bay in Cornwall and the Longships off Land's End. The gale was very localized and the leaders among the big yachts were sufficiently far ahead to avoid more than Force 6 or Force 7 as they sped into the Irish Sea, but the main body of the fleet were properly caught out in a potentially dangerous position between Land's End and the Scilly Isles.

The cause of the trouble was a small but intense secondary depression which moved quickly in from the Bay of Biscay. Gale warnings were received in advance. The barometer was falling smartly, the wind had backed to the SE. and the sky had become heavy with rain when, in *Cohoe III*, we were off Mount's Bay in company with several other yachts of all three classes on Monday afternoon, 7 August.

It was not until the late evening, when we were about 5 miles north of the Wolf lighthouse, that the gale really caught us. In the previous year *Cohoe III*'s sail plan had been altered by the addition of a masthead rig and a stainless steel bowsprit which enabled a huge spinnaker to be carried. We hung on to this big sail, because I had a stout-hearted crew, who optimistically hoped that we might slip ahead of the worst of the gale into the Irish Sea, for which the weather forecast predicted only Force 6 winds. The leaders among the big class, probably 20 miles ahead, succeeded in doing this, but we had no such luck.

The wind rose quickly. *Cohoe III*, only $32\frac{1}{2}$ ft. overall, pressed by over 1,000 sq. ft. of spinnaker, became almost unmanageable. No sooner than I had given the order to lower it, at 1935 B.S.T. (1835 G.M.T.), and as the watch below were tumbling out on deck, *Cohoe III* broached-to. In an instant the spinnaker split right across and the halyard had to be let fly to relieve the yacht of the strain. The pressure (probably nearly 2 tons), was so tremendous that the 4 in. $\times$ $\frac{1}{2}$ in. galvanized steel bolts which took the sheet blocks bent and drew half an inch through the toe-rail and the planking below, leaving half-inch fractures in the upper plank.

The spinnaker was quickly recovered, but, while the mainsail was being roller reefed, the leach line got snarled up in the folds and it had to be lowered. It was cleared by Tim Laycock, one of our crew, poised dangerously on the end of the transom. In these few minutes the wind had increased so violently that the new terylene storm jib had to be set, and under this small sail alone the yacht ran as fast as she had under spinnaker.

Everything was blotted out by rain. The gap between the Longships and the Seven Stones lightvessel is 12 miles wide. We set a compass course and raced in the gathering gloom seeing nothing at all, though we must have passed near the Seven Stones lightvessel (where the tanker *Torrey Canyon* came to grief in 1967) before emerging into the open sea in the Irish Sea approaches. The barometer touched its lowest at about midnight and the wind veered to SSW., followed by a veer to NNW. two hours later.

I shall always remember that night. It was intensely black. The rain was absolutely torrential and the visibility nil. The wind was exceptionally strong and gusting well above gale force. The odd thing was that the seas never ran high. This was because the depression, although intense, was small in area and moved so quickly that the seas never had a chance fully to build up. The violent rain also flattened them.

I also remember wondering what would happen if any yacht ahead of us had hove-to. The visibility was so bad that we might have run her down. Equally, had *Cohoe III* laid-to she might have been run down by an overtaking yacht. We held on course, as in any case we wanted to get clear of the land as fast as we could. I also wondered what would happen if one of the tankers bound for Bristol crossed our path. I wished we had *Cohoe I*'s false bow to take part of the impact. This gale was very comfortable for me navigating below, as the cabin was dry and with a following sea the motion was tolerable, but it was hell on deck for the crew, striving to keep a look-out in the blinding, searing rain. There was one brilliant flash of lightning, but it lit nothing but the rain-swept smoking sea.

When daylight came the wind moderated and the rest of the race was uneventful.

Conclusions

This gale was caused by a vigorous secondary of 996 millibars forming off the Bay of Biscay and moving rapidly across to the Scillies, intensifying as it went. The centre crossed immediately over the ocean-racing fleet at a pressure of 992 millibars, giving rise to sustained winds of Force 9, possibly Force 10 for a short while, with gusts approaching hurricane force.

The gale caused some anxiety to the Committee of the Royal Ocean Racing Club, because the yachts were caught in narrow waters between Land's End and the Scilly Islands. When the centre of the depression went through there was a risk of the shift of wind putting some of the yachts, which were under bare poles, on a lee shore. However, there were few mishaps and the tail of the fleet sensibly took temporary shelter or retired, rather than go through the gap when visibility was nil and with the prospect of a lee shore.

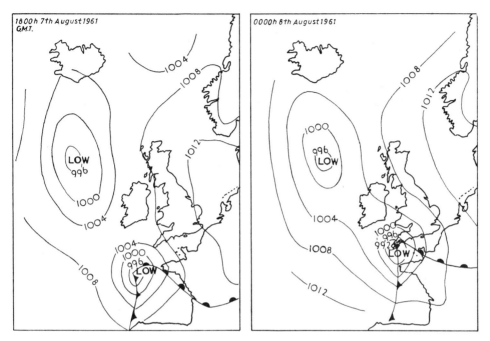

26 Synoptic charts covering Fastnet Race, 1961.

I have tabulated the wind direction and force for each hour (that is, the mean velocities over the past hour as recorded by anemograph) of the gale at the shore stations at Scilly and the Lizard, which are as follows:

Monday, 7 August 1961

Hourly values as recorded by an anemograph

	SCILLY			LIZARD		
G.M.T.	Direction	Knots	Force	Direction	Knots	Force
1800	SE.	17	5	E. by S.	21	5
1900	ESE.	18	5	E. by S.	23	6
2000	SE. by E.	23	6	ESE.	25	6
2100	SE. by E.	23	6	ESE.	26	6
2200	SE. by E.	21	5	SE. by E.	33	7
2300	SSW.	21	5	SE. by S.	32	7
2400	SW. by S.	21	5	S. by E.	26	6

Direction changed suddenly 2330 and 2345
Highest gust 2359, 52 knots   Highest gust SE., 49 knots

163

Tuesday, 8 August 1961

G.M.T.	SCILLY Direction	Knots	Force	LIZARD Direction	Knots	Force
0100	N. by W.	35	8	S.	24	6
0200	NNW.	34	8	SW. by S.	15	4
0300	NW. by N.	32	7	WNW.	40	8
0400	NW.	29	7	NW. by W.	41	9
0500	NW.	26	6	NW. by W.	35	8
0600	NW. by W.	27	6	WNW.	28	7
0700	NW. by W.	24	6	WNW.	30	7
0800	WNW.	21	5	W. by N.	28	7

Direction changed suddenly 0155
Highest gust 0100, NNW. 53 knots   Highest gust 0235, NW. by N. 63 knots

These records from the coastal stations are most interesting, but what we need to arrive at is the strength of the wind at sea, in the gap between Land's End and the Scillies. Applying the methods recommended by Alan Watts in Chapter 21, making a deduction of 25 per cent for height and multiplying by the appropriate factors, I arrive at the wind at sea at night to have been as shown in the right-hand column of the following table.

Time 8 August Scilly	Wind at coastal station Knots	Force	Wind at coastal station less 25% for height Knots	Force	Multiplication factor for wind at sea	Estimated wind at sea Knots	Force
0100	35	8	26	6	1.8	47	9
0200	34	8	26	6	1.8	47	9
0300	32	7	24	6	1.8	43	9
0400	29	7	22	6	1.8	40	8
0500	26	6	19	5	1.6	30	7
0600	27	6	20	5	1.6	32	7
Lizard							
0300	40	8	30	7	1.6	48	10
0400	41	9	31	7	1.6	49	10
0500	35	8	27	6	1.8	48	10
0600	28	7	21	5	1.6	34	8

This gives an average of 44 knots (Force 9) for three hours to 0300 off the Scillies. The full force of the gale was felt at the Lizard about two hours later and averaged 48 knots (Force 10) for three hours to 0500, but this could be an

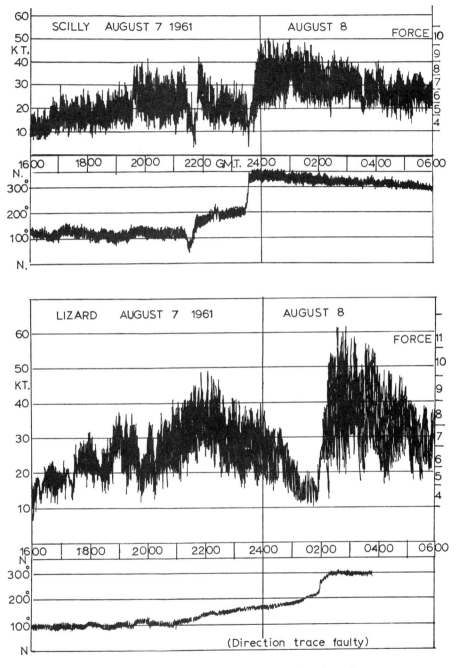

27   Anemogram traces, Scilly and Lizard, 1961.

overestimate owing to the great height of the anemometer at the Lizard, which is 240 ft. above sea-level. Force 9 is probably nearer the mark.

Unfortunately I have only one record at sea and that is from the Seven Stones lightvessel in the middle of the gap. It is at 0600 on 8 August, after the worst was over, but the hourly value was Force 8, which is two grades higher on the Beaufort Scale than at the shore station at Scilly, only 10 miles to the westward, but almost agrees precisely with the Watts method of computation. This once again emphasizes that the wind at sea is higher than at shore stations, especially at night, though the gusts at sea are not necessarily higher than over the land. It also explains why in the Dinard Race of 1948 the ocean racers reported Force 7 when only Force 5 was registered at the shore station at Guernsey Airport only about 10 miles to leeward.

The features of the gale were the gusts and squalls when the wind veered, which are shown on pp. 163, 164 and also in the anemograph (p. 165). For example, following the wind shifts at the Scillies near midnight on 7 August there were gusts up to 52 knots, but these were apparently not enough to put the average of the past hour above 21 knots, although wind increased in the following hour to a mean of Force 8. At the Lizard there was a gust of 63 knots (nearly hurricane force) and several of near that velocity with the veer of the wind. These gusts were at more than double the mean velocity for the previous hour, but they may have been less at sea, where the wind is steadier, though the mean force is higher than over the land.

I mention that at no time did the seas run particularly high and on this occasion I can give the measured height. The figures from the Seven Stones lightvessel show that at 0600 on 8 August, after the gale had been blowing from NW. for some hours, the period was 8 to 9 sec. and the *mean* height of the waves was 11 ft.

The following points are of interest:

1. Any boat which set more sail in the weaker winds preceding the veers would have been badly caught and possibly knocked down on her beam ends in the violent squalls which rapidly followed.

2. The anemograph shows that it is impossible to estimate the mean wind force on the Beaufort Scale, which might be logged as a near hurricane, Force 11, 10 or 9 according to the temperament of the skipper.

It shows why gales are so often described, even by experienced sailing men, in relation to the strength of the gusts rather than the mean force on the Beaufort Scale. Without an anemometer it is sheer guesswork and later in this book this opinion is endorsed by experienced yachtsmen on the other side of the Atlantic.

3. *Quick reduction of visibility*. The speed at which the wind can rise in a small intense depression is remarkable. Visibility can be reduced equally quickly in the belt of rain accompanying it.

4. *Sail area.* Although *Cohoe III* sailed at her maximum speed under storm jib alone she would have been better with a corner of the mainsail left set. She could have carried this and it would have enabled her to have pointed closer to the wind when it veered. This would have been of importance if, when the centre of the depression had passed through, the shift of wind had put her on a lee shore, but she was in open water by that time.

1963—INSIDE PORTLAND RACE

All records up to that year were eclipsed in the Fastnet Race of 1963, when for the first time entries were well in excess of a hundred, and the Admiral's Cup was recovered from America, against hot international competition.

At the start of the race there was half a gale of wind from the south-west, which was quite enough with from forty to fifty yachts in each class milling around, battling to get into the narrow fair eddy inshore off Cowes Green. It was not surprising that in the mêlée there were two collisions, one of which was serious. The wind and sailing conditions were similar to the early part of the Fastnet Race of 1957, but with rather less wind.

I was racing a new Class III yacht, the 11-tonner *Cohoe IV*. She was one of the successful class of fibreglass Nicholson 36-footers, a boat of about the same displacement and waterline as *Cohoe III*, but drawn out to provide a more easily driven hull. With greater overall length and beam and with higher freeboard she was a much roomier boat, and her longer immersed waterline when heeled gave her a higher theoretical maximum speed, but there was not any very marked difference in racing performance. The principal difference was that she carried a total crew of six instead of five, which made ocean racing lighter work, especially as her sail area was smaller. I had bought *Cohoe IV* for entry in the Bermuda Race 1964, but the C.C.A. rule was altered, as a result of which she was too small, my mistake always being to build too near the minimum size eligible for that race. Accordingly, I sold *Cohoe IV* at the end of the season and kept *Cohoe III*, which my wife preferred for cruising, since she is more comfortable for two.

In the Fastnet Race of 1963 *Cohoe IV* started under small genoa and two rolls in her mainsail, the wind being about Force 6. In the rough and tumble of breaking weather-going seas in the West Solent, and off Anvil Point and S. Alban's Head, she worked out a lead in the same way as *Cohoe III* had done in 1957. In fact, she proved herself to be rather better, as off Portland Bill she was lying sixth in the whole fleet on elapsed time, boat for boat without handicap.

However, *Cohoe IV* probably saved at least an hour by taking the inside passage in the gap between Portland Bill and the Race. When bound westward in moderate weather this affords a short cut with a fair tide between one hour before and two hours after H.W. Dover. What is not so generally known is that this passage can also be used (with care and under suitable conditions) against a foul tide. There is a southerly eddy along the SE. side of Portland as far as the Bill, which is where the danger lies as the stream sets strongly into the Race.

Besides Ross (who knew Portland and the Inner Channel well) I had a strong crew in Alan Mansley, Dr. Rex Binning, David Colquhoun and Keith Hunt, so no one was perturbed at the idea of the short cut at night through the unlit channel at the wrong state of the tide.

When *Cohoe IV* approached Portland breakwater at 2236 we were lucky, as the wind moderated to little over Force 5, permitting the mainsail to be unreefed and the big genoa to be set in smooth water under the lee of the peninsula. The lights on the breakwater were close when we tacked, and behind them lay the bright lights of Castletown with the high dark land mass of Portland itself fading into the sky to the southward. Four of us were on deck: the watch of two with Ross to hand the genoa sheets round the mast and act as local pilot, while I navigated.

At first progress was slow, as we had a weak foul tide against us, but off Grove Point we came into the fair eddy and passed through modest overfalls. The interesting part lay between Grove Point and the Bill, as we tacked between Portland and the Race. Except for occasional breakers it was not rough inshore, because the overfalls in the Race of Portland formed a kind of breakwater. On the offshore tacks the brilliant group flash of Portland lighthouse gave us something on which to take bearings. The inshore tacks were more difficult. The closer we could get to the cliffs the better, but here Portland light was obscured and it was difficult to judge distance at night. We used the echo-sounder constantly. Soon we had over a knot of fair eddy, but the farther south we got the nearer to the land we had to keep.

Progress as we approached the Bill was increasingly fast and each tack had to be shorter, for the Race lay close to the south. At the Bill we came close in to the rocks. I have never viewed the lighthouse at night from so near at hand. It was a lovely sight, with big windows, the upper one with a white light and the lower with a red. In the background were car lights and lights in a big building. To seaward all was dark.

It was only a glimpse, because we tacked close to the lighthouse just before midnight and only made a short board before coming round again. Here lies the crisis of the inside passage against the flood stream. At that state of the tide the whole weight of the easterly-going stream is diverted off the west side of Portland and accelerates southwards, pouring past the Bill at 5 knots or more headlong towards Portland Race, less than half a mile to the south-east.

Throwing *Cohoe IV* on to the port tack, we stood as close to the end of the Bill as we dared in the darkness; but very quickly the yacht was seized by the southerly set of the stream. We responded by easing the sheets and reaching at

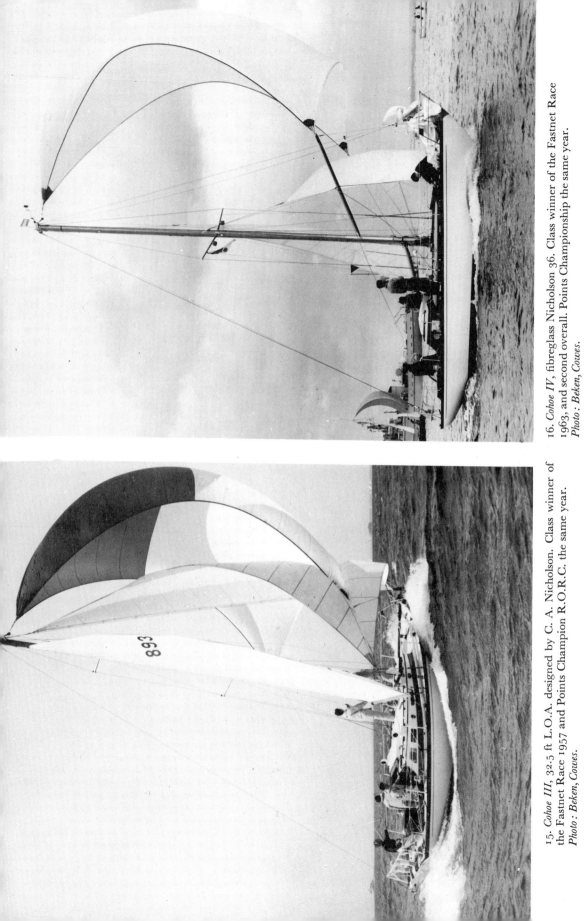

15. *Cohoe III*, 32·5 ft L.O.A. designed by C. A. Nicholson. Class winner of the Fastnet Race 1957 and Points Champion R.O.R.C. the same year. *Photo: Beken, Cowes.*

16. *Cohoe IV*, fibreglass Nicholson 36. Class winner of the Fastnet Race 1963, and second overall. Points Championship the same year. *Photo: Beken, Cowes.*

17. Seas in overfalls between St. Catherine's and Dunnose. Here the wind is only Force 6 to Force 7, but in the Channel gale it was Force 10, gusting 80 knots, and the whole area was dangerous

18. The ketch *Melanie* approaching Needles Channel when mean wind velocity at Needles and St. Catherine's is 40 knots, gusting 52 knots.
Photo : D. Ide from Cohoe III.

19. *Cohoe III* at Force 8. It is smooth as she is under the lee of *Melanie*. The forestay is set to the stem head as the bowsprit collapsed in the race to Spain, and there is no kicking strap as the goose neck fitting is cracked. *Photo from Melanie.*

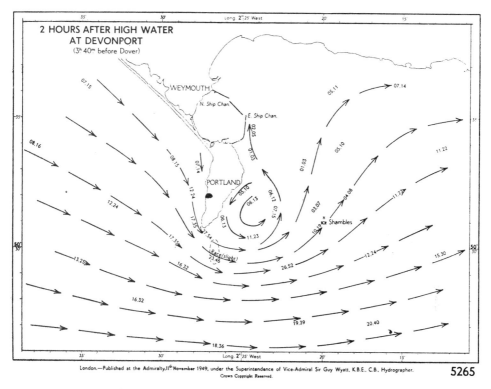

28   Portland Tidal Stream – 3 h. 40 m. Dover.

Cohoe IV's maximum speed, but even with the strong free wind off the Bill and lee-bowing the tide we were set almost a cable towards the Race before we gradually broke through into the weaker stream. The seas were rougher SW. of Portland Bill, but we had only Force 5 SW. and a left-over sea from the Force 6 to deal with.

The paradox in using the Inner Passage against a foul tide is that a fresh or strong wind and a fast boat are needed to cope with the stream off the Bill (which on a big spring tide can attain 7 knots setting into the Race), but the stronger the wind the rougher the seas, which can be dangerous in gales. Everything turns on time and the tidal streams, and the key to these is the Admiralty Pocket Tidal Stream Atlas for the Approaches to Portland.

Portland Bill marked the end of the heavy weather part of the race so far as we were concerned, for over the rest of the course there were only moderate winds and almost a calm off the Irish coast and near the Fastnet Rock. We managed to win in our class, with our sporting French rival *Pen-ar-Bed* second, but we lost the Fastnet Cup for first place overall in all classes by six minutes, being beaten by the Class II *Clarion of Wight*, then owned by Derek Boyer and Dennis Miller. This was the nearest we had ever come to winning the Fastnet Cup, but we lost no sleep over losing by so small a margin. The winner of Class I was the American yawl *Figaro* owned by William Snaith, but the Admiral's Cup was regained by Great Britain.

Conclusions

From data supplied by the Meteorological Office, I find that the wind at the start of the race was Force 6, and the maximum was nearly Force 7 at 1600, with the highest gust 34 knots. The tidal stream through the Needles Channel and outside is about 3 knots, so that at times the *apparent* wind might have been as much as Force 7. With wind against tide, conditions may fairly be described as rough.

It was in this part of the race, when all the yachts met the same conditions that the results were so surprising. In view of the fact that they contributed towards an alteration of the Royal Ocean Racing Club's handicapping allowances for the first time in nearly forty years it is necessary to state them. The elapsed times at Portland, without adjustment of handicaps of the first ten yachts were:

1. *Bolero* (Class I) 7.05; 2. *Capricia* (Class I) 7.30; 3. *Dyna* (Class I) 8.45; 4. *Outlaw* (Class I) 9.35; 5. *Stormvogel* (Class I) 9.40; 6. *Cohoe IV* (Class III) 9.50; 7. *Clarion of Wight* (Class II) 10.05; 8. *Striana* (Class I) 10.00; 9. *Martlet* (Class II) 10.15; 10. *Figaro* (Class I), *Kay* (Class I) and *Belmore II* (Class III) 10.30.

It will be seen that out of 127 starters two comparatively small yachts in Class II and two in Class III were among the leaders in the rough going, boat for boat without handicap allowance. For some years there had been growing feeling in the R.O.R.C., especially among the owners of the larger yachts, that the smaller boats came off best under the handicapping system. The results of the 1963 Fastnet Race may have brought matters to a head. The argument was that the time allowance favoured the small yachts in light and fluky conditions (as they do), but the large competitors no longer enjoyed the advantage in heavy weather hitherto conferred by their size and power.

In the words of the Committee of the Royal Ocean Racing Club: "It now seems apparent that in a quarter of a century the small yacht has improved her efficiency more than the big one, so that the latter can only hope to win in exceptional circumstances." Accordingly, the time allowances granted by large yachts to small were reduced. I will not comment on the appropriateness or otherwise of this decision, as we are not here concerned with racing rules. What is important was the official recognition of the increased ability of the modern smaller yacht.

It was a far cry from 1949, when Class III yachts were excluded as being too small and too slow for the Fastnet Race, to 1963, when time allowances were altered because they were considered too fast.

15

BERMUDA RACE GALES

The greatest ocean race on the other side of the Atlantic is the Bermuda Race, which attracts so wide an entry that it is now divided into six divisions, in which the latest of design, sails and equipment is tried out. The Bermuda Race is 630 miles across the ocean, with the Gulf Stream as the principal hazard. The roughest Bermuda Race before the war took place in 1936, when there was a cyclonic low which produced a prolonged spell of heavy weather in the Gulf Stream.

It was not until 1960, twenty-four years later, that an equally severe gale occurred in a Bermuda Race. I record it here, in the light of what I have read by Alfred F. Loomis and Bill Robinson in *Yachting*, because it was an important gale in which 135 competitors were caught out.

The 1960 Bermuda Race started off in a fog on Saturday, 18 June in a light south-south-westerly. Winds continued light and the first part of the race was slow going, the principal object being to enter the Gulf Stream at the right place, some 45 miles west of the rhumb line, in order to find the favourable meander which had been discovered by the Woods Hole experts.

It was not until 22 June that things changed. A cold front had been slowly moved southward owing to a "high", which had drifted eastwards from the area of the Great Lakes to arrive over the Atlantic seaboard on 22 June. The front took a position extending more or less eastward near the thirty-fifth parallel. Meantime, an area of modest low pressure which was off Charleston on 20 June travelled NE. slowly, deepening as it moved. Early on 22 June it lay SE. of Cape Hatteras, and, deepening further as it went, it sharpened on a faster course eastward south of the cold front and over the racing fleet.

The strength of the ensuing gales was to vary considerably with the local frontal squalls, and their effect on the racing fleet was to depend upon the positions of the individual yachts relative to the centre of the low as it passed by. A considerable number of them went through the eye, experiencing abrupt shifts of wind from SE. to SW., but others escaped the extreme.

Estimates of the wind strength varied considerably, in the same way as they did in the reports of the Channel Race. The velocities of the gusts would have varied locally, but broadly speaking it is clear that the lowest estimates come from the yachts which won places in their classes, among whom would be found some (but by no means all) of the most experienced owners. The highest esti-

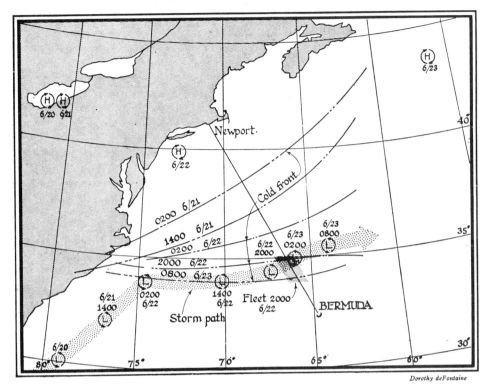

Dorothy deFontaine

29(a)   Development of weather, 1960 Bermuda Race.

mates come from the yachts which hove-to, no less than twenty-three of whom reported gusts of near or above hurricane force. I noted Bill Robinson's comment that "it is difficult for the average person, even an experienced seaman, to estimate wind accurately". This is exactly what I have pointed out earlier; in the absence of a masthead anemometer, wind strength estimating must be sheer guesswork when it is above the forces commonly experienced. By taking the estimates of the class prize-winners and averaging them out I arrive at a mean speed of 42½ knots, which is near the bottom of Force 9. with gusts around 55–59 knots.

There were few retirements, but the Atlantic is like the Bay of Biscay in that there are no ports of refuge to retire to. More creditable is the fact that the great majority of the yachts continued to race and were driven hard throughout the gale, among them the British entry *Belmore*, skippered by Commander Erroll Bruce, placed second overall. Apart from allowance for the Gulf Stream, the best tactic appears to have been to hold on to the starboard tack, as the wind freed in time to bring the yachts that did so quickly to the finishing line. The class-winners were Clayton Ewing's *Dyna,* T. J. Watson Jr.'s *Palawan,* Henry B. du Pont's *Cyane,* Fred Adam's *Katama* and Carlton Mitchell's *Finisterre.*

Conclusions

The lessons learnt from the Bermuda Race of 1960 were in general much the same as those of the Channel Race of 1956. They will not be repeated here other than as endorsements, together with some additional information derived from the reports.

1.   *Man overboard.* The class A *Djinn* was knocked down flat in the water, presumably in the same way as *Tilly Twin* in the Channel Race. Six men were washed out of the cockpit into the sea. They got back aboard, aided by the lifelines which they were wearing. *Royono* likewise lost and recovered a man by his safety belt when he was thrown overboard between the lifelines when the yacht was caught aback at the outset of the gale. A more dangerous accident occurred in *Scylla.* A member of her crew, having completed his watch, detached himself in the usual way from his personal lifeline and started to go below. At this moment the yacht lurched and overboard he went. It was night, but *Scylla* was equipped with an electronic flare waterlight, so brilliant that it is said it can be seen from the air at 50 miles range. This was thrown immediately and *Scylla*'s sails were lowered, but before the engine could be started the leads had to be changed over to a new battery. In all, it took about half an hour before the yacht returned to the scene guided by the brilliant flash of the light. The man was found, for in the meantime he had somehow managed to get out of his oilskins and strip to his shorts. His was a miraculous escape, all the more so because sharks are not unknown in these waters. It says something for *Scylla*'s crew that immediately after the rescue she continued in the race to finish sixth in her class. Except that it occurred at night, the incident in *Scylla* was on all fours with the accident in *Galloper* in the Fastnet Race. In each yacht a man was momentarily without a lifeline attached.

These near misses from disaster serve as a reminder that in a gale, when all seems well, there is always the chance of the exceptional squall or the freak wave (or both occurring at the same time) which may knock a boat flat on her beam ends and sweep her crew overboard. There were 135 yachts at sea and this accident happened in *Djinn,* one of the largest. It emphasizes the need to wear safety harness, however hampering and uncomfortable this may be.

2.   *Masts and rudders.* It appears that only two yachts were dismasted in the Bermuda Race and one disabled. This is a small proportion when it is remembered that 135 yachts were involved in the gale. I gather that one or both made St. David's under jury rig, aided by auxiliary power.

What was more unusual was that two yachts lost their rudders. *Highland Light* refused to answer her helm. A long emergency tiller was shipped and handled by two men in relays, and in the closing miles a spinnaker pole was lashed to the taffrail and manned by eight or ten men to assist in steering her. In the meantime her course had been maintained principally by trimming sails.

Cotton Blossum IV was caught aback, got in irons and with sternway drifted down on her rudder which broke. To be caught aback in a sudden shift of wind when a cold front goes through is not uncommon, but it has probably not occurred to many yachtsmen that this can throw enough strain on the rudder to break it. The experience also adds strength to the argument that lying to a sea-anchor head on in a full gale involves real risk of damage to the rudder.

The encouraging feature of these accidents, was that by good seamanship both these rudderless yachts were able, by careful sail trimming, to make port without assistance.

3. *Damage to transom. Stormy Weather* damaged her transom. It apparently occurred when she was caught aback and a great strain was thrown by the backstay on her bumkin, which in turn played havoc with her transom. Repairs were effected by wrapping cable around the stern overhang and securing the backstay to it.

4. *Rain.* Once again it is noted that violent rain has the effect of smoothing the seas, if only temporarily. It was reported from *Barlovento* that "the biggest problem was vision with the rain lashing in horizontally".

5. *Heaving-to.* Twenty-six of the competitors lay to during the gale. It seems that the majority who did so hove-to, whereas in the Channel gale the majority lay under bare poles, usually trailing warps.

THE BERMUDA RACE 1972

Twelve years elapsed after the Bermuda Race of 1960 before there was another severe gale in this great blue-water event, for which again I thank Bill Robinson and *Yachting* for information and the accompanying weather diagram.

As in 1960 the 1972 Bermuda Race started in good weather with a forecast of a cold front advancing along the rhumb line with a northwester behind it. It was not until the last two days that there was a sudden change. This was due to the development of a slow moving but large tropical depression to the SW of Bermuda, bringing with it a 40 knot fresh gale giving SE winds over the Bermuda area. This 60° shift of wind greatly benefitted the boats which had navigated east instead of west of the rhumb line. The presence of hurricane (rare in June) Agnes over Georgia and few reports from the boats at sea, added anxiety among those awaiting their arrival on the usually sunlit shores of Bermuda.

The strength of the wind may in fact have been a little less than in 1960, but the race proved a greater test of navigation and seamanship owing to the truly shocking visibility in which the first half of the fleet ended it.

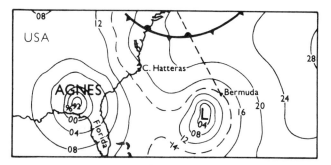

29(b) Weather map 0600, June 20, 1972, shows storm centre L to SW of Bermuda which caused SE winds on the rhumb line. Hurricane *Agnes* was then over Georgia.

The lack of sun sights, the erratic RDF bearings taken in rough seas (confirming similar experiences in other gales) and the uncertainty about local currents (setting northwards) made the approach to Bermuda hazardous, coming in during a gale on far-extending reefs on a lee shore with confused seas over shallow water. Still more hazardous was the actual finish with land completely obliterated by driving rain and with the marker frigate at sea engaged in rescue operations. It was under such conditions that the Bermuda Race 1972 was won by Ron Amey's *Noryema IV*, skippered by Ted Hicks. This British success marked the first occasion that the Bermuda Race has ever been won by a foreign yacht.

Conclusions

Few lessons were to be drawn from the 1972 race other than those already learnt in 1960. There were three dismastings and the usual crop of minor troubles of stays breaking, sails tearing and the breaking of track slides and jib hanks. Less common were reports of wire rigging unlaying and in *La Forza del Destino* the steering quadrant came adrift and her emergency steering also broke. There were several reports of damage owing to falling off waves. *Windward Passage* brought down a lower shroud with the impact, *Crusade* broke her port intermediate shroud and cracked a bulkhead and *Nephente* fell off three waves in succession and the third dismasted her.

To sum up, the 1972 Bermuda Race proved a big boat race and, although the smaller yachts had their share of the bad weather later, they missed the appalling visibility at the finish. Mishaps were relatively few and the race was a credit both to the ability of modern yachts and to their skippers and crews. Class winners were: R. H. Grant's *Robon* in A, Jesse Phillip's *Charisma* in B, Ron Amey's *Noryema IV* in C and overall, Stewart Green's *Dove* in D, Rodney Hill's *Maverick* in E and Alexander R. Fowler's *Aesop* in F.

16

BISCAY GALES

When first I drafted this book I left out a description of a near gale in the Bay of Biscay, as I felt there was already a surfeit of gales, but owing to a parallel gale which has occurred since, in which there was a tragic loss of life, I think both gales should be recorded, because of the lessons to be drawn from them.

In the Cowes to La Coruña Race of 1960 there were twenty-four entries, divided into the usual three classes. In the south of the Bay of Biscay a near gale was experienced, but it was not a severe one and the forecast was of strong winds rather than of gales (see charts, pages 68 and 181).

I was racing *Cohoe III* and on Wednesday, 10 August, in the south-west of the Bay of Biscay, there was a strong headwind from the south-west. The strength was logged at about 25 to 30 knots (Force 6 to Force 7). The sea was confused and the boat, driving fast under staysail and mainsail with two rolls in the reefing gear, occasionally fell off a wave with such a shock that it seemed best to heave-to for a while. The yacht lay very comfortably, but in the evening we took another two rolls in the mainsail and let draw.

We had a wild ride that night, with dense rain. I see that I logged two squalls at "over Force 8". They were accompanied by hail and rain and occasionally thunder and lightning. *Cohoe III* hove-to during these, and I remember being surprised how quietly she lay despite having so much sail set.

After the worst squalls were over, we reefed the mainsail right down to the lower spreader and set the storm jib. I was on deck at the time, rolling down the mainsail, and then took the helm. We let draw, and I remember how impressive and beautiful the scene was as the yacht sped her way through the gale. Black clouds were tearing across the sky, with a brilliant moon breaking through between them and silvering their edges.

Next morning, 11 August, conditions remained rough and the yacht sailed very fast, but at times not so close to the wind as she should have done. There were occasional severe squalls.

At noon I again logged Force 7, but the wind had veered to the north-west. There was a high swell and a confused sea, with small irregular crests. *Cohoe III* was still moving fast, with spray flying over her and heads of seas occasionally breaking on board, but conditions in the cockpit were not at all bad. At 1400 we hove-to again, but two hours later, as the barometer was steady and the wind had moderated, we made sail. During the night we had to lie a-hull again, but the midnight forecast gave only a continuance of Force 7 winds for the Bay of Biscay. At dawn the mountains on the north-west extremity of Spain were sighted. Of the twenty-four starters all but seven completed the course and came to anchor off the Real Club Nautico of Coruña. If there had been any hardships at sea, they were soon forgotten in the happy surroundings. *Cohoe III*, incidentally, was beaten in Class III of this race by *Meon Maid II* by three-quarters of an hour on corrected time, which is as it should be, since *Meon Maid II* had sailed harder. Class I was won by the French *Striana* and Class II by *Martlet*.

It was not until I returned to England that I learnt that a yacht had suffered serious damage during the gale. This was *Tandala*, a new Class II ocean racer designed by Fred Parker for Mr. B. V. Richardson. She was a well-found vessel of 40 ft. overall length manned by a crew of six. Here is her story.

"At 0245 on 11th August, we were some 100 miles NE. of La Coruña with the wind blowing Force 6 from the SE. when the goose-neck of the main boom broke, the boom itself having commenced to show signs of deterioration and splitting where it was glued, with the track having pulled out some little time before this.

"I thereupon gave up the race, and fixed a jury rig for the main boom, by means of a lashing with the mainsail well reefed down, and the small No. 1 staysail set.

"At 1300 it was blowing a full gale Force 8, and I decided to set a course for Santander, the wind having gone to the NW. At 1400 the wind was gusting Force 9, and I decided to lie a-hull with no sail set, and ride out the gale, with two crew with safety belts on duty in the cockpit.

"At approximately 2230 I and three of the crew were sleeping below, when a terrific crash occurred, a wave having smashed in the starboard [lee] side of the doghouse, and carried away the cockpit coaming, and also the dinghy.

"There was some two feet of water above the floor boards in the interior of the yacht.

"The storm jib was used for closing up the gap in the broken doghouse, and in order to lash it four holes were made in it, which as time went on enlarged owing to strain. The yacht was then put stern on to the following waves, with a looped warp towed over the stern, and the water eventually baled out, and the bilges pumped, the wind by this time having moderated to Force 7. Some little later, we hoisted a small amount of mainsail and No. 1 staysail and eventually entered Santander harbour in the early hours of 13th August, where arrangements for immediate temporary repairs were put in hand.

"The 7 ft. dinghy was carried on the coach roof, with webbing straps holding it down. The force of the water sheared the webbing and carried away the dinghy, and also bent the metal pedestal of the Sestral Moore Compass, the latter being thrown into the cockpit."

This is a brief seamanlike report. *Tandala* was badly damaged (I saw her later) and the yacht and her crew had a narrow escape. The occurrence was exactly parallel to that of *Vertue XXXV* when she was struck by a sea in the Atlantic Storm north-west of Bermuda, except that it was not blowing so hard in the Bay of Biscay and there were more men in *Tandala* to cope with the inrush of water. It is to be noted that in both yachts the damage was done on the lee side.

The second Biscay race to which I want to refer took place in 1964 from Santander to La Trinité, a distance or 240 miles of open water. I was not in this race myself, and this report is based on the analysis of the race by the R.O.R.C. coupled with information on the weather conditions which Commander Erroll Bruce obtained from the Meteorological Office and published in *Motor Boat and Yachting*, together with information which I have obtained myself from the Meteorological Office and other sources.

Forty-six yachts started the race at Santander on Sunday, 16 August, in light airs. By Monday the wind had freshened to Force 7 with heavy rain squalls and in the evening there were gale warnings for many sea areas to the northward. Several yachts gave up the race, and the remainder carried on. There was a very big sea running when the leading yachts were approaching the finish, and this, together with the rain squalls, made it difficult to identify the lights around Quiberon Bay in the early hours of Tuesday morning. However, most of the fleet made La Trinité without mishap during the day.

Three Class III yachts, *Lundy Lady*, *Zeelust* and *Vae Victis*, hove-to with plenty of sea room, rather than close the coast with restricted visibility, and these experienced the worst of the weather. They did not finish until Wednesday afternoon and were the last to arrive. No doubt there was some uneasiness about the yachts which had not so far reported, but in heavy weather it is sometimes two or three days after the conclusion of a race before all the yachts are accounted for, as there are many factors which may cause delay before all are safely reported. But the La Trinité race was to prove an exception, for one yacht and five lives were lost.

At about 1800 on Monday evening the small French Class III yacht *Aloa* lay a-hull, heading about north magnetic on the port tack with the wind probably westerly, about abeam. Her position was then estimated about 25 miles SW. of the Rochebonne shoals, and she remained hulling for nearly twenty-four hours. It was not until about 1700 on Tuesday, 18 August (when the weather was its worst), that a big sea threw her on her beam ends, which stove in a part of the lee side of the coachroof and part of the cockpit coaming. The boat was flooded and in one report it is stated that her motor was put out of action, which may mean either that she was under power when the sea hit her, which is unlikely, as the propeller would have been out of water much of the time or, more probably, that the sea soaked the ignition so that it could not be started later.

The crew pumped the boat out and attempted to cover the gap in the coach-roof by plugging it with sails and mattresses.

At about 1800 *Aloa* shipped a second breaking sea which once more flooded the yacht. She was pumped out again, and the skipper decided to run off to the eastward under bare pole. As warps were not mentioned, it may be assumed that they were not streamed.

Two hours later, at about 2000, *Aloa* was struck on the port quarter by another breaking sea and this time she was capsized. This is evidenced by the facts that the wind vane and anemometer at the masthead were bent and the dinghy (presumably rubber) was caught in the cross-trees.

The three men in the cockpit were thrown into the sea. Two were able to get back on board by means of their safety harness. The safety harness of the owner was not attached to the ship, some say because he was emerging at that moment from the cabin, where possibly he had been navigating, since there was a lee shore only about 35 miles distant. When the boat righted he was 50 yards astern and was wearing a Swedish-type inflatable life-jacket.

The remaining crew pumped the ship dry, made emergency repairs, set the mainsail and hove-to. Rockets were fired, but there was little hope of recovering the owner, who by then must have been out of sight in the seas far out of reach to windward, and he was lost. It was not until the following evening, Wednesday, at 1800 that *Aloa* was sighted by the French trawler *Giralda* about 10 miles SW. of the Rochbonne and taken in tow.

Marie Galante II, one of the smallest of the Class III ocean racers, gave up the race on Monday evening and ran for the River Gironde about 80 miles to lee-ward. She reached the entrance safely on Tuesday evening, 18 August, running under bare pole with two warps streamed aft, but at about 1800, when 4 to 5 miles NNW. of Cordouan lighthouse, she was struck by three heavy breaking seas. The first smashed the transom and stove in the cabin doors and flooded her. The second capsized her and broke her mast, and the third caused her to fill and sink. The owner was wearing a safety harness which was made fast to the rigging and he was either unable or unwilling to free himself (it is stated in one report that he could not swim), and went down with the yacht. In the meantime the crew had attempted to inflate the rubber dinghy. It was punctured, but they were able to get it into the water and cling to it. One of the crew had been very badly injured by the ship's ice box when *Marie Galante* was turned over by the second breaker, and he and one other died shortly afterwards. The remaining two were wearing submarine diving suits which enabled them to survive the cold water. They were washed up on the beach in the early hours of Wednesday morning.

A third Class III yacht also got into difficulties. This was *L'Esquirol II*, which was making for shelter behind the Île de Ré. Some reports state that the Pertuis Breton (which is the channel on the north side of the Île de Ré to La Rochelle) was entered by mistake, as the usual channel is the Pertuis d'Antioche on the south side of the island. It is more likely, however, that the skipper (who was familiar with the coast) chose the Breton channel to avoid the rough water at the entrance of the Pertuis d'Antioche or the rocks off the Point des Baleines. *Esquirol II* safely gained shelter under the lee of the Île de Ré, where she spent the night. It was the following morning, when she was under way again, that a jib sheet parted, and whilst it was being repaired, or for other reasons, she drove ashore east of the Grouin du Coup lighthouse about 5 miles north of the Île de Ré. Her crew were able to walk ashore when the tide fell and the yacht was not badly damaged.

Conclusions

The feature common to these two races in the Bay of Biscay was that damage was suffered in strong winds of Force 7, under gale force except locally, probably Force 8, with squalls and gusts probably about 40 to 50 knots. Damage was not anticipated by the Committee in either race, and it was only after the events were over that reports were received either of damage or casualties.

As will be seen from the weather charts for La Coruña Race, a shallow depression was approaching the English Channel on the morning of 10 August 1960. It deepened a little and moved slowly in a south-easterly direction to be centred off Ushant at noon on 11 August, with a complex frontal system stretching across the Bay of Biscay and crossing the course of the yachts racing to the NE. of La Coruña. The isobars are fairly widely spaced and do not suggest more than strong winds of mean Force 7 except frontally.

The cause of the bad weather in 1964 during the La Trinité Race was a deep depression which had moved in from the Atlantic and which on Monday evening of 17 August was centred near the Isle of Man with a minimum pressure of 979 millibars. This caused severe gales in the Irish Sea and the English Channel and strong winds up to Force 7 hundreds of miles south in the Bay of Biscay. I understand that none of the French shore stations in the Bay of Biscay recorded more than Force 7, but the wind is stronger at sea and off the coast on Tuesday evening it was probably gale Force 8, and the seas in the Bay of Biscay with a westerly wind would have been very high.

The lessons to be learnt from these gales are mostly underlining of previous ones.

1. *Tandala.* Twenty-four yachts were in the 1960 La Coruña race and, out of this number, only *Tandala* suffered damage, and she was an almost new and well-built boat. Damage such as this is fortunately rare. It depends upon the build-up and character of the particular freak sea and the angle at which it

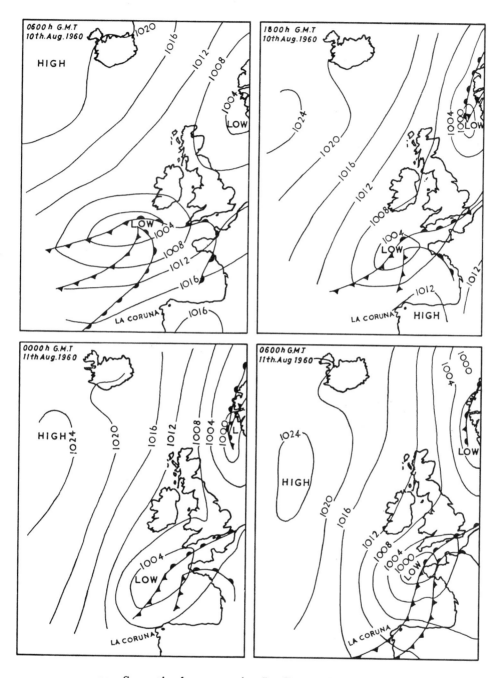

30 Synoptic charts covering La Coruña Race, 1960.

happens to strike the yacht. Unstable seas (and therefore potentially dangerous ones) are liable to occur with the veer of the wind when a cold front passes through, accompanied by violent squalls, possibly 50 knots or more, forming new trains of waves across the existing run of seas.

2.   *Aloa.* The loss of her owner and the damage to this boat has been attributed to her being in the vicinity of the Rochebonne shoals, and I believe this follows on the official inquiry.

The Plateau de Rochebonne is situated in the Bay of Biscay, about 35 miles

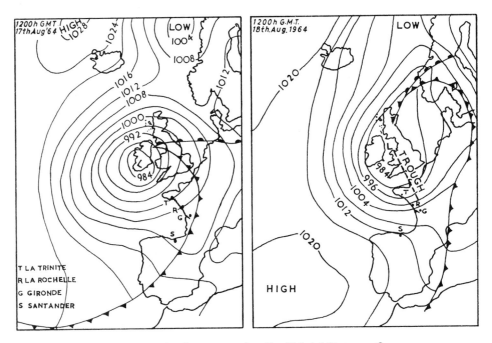

31   Synoptic charts covering La Trinité Race, 1964.

west of Île de Ré, the island situated at the entrance to La Rochelle. The Rochebonne is a rocky shoal with heads, over which there is as little as $2\frac{1}{2}$ to 4 fathoms, with deeper water between them. The shoal extends in a NW. to SE. direction for about 5 miles and is about 2 miles wide. It is marked by four buoys, but these might not be seen during a gale, owing to the high seas restricting visibility until near approach. In the *Bay of Biscay Pilot* the Rochebonne is described as "one of the most dangerous shoals off the west coast of France. The sea often breaks heavily on it and, in bad weather from the westward, is extremely dangerous." On the Bay of Biscay chart, the 20 fathoms contour is shown well within the buoys and the nearest soundings marked outside to the west and south are 45 fathoms, but it is stated that the WSW. approaches to the bank are particularly dangerous in bad weather up to a distance of 4 to 5 miles from the bank itself. This is probably local knowledge, derived from fishermen, and is a warning, as although I know this part of the Bay of Biscay I would not have expected danger so far from the actual shoals.

The general opinion is that the accident to *Aloa* was caused by her being in the vicinity of the Rochebonne, but there remains a possibility that she was in deep water the whole time, as when she was picked up by the trawler she was reported to have been 10 miles SW. of the shoals. Like *Tandala*, she may have been knocked down by freak seas when the cold front went through with a wind veer accompanied by violent squalls and gusts. A point which I have not seen mentioned is that the tidal stream had turned contrary to the wind, which (as explained in Appendix I) would have caused a considerable increase in the height and steepness of the waves, even if the rate were as low as half a knot. There would have been a tumult of high, broken and dangerously irregular cross-seas in what, in westerly winds, is virtually the Atlantic ocean. The damage may thus have been caused by stress of weather, rather than shoaling water. This will never be known with certainty, but the tragedy underlines several lessons:

(*a*) During gales, areas where there is irregularity on the bottom or rocky ledges (even if deep down) cause seas to break and can be nearly as dangerous as lee shores.

(*b*) The experience of *Aloa* confirm those of *Tandala* that freak waves may attain dimensions dangerous to small yachts at Force 8 (34–40 knots mean) and even lower, as will be shown in the next chapter.

(*c*) The damage is nearly always on the lee side of a yacht, and is caused by a breaking crest throwing her down on her side into the trough, striking the solid sea to leeward like falling on a pavement. It is usually the dog-house which suffers, and its construction is often a source of weakness.

(*d*) That despite damage, provided temporary repairs are made in time, the yacht may survive, as did *Vertue XXXV*, *Tandala* and *Aloa*.

(*e*) The accident to *Aloa* illustrates once more that the danger of losing a man overboard is greatest when the safety harness is temporarily disengaged, either when coming on deck or when changing helmsmen.

3. *Marie Galante II*. When the skipper of this yacht decided to retire, the strength of the wind was Force 7, and he made for the nearest port, which was the Gironde. The yacht appears to have been well navigated, but her arrival off the Gironde coincided with the height of the gale, which off the coast may have been Force 8, accompanied by violent gusts. The approach channel is dangerous even to large merchant vessels during onshore gales and it would be at its worst near low water, with wind against the ebb tide. *Marie Galante II* may have

missed the deep channel in bad visibility during squalls or been obliged to cut across the shoals in order to keep stern-on to the seas.

The seas in the channel might be enough to account for the loss, but it appears more probable that she was lost in the breakers on the Corduan shoals.

In either case the first two of the following points are clear:

(a) *Marie Galante II* suffered no damage when running before the gale streaming warps in deep water.

(b) It is safer to ride out a gale at sea rather than run for shelter to leeward. Even the deep approach to La Rochelle farther to the northward can be very rough when the wind is against the stream.

(c) The owner of *Marie Galante II* is thought to have been unable to unclip the hook of his safety line. His hands may have been numb from exposure, but hooks of safety harness sometimes get stiff from lack of use or from rust. The tragedy serves as a reminder that the hooks should be checked and greased so that they can be unclipped easily.

(d) The accident also serves as a reminder that life rafts should be capable of carrying the whole crew as prescribed by the R.O.R.C. safety regulations.

(e) In the event of a roll over, with the yacht thrown by a sea beyond the horizontal, there is danger from anything heavy, such as a refrigerator or batteries, which can break loose and injure the crew unless they are really strongly secured.

17

MEDITERRANEAN MISTRAL

I have never sailed in the Mediterranean, but the following story by Mr. Edward R. Greeff which appeared in *Yachting*, and described an experience when his yacht *Puffin* was caught-out in a mistral, is instructive both in regard to local conditions and the wider implications of heavy weather sailing wherever it may be.

Puffin is a yawl with a masthead foretriangle rig and a total measured sail area of 778 sq. ft. She is 40 ft. in length overall, 29 ft. 3 in. on the water; the beam is 10 ft. 7 in. and she has a lead keel of 8,200 lb., relatively slack bilges and quite a raking rudder-post. Total weight 25,400 lb. The hull form was in line with Olin Stephen's current thinking in 1963 of an able ocean racer.

Edward Greeff had competed in the Bermuda Race of 1966, in which *Puffin* was third in class and twelfth in the fleet out of 176. He then crossed the Atlantic and sailed to Port Mahon on the Isle of Minorca, easternmost of the Balearic Islands. Here her crew consisted of her owner and his wife Betty, Braman and Marjorie Adams, together with David Smith and Kim Coit, who had been with the owner during the whole of the cruise.

Puffin left Port Mahon at noon on 15 August 1966, bound for Bonifacio on the island of Corsica, about 240 miles distant. The forecast from the airport said the weather would be fair, visibility good, with winds 10 to 12 knots, NNE., but would become variable when approaching the coasts of Corsica and Sardinia, with seas not exceeding 1–1½ ft. in height. I will now take up the story from Edward R. Greeff.

"We had a fine breeze standing out of the harbour and found that we could nearly lay the course of 070°, and later the wind freed. We had the big No. 1 on and were moving along at about 5½ to 6 knots. Later during the evening at 2000 the breeze died down and we started our old faithful Westerbeke, again making good our course and 5 knots.

"At sundown I had noticed a rather heavy cover of clouds appearing in the west with some high cirrus preceding them. It looked like trouble, but the barometer still remained at 30.05 in. (1018 mb.) where it had been for weeks with only slight variations. In view of the weather report, I thought there was no point in alarming anybody by mentioning ominous clouds.

"By 2050 the breeze returned and started to freshen. We also began to get a big swell from NNW. By midnight we had gone from the No. 1 genoa to the

No. 3 and then to the working jib and soon decided to put a single reef in the main and lower the mizzen. We were still making good our course with our sheets eased a bit, wind N. by E. at about 30 knots. By 0200 we had a double reef in the main and ran into some rain. Sleep was rather difficult for me as I was worried about this change in the weather, but as there was no change in the glass I felt that it would probably not last very long. At 0400 I decided to take the main off and we proceeded on under working jib and mizzen, wind now N.,

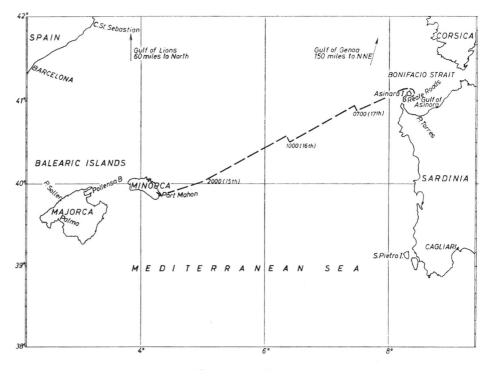

32   Western Mediterranean.

35–40 knots, which was a little forward of our beam. By this time we realized we were in for trouble as a French broadcast from Monaco confirmed the existence of a very severe storm moving east from the Golfe du Lion. All of this time the seas were building quite rapidly. I do not know how many people reading this account have cruised in the Med., but one of its peculiarities is the shortness and steepness of the seas.

"By sunrise, Tuesday, 16th, *Puffin* was again going too fast with the working jib and mizzen, so we shifted to the storm jib. I found that by keeping the speed down to 5 or 5½ knots, *Puffin* did not labour and with two girls on board I naturally did not want to make it any more difficult or uncomfortable for them than was necessary. After dawn the skies cleared and the wind now west of north had increased to a good 40–45 knots and perhaps more in the puffs, and seemed to increase more as the morning wore on. I must say it was a magnificent sight to see the crest of these waves blow off in the sunshine. During this period I had been rereading the Hydrographic Office Sailing Directions about mistrals. They point out that a mistral can last for 25 days with winds as high as 60 or 70 knots. In the summertime, however, they do not occur very often and their duration on the average is not over 3 to 6 days. At a time like this, one always wonders what to do, whether to take everything off and run before it or heave-to. With the wind on our beam west of north we had Africa to leeward of us, and I therefore decided to continue. At 1200 we set the storm trysail and lowered the mizzen. We continued on this way, fortunately, with only one case of sea-sickness and everybody else in good spirits, safety belts being worn on deck, *Puffin* dry below.

"During the afternoon the wind increased still more and it seemed that it was blowing 50 and certainly higher in the gusts. By 1800 the storm jib was taken off and we kept on under storm trysail. The wind continued to back more to the north-west and by early evening was about west-north-west. Rather than continue on course for the night, I decided to trim the storm trysail flat and heave-to, but with a man at the tiller. *Puffin* rode very comfortably taking the seas about a point on the port bow and making perhaps a knot and a half to two knots through the water, but certainly not over the bottom. The seas, as mentioned, were very steep and occasionally a crest would break on deck partially filling the cockpit but it did not amount to more than a soaking. I was now pretty tired and got my first four hours of sleep. Dave Smith and Kim Coit were standing one watch and Braman and I the other, using the Swedish system. Tuesday night passed relatively comfortably except for a heavy cloud cover and some rain which followed tremendous lightning to the north. The Monaco radio at 0400 said that this very bad storm had stalled over the Gulf of Genoa and had done great damage along the French and Italian coasts.

"When Braman and I came on deck for the 4 to 8 watch, the wind had moderated somewhat but there would be gusts which were quite severe. We both felt, as time passed, however, that these gusts were lessening and during the lulls the wind dropped to possibly 20 knots. At 0600 Wednesday morning, 17th, the seas seemed to be down as was the wind, and I felt that we could hold off and go on course again. It was almost impossible to take sights during Tuesday and, as there are no radio beacons on the west side of Sardinia, our position was only an estimate, which worked out to about 40 miles WSW. of Punta Scorno.

"The breeze by this time was on our port quarter and considerably down. With just the storm trysail our speed was about 3 knots, so I decided that we could set the storm jib with the hope of getting up to 5. Things shortly looked so encouraging that I thought we would set the mizzen rather than wake one of the boys to set a larger jib. About 0645 I went below to try to improve my estimated position, and while below had the feeling that the wind had increased slightly and so came up on deck to look around. It had increased but I still didn't think it was blowing more than 30 at the most in the puffs. Braman, who had the tiller, said that he felt she was all right.

"About 0715 I was standing on the lee side of the main boom watching the seas and chatting when I heard a roar astern and turned to see a huge wave much larger than anything we had seen with a broken crest tumbling down the face. The width of it must have been about 75 yards and the height of the crest 8 to 10 feet. I yelled to Braman something to the effect that 'this is coming aboard, hold her off and steady'. I was not actually worried because everything was battened down, slides were in the companionway and all hatches shut.

"As this sea broke over our stern I put my arms around the main boom. The sea went over both of us, and the next thing I knew there was a force of water around my waist so great that I was torn off the boom. Seconds later I was under water being pulled along by my safety line. *Puffin* had obviously broached, starboard side down, and was carried in the breaking sea on her beam ends, laying her masts in the water. I pulled myself up until I could get my hand on the rail, and by that time the boat had righted herself. Braman was still at the tiller, but we were laying in the trough.

"I climbed aboard as Dave Smith came up to lend a hand and yelled to hold her off again. She paid off on course without difficulty though a bit sluggishly. Betty, who had been thrown out of her bunk smashing her nose, informed me there was about $1\frac{1}{2}$ feet of water over the floor boards. I could not believe my eyes when I saw that 8 feet of the trunk cabin on the starboard side was broken in. Water had apparently rushed through this hole with such force that it tore the plexiglass slides in the companionway out aft into the cockpit.

"Realizing that we had to work fast as *Puffin* was in a very dangerous condition, we took the mizzen off immediately and lashed the gangplank (used for the stern-to moorings prevalent in the Mediterranean ports) along the side of the starboard trunk. I hoped that this might keep out another sea until we could get the water out of the boat. *Puffin* has two hand operated bilge pumps, one that can be worked on deck and one below. However, everything was such a mess in the cabin that gear had gone down into the bilge and the suctions of both pumps were clogged. Dave and I proceeded to bail with a bucket until we got enough water out of her so as to hold our hands over the pump suction to keep it clear without putting one's head under water. With Dave's long arms down in the bilge, I pumped and we soon were free of water.

"The next job was to secure the gangplank properly to the deck house. It was 14 ft. long by 18 in. wide and 1½ in. thick. To do this we took the treads off, bored holes through the plank, put the treads on the inside of the trunk cabin in a vertical position, and then passed lines through the holes and around the vertical treads which held the plank very securely, Because the plank was so heavy, it could not conform to the sides of the trunk cabin, and we had to resort to stuffing towels in the open spaces. This was completed by about 0900.

"As Betty was bleeding badly and we could not seem to stop the flow, I sent out a May Day. I could not raise anybody and so kept calling periodically for about an hour and a half. Finally an Italian yacht answered and offered to relay our message. By this time things were under control, and I informed them that we were in no immediate danger and were proceeding to Bonifacio—we would like a vessel to stand by, however, and that we would need medical assistance on arrival.

"Kim Coit who had been sleeping in the lower port bunk had been thrown out and landed in the starboard upper bunk and had received a bang on the head and shoulder, fortunately no permanent injuries. Dave Smith who had been in the port upper bunk was not hurt at all because the dacron bunk boards prevented him from being thrown out. Marjorie Adams had been in the starboard bunk in the forward cabin and had nothing more serious than some bruises. Betty, who had been in the port bunk in the forward cabin had been thrown out hitting her face on something—she doesn't know what.

"In the meantime *Puffin* was moving along at about 4 to 4½ knots on course, and I estimated our position to be about 20 miles west-north-west of Asinara Island which is the north-western tip of Sardinia.

"After a quick breakfast I went on deck to take a careful look at the damage. Our survey showed that when *Puffin* broached almost everything on the starboard side was torn off or damaged. This included the spinnaker pole which was resting in its chocks on top of the trunk cabin, the dorade type ventilators, one on the starboard side of the mainmast and the other on top of the lazaret hatch. The stanchions on the starboard side were bent and the life ring, Strobe lights and floats were missing. These could have been torn off by me as I went over the side. The mizzen rigging was all slack which was a puzzler. On checking we found that the mast had crushed the step which was a bronze plate and the mast was resting on the horn timber. The mizzen mast itself seemed to be intact as was the main mast. I think there are two things that contributed to the crushing of the mizzen step: the sea breaking into the mizzen sail created a tremendous compression load and also the force of the water on the top of the main boom contributed to the compression strain as the boom was hanging on a wire strap from the mizzen. Fortunately the mizzen did not break, and I think it was partly due to the fact that I had a mizzen backstay set. Incidentally one was set at all times at sea, whether I had a mizzen staysail on or not.

"The dinghy which was a Dyer Dink sailing type was secured in chocks on top of the trunk cabin. These chocks were through bolted through the top of the trunk cabin and the line holding the dinghy went through the chocks over the dinghy, crossing it several times. The painter was secured around the main mast. It is interesting that the dinghy did not move in its chocks but both sides were crushed in so that the thwarts punctured and broke the fibre glass. This gives you an idea of the force that was exerted on the dinghy.

"By 1100 our progress was quite slow as the wind had decreased further and Dave Smith said 'why don't you try the engine?' It never occurred to me to try it as I knew that the water had been over the battery—a foot and a half of water over the floorboards was enough to cover it. But miracles do happen and the engine started. It was probably lucky that the terminals on the battery were heavily greased but more important than that, we had a diesel. With the engine running our speed increased again to over 5 knots and we picked up the coast and identified Punta Scorno, the northern tip of Asinara Island. Shortly after 1200 the Italian yacht called again asking for our latest position. At this time we were approximately 3 miles due west of Punta Scorno. The yacht directed us to Reale Bay on Asinara Island to meet a tug which would have a doctor aboard. We proceeded to Reale Bay and anchored at about 1430. The tug came alongside and put a doctor aboard who had no equipment whatsoever to make any examination. We were naturally all quite annoyed. We did, however, gather that he requested us to go to Porto Torres—13 miles away—so that Betty could go to his office and to a hospital. We then asked the tug to give us a tow so as to save time as they could tow us at 9 knots versus our 5 plus. We arrived at Porto Torres at about 1730. Betty was under medical care shortly thereafter.

"The principal thing that we all want to know is how did it happen—what to do at such times and how to avoid a similar situation. Normally if the going gets really tough, blowing very hard and dangerous seas, one is apt to take everything off and run before it and at times tow things to slow the vessel down. In our situation we were sailing because it was not blowing hard and we had good control steering. I might say that there were moments, however, as each crest passed under us that *Puffin* did not respond quickly. At all other times we had excellent control.

"In my opinion there are two reasons for our broach. One is that the sea was so high and steep that it broke into the mizzen sail exerting great thrust which spun *Puffin* around. The other reason is that Braman Adams was hit so hard in the back by the sea coming aboard that he was thrown over the tiller, and to starboard. Although he never lost his grip on the tiller, it went down to leeward and we broached to port. Fortunately he had his safety line attached but perhaps he should not have had as much slack in it. If there had not been that slack he would not have been thrown so far.

I have no doubt at all that this could only happen in the Mediterranean where the seas are very short and steep. We had been through a severe gale in the Atlantic and at no time were there any seas that could have done this to us. I would hazard a guess that the seas in the Mediterranean are only half the length of those that we experienced in the Atlantic and twice again as steep. I think it was only because of this steepness that a sea would break as this one did with the wind decreasing and at most not over 25–30 knots.

"One principal reason, however, for out trouble was that *Puffin*'s trunk cabin sides did not have the vertical through bolts called for in Sparkman & Stephens specifications. These bolts go down through the sides of the trunk cabin, through the sill which sets on the deck, through the deck and through the header which is below the deck. The bolts called for were $\frac{1}{4}$-in. silicon bronze and there should have been at least six in the 8 foot span of trunk cabin which was broken in. Obviously these bolts would have added considerable strength."

Conclusions

The notable feature of this experience is that the sea which did the damage occurred after the storm was over at no more than 25 to 30 knots, indeed not more than 30 knots in the gusts, which suggests about Force 6 on Beaufort Notation. This is confirmed by the fact that *Puffin* was only making $4-4\frac{1}{2}$ knots under storm jib, trysail and mizzen, for had there been more than a strong wind one would expect at least 6 knots. It was a huge wave with an 8 to 10 ft. crest tumbling down its face, much larger than any which occurred even when

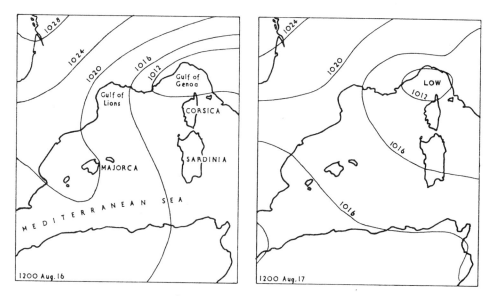

33   Synoptic chart, Mediterranean.

the mistral gusted over 50 knots with the crests of the seas blowing off in the sunshine, or during the severe weather experienced by *Puffin* in the Atlantic. In the previous chapter examples were given of freak waves in winds of only Force 7 or Force 8, but this experience shows the possibility of a rogue sea occurring even at Force 6. I do not believe the Mediterranean can be blamed for this. It can occur anywhere, though happily very rarely. Once again, the damage was done on the lee side.

There was no warning of this storm either by weather report or by barometer. As can be seen from the synoptic charts, the depression developed very quickly. It is the same story as occurs in several other gales described in this book. Meteorological experts can (though rarely) be foxed by sudden and unpredictable changes in meteorological conditions, especially locally.

Among the observations Edward Greeff makes in his article are the following, to which I have added my own comments in italics where appropriate:

1. If *Puffin* had been a centreboard boat, I doubt very much that she could have come back with as much water below as we had. *Puffin* snapped back very quickly. I strongly recommend a keel boat to anyone planning an ocean cruise in a small boat such as *Puffin*. *This is interesting because a number of ocean cruising men have come to the same conclusion.*

2. When running off in a big sea never carry any sail aft. *I have recommended the yawl rig because Cohoe II ran so well under mizzen and jib. Puffin's experience is a logical objection to the use of a mizzen which I had not foreseen, but it applies only if seas become really dangerous.*

3. Safety belts should be of the harness type. The snap hooks should be very strong—not the bronze boat snap kind, but a drop-forged galvanized snap.

4. Sheets of $\frac{3}{8}$-in. plywood should be carried as wide as the cabin is high and besides plenty of screws and bolts of all sizes—nails if you have a wooden ship. *This confirms advice already given, but note I have carried them around for twenty years without using them.*

5. I would run a $\frac{3}{8}$-in. line fore and aft on deck, port and starboard sides, very taut inside the shrouds and made fast to padeyes or stanchions on the foredeck and near the transom, this to which to attach the snap of your safety line. This then gives one freedom to move fore and aft and to be hooked on all the time. *Note also that Mr. Greeff recommends that the helmsman's personal lifeline should be short and have no slack in it.*

6. The Bermuda Race requirements on pumps are very sound—two hand-operated pumps. Don't rely on an electric one, because if you get into trouble you may need the juice to call for assistance or to start the engine.

7. The area between floors in a wooden vessel or where the bilge pump suction is located should be covered with a wire mesh to prevent material from clogging the suction hoses. *It is, of course, essential that pumps must not clog. This*

can be achieved by copper-mesh strum boxes at the foot of the pipe, or as suggested here or better still by using both methods.

8.   Strong wood lath is handy for battens holding down cloth besides many other uses. A full set of tools is needed for working in metal or wood, including three types of drills: electric, hand "eggbeater type" and brace and bits.

9.   Emergency running lights and binnacle light—battery type—should be carried.

10.   Carry at least two buckets—one can be of plastic and one of canvas.

I would like to add the following notes:

(*a*)   *Heaving-to.* During the worst of the storm *Puffin* hove-to, and she did this under trysail only, trimmed flat, but with a man at the tiller steering. Edward Greeff had adopted this system when *Puffin* was caught-out in the tropical storm *Becky*, five days out of Bermuda. He found that by this means the boat could be manoeuvred sufficiently to minimize the danger of bad breaking seas. *Puffin* had no trouble in the Atlantic storm because the seas were so much longer and therefore less steep than those in the Mediterranean.

(*b*)   *Coachroof.* Edward Greeff's recommendation of the Sparkman & Stephens method of strengthening the coachroof sides is interesting, and it is adaptable where the sides are 1 in. teak, as in *Puffin*. The alternative is steel, bronze or aluminium stiffening to the whole coachroof and coamings, carried down to the deck beams and frames, thus tying the superstructure to the hull. The form of strengthening is a matter for the individual designer, but what is clear is that coachroofs and doghouses can be a source of weakness in the event of meeting freak seas and receiving a knockdown.

18

TWICE ROLLED OVER

For a yacht to be completely rolled over through 360 degrees is a rare occurrence, but it does occasionally happen in the ocean. The two classic examples which come immediately to mind are Voss's 19-ft. *Sea Queen* in the North Pacific and the 45 ft. ketch *Tzu Hang*, which was both pitchpoled and later rolled over in the South Pacific. There are several other examples.

The following is an account of a yacht which was completely capsized twice off the coast off North Carolina. I am indebted for the particulars to her owner and to the editor of *Yachting*, in which an article describing the incidents first appeared. The experiences are of particular interest, as the yacht involved was a normal ocean racer of moderate size and the incidents occurred while making a normal passage, subject only to the special hazards of the Gulf Stream.

Doubloon is a 39 ft. centreboard yawl designed in 1957 by Aage Nielsen and then owned by Mr. Joe C. Byars. She measures 27.5 ft. on the waterline and has a beam of 10.8 ft., draught 4.5 ft. and a C.C.A.-rated sail area of 823 sq. ft. Her displacement is 9 tons and the ballast keel about 2½ tons.

The yacht departed from St. Augustine, Fla, on Saturday morning, 2 May 1964, bound for Morehead City, N.C., where she would join the Intra-Coastal Waterway and thence sail to Newport, R.I., to arrive in time for the start of the Bermuda Race. The distance from St. Augustine to Morehead City (some 50 miles south of the notorious Cape Hatteras) is about 360 miles, and as the course was on the axis of the Gulf Stream, the passage would, in the ordinary way, take about a couple of days. (See chart, page 199.)

Doubloon was skippered by her owner, Joe C. Byars, who had as crew Gene Hinkel and two other young men, Mel Burnet and Roger Ryall, who were inexperienced at the start, but finished as the owner puts it, as "graduates of some of the rougher courses the sea has to offer". When she left St. Augustine at 0600, there was no wind. The marine weather forecasts had not been kept up with, but from Daytona a commercial report forecast no bad weather and the only hint of trouble came from another commercial station which reported a small craft warning for the Charleston area. The barometer was about 1,013 millibars.

The engine was used until 0800, when the wind came in SE. moderate, dying away about 1100. It then came in as a whole sail breeze from the east, but later hauled round to SE. and freshened, necessitating close reefing. During the night

Doubloon sailed at 8 knots under mizzen and jib. On Sunday morning (3rd May) the wind moderated to 12–14 knots (Force 4), and shifted to west. Later in the morning a swell was encountered which Joe Byars described as the largest he had ever experienced. It came from NNE. and the height of the waves was estimated at about 15 ft. The wind was blowing their crests backwards in large sheets of spray and, although *Doubloon* had a good wind, it was almost impossible to keep her sails filled, as the huge swells were large enough partially to blanket them. A preventer was necessary to keep the main boom outboard and progress through the water was poor. This is an interesting corroboration of my own experiences off Ushant, described in Chapter 13. It confirms the little-known fact that a very big swell can make it almost impossible to sail in light or even in moderate winds.

Byars at first assumed that the swells came from an expired gale to the northward, but by 1500 the barometer had fallen to about 999 millibars, and when the wind shifted to the north-east (the same direction as the swell came from), he decided to alter course for Charleston, which was about 105 miles to the west-north-west. It was just on 1700 when the skipper noticed what looked like a line squall or a front to the north. Preparations were made for a blow. All sails were lowered and the storm jib hanked on in readiness. All hatches and ports were secured.

A few minutes later the wind backed to north and freshened to 35–45 knots (Force 8 to 9) and *Doubloon* was run off under bare poles. A north-easter had started in real earnest and soon rose to 50–70 knots (Force 10, gusting above hurricane force). The tops were blowing off the seas, filling the air with spray.

By sunset Byars estimated the height of the seas to be between 15 and 18 ft. and by the morning 18–25 ft. The seas, larger than he had ever seen before, were vicious, very steep and white capped. Now and again *Doubloon* took a sea over the stern, half filling the cockpit. This is normal in yachts during gales, but what followed during the night was near disaster. The storm jib was set to steady the yacht on her helm, and her skipper thought that it helped, but the boat began to surf, so it was lowered again. Later and during the night followed "five full smashes from breaking seas". Let us examine them.

The first smash. The sea came from dead astern shortly after 1800, and engulfed the cockpit. Byars was wrenched from the tiller and thrown hard against the aft end of the deckhouse. Burnet went overboard to port, but his safety-belt line held and he was quickly back aboard. Neither was hurt. The cockpit was full to the top and as usual, the cockpit drains proved to be too small. Nearly all yachts are the same in this respect. A large stewing pot was brought into operation. The cockpit was emptied and the bilges were pumped out. There were only about 10 gallons of water in them.

It was then decided to put *Doubloon* on a south-west heading, bringing the wind and seas on her starboard quarter. She rode well and this seemed to be the best chance to work out of both the storm and the Gulf Stream.

Second smash. This course was held for nearly three hours until about 2100 taking no seas aboard. Then *Doubloon* was struck by the second full breaking wave. Once more the cockpit was completely engulfed and the yacht went right down on her beam ends. Byars and Burnet were swept out of the cockpit and overboard, but their safety-belt lines held and they floated back aboard as she righted. The stewing pot and the pump were brought into operation again. A porthole which had been smashed was repaired by nailing the lid of a bunk bin over it with large nails, and later a piece of plywood was also nailed over it from the outside.

The skipper then decided to try to get *Doubloon* closer to the wind, and put the helm hard down. The best she would lay was about 60 degrees to 70 degrees from the wind, about 300 degrees on the compass, which is rather better than I have usually found when lying a-hull, and was perhaps due to the windage aft on her mizzen. The centreboard was then let down to try to make her hold up closer. The yacht seemed to handle better lying a-hull heeling about 20 degrees and taking over no seas for four hours.

First roll over. About 0100 the following morning (Monday, 4 May) there was a tremendous crash. The boat was slammed down on her side to port. It seemed that she might have paused for an instant, but instead of coming back she went right over. Her crew were all thrown to the port side, then on to the cabin ceiling. Before they could think about it, they were back upright. The complete 360-degree roll over was estimated to take only three to five seconds.

Joe Byars was in the cabin at that time, but he knew what had happened and his immediate thoughts were of the survival of the crew. He felt certain that *Doubloon* was lost and hurried up the companionway. He can remember the dreadful feeling of seeing the tiller moving back and forth with no one at the helm. He yelled for Gene Hinkel, who had been steering, but got no answer. A quick survey showed the main and mizzenmasts and booms were gone. Byars rushed to the stern and tried to remove the U-shaped life-ring, but the stern pulpit was bent over it, so that it could not be detached. A light buoy was bobbing to leeward which must have been the other life-ring, and as it was not drifting away it was hoped that Gene would make for it if possible. Byars shouted for Gene again and again, but there was no response.

Down below it was reported that the bilge water was not rising. With the aid of a portable pump the water in the bilges was kept under control. Gene had to be given up for lost, because there is no chance of survival for a man overboard from a disabled yacht at night.

The first thing to do was to cut away the masts and rigging. They were along-side, mostly to windward, but they were not hitting the boat, and it was decided to make no attempt to clear the rigging until daylight. Byars went below, but before he did so he noticed that the styro-foam life-raft, which had two other life-rafts lashed to it, was gone. The starboard padeye had pulled out, releasing the tie-down strap.

Roger Ryall and Mell Burnet asked where Gene was, and Joe Byars had to reply that he was gone. They were stunned at the loss, but there was nothing that could be done.

Fifteen minutes later their spirits were immeasurably raised when who should appear in the companionway but Gene himself. They were astounded and overjoyed.

"I heard you, Joe", said Gene, "but you couldn't hear me. I had her helm at 300 degrees and I got the life-rafts." He had been overboard on the windward side, where he had found the main raft, with two inflatable rafts strapped inside, wedged in the tangled mass of rigging. His safety line was on, still secured to *Doubloon*, but he could not get himself free. The screaming wind and the pounding seas together with the darkness of the night had put him out of communication, so that he could not be heard, but he managed to get himself back aboard *Doubloon*.

Gene immediately got to work. The batteries had fallen out of their boxes in the roll over, and he got them back in place so that at last light could be restored in the cabin. He wanted to go on deck to cut the rigging away, but the skipper wouldn't let him. All turned in in their bunks to rest and Gene picked up a book and started reading. As the skipper puts it, "This was the same man whom minutes before we had given up for lost."

Fourth smash. Shortly after dawn there was another tremendous crash, *Doubloon* went over to her beam ends, but came quickly back. The rigging had been washed completely over the yacht to the lee side. The mainmast was in three pieces with a sizeable piece held vertically against the lee side protruding 6 or 7 ft. above the water, but it was not pounding the boat.

Second roll over. Between 0800 and 1000 *Doubloon* received the hardest blow of all. She went over on her side and continued going. The cabin darkened for an instant, and then she came upright again. All hands were below at the time. As the yacht rolled over Byars fetched up hard twice, once against his head and once against his body. He was bleeding about the face and felt he had been hurt, but it was not until later that he found he had broken a rib. Everybody suffered cuts and bruises in the roll over and later it was found that Roger Ryall had suffered three partially crushed vertebrae.

It is surprising that despite this complete roll over *Doubloon* had taken in very little water, which says a lot in favour of her construction and hatches. The water never rose above 3 or 4 in. below the cabin sole, which could easily be dealt with by the crew.

It seems that *Doubloon* could stand anything more that would come her way, and the spirits of her crew rose a little. The next thing to do (it was now daylight) was to clear the rigging. The wire cutters had been in the cockpit and had gone to the bottom when the yacht rolled over. Nevertheless, Gene managed to cut the halyards and remove all clevis pins to rigging except the forestay, which was attached to a good piece of the mast which acted as a sea anchor. He then rigged another sea anchor out of a No. 2 genoa, a sail bag and an anchor. *Doubloon* was riding 60 degrees from the wind. Yet another sea anchor was put out comprised of a working jib, with the head attached to the tack to create more drag. Two mattresses were lashed on what remained of the stern pulpit, in order to create windage aft to help hold her head up. The effect was to keep the bows at about 50 degrees to 60 degrees from the seas and wind.

All that remained to do was to check over other damage. Both ventilators had been torn off, but the holes were plugged. Both spinnaker poles had torn loose, and no spars were left other than the 2-ft. high stumps of the main and mizzen. A starboard winch was partially uprooted and every stanchion on deck was bent, as were both pulpits. The tiller was broken off at the head, while the binnacle was gone.

The barometer had risen to 1,004 millibars, but wind and sea remained at full force for some hours. However, *Doubloon* was making appreciably better weather of it and took no more knockdown blows from seas. Her skipper attributes this to the sea anchors holding her up to the wind. Her weary crew turned in to rest in the cabin, which was now a shambles.

That was the end of the adventure, but it was still blowing hard on Tuesday morning. It was not until around noon on Wednesday that her crew got in the sea anchors, and a jury mast was rigged out of the only spar left. This was a $6\frac{1}{2}$ ft. aluminium spinnaker guy strut for keeping the aft guy off the shrouds. It was rigged inside the stump of the mainmast and put the head perhaps 10 ft. above the deck. To this a mizzen spinnaker was set, which was sufficient to give *Doubloon* a speed of 4 to 5 knots on a westerly course.

To cut a long story short, two ships passed *Doubloon*, one only a mile away, but neither saw her flares. It was about 1600 on Wednesday that the freighter *Alcoa Voyager* stood by for rescue operations. Joe Byars was pressed to abandon *Doubloon*, but he refused, as she was not leaking and was making progress towards the coast under jury rig and had plenty of supplies. The *Voyager* then made a wide circle and came back close to leeward and took the yacht in tow until relieved by the coast-guard cutter *Cape Morgan*, who gave her a lively ride at 12 knots to Charleston Harbour.

Doubloon had been towed for over 160 miles east of Charleston, her position when picked up by the *Voyager* on 6 May being 32° 41′ N. 76° 36′ W. Her skipper notes that the Gulf Stream had carried the yacht to the north-east in

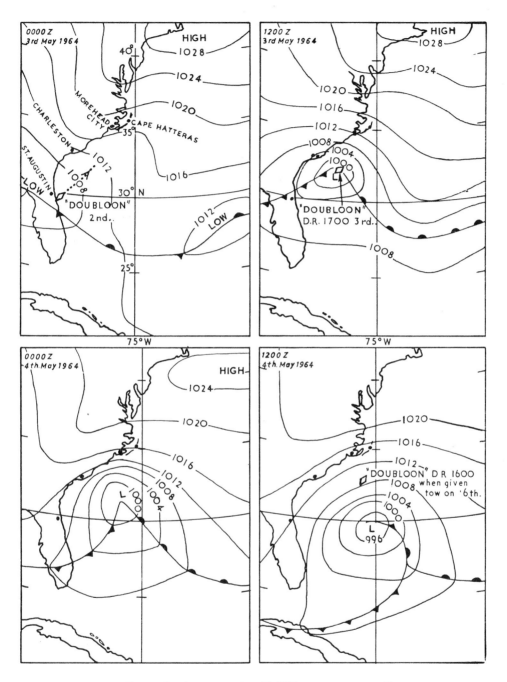

34   Synoptic chart covering Gulf Stream storm, 1964.

spite of gale winds against it. The sea anchors must have accounted substantially for a part of this.

Doubloon was skippered with tremendous determination, for despite the ordeal, Joe Byars refused to abandon her when asked to do so by the *Voyager*, and despite somersaults and dismasting he managed to get the yacht to Newport R.I., and have her repaired in time to take part in the Bermuda Race in June and to win second place in Class E.

Conclusions

I have obtained particulars of this storm from the U.S. National Weather Centre. It was an extra-tropical cyclone which formed as a wave on the polar front over northern Florida and adjacent Atlantic waters. Whole-gale winds were reported from several ships in the area of cyclogenesis over the warm Gulf Stream waters. S.S. *Santa Rita*, 34.1° N. 75.7° W. at 1800 on 3 May logged Bar 1009, wind E. 50 knots, and at 1200 on 4 May S.S. *Platano* 33.0° N. 75.5° W. reported Bar 1009, wind ENE. 50 knots.

Doubloon must have been nearer the centre of the low when her barometer reading was 999 millibars and may have experienced higher winds of 55 to 60 knots. A fair guess would be Force 10–11, gusting at hurricane force.

The storm seems to bear a marked similarity to that experienced by the British yachts north of Bermuda. Both were extra-tropical cyclones with predominantly easterly or NE. winds. In neither storm did the barometer fall exceptionally low, only to 993 millibars in 1950 and 999 millibars in 1964.

The principal difference between the experiences of the yachts was due to the Gulf Stream. Of the British yachts, only *Vertue XXXV* and *Samuel Pepys* appear to have been in the Stream (near its southern boundary) during the earlier storm, whereas *Doubloon* was on the axis of the Gulf Stream, where the current was running near its maximum speed directly contrary to the wind, so she must have experienced phenomenal seas.

Joe Byars estimated the height of the waves at 18–25 ft., which is remarkably accurate, for the guesses are confirmed by S.S. *Platano's* report of 16 ft. and S.S. *Santa Rita's* of 24 ft. height.

Comments are as follows:

1. *Gale tactics. Doubloon's* skipper does not like running dead before a major gale, but he did not try towing warps, which are certainly a help. Streaming warps might not have saved *Doubloon* from her roll over in the exceptional seas of the Gulf Stream, but, as her skipper says, they might have worked well enough running in more normal seas in a gale. Despite his experiences, he thinks that once the wind had risen to Force 10 *Doubloon* would have been in greater danger running off either with or without warps. He is firmly of the opinion that he

20. Typical sea in the English Channel, when the wind is confirmed by shore stations at Force 8. The breaking crest is the other side of the sea. With a weather-going stream the seas would be very rough.

21. The 40 ft yawl *Puffin*, designed by Sparkman & Stephens. After crossing the Atlantic and being involved in tropical storm *Becky* she was

22. The 40 ft masthead sloop *Force Seven*, designed by William Tripp. She survived Hurricane *Cleo* running under bare pole, taking the seas on

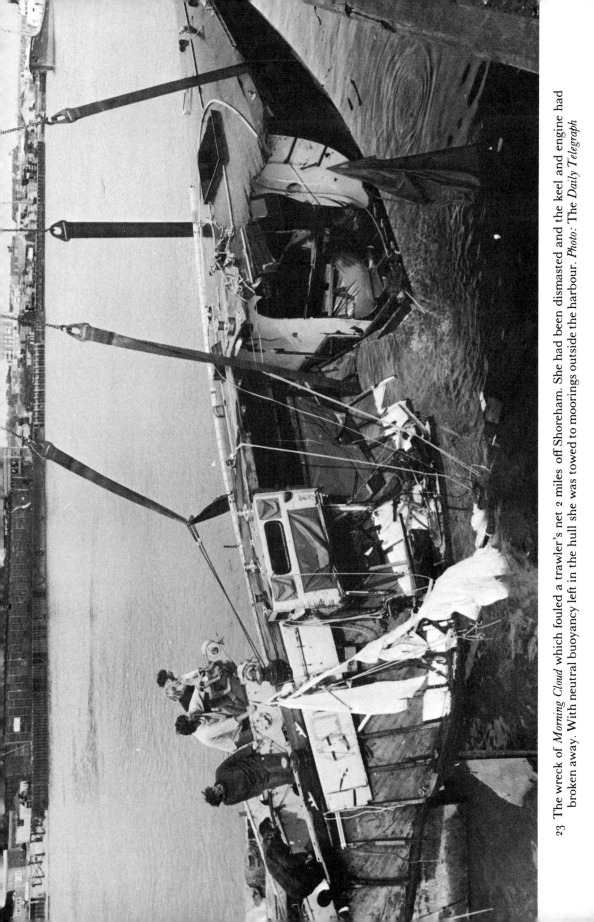

23 The wreck of *Morning Cloud* which fouled a trawler's net 2 miles off Shoreham. She had been dismasted and the keel and engine had broken away. With neutral buoyancy left in the hull she was towed to moorings outside the harbour. *Photo: The Daily Telegraph*

24. The schooner *Curlew* in distress in the Atlantic storm, north of Bermuda, with winds gusting up to 85 knots. *U.S.S. Compass Island photo.*

would rather take his chances in a gale by lying as near as possible head-to-wind. For a boat of *Doubloon*'s size, a storm mizzen is recommended with 9 ft. on the hoist by 4 ft. on the foot, made out of 12-oz. Dacron with wire mast-hoops and rollers which can be shackled around the mizzenmast. A sloop could hoist a storm jib with the main halyard, with the luff hanked to the backstay and with the clew forward sheeted in flat. Byars believes that this would hold the bow up to about 30 degrees to 50 degrees from the wind without a sea anchor, and that the boat should make the proper leeway, giving with the seas, although a small sea anchor might be necessary to slow her and to reduce leeway or hold the bow closer to seas.

The rudder would have to be adjusted to suit the requirements of the individual yacht and conditions, lashing it amidships or allowing it to swing through a small angle. He considers this should work for most yachts without endangering the rudder by backing down on it.

It cannot be denied that the bow is the stronger end of a yacht and less vulnerable to seas than the stern with a cockpit which is an invitation to the head of any "freak" sea to flood it and sweep the crew overboard, as has happened time after time in severe gales and storms. The crew can usually be recovered by their safety belts, but it is preferable that they should not go overboard at all. It is instructive to note that on the second occasion that *Doubloon* was rolled over she was without masts. This contradicts the theory that a hull without masts will float like a cork through anything.

2. *Centreboard*. From this experience it appears that the centreboard helped to hold *Doubloon*'s head closer to the wind, but her owner thinks it probably contributed to the roll-overs by tripping the yacht. The centreboard was $\frac{3}{4}$-in. bronze and it was found to have been bent about 30 degrees, probably when it hit the water as the yacht came back to even keel after the roll over.

The beamy centreboard yawl is a proven type of good seaboat, tested by many gales, among them the 1957 Fastnet Race, which was won by the American yawl *Carina*. It is possible, however, that in "survival" storms there comes a point of heel where stability is lost compared with the conventional deep-keeled yacht. *Doubloon*'s draught is 4.5 ft. and her keel is $2\frac{1}{2}$ tons. Once thrown so far over on her side that most of the stability afforded by her 10.8 ft. beam was lost, the righting moment of her ballast keel would be far less than that of a narrower boat with say $3\frac{1}{2}$ tons of lead at the bottom of a 6 ft. keel. It is purely a matter of conjecture, as "survival" storms are rare, and some authorities believe that reasonably shallow draft is no handicap. On the other hand, a centreboard or a deep fin keel tends to provide a pivot on which a boat can be rolled over.

3. *Doghouse windows*. The year before the storm *Doubloon*'s four fixed windows had been replaced by smaller ports. The seas struck with tremendous force,

giving somewhat the impression of an explosion on deck. It seems doubtful whether she would have survived if she had still been fitted with big windows, such as are found in the doghouse of the average yacht. In my own boats since 1950 I have carried shaped plywood panels, with holes drilled in them, ready to be quickly nailed over a broken coachroof window or port. I have never had to use them, but they are light and stow easily under the quarter-berth mattresses and might prove invaluable in an emergency.

4. *The watch below.* *Doubloon*'s owner recommends staying below to get rest after making everything on deck secure, thus eliminating the chance of injury on deck, or being washed overboard.

5. *Other recommendations.*

(*a*) Cockpit hatches (lockers) should be raised, strong, and have a good means of fastening to be watertight. Cockpit-hatch leaks will allow a significant amount of water in. This adds to the burden of keeping buoyant. The usual gutters and small drains are near useless under such conditions. Two additional cockpit drains were installed after the gale.

(*b*) The bilge pump was altered, so that instead of emptying into the cockpit it discharges on deck. The emergency pump was changed to a large-capacity Edson Diaphram pump, which is nearly 100 per cent clogproof.

(*c*) Everything on deck must be well secured. Ventilators should be removed and the pipes stuffed with rag if they are not fitted with deck plates to screw down to make them watertight.

19

SEPTEMBER HURRICANE

Tropical storms are known in the northern Indian Ocean simply as cyclones, in Australia as "Willy Willies", in the west and north Pacific as typhoons and in America and the Caribbean as hurricanes. It is the latter which yachtsmen have most often to reckon with, because they so often move up the eastern American seaboard, leaving a trail of havoc among yachts in harbour or those unlucky enough to be caught out at sea in one. Hurricanes are not entirely unknown even in European waters. For example, Hurricane *Carrie* in 1957, after meandering thousands of miles, ended her travels in southern Ireland, though over a month too late to add to the entertainment of the Fastnet Race of that year. In 1958 *Helene* developed east of the West Indies and proceeded off the New England coast to Newfoundland. She then went ocean cruising towards Greenland before changing her mind and paying a courtesy call at Cardiff. Happily by the time hurricanes reach our waters most of the sting has been taken out of their tails and there is more buzz than bite.

Hurricanes are carefully tracked by the American meteorological experts and repeated warnings are given of their anticipated course, but they are temperamental, wayward things that from a met. man's point of view are perhaps not quite house-trained. Their courses are sometimes unpredictable. Here is the story of one such which appeared in the American magazine *Yachting*.

The yacht concerned in it was *Force Seven*, owned by Mr. Warren Brown of Bermuda. She is an ocean racer, designed by William Tripp and raced in Class 'E' of the Bermuda Race under the Cruising Club of America or Class II under the R.O.R.C. She measures 40 ft. in overall length and 27 ft. 6 in. on the waterline. Her beam is 11 ft. 8 in. and draught 5 ft. 10 in. She is typical of the modern boat that races on both sides of the Atlantic. I know *Force Seven* and I exchanged greetings with her owner and crew when she and *Cohoe IV* were off the Lizard in the Fastnet Race of 1963, and the two yachts lay alongside later at Plymouth.

Force Seven took her departure from Bermuda on 30 August 1964, bound for Newport, R.I. The owner was skipper/navigator and with him were Herbert Williams as mate and four undergraduates as crew. There were also two youngsters on board, the mate's daughter and a schoolboy. Both skipper and mate had many year's experience of ocean sailing and racing, and the yacht was in first-rate condition and well fitted out.

The September hurricane belt lay between Bermuda and the United States and a careful eye had to be kept on the progress of storms coming up from the south, though with the new weather satellites in orbit most of them can be tracked more accurately than in the past.

Departure had been delayed a day because hurricane *Cleo* was at that time lying between Bermuda and the mainland, but on Sunday morning, 30 August, it was reported that the winds had dropped to about Force 9, and that *Cleo* had moved over North Carolina and had started to break up. So with no indication of any further disturbances *Force Seven* left Bermuda in beautiful weather.

It was decided to enter the Gulf Stream approximately 30 miles to the west to allow for it to set the yacht back to a rhumb-line course. There was enough fuel on board for the diesel engine to give a cruising range of almost 400 miles, because during September there are sometimes calms which may last two or three days. Winds proved to be light and variable and the engine had to be used at times to push ahead as fast as possible. (See Figs. 35, 36, pp. 208, 209)

The first indication of an approaching storm came on Wednesday morning, 2 September, at about 0800, when the barometer started to fall very rapidly. *Force Seven* was then under full main and genoa, averaging about 7¼ knots with the wind on the starboard beam from the east. As the barometer fell the wind increased and by 1030 the jib had been lowered and stowed and the boat was making roughly the same speed under mainsail only. Here I will pick up Warren Brown's account in his own words of what was to follow.

"Soon after this, the sky started to darken and contrails high in the sky were replaced by low cloud and rain squalls. The wind increased rapidly from 30 to 45 knots, and we dropped our mainsail at noon, just before a vicious squall hit, with gusts of well over 50 knots. The seas by this time had built up considerably, and with the barometer dropping alarmingly, I realized that we were in for what I thought at the time would be a severe depression of relatively short duration. We were on the southern edge of the Gulf Stream by our dead reckoning position and water thermometer readings, which we had taken since early that morning, which showed that the water temperature had increased six degrees.

"Shortly after 1300, when we had been under bare poles for one hour, I picked up a radio report from the United States that hurricane *Cleo* had reversed herself off the coast and had picked up speed and intensity. She was once again a full-fledged hurricane. Her estimated position was, according to my dead reckoning, almost exactly the same as ours! I now realized why the barometer had fallen so rapidly, and knew that we were in for a jolly good pasting.

"Not wishing to alarm the crew, I did not report this fact to them, especially since we had youngsters aboard. However, we set to work immediately to rig the ship for severe weather conditions. All ventilators were removed and stowed below, and the appropriate ventilator plates were fitted to replace them and screwed into position. The deck was cleared of everything movable and the main boom was lashed amidships by handybillies, making it completely immobile. All jibs were stowed below and the mainsail itself was securely lashed so that no matter how hard it blew, it could not shake itself loose. All hatches were secured.

"By four o'clock in the afternoon the seas were masthead height, the wind was still increasing, and visibility had diminished considerably. Tops of seas were already breaking over us. One factor which worried us at this point was the dinghy lashed to the top of the cabin. We decided that, secured in this way, the dinghy definitely placed extra strain in the cabin roof, so we moved the lashing to the base of the stanchions. By five o'clock we were in the full force of the storm, and averaging six to seven knots downwind. One minute we were on top of a huge sea, and the next we were down in a hollow out of the wind. The only visibility we had was on top of each wave. In the late afternoon we sighted a huge tanker, also running away from the storm, keeping the wind on her port quarter.

"In the meantime we tried to keep the seas on our starboard quarter. The wind by this time had swung from the east into the north so that we were running approximately southwest, and I realized that the storm must be passing very close to the south.

"Since I had experienced gales off the coast of the States as well as in the North Atlantic, I knew *Force Seven* was encountering a very different set of sea conditions. The reason for this was that the wind was blowing against the current of the Stream, and the seas were very much shorter between the crests, and very much deeper than they would have been in the open ocean. Every sea was extremely steep and every wave was breaking at the top.

"How hard was it blowing? Quite frankly, I do not know. When conditions increased above 65, it is impossible to tell from the deck of a small boat whether it was blowing 70, 80 or 90. Visibility was so restricted and the weather so dark that everything was a confusion of sea, wind, foam, and driving rain. We learned afterwards, however, from the Coast Guard in New London, that the tanker we had spotted reported winds of 83 knots at the time.

"By 1700, steering had become extremely difficult, and of concern for the deck watch. We criss-crossed the cockpit completely with rope, giving handholds for every movement in this area as a safety measure additional to safety belts. Watches were put at two hours, one man watching the sea while the other steered. The problem facing us was keeping the boat going fast enough in order to keep out of the way of the huge breaking seas by sliding down their sides and keeping them on the quarter. If we failed to react fast enough, the sea would break completely over us and would fill the cockpit. If, on the other hand, we kept the sea directly on the stern, we were in the dangerous position of surfing on a downward slope for a quarter of a mile at a speed of about 15 knots. This was not a safe thing to do, as we might have had the full weight of one of these seas break on top of us.

"The question of being scared never came into the picture of our predicament; it was more a question of apprehension. We knew that if we broached at any time we could very easily lose the top of our cabin, the most vulnerable part of the boat.

"At 1745 one exceptionally bad wave hit us on the stern and put us on our beam ends, filling the cockpit from leeward as we went over on our side. Luckily we righted in time to keep out of the way of the next sea.

"We learned one very valuable lesson. In order to keep manoeuvrability we should have had larger cockpit drains. The two that we had could not drain the water fast enough and the boat became sluggish as the cockpit filled. After this experience, I would never build a boat with a large cockpit in which the forward end leads directly into the cabin. If the hatch were to be broken by a heavy sea, any flooding of the cockpit would drain directly belowships.

"It was so rough by 1800 that the constantly filling cockpit and our being knocked down by breaking waves became a matter of routine. The brackets on the stern in which the life-rings rested became useless, as the rings were plucked out by the sea. One was washed away and the other was grabbed by an alert crew member as it went over the side. It was obvious that our life-ring brackets were not designed for this kind of weather.

"The radio insulation blocks on our backstay started to break up under the strain, but, fortunately, the backstay did not slack enough to allow the mast to whip around. Our great danger was the possibility of broaching and being rolled over sideways or being turned head to wind. It would have been virtually impossible for any sailing boat to heave to under the conditions we faced that evening, without being torn apart completely. The waves were so steep and such a short distance apart that the seas would have broken over our decks and would have swept our small boat clean.

"A second great hazard was our dinghy. We were tempted to throw it overboard, but did not do so as we felt it might be picked up and a report given out that we had been lost at sea. Given the same circumstances again I would not hesitate to do so, as the dinghy constituted a danger not only to the boat, but to the crew, in case it was swept aft. I would also strongly recommend two life rafts in place of a dinghy for anyone making a sea voyage at this time of the year.

"If we had dragged warps, we would not have been able to control the speed of the boat to get out of the way of the huge breakers and it would not have been long before we had the full weight of one, which would have caused major damage.

"From 1800 until about 2200 that night it was a constant battle, with one man watching the sea and the other steering. The boat was continually being flooded by breaking tops of the waves, or being filled from leeward by knock-downs. Every small opening in the superstructure was leaking and despite the small hatch opening, it was a continuing race to stop gallons of water from flooding below. By 1100 the following morning [3 September] the wind had abated to about 45 knots, but we did not put the sail back on again until midday as the seas had still not improved. To have made any headway directly into them would have been impossible.

"During the course of the storm we had travelled under bare poles approximately 120 miles in a southwesterly direction, but had actually covered only about 70 to 80 miles over the bottom, as we were running against the flow of the Stream.

"It was not until Saturday, September 5th, at about 1600, we found ourselves just off Block Island, at which time the Coast Guard picked up our weak radio. They forwarded the news to Bermuda and sent out a plane which flew over us a few hours before our arrival in Newport.

"Upon our return to Bermuda we plotted our position against the track of the storm with the local C.G. units and with one of the C.G. ships stationed in the Colony. The plottings confirmed that *Cleo* was indeed a fickle lady. Not only had she reversed herself and turned into a full fledged hurricane again, but had actually gone south to pick up speed. At one point she had moved over 100 miles in just six hours. Our estimated position when she crossed our bow at approximately 1800, September 2nd, at the height of the blow, was approximately 45 miles from the centre, and the fact that she was moving so rapidly probably kept us from a worse beating than if she had stopped in her tracks."

Conclusions

This is one of the most modest and instructive accounts which I have read of the experience of an averaged-sized yacht in a hurricane. Let us attempt to assess the force of the wind when hurricane *Cleo* passed close to the yacht.

First of all, it will have been noted that Warren Brown states frankly that he does not know the strength of the wind. I have long put forward the view that one cannot estimate wind forces above those with which one is familiar. For the average cruising or ocean racing man, this is about Force 7 to Force 8. As Warren Brown says, how can one possibly tell from the deck of a small boat whether it is blowing 70, 80 or 90?

I have obtained full particulars of *Cleo* from the U.S. National Weather Center and the track of the hurricane is reproduced here by their permission. Superimposed on this, are the approximate positions of *Force Seven*.

The early stages of development in hurricane *Cleo* moved off the West African

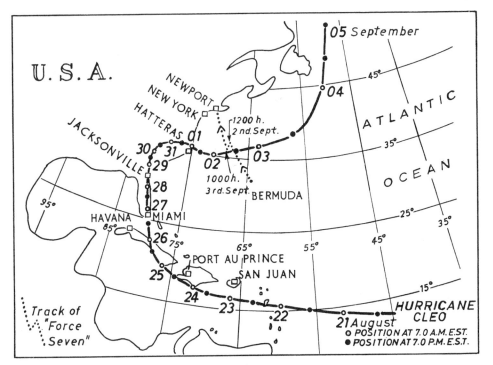

35   Track of Hurricane Cleo, 1964.

Coast south of Dakar on 15 August, with a minimum pressure of 1006 millibars. The disturbance intensified rapidly with a central pressure of 992 millibars and with winds of hurricane force by 21 August. It swept through the West Indies and the bulletins described it as "a small but extremely dangerous hurricane". The highest winds were estimated to be 120 knots near the centre, with hurricane winds extending 40 miles from the centre in all directions and gale winds extending 150 miles north and 100 miles south. The coast of Florida was reached on 27 August, and sustained winds of over 80 knots were recorded at Miami on the western edge of its eye as it proceeded along the coast. On 28 August *Cleo* moved inland near Savannah, Georgia, and the wind diminished. By Sunday, 30 August, no strong winds were left, but the depression moved out to sea between Norfolk and Hatteras early on 1 September. By the afternoon tropical storm force had been regained and on 2 September *Cleo* had intensified and regained hurricane status over the warm water of the Gulf Stream. The highest winds in the centre, just outside the eye, were 80 knots and gales extended 200 miles from the centre in all quadrants. On 3 September, *Cleo* then curved north-east and northwards and the weather conditions remained much the same. The bulletin on 4 September at 1100 still gave 80 knots near the centre and gales

208

extending 250 miles in all directions. A diminution of the wind force was forecast at the centre, but gale force winds were expected to extend 500 miles to the south-east of the centre.

The words "highest winds" used in the American bulletins appear to mean sustained winds and not merely the gusts at the highest velocity. The official reports therefore corroborate everything that Mr. Warren Brown has stated. It is probable that when *Force Seven* was nearest the eye of the hurricane she experienced winds which, according to the accompanying graph, were of a mean strength of about 68 knots (hurricane force) with gusts of 83 knots as reported by the tanker when near by.

I have seen the list of the observations from ships passing in the vicinity of *Cleo*, but unfortunately there is a gap between 29 August and 4 September. After *Cleo* had passed *Force Seven* and proceeded to the north-east, there is a report on 4 September from S.S. *American Challenger* in position 45.5° N. and

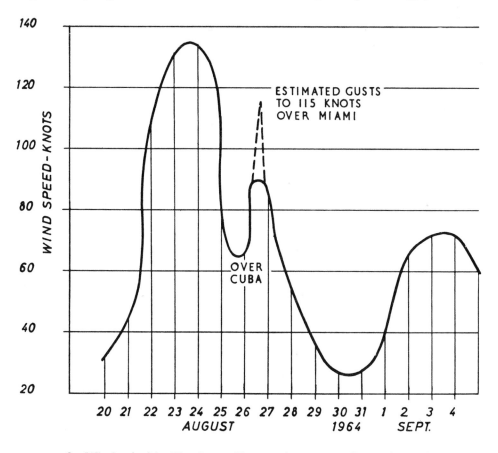

36 Wind velocities Hurricane Cleo, 20 August to 4 September 1964.

50.0° W. of the westerly winds of 80 knots. The master of the *Queen Mary* reported it as the worst blow he had experienced since 1939, and that the *Queen Mary*'s stabilizers had rolled out of water.

The height of the waves was observed to be about the height of *Force Seven*'s mast, which would be about 50 ft. if my formula of three-fifths the observed height of a wave is accepted as a fair estimate of the real height, that gives a height of 30 ft. However, recent oceanographic research and methods of measurement suggest that the height of the highest waves might have been considerably greater.

The principal lessons to be learnt from the experiences of *Force Seven* are:

1. *Storm tactics*. Warren Brown had given considerable thought to what he would do if he was caught out in a yacht in such an exceptional storm as this. He adopted what appear to me to be new tactics for survival in a hurricane. He considered the seas in the Gulf Stream were too dangerous for heaving-to or lying a-hull. He did not experiment with the general accepted practice of dragging warps. He had two very long heavy warps in the cockpit ready to stream astern in a bight, but he did not use them, because had he done so he believes he would not have sufficient control of the boat to avoid the worst of the seas. He says that if he had trailed warps it would not have been long before the full weight of a breaking sea would have caused major damage.

He found that when running with the seas directly on the stern the yacht surfed on the downward slope of a big wave for a quarter of a mile at a speed of about 15 knots, risking being pooped. Warren Brown is a master of understatement when he writes: "This was not a safe thing to do . . . as we might have the full weight of one of these seas break on top of us." Accordingly, he altered course to bring the seas on the quarter, though I get the impression that he kept *Force Seven* maintaining about 5 to 7 knots under bare pole. He states that he found speed essential to safety, for if the helmsman failed to react fast enough, "the seas would break completely over the yacht and fill the cockpit".

In Chapter 8 in this book I commented that *Cohoe* got pooped in a moderate gale because she was not running fast enough to give the helmsman sufficient control to hold her stern to the bigger seas. But this is the first time I have read of a yacht running through a hurricane under bare poles at such a speed without streaming warps. Some may consider this rank heresy, of course, but I would point out that, apart from knockdowns, *Force Seven* came through the hurricane unscathed in conditions in which many yachts might have gone to the bottom. More evidence in favour of this tactic in exceptional gales is afforded by *Joshua*, when caught out in a storm in the South Pacific, to which I refer in the next chapter.

2. *Preparation for gales*. As soon as the radio warning was received by *Force Seven* everything on the yacht was properly secured and she was prepared to cope

with the approaching storm. In this connection, two points are of particular interest.

The first is that the dinghy lashed to the top of the cabin was regarded as a potential danger, because of the strain it would have imposed on the cabin structure if it had been struck by a heavy sea, and because if the dinghy were torn away it might injure the crew. Yachts have carried dinghies on their cabin tops without experiencing trouble in countless gales of Force 8 or Force 9, but the possible danger of a dinghy if a yacht is caught out in a survival storm may not have occurred to everybody. This is a point stressed both by Joe C. Byars and Warren Brown. Happily, most yachts now carry rubber boats which make less resistance than a rigid dinghy.

The second point is that Warren Brown gives a useful tip as a safety precaution in a storm. By criss-crossing the cockpit completely with ropes, he provided handholds for his crew to grip when *Force Seven* was knocked down. It is not uncommon for part of the crew to be swept out of the cockpit if a yacht is knocked down in a heavy gale, and several went overboard even in the gale of the Bermuda Race of 1960. In most cases crews are saved by their safety harnesses, but obviously it is preferable not to go overboard at all, and the criss-cross of ropes seems a practical idea to help prevent accident of this sort..

3. *Fear.* A major storm or a hurricane is something of an ordeal in a small yacht. However, I think Warren Brown hits the nail on the head when he says: "The question of being scared never came into the picture. It was more a question of apprehension." The word "apprehension" is the right one, because there is always an element of the unknown in a real gale.

4. *Cabin entrance.* Warren Brown states that he would never in any circumstances build a small boat with a cabin entrance (with doors or wash boards) entered directly from the cockpit. *Force Seven* has a very small companionway entered from above and this probably saved her, as the seas which broke into the cockpit time after time might have stove in doors from the cockpit to the companionway as arranged in most yachts.

5. *Working on deck.* The tremendous violence of a hurricane will be appreciated when it is stated that it took twenty-five minutes to move the Beaufort life-raft from its position forward of the mast to the cockpit, where it might be wanted. A man had to inch his way forward with two safety lines. Lines had also to be run forward so that the raft would not be washed away. Difficulty in working on deck occurs at Force 10 (as was experienced by *Tilly Twin* in the Channel Storm of 1956), and at Force 12 any movement on deck becomes dangerous.

6. *Other points. Force Seven* confirms experiences in many lesser gales. The bad visibility when seas are very high, the way water finds its way below like penetrating oil, and the inadequacy of drains of the ordinary "self-emptying" cockpit. It is also interesting to note that *Force Seven's* life-rings were washed away,

like those of *Doubloon* when she was capsized. Normal brackets for lifebuoys appear to be useless in this kind of weather, though it is difficult to think of a substitute, as if lifebuoys are lashed down they cannot be cast off quickly. A final point is that radio insulation blocks on the backstay can be a source of weakness. I have never had these blocks in my own boats as I always suspected them. Warren Brown has confirmed that these doubts are not without foundation.

20

SURVIVAL STORMS

The difference between a gale and what has become known as a "survival" storm is that in the former, with winds of Force 8, or perhaps 9 (say 30 to 45 knots mean velocity), the skipper and crew retain control and can take the measures which they think best, whereas in a survival gale of Force 10 or over, perhaps gusting at hurricane strength, wind and sea become the masters. For skipper and crew it is then a battle to keep the yacht afloat. There is no navigation, except rough D.R., because the course is dictated by the need to take the breaking crests of the seas at the best angle.

In this chapter I shall deal broadly with a few further experiences of yachts involved in survival storms and hurricanes and the lessons to be drawn from them.

Where yachts more commonly get caught out in storms and hurricanes is on the western side of the Atlantic. It is for this reason that I have turned to America and the American magazine *Yachting* for information about survival storms, as the principal danger area lies on the route between the New England yachting centres and Bermuda, Florida and the Caribbean. The principal hazards are the tropical storms, with closed isobars and mean wind force between 34 and 63 knots, and the hurricanes with wind force of 64 knots or more, with gusts possibly reaching 170 knots. The maximum velocity is not exactly known, as most anemometers disintegrate at about 125 knots. Hurricanes as a rule occur betweem June and November and principally in September, but there can be out-of-season ones at pretty well any time of the year. According to Captain Edwin T. Harding, U.S. Navy (the author of *Heavy Weather Guide* and a meteorological specialist in the subject), waves of 35 to 40 ft. are not uncommon in an average hurricane and, in giant storms, build up to 45 to 50 ft. Waves even higher have been reported, but happily they are very rare.

Bermuda yachtsmen tell me that during the winter there are severe storms in the Atlantic which, while not termed hurricanes, are equally formidable. They may last for a duration of three days with winds reaching the vicinity of 85 knots, well above hurricane force. Yachts do not always survive such severe storms. For example, the 70 ft. schooner *Margot* or *H.S.H.* (Home Sweet Home) left Bermuda at 1700 on a January evening bound south. The weather forecast was good for fifty miles south of Bermuda, but by 2000 the same night the wind reached 85 knots locally and for the next week the minimum winds recorded at Bermuda were 50 knots. The schooner has never been heard of since. It is thought that she went down on the first evening while running under bare poles, and that her extra large cockpit and unsafe companionway resulted in her being flooded by a following sea. It is not known whether she was towing warps or whether her loss could have been averted had she done so.

Another example of a winter storm was that experienced by the 68 ft. schooner *Curlew*, which left Mystic, Conn., in a fresh north-wester on Sunday, 11 November 1962, bound to the Caribbean for charter service. She was skippered by Captain David Skellon, an Englishman, and the mate was Ed Lowe, a Connecticut sailor. The two of them were the only deep-water sailors aboard and they took the helm in turns during the whole of the nights in the bad weather which followed. By Wednesday morning the wind was northerly, about Force 10, and the yacht was running under bare poles. A number of troubles had already developed, the most serious being the failure of the braking screw that kept the propeller shaft from turning and a bad leak in the propeller-shaft packing. The bilge pump operated by the main engine was only just capable of keeping ahead of the leak.

The storm steadily increased during Wednesday and throughout the night. *Curlew* had entered the Gulf Stream, where the seas became more dangerous. In the second watch the following morning she suffered her first real broach-to, and was knocked flat on her beam ends for almost three minutes before she slowly righted. After straightening the yacht out before the storm, the crew streamed a 3 in. warp astern in a long loop, with drags lashed to it.

On Thursday the seas were higher than ever and the wind was estimated as gusting 75-80. At 0700 a mountainous sea broke over the full length of the ship and stove in the main cabin skylight. As a result of Mayday calls to Bermuda *Curlew* was spotted by a search plane and at 1400 the U.S.S. *Compass Island* hove into sight.

The yacht then continued to run under bare poles on her course for Bermuda, with *Compass Island* standing by and giving course instructions by radio telephone. This says a lot for David Skellon's tough efficiency, operating the telephone and navigating below with water almost up to his waist, swilling over the charts and chart table. That night *Curlew*, under a lee created by *Compass Island*, succeeded in getting within a quarter mile of the flashing buoy off St. George's Harbour. Shelter was at last at hand. But the wind must have shifted and it was so violent that no further progress could be made against it, even with the help of her powerful engine. Like *Dancing Ledge* off Cherbourg it was impossible to gain harbour and *Curlew* had to run off. By then the yacht's condition was critical and, as the weather forecast predicted a continuance of the storm for another 24 hours, there was no alternative left but to run off and abandon her.

Curlew manoeuvred alongside, under the lee of *Compass Island*, but in doing so broke her bowsprit and carried away her foremast and shrouds against the ship's side. Nevertheless, all the crew were rescued by *Compass Island* without injury by means of cargo nets—a creditable performance at night with wind little below hurricane force.

Now comes the strange ending to this story. Three days later it was reported that *Curlew* had been sighted. She was located and towed back safely into St. George's Harbour. By then there was some 5 ft. of water above the cabin sole and everything below had been smashed, but after survey it was found that the hull was undamaged. All her seams and fastenings were as good as new. She is Everdur fastened, mahogany planked over white oak, with teak decks.

Curlew's was a remarkable survival of a storm stated to be the largest low-pressure in the area for forty years. The 56 ft. schooner *Windfall*, which left Mystic at the same time as *Curlew* on the same course for Bermuda, was never heard of again, as she broke up. All four of her crew were lost, and when last seen by a freighter they were hanging on to wreckage, but the weather was so bad that the freighter was not able to do anything to help them. Nine other ships were in distress at the same time as *Curlew*, and altogether the sea claimed over 144 seamen.

What is confirmed by the experiences in this storm is that once wind and sea have risen to or near hurricane force there is no knowing what will happen. *Windfall* was sunk, but *Curlew* survived, despite being partially waterlogged. Her tactic of running off, streaming warps, may have saved her, but despite this she broached several times. It is probable that *Windfall* may also have streamed warps, because it was the recognized method of coping with following seas.

Captain Skellon's log of *Curlew*'s ordeal appeared in *Yachting*, February 1963. There are several comments I should like to make:

(1) The value of *mechanical aids*. It was the engine-operated bilge pump in *Curlew* which enabled the leak to be kept under control, and the radio telephone which summoned assistance.

(2) The weakness of many *steering wheels*. Five spokes of *Curlew*'s wheel were broken when a man was swept against it by breaking seas. Damage to wheels is by no means rare in gales.

(3) That *broaching to* in a storm, however violent, is not necessarily disastrous.

(4) That a yacht may survive despite being *partially waterlogged*. This is evidenced both by *Tzu Hang* (to which I refer in this chapter) and *Curlew* in circumstances where one would imagine survival to have been impossible. After she had been abandoned *Curlew* must have drifted out into the full force of the storm and yet left to herself she remained afloat lying a-hull with water several feet above her cabin sole.

(5) The difficulty, or virtual impossibility, experienced by a *rescuing ship* in lying alongside without damaging a yacht in order to take off her crew. A ship has to lie close alongside to ensure saving the men, and in heavy

seas there is grave risk of the yacht's mast breaking against the ship's side. The mast may then provide an additional hazard, as the broken part and rigging will flail around, and may prove a lethal weapon if it strikes the crew or rescuers as they are climbing the scrambling nets. I am told that an alternative procedure which might be used today for rescue (such as the survivors of *Windfall* clinging to wreckage) would be

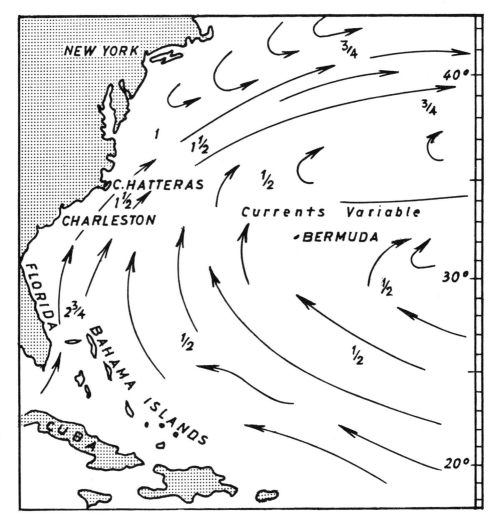

37(a) Gulf Stream current (approx. rate in knots). The diagram shows average summer conditions, but the stream varies in direction and rate in knots and is often much stronger than shown. It causes exceptional seas when the wind is contrary to the stream and its meanders provide a time-honoured speculation for navigators in the Bermuda Race.

25. *Ultimate Storm.* The following series of incredible pictures were taken by Captain de Lange in North Atlantic gales of about Force 10/11, between 35 and 45 N. Seas such as are depicted are experienced by freighters on the West Indies run about once in four years, and hence might not be encountered by a yacht even in a lifetime of voyaging. The pictures show the height seas can attain. A yacht might ride the huge sea in the foreground but look at the 'freak' wave coming up astern.

26. Bernard Moitessier describes the seas which *Joshua* encountered in the South Pacific as 'breaking without interruption from 650 to nearly 1,000 ft.' He ran under bare pole taking them 15° to 20° on the quarter to avoid being pitchpoled. The yacht was of steel construction, steered from within a steel cupola. *Photo: de Laage*

27. Close up picture of a following sea. It is difficult to understand how any yacht, or even a small ship, can survive in such seas.
Photo: de Lange.

28. In storms of extreme violence seas can become absolutely chaotic. Note the perpendicular wave rising against the sky at the left centre. This remarkable picture looks as if it comes from another world. *Photo: de Lange.*

to try and make a lee and drift rubber life-rafts to anyone overboard, as ships lifeboats are useless under these conditions. The difficulty would be that the ship would drift rapidly to leeward down on the yacht, so great skill in handling the ship would be required.

Curlew may not have experienced the worst conditions of the Gulf Stream, as in her position the wind appears to have been blowing across rather than against the stream, though I am told that there is nothing certain about its course or velocity. Normally, the maximum strength of the Gulf Stream is found in the Straits of Florida and where it flows northward towards Cape Hatteras. Here, in northerly gales against the stream, the seas in the axis of the stream are more dangerous to a yacht in an ordinary gale than those in a storm or possibly even a hurricane in the open Atlantic. This accounts for *Doubloon*'s experience of being twice turned over and possibly for the loss of *Revenoc*, one of the most deeply felt yachting disasters on the American side of the Atlantic.

Revenoc was a Sparkman & Stephens designed, outside-ballasted, centreboard yawl. Her dimensions were 42 ft. 7 in. L.O.A., 29 ft. 7 in. L.W.L., 11 ft. 10 in. beam, 4 ft. 6 in. draught, with a sail area of 883 sq. ft. She was built to the highest specification and particularly well equipped for cruising and ocean racing.

On 1 January 1958 the yawl sailed from Key West bound for Miami. In her sailed her owner and skipper, Harvey Conover, his son Lawrence Conover, their two wives, and William Fluegelman. The crew were highly experienced. Harvey Conover was a veteran deep-water sailor who had sailed since boyhood and was a former commodore of the Cruising Club of America. His son, aged 26, had been brought up with boats and was a first-class seaman. William Fluegelman had sailed a great deal with the Conovers and was a former Coast Guardsman. Mrs. Harvey Conover was an able and experienced hand and Mrs. Lawrence Conover had also sailed extensively in the two *Revenoc*'s.

On 2 January a NNE. gale gusting 65 knots struck the area without warning. The Weather Bureau summary as reported in *Yachting* read: "A big high pressure area over south-eastern U.S. was pushing back a broad, not especially severe, cold front south-easterly across Florida, the Florida Straits and the Bahamas. Meanwhile a small, intense low pressure centre [not reported until Thursday, when *Revenoc* was expected at Miami] suddenly developed on Wednesday over western Cuba, moving north-east across the path of the front. As they approached each other, the clockwise wind pattern of the front and the counter-clockwise wind around the low centre, both blowing from a generally NNE. direction, combined to set up a sudden gale with terrific gusts in the Florida Straits before daylight Thursday."

The seas under these conditions on the axis of the Gulf Stream would have been fantastic. It was in this storm that *Revenoc* was lost with all hands. No trace of her was ever found except for her swamped dinghy, which drifted ashore near Jupiter Inlet on 6 January, having been carried northward by the current.

The loss may have been caused by many things. Most probably, as *Yachting* suggests, it could have been by being run down by a ship at night, because shipping is heavy where she was caught out and, as I have remarked, a yacht's lights may be lost in the seas and spray of a gale. It could also have been accounted for by a mast over the side damaging the hull beyond repair before it could be cleared away, by the yacht being driven on to outlying coral reefs, or by a rogue sea stoving in the superstructure or decks or rolling her over like *Doubloon*.

The answer will never be known, but the tactics adopted in *Revenoc* can be guessed at. In an article by Carlton Mitchell in *Yachting* of June 1956 an extract was quoted from a letter by Harvey Conover, after he had been caught out before in a Gulf Stream storm in *Revenoc*. In this gale (gusting 56 to 65) he had run at 2 or 3 knots under bare poles towing warps so satisfactorily that he thought the yawl would take almost anything by this means. So, provided he had enough sea room, it is most probable that *Revenoc* was running before the storm trailing warps (and perhaps sails) on her last voyage. This is conjecture and the only lesson to be learnt from the tragedy is that no yacht, however sound, and no crew, however experienced, are immune from the dangers of the sea.

Returning now to the subject of hurricanes, let us consider Jean Gau's 29 ft. 6 in. ketch *Atom*, caught out in the path of hurricane *Carrie* in September 1957, about 360 miles south of Montauk Point, Long Island. She survived lying a-hull streaming one warp and with oil bags secured to the weather rigging screws. There are four points which may have helped her in weathering the storm. After crossing the Atlantic, her bottom was so foul that she lay almost dormant in the water. Her draught was only 4 ft. 6 in. and she had 2 tons of iron on her keel and 2 tons of inside ballast. She was thus of a type that would be difficult to capsize and there would be less tendency to be tripped by a long shallow keel than a deep narrow one. It is probable that she had a low rig, though I have no particulars of this. *Atom* was in the track of *Carrie*, but about 160 miles to the northward of Bermuda *Carrie* changed her mind, and sped off eastward across the Atlantic and finally made a precise landfall on the Fastnet Rock off south-western Ireland. As I have no particulars of *Atom*'s course to compare with the track of the hurricane, I do not know whether she was anywhere near the centre, but even if she avoided the worst she would have been involved in gales so severe that they might come into survival storm category.

Atom's evidence is thus in favour of lying a-hull, but on 26 February 1966 the ketch was caught again between Durban and Cape Town. She lay a-hull with wind and sea on her port beam, but on this occasion she was completely rolled over through 360 degrees. She lost all her spars and sails. Jean Gau was asleep below at the time and fortunately suffered no incapacitating injury. He spent the next fourteen hours pumping the bilges (filled to the cabin sole), cutting away spars threatening to damage the hull, clearing rigging and finally coping with the horrid job of drying out the engine. Then under power he managed to get to Mossel Bay, some 75 miles distant.

The *Atom* had a reliable anemometer, which recorded the wind velocity of 60 knots. Whether this was in gusts or at the mean speed on the Beaufort Scale (which at 60 knots would be Force 11) I do not know.

Jean Gau's experiences show that one can voyage time after time across the oceans without harm, but it takes only one freak wave of particular size and shape, catching the boat on the wrong foot, to do real and sometimes disastrous damage. In this connection it is interesting to turn to Laurence Draper's Appendix 2, in which he refers to experiences of big ships between Durban and Cape Town and explains the possibility of freak troughs as well as freak waves.

One of the most remarkable stories of yacht survival in a hurricane was that of *Pendragon*, which was involved in *Carol* in 1954.

Pendragon was lying in the somewhat insecure Gosport harbour at the Isles of Shoals, situated in the Atlantic to the north-east of Boston. She is a cutter measuring 41 ft. L.O.A., 30 ft. L.W.L., 10 ft. beam and 6 ft. 3 in. in draught, built by Nevins in 1935. Her crew consisted of William H. Mathers and his wife Myra and two friends, Mr. and Mrs. Smoot.

Meanwhile hurricane *Carol* had stalled over North Carolina, but on the Tuesday morning, 31 August, came the startling news that she was well on her way again, moving up the New England Coast. The warning arrived too late to make a better harbour. In *Pendragon* all preparations were carried out for *Carol*'s arrival, but at the height of the storm a ketch began to drag and *Pendragon*'s cable had to be cut to clear her. The wind was too strong to enable them to regain shelter under the lee of the breakwater upwind under engine, so in order to avoid going on the rocks *Pendragon* proceeded to sea in the dangerous quadrant of the hurricane.

Once in the open the seas were found to be mountainous and the full weight of the hurricane winds was experienced. What we are concerned with here, however, is the method adopted so that the yacht could survive. The extraordinary thing is that she was handled under engine. This is the only occasion that I have heard of where an engine was used in an auxiliary yacht in open water during a gale, let alone in a hurricane. It seems to me that the average auxiliary engine would be useless even at Force 7, though I have never tried the experiment at sea. So I wrote to Mr. Mathers and from his answer it appears that it was done in this way.

The engine was a four-cylinder Gray with a rating of 25 h.p. It was fitted with a 2:1 reduction gear giving a propeller speed of about 800 r.p.m. in the hurricane. The propeller was 18 in. in diameter with a relatively flat pitch. In the hurricane *Pendragon* was steered in the troughs beam to the seas. The crests were about 300/400 ft. apart. In the troughs (where the yacht was under the partial lee of the waves), the engine gave enough power to give a speed of about 2½ knots, which gave her skipper sufficient control to luff to the breaking crests of the seas, sufficiently to prevent her from being rolled over.

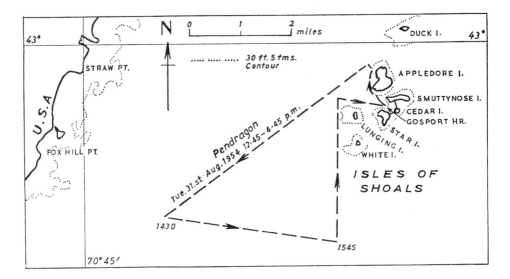

37(b)   Course of *Pendragon* during Hurricane Carol.

Pendragon's course is shown on the accompanying diagram. First she ran before the storm and her rather fine bow seemed to bury and "her stern would lift, which made the rudder almost useless. At the bottom of each wave she would turn one way or another at her own discretion and roll badly. In one of the troughs she rolled so far that she took in green water over the cockpit coaming."

Owing to the dangers and the outlying rocks off Duck Island, *Pendragon* could not be run off to east or north-east away from the centre of the hurricane. For this reason, after clearing Appledore Island, William Mathers rounded on to the port tack heading SW., although this would bring her nearer the centre of the storm. At about 1400 the sky cleared considerably in the west and the wind definitely let up. Half an hour later the wind veered from SE. to S. and SW., and *Pendragon* was able to lay to the E. and SE. A tiny patch of blue—a beautiful deep blue—appeared and disappeared before returning again and gave moments of warmth and better visibility. At 1545 the lighthouse on one of the islands in the Isles of Shoals was seen. The yacht was run off to the northward and an hour later she was safely back in harbour. As Myra Mathers puts it "it did seem somewhat incongruous to crash around for four hours unable to see anything and end up exactly where we started".

The only accident occurred when a sea hit *Pendragon* on the port quarter, just as the helmsmen were being changed and the yacht was momentarily off course. Myra Mathers had handed the tiller to her husband and was sliding past him when she was catapulted head first into the sea and drifted 25 ft. to leeward. Her head struck a stanchion as she went overboard.

By a stroke of good fortune, the sea had knocked the yacht to a standstill and the hurricane winds quickly drove her to leeward to Myra Mathers, who was then picked up. Much the same thing happened when *Tzu Hang* was pitchpoled in the Pacific, to which I refer later, and Beryl Smeeton was thrown 30 yards to leeward. As the yacht had been dismasted, she was partially waterlogged and lay motionless. Beryl Smeeton, although injured, swam to the floating wreckage of the mizzenmast and pulled herself along to the side of *Tzu Hang*.

In both yachts the difficulty was to pull the survivor, weighed down by sodden clothes, out of the water into the safety of the cockpit. Myra Mathers was temporarily entangled round a stanchion, but once this was realized, she was quickly hauled on board *Pendragon*. The rescue of Beryl Smeeton in *Tzu Hang* was even harder, because she was unable to help with one arm owing to the injury to her shoulder. It took the combined strength of the two men to get her on board.

Hurricane *Carol*, in which *Pendragon* was involved, was intense, causing tremendous damage and insurance claims. During its unexpected dart up the New England coast, it blew down a 630 ft. television tower on the roof of the radio station at Lynn, Massachusetts, so no further weather forecasts were received from that source. It also toppled over a crane on the breakwater at the Isles of Shoals just before *Pendragon* started on her hurricane cruise. It is remarkable that, although *Pendragon* was rolled over until her spreaders were in the water and the cockpit filled, she survived with no more damage than might occur in an ordinary gale. She fared better at sea in the hurricane than most of the yachts which had taken shelter in harbour, where houses broke up and floated down on the anchored vessels and boards, planks and other land objects took to the air, striking rigging and endangering crews. Great numbers of yachts broke their moorings or dragged their anchors and went ashore.

Points to note are:

(1) It was only William Mathers's quick decision to put to sea that saved *Pendragon* from the fate that befell many yachts in harbour. Big ships sometimes leave port when hurricanes are anticipated, as they are safer in deep water far from land, but I have not heard before of a yacht doing so. However, I am not familiar with hurricane areas, so I write with no authority on this matter.

(2) Attention is drawn to the difficulty of recovering a man or woman overboard even when alongside the yacht. The added weight of sodden clothes and the violent motion of a yacht in a storm combine to make the task unexpectedly difficult. This is particularly significant when a yacht's crew consist of two only, such as the owner and his wife. If one goes over the side, even if a hold is retained, the weight could be too much for the one remaining on deck. In such an event a rope ladder or steps could make all the difference.

(3) A yacht provided with enough power and with a big slow-revolving propeller, may be able to survive a hurricane, as *Pendragon* did. In her case, the seas seem to have been so immense and so long that enough speed could be obtained in the troughs to luff to the crests, but I doubt whether this would be possible in short and very confused seas. Furthermore, I do not think *Pendragon*'s tactics could be adopted by a yacht equipped with a high-revving propeller, as the strain would be too great on the shaft with the propeller alternately racing in the air and at full load in the water.

Most of the gales and storms which I have described occurred in waters frequented by yachts and thus they afford practical examples of what can happen when engaged in ordinary cruising on the American side of the Atlantic, but some of the worst storms and the highest seas are found in the high southern latitudes, where yachts rarely sail except for the occasional world voyagers or Cape Horners.

The classic example of a storm of supreme violence in the South Pacific Ocean was afforded by William Albert Robinson when he was caught out in one in 1952 about 40° 45′ 50. Robinson had circumnavigated the globe and is one of the best-known and most experienced deep-sea cruising men of this generation. He had had experiences of other storms and recorded hurricanes, but the storm which he describes as "The Ultimate Storm" in his book *To the Great Southern Sea* was by far the greatest that he had experienced in a lifetime of deep-sea voyaging.

His yacht was named *Varua*. She was a brigantine of 70 ft. overall length, designed by the late Starling Burgess in consultation with her owner for deep-sea voyaging, to be capable of weathering exceptional gales and storms and able to run before them cleanly with little risk of broaching-to. As yachts go she was a big ship, and she owes her survival to size, design and her owner's experience. I do not think any ordinary yacht, such as yours or mine, could have lived through the ordeal which she encountered.

During the storm *Varua* lay-to under forestaysail and lower staysail until the seas reached such a height and steepness that her sails were alternately blanketed in the troughs and blasted by gusts on the crests. They were then lowered and *Varua* lay a-hull. Instead of lashing the helm down (as I do, rightly or wrongly) the wheel was lashed amidships and, finding her natural drift, the brigantine fell off several points and headed slowly downwind with the seas on her quarter. Oil was used and Robinson states that the slick was more effective than when the boat was hove-to, when most of it was blown to leeward.

The gale backed slowly from north-east to north, and towards midnight *Varua* began to get out of control. "The seas were so huge and concave at this point that the whole upper third seemed to collapse and roar vertically down on us. Our oil had little or no effect now, as the surface water was all being blown to leeward."

Robinson unlashed the wheel and ran her off downwind dead before the storm, gathering speed under bare poles to 6 or 7 knots. As he considered this dangerous, he let go five 75 ft. lengths of 2 in. warps plus 100 fathoms of smaller lines. This reduced her speed to 3 or 4 knots and she steered under perfect control, and the oil slick seemed more effective at this lower speed. Nevertheless, at times she ran down a sea and buried her bowsprit in the trough before rising again. Robinson says that if *Varua* had not been trailing drags she might have run right down. As he puts it, "When a fifty-ton, seventy-foot vessel surfboards shudderingly down the face of a great sea on its breaking crest, you have experienced something."

The detailed description of this storm should be read in Robinson's book, but briefly his points are:

(1) Conventional methods of riding out the average gale are totally inadequate in exceptional storms in the ocean. He absolutely condemns sea anchors for deep-keeled hulls in extreme storms. He contends that "the greatest effort of wind and wave-crests is exerted on the forward part of the ship, which has the least grip on solid water. Thus as the vessel makes sternway, as it is bound to do while riding to a sea anchor, the bow falls off, pivoting on the after-part of the hull, which has deeper grip on the water." This explains the reason for what many cruising men have found in lesser gales. He goes on to question the value of a riding sail in an ocean storm, as, even if it stood up to the blasts of wind

on the crests, it would be becalmed and ineffective in the troughs. He also draws attention to the risk of the sternway causing the rudder to break.

(2) Robinson states that no ship would have been capable of holding her bow up into such seas as *Varua* experienced without sustaining major damage, and he proved his theory that to survive in such a storm a yacht must be allowed to take her natural position, running dead before the seas under bare poles, "moving just fast enough to retain good steering control, using drags as a brake to prevent going too fast". For *Varua* this meant 3 to 4 knots. As he puts it, "The ship was alive and responsive . . . we had flexibility, choice of action when the wind shifted, freedom to swerve to meet a great sea coming in out of line with the others. And when a monster of a sea did come along and break over us we met it end on, offering the least possible resistance and gave with it."

(3) *Varua* used oil with some effect when she lay-to at the start of the gale, but she was forereaching too fast and much of the oil was left astern. When she was lying a-hull the seas were so concave that the surface water and the oil on it was blown to leeward. Oil seems to have helped when running streaming warps, but a considerable amount must have been used, for besides two oil bags on each side, oil was pumped out through the forward heads.

Tzu Hang in her attempts to round Cape Horn from the Pacific to the Atlantic was involved in survival storms in much the same latitudes as *Varua*. On the first occasion she was manned by a crew of three, consisting of her owner, Brigadier Miles Smeeton, his wife Beryl, and John Guzwell of *Trekka* fame. In this attempt to round Cape Horn she was pitch-poled, stern over bow, when running streaming 60 fathoms of 3-in. hawser. During the second attempt, when she was sailed by Miles Smeeton and his wife alone, another storm was encountered. This time *Tzu Hang* lay a-hull, but she suffered a complete roll over. On both occasions the yacht was dismasted, severely damaged and partially waterlogged. The seas which did the damage must have been "freak" waves, formed by a combination of wave trains with unlimited fetch in the wastes of the Pacific. "Sometimes", wrote Miles Smeeton, in *Once is Enough*, "a wave would seem to break down all its front, a rolling cascading mass of white foam, pouring down the whole surface of the wave like an avalanche down a mountainside."

In weather conditions such as these few yachts would live without sustaining damage, whatever their type and whatever the method of defence adopted. The astonishing thing was that she survived at all. *Tzu Hang* had a tough crew, and temporary repairs were effected on each occasion, but had the seas which did the damage been quickly followed by others equally formidable she surely must have gone to the bottom. Possibly the dismastings enabled her to ride the seas better and thus saved her from this catastrophe, but *Doubloon* was rolled over again after she had been dismasted so one cannot be sure of this.

On the other hand, there are many examples of yachts which have sailed in the Roaring Forties and round Cape Horn without incident or near disaster. This was the "impossible route" chosen by the Argentine, Vito Dumas, for the great single-handed voyage he described in his book *Alone through the Roaring Forties*. Dumas's yacht *Lehg II* was a 31 ft. 2 in. Norwegian type from the board of Manual M. Campos, and was a modernized version of the old Rio de la Plata whaleboats, somewhat akin to a Colin Archer double-ender. She was designed for the purpose of ocean voyaging, with a long keel, and to be easy to steer in all weathers. The ballast keel was $3\frac{1}{2}$ tons of iron and the design provided a high degree of reserve buoyancy. No inside ballast was carried. The success of the design was proved by the apparent ease of steering single-handed without the modern aid of self-steering. There must have been plenty of buoyancy in her pointed stern to have survived the seas which Dumas experienced. In his voyage it was not a matter of a gale here and there but of almost continuous dirty weather, with winds on occasions estimated to be gusting up to 70 knots. His tactics in heavy weather were original. "As regards a sea anchor," he writes, "I have one point of view which settled the question for me; I would never give such an object sea room. I am convinced that a boat can stand up to any sea, comfortably enough, under sail. She has freedom of movement and can lift to the sea. Should the wind force exceed 50 knots I would say, contrary to the opinion that following seas play havoc by breaking on deck, that one of my favourite pleasures was to run through squalls on a mattress of foam. My speed on these surf-riding occasions exceeded 15 knots: I then presented the stern to another wave and began this exciting pastime anew."

Some readers may regard the speed of 15 knots as exaggerated, but the exact speed is immaterial and what is clear is that *Lehg II* experienced the right length of ocean sea which enabled her to surf for appreciable periods at far above her theoretical maximum speed. Dumas does not give any detailed description or advice on how this surfing was accomplished, or of how he managed without self-steering. Surfing in ocean seas can be dangerous on account of the risk of being thrown down into the trough and pitch-poled. However this may be, Dumas ran before gales at about 5 knots and succeeded in sailing round the world in the most dangerous waters that can be found and arriving at the end of the voyage with his boat in perfect condition.

There are more recent examples of yachts which have voyaged in the dangerous waters of the South Pacific and rounded the Horn without resort to streaming warps or any of the conventional methods of weathering gales and storms. When Sir Francis Chichester rounded the Horn in *Gypsy Moth IV* in March 1967, after making a remarkably accurate landfall without a fix of sun or stars for three days and little sleep for a week, he was running under storm jib. It was evidently blowing very hard, with the violent gusts and high seas for which the Horn is notorious. *Gypsy Moth*'s cockpit was filled on five occasions and once it took fifteen minutes for the water to drain away, which provides further evidence of the inadequacy of the drains in self-emptying cockpits.

Gypsy Moth IV ran under storm jib and there is no mention of her streaming warps. Her speed seems to have been between 5 knots and later 7 knots, so this affords another example of a yacht maintaining considerable speed when running in heavy seas before a gale.

Much valuable evidence on the subject of running before storms comes from Monsieur Bernard Moitessier, who, in 1967, was awarded the Blue Water medal of the Cruising Club of America and the Wren Medal for Seamanship of the Royal Cruising Club for his outstanding voyage from Moorea to Alicante via Cape Horn. He has written a book entitled, *Cap Horn a la Voile*, on his experiences but, in the meantime, I am indebted to him and the *Royal Cruising Club Journal* and *Cruising Club News* (published by the C.C.A.) for the following information.

Joshua, in which the voyage was made, is a 39.6 ft. double-ended Bermudian ketch of 12.1 ft. beam and 5.25 ft. draught, designed by Jean Knocker. She is of steel construction and has a fixed keel. The sail area of 960 sq. ft. is considerable for a yacht undertaking such long-distance voyages. A feature of her design is the "pilot's post", which is a metal cupola from which she is steered. *Joshua* left Moorea (the island west of Tahiti) on 23 November 1965 and rounded Cape Horn on 11 January 1966, forty-nine days later. As it chanced, the wind was moderate from the NW. when Cape Horn was rounded. No difficulty was experienced and as with *Tzu Hang* it was in the South Pacific that *Joshua* encountered a "survival" storm in which she nearly foundered. This storm lasted six days and was caused by two low-pressure systems. Moitessier had no anemometer, but he estimates that the wind was at hurricane force in the gusts, which suggests that the mean strength would be about Force 10 or perhaps Force 11 on Beaufort Notation. In the South Pacific, given six days for the seas to build up, this would be a "survival" storm. The seas were reported to have been absolutely gigantic and their length was estimated to be about 500 to 560 ft., breaking without interruption for from 650 ft. to nearly 1,000 ft., leaving acres of white water behind them. They were described as being "absolutely unbelievable".

Joshua at first ran before this storm towing five long hawsers, varying in length from 100 to 300 ft., with iron ballast attached and supplemented by a heavy net used for loading ships. These afforded so much drag that the yacht failed to respond quickly enough to the wheel. They also failed to prevent her surfing on the crests of the gigantic waves. On one wave, which Moitessier says was not especially large, but just about the right size and shape for surfing,

Joshua took off like an arrow, with the warps behind her as if "dragging a fishing line", and buried herself in the wave at an angle of 30 degrees, so that the forward end of the boat was buried up to the ventilator abaft the mast.

Another wave taken in the same way might have caused *Joshua* to pitch-pole just as *Tzu Hang* had done and been dismasted, but happily the next really dangerously breaking sea caught the yacht at an angle and Moitessier thinks it is this that saved her from surfing and pitch-poling. It was then that he remembered the Dumas technique of running in gales at about 5 knots and putting the helm down on the arrival of each wave sufficiently to luff a little so as to take the wave at about 15 degrees to 20 degrees on the quarter. By this means a yacht will not be thrown forward surfing and in danger of pitch-poling because she is at an angle to the sea, nor will she be rolled over as she is not abeam to the sea, but there must remain some risk of a broach-to.

Accordingly Moitessier cut the warps and released *Joshua* from the drag. From that moment she was safe, following the Dumas technique of running fast and taking the seas 15 degrees to 20 degrees on the quarter. Moitessier says that *Joshua* could not possibly have survived except by this means. This ties up very closely with the experiences of Warren Brown, who ran in *Force Seven* before a hurricane at speed taking the seas on the quarter.

There is much to be learnt from Moitessier's theory of running to which I refer below:

1. In extreme storms in the South Pacific the ordinary methods of surviving storms are not enough. A sea anchor would be useless. Heaving-to would be out of the question. Streaming warps may not prevent surfing at perhaps 15 knots with the risk of pitch-poling.

2. *Joshua* was of steel construction and in her owner's opinion would not have survived without it. She was constantly struck by seas sweeping over the whole vessel up to the mast. These would have carried away any timber deckhouse and disaster would have followed. *Joshua* was steered from a steel pilot cupola. It was not safe on deck, even with lifelines, as the yacht sometimes disappeared completely below the sea. Moitessier also recommends that any yacht planning world voyaging should have a flush deck if she is of wood construction.

3. It is recommended that storm sails should be small and not too heavy and cumbersome. I think this applies to any sails such as a storm trysail. The old-fashioned ones used to be very heavy for the sake of strength, but cumbersome heavy-weather sails are difficult to handle and to set. There is no need for very heavy sails, especially now that terylene is used, because the area is so small that canvas of even moderate weight is very strong in relation to the area.

4. Moitessier states and then repeats that "no one can claim he will not founder in these latitudes". This confirms the opinion of other deep-sea cruising men that a time can arrive when no yacht can be certain of survival, whatever her size or rig may be.

5. Moitessier does not say a great deal about the form of the seas which he found most dangerous. He describes such seas as "crazy", which is, of course, the equivalent of "freak" or "rogue". Such seas usually have heavy cascading crests, but Moitessier states that this is not necessarily the case, as the most dangerous seas in the South Pacific are very steep, not necessarily breaking, which pick up and throw the boat into the trough and cause pitch-poling. He also refers to waves much bigger than the others and coming from a different direction. The theory of these is explained in Appendix 2, but for a yacht to be pitch-poled requires a sea of such immense size that it is not likely to be encountered except in very exceptional storms and with the unlimited fetch of the ocean.

I give a general summing up in Chapter 22 of the experiences of yachts in gales and storms and of the theory of running before them at speed.

THE METEOROLOGY OF DEPRESSIONS

Contributed by ALAN WATTS

The Channel Storm of 1956 was a very odd storm. It would have been phenomenal even without the experiences described in Chapter 11 to back it up.
Meteorologically it did not look to be much of a depression and we can pick it
up in Fig. 38 (page 231) at midnight on Saturday, 29 July (0001 G.M.T.), when
its central pressure was 985 millibars and the only sizeable wind was 35 knots at
Ushant. It looked a simple little low which would produce a Force 8 blow in the
Western Channel and nothing very much more. By 0200 it had deepened by 6
millibars, but that is not unusual, and while Scilly and Cork had 35 knots mean
speed, winds in the Channel were only 25 to 30 knots (Force 6-7), as forecast.

In the early stages several frontal troughs were recognizable, there being the
usual veer of wind across each. During the hours 0200 to 0400 the low deepened
very slowly at about 1 millibar per hour. The remarkable and significant feature
of this depression's progress lies in the fact that during the time when the really
excessive winds developed over the Channel it did not deepen at all. Thus some
other explanation has to be found for the wind torrent which swept the English
coastal region that morning. At 0400 (Fig. 38) the low centre and its central
region were coming into conflict with the high ground of Cornwall, Devon and
Wales. Between lay the pass of the Bristol Channel. It might be assumed that a
depression stretching its circulation many thousands of feet aloft would not be
influenced by surface features of a few thousand feet. Yet this is not always the
case. The depression's whole inclination was to move on its original track
slightly north of east, but by 0600 the isobars were slipping eastwards very
slowly and the low had developed two centres. The energy of the surface low,
thwarted on its leading edge by the high ground, began to find its way into a
wind corridor on its trailing side, so that incredible things happened like the
wind being a few knots from the south-east at Hartland Point and 60 knots from
the opposite direction in Watergate Bay, a mere 45 miles down the coast to the
south-west. It will be seen that the reason the Channel Islands had a mere 25 to
30 knots and that *Lutine* reported Force 4 at this time is that they lay on the edge
of the wind corridor, while Portland was equally on the north of the corridor and
so also had a mere 30 knots.

In the next hour the depression decided that it could not force its second centre over the barrier of the Welsh mountains and began to put all its energy back into the main centre and to swing around the mountains it could not cross, taking the wind corridor with it.

By 0800 a real torrent of 40–45-knot winds with gusts to over 60 knots had built down the after side of the thwarted low. Yet over the Channel fleet the isobars were still deceptively wide apart. However, Plymouth now had Force 9, as did the exposed coasts of Cardigan Bay and the Bristol Channel.

Between 0800 and 0900 the depression took the line of least resistance by tracking through the Severn Valley, and the wind corridor, swinging down around it, forsook Wales and began to concentrate its energies on sea areas Portland and Wight. It was in this period that the hard-pressed yachts in the region of the Owers were overwhelmed. The corridor of storm-force winds was moving over its prey.

By 1000 the wind's main energies were concentrated in the area between Portland and Beachy Head, with mean speeds of 50 to 60 knots (Force 10–11) in the Owers region. Chapter 11 tells the sorry tale.

It is important to realize from this sequence the tremendous effect near the surface of what might appear to be minor land barriers. In the hour 0900 to 1000 the wind corridor skipped over the moors and was all in the Channel, as the 2,000–3,000 ft. ranges to the south of Snowdon doggedly determined not to allow the isobars to pass.

By 1100 the depression finally made its way across the Welsh mountains and the winds began to become more normal, even if they did re-extend their sphere of influence all the way across southern England from the Bristol Channel to the Thames Estuary. But the worst was then over and while it still blew at 45 knots at St. Catherine's Point and there was 40 knots at Boulogne and 45 at Dungeness, there is no point in continuing the saga. The storm corridor—best described as a surface jet stream—had swung around its parent centre, whose pressure was now rising, and was spent. *Right Royal* managed during this time to be always within the Force 8–9 sector and to run along with it, so unfortunately remaining within its influence for an extended period, even if she did miss the worst that there was.

This storm has been covered in some detail, not only because, as is said in Chapter 11, it is the most important storm in the book, but also because it indicates a lot about such storms. It shows, for instance, why winds in the coastal sea areas bordering hilly or mountainous terrain (over which local depression centres have to track) may be the strongest there are. The Channel depression is obviously an entity which will intimately affect the offshore and cruising fraternity, and when it swings into the maw of the Bristol Channel (Chapters 6, 12 and 14), then the effects described for the Channel Storm are likely to occur, so that the West Channel and immediate South-west Approaches become areas of severe gales resulting from the ire of thwarted and previously innocuous lows.

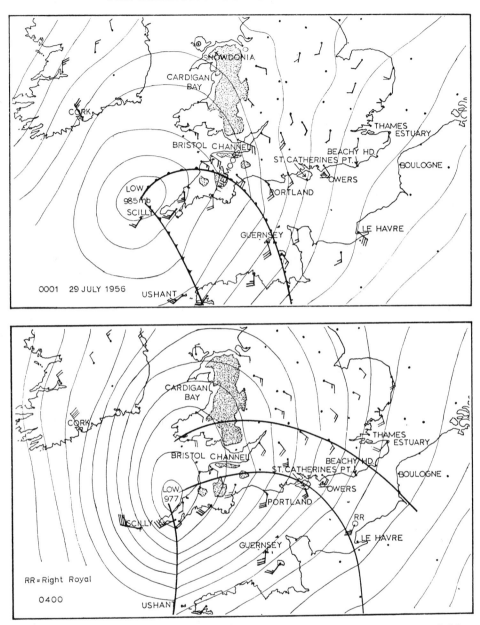

38(i) How the Channel Storm developed. All times are G.M.T. and yacht and ship positions are only approximate at these times. The 1200 chart shows the path of the low from midnight 28 July to 0900 29 July and from then on the re-formation of the centre and its motion from 0900 to 1200. Isobars are at 2 millibar intervals and full and half barbs on the wind arrows mean 10 and 5 knots respectively. Triangles mean 50 knots.

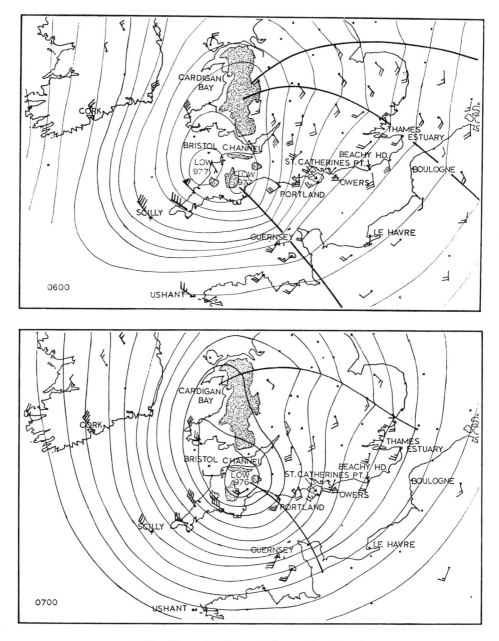

38(ii)   How the Channel Storm developed.

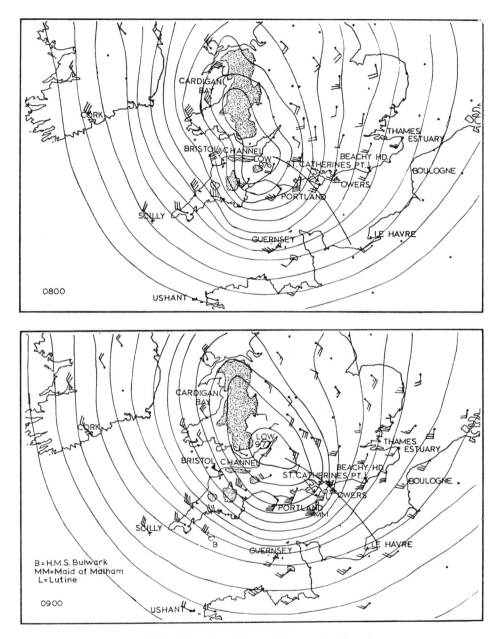

38(iii)   How the Channel Storm developed.

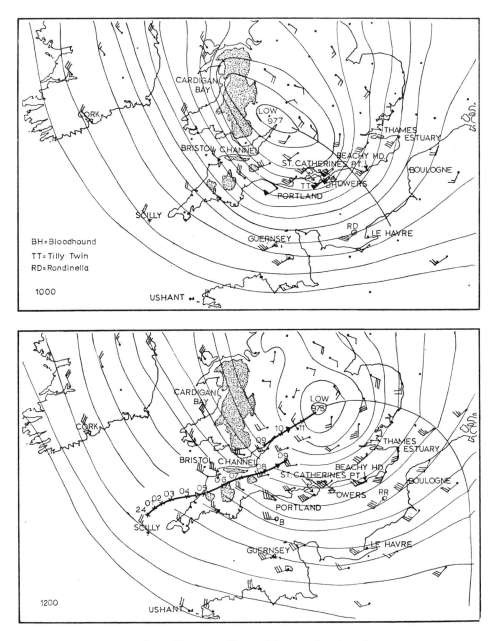

38(iv)   How the Channel Storm developed.

What the charts (Fig. 38) also show is the extreme influence that the land has on the wind strength. For instance, on the same wind track on the 0900 chart we find the triangular storm symbol for 50 knots at Chivenor (near Ilfracombe), while at Exeter, in the same isobaric tramlines but on the other side of the moors, the wind is only 35 knots. Similarly at Aberporth, on the shores of Cardigan Bay, the wind is 30 knots, while at Swansea on the other side of the Cambrian Mountains it is only 20 knots.

WIND AT SEA AND AT COASTAL STATIONS

As is well known, the wind increases with height in the extreme conditions discussed above, so not only the position but the height of any anemometer readings must be taken into account. The standard height for wind observations is 33 ft. (10 metres), which is luckily not far above, or below, the masthead height of an average yacht. When the "effective height" of an anemometer is about this value, then the winds recorded are the mean ones to be expected in a yacht. However, the winds as plotted on the weather charts are the actual ones read at the time of the observation. Often this does not matter, but in the case of anemometers like the one on the Portland Bill lighthouse (now with an effective height of 155 ft.) the height makes for stronger winds being recorded there than would be felt at 33 ft. above sea-level. In this case a whole 25 per cent has to be subtracted from the Portland wind speed to make its value comparable with a level of 33 ft. in a yacht skirting Portland, or farther out to sea, apart from local influences such as a wind corridor and the fact that at sea the wind is sometimes stronger than it is close to the land.

When we take the actual winds of the summer months of 1965 and compare them at Portland and Hurn Airport (inland from Bournemouth), both by day (0800–1700) and by night (1800–0700), as recorded by the anemographs (chart-drawing anemometers), then we find the following. With winds which blow in off the sea at Hurn (120–240 degrees) the Hurn wind needs to be multiplied by the following factors in order to get the wind offshore in the vicinity of Portland Bill. All the winds are reduced to the same standard 33 ft.

Wind force at sea when coastal station winds are onshore	*Factor by which to multiply coastal station wind to obtain wind over the sea*	
	By day	By night
4	1.1	1.7
5	1.3	1.6
6	1.4	1.8
7	1.3	1.6
8	1.3	1.6
9	no figures	1.6

It will be noticed that the factors are bigger by night than by day and that the winds of Force 6 are the most affected by the friction of the land. These figures are representative of those by which a prudent skipper multiplies the wind he has in harbour (or obtains from a local met. office) to assess the wind outside, though in some harbours he may be so close under the lee of high land or buildings that the wind outside is difficult to guess at all.

A further complication is the wind direction. We can divide wind directions around a coastal station into three sectors: (1) winds off the sea; (2) winds off the land, but excluding easterlies; (3) easterlies. Of course, an easterly on the East Coast is a wind off the sea, but on the South and West Coasts these three divisions serve to separate the different winds.

Again, comparing Portland and Hurn for winds which were between SW. and NW. (i.e. routed over land, but from the west), we find the following:

Wind force at sea when coastal station wind is routed over land	Factor by which to multiply coastal station wind to obtain wind over the sea	
	By day	By night
5	1.2	1.6
6	1.4	1.9
7	1.6	1.6
8	1.7	1.8
9	no figure	1.8

We see that the effect on the Force 5–6 winds of flowing over land is not much different than flowing off the sea, but that the effect on the strong to gale force winds is greater. They are, in fact, slowed up more over the land than is the case with winds off the sea.

Finally the easterlies. Easterlies in Great Britain are notoriously variable and gusty and it must be pointed out that these figures are obtained from analysis of the mean wind taken over a series of full hours, so that gusts must be added to the figures.

Wind force at sea when winds are easterly	Factor by which to multiply coastal station wind to obtain wind over the sea	
	By day	By night
4	1.5	2.1
5	2.0	2.5
6	2.0	2.5

(Easterlies above Force 6 mean speed are rare)

It is obvious from these figures that what may look on a weather map like a coastal station need not be unfettered by the local terrain. Cliffs may rise on one side or the other. Only a certain sector of direction may give a flat inroad for the wind. For example, the winds at Scilly and Lizard compare until the wind swings into the northerly quadrant (315—045 degrees) from which directions Lizard is sheltered. We have already mentioned the fact that not all anemometers are at the same height, and for real comparisons one really needs to know their exact location. An example is the anemometer on the top of the Headquarters Building at Thorney Island in the middle of Chichester harbour. On the map it looks completely surrounded by nothing, but in actual fact its effective height of 40 ft. is bedevilled by the buildings which cluster about it and more immediately by the trees which soften the view. Thorney's winds were never representative of those in the open sea area, but the anenometer has since been moved to the middle of the airfield well clear of all obstructions.

Only comparatively few anemometers whose readings appear on the charts are therefore representative of the wind offshore. Those on lightvessels will be, and those on lighthouses may be; the pictures in the pilots will often give a good idea of the extent to which they are well exposed. Thus when winds recorded on the coasts do not measure up to those experienced (and accurately assessed) at sea there may be many reasons, not the least of which is the sort of wind corridor effect described for the Channel Storm.

OTHER DEPRESSIONS

Let us now turn to the other depressions which have made the experiences of this book possible. They fall into three distinct groups, plus a small miscellaneous collection.

The first group can be called "deep lows". The weather maps (Fig. 25) accompanying Chapter 13, "Swell east of Ushant", for 6–7 September 1957, are classic examples of a deep low. The centre below 970 millibars is really deep by summer standards and is very unusual for September, which according to statistics is the time of minimum wind over the southern half of Britain. This depression we find becoming a slow-moving whirl of air sweeping on its fronts out of its circulation, and then sticking. It stuck all the following week, as I have reason to remember, being in the act of introducing my non-sailing wife to the joys of a yachting honeymoon. The low was not the only entity which did not move that week. We decided to stay on our moorings in Wootton—and had a very restful week!

It is noticeable that many of the lows which produce blows are not many millibars below the magic number of 1,000 millibars (normal pressure is 1013 millibars) and such depths need not be parts of depressions at all. But when the barometer falls to below 980 millibars, then that is a deep depression. This is not a definition of the term "deep", but a practical figure which tends to fit the facts. Such pressures must be surrounded by dartboards of isobars as the pressure climbs up to the highs within which the lows exist. They must, therefore, produce blows and these are often long-drawn-out periods of strong if not gale-force winds. As well as this unusual September gale, we find other examples of deep lows covering the Santander gale of 1948 (Chapter 5), La Coruña gale of 1954 (Chapter 9), and the Fastnet gales of 1957 (Chapter 12).

The latter had a reflection of the Channel Storm in it in that the Saturday-evening chart (10 August) shows another of those Bristol Channel depressions with the strongest of winds along the West Channel and a great no-man's-land of slack pressure and light winds up the Irish Sea. We can call such depressions, whether they track through the Severn pass or not, *"land-aggravated lows"*. Their characteristics have already been covered at their worst in the opening paragraphs. It only remains to show how prevalent they are in the examples of this book. We find two examples in Chapter 6, the Belle Île race of 1948 and the Wolf gale of the following year, while the Fastnet race of 1957, the Channel Storm of 1956 and the Fastnet gales of 1961 add to the list. There is one chart which is both deep and land aggravated and that is of the La Trinité gale of 1964 (Chapter 16). The rest are relatively shallow.

The third main division is the *multifront* system typified by the chart sequence covering La Coruña Race of 1960. To those brought up on the classic frontal depression drawings found in textbooks the double frontal system does not make much sense. However, weather maps as drawn by the professional meteorologists are seldom textbook and like them we must accept what nature gives us. Fronts separate air with significantly different temperature régimes and a front has the same name as the air behind it. For example, the air behind a cold front is colder than the air ahead of it. So if we start off in the col between the lows on the 1800 (second) chart for 10 August 1960 (Page 181) and move south we cross a warm front into warmer air over the Channel Islands and Brest. Then we cross another warm front into even warmer air over the Bay. Then turning westwards across the South-west Approaches we cross a cold front into cooler air and then another into cold air. As a depression whips up its wind energy by virtue of the difference in temperature between its coldest and warmest parts so such systems have a strong tendency to develop and blow hard.

We have signs of a similar situation in both the Channel Storm chart for Saturday, 28 July (Chapter 11), and the 1960 Bermuda gale (Chapter 15), where a low makes in towards an already waiting cold front and again the cold air to the north of it is drawn into the circulation and the energy of temperature contrast finds its way into a real blow. In the Saturday-evening chart for 10 August 1957, covering the Fastnet Race of that year (Fig. 22, p. 152), the same kind of consideration obtains. The occlusion bending down across France separates cool and cold air, but behind a sharp cold front (from Cork towards the south-west) must come even colder air compared to which the air behind the occlusion is relatively warm. Whatever the synthesis of fronts that follow, this sort of chart signifies that air which is potentially cold is close by and when drawn into the circulation of the already extant low must lead to its deepening at some later time. There are other examples of this principle in other weather charts, e.g. Belle Île (Fig. 13, p. 87). Sometimes careful attention to shipping and other forecasts may suggest the multi-front system, which is likely to lead to a real blow.

Finally there are *other systems* which do not fit these categories. We find a curious pair of lows in a col producing a tightening of the isobars over the waters along the South Coast in Chapter 2, page 35 and a "two-fried egg" situation in Chapter 10, page 124 covering the Cork Race of 1954.

But the main divisions fit nearly all the examples, except, of course, the hurricanes.

HURRICANES

A hurricane is fundamentally different from the most potent of depressions and a cross-section of a typical one is shown on page 240. What makes a hurricane is not so much what happens at the surface (although that is important) but what happens at 6–8 nautical miles aloft. The incipient hurricane is probably not much different at the surface to any ordinary embryonic depression, but it breeds great deep cumulo-nimbus clouds over the warm oceans and these spread anvils towards the periphery of the developing system. This happens below the tropopause (the permanent inversion which divides the troposphere from the stratosphere) which is some 50,000 ft. aloft over the tropics in summer. Such spreading at great heights leads to a rotation in the same direction as the winds nearer the surface. Thus the winds have a solid rotation in the same direction at all levels.

The depression, on the other hand, has winds aloft, whose rotation oppose their surface rotation, and this opposition exerts a control on the build-up of the surface winds. There is no similar control over the winds of the hurricane, added to which there is the feeding of the cloud-free eye of the hurricane with air drawn down from the stratosphere. Depressions do not communicate with the dry air of the stratosphere in quite such a direct way and do not usually have a central area curiously and ominously clear of cloud, although the 0600 chart of the Channel gale sequence (p. 231) shows that such depressions can have light winds (5 knots) in their centres and 60 knots only tens of miles away.

The general tendency of hurricane tracks, their main locations and the avoidance courses are all adequately covered in any Admiralty Pilot and do not need reiteration here. The all-seeing eye of the weather satellites have made the tracking of hurricanes very much surer than before, and the hurricane warning services of the U.S. Weather Bureau provide early warning.

When old tropical cyclones reach British shores, then they have been demoted to depressions, and this is not just a way of describing their diminished intensity. It also means that they have lost the direct link with the stratosphere that they had before and will now have winds aloft which, although strong, exercise control over the winds at the surface. For example, the Low D, which

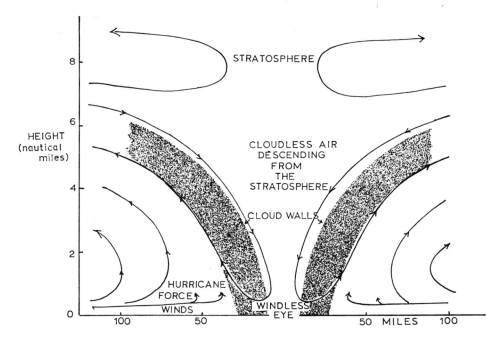

39   Cross-section through a typical hurricane. The way the winds descend in the eye and ascend elsewhere is characteristic of the hurricane.

had been Hurricane *Debbie*, lashed Ireland and West Scotland with winds approaching 90 knots in September 1961; and Hurricane *Carrie*, which sank the *Pamir* on 21 September 1957 in mid-Atlantic, finally crossed Cornwall and went into northern France on 25–26 September as a depression. Yet the full hurricane is most unlikely to ever be experienced even in the South-west Approaches to the English Channel. It is worth noting, however, that *Carrie* was still considered to be a hurricane to within a couple of hundred miles of the Scillies.

September is the peak of the hurricane season in the Caribbean and of the "old hurricane" season here. We do not get many old hurricanes, but if we do they are usually vigorous lows and should be allowed for especially off the western seaboard in September.

TORNADOES AND WATER-SPOUTS

Tornadoes are another matter. Tornadoes in the British Isles have been, in recent decades, products of inland areas and form under intense thunderstorm areas, particularly where the air can get an upward push over rising ground. Once formed they may proceed out to sea, pick up a great writhing spiral of water and may deposit it in the cockpit of some unfortunate yacht. At least one liner at sea has had its crow's nest at 70 ft. above the sea surface filled with water from a tornado storm spout. That was in the Atlantic. Cowes had a tornado in the last century, so it might happen again, although such things are rare.

Far more likely is the waterspout which will often form under vigorous cumulo-nimbus clouds over the sea. The funnel of the spout is not usually solid water and so it is not likely to swamp a yacht as a tornado storm spout may do. However the circulating winds can be temporarily dangerous and if spouts are sighted then it is prudent to shorten sail. Tornadoes and spouts come under the general heading of funnel clouds and the latter need not extend from cloud to the surface for their effects to be felt. I have only once experienced the effects of a funnel cloud and that was off a windward shore in landlocked waters. It was not a spout, as it came in an easterly wind off the land mass, having no time to pick up water. Still, the boom swung violently from side to side and the sails shivered and trembled as if they had the ague. The rotation of the wind turned us until we were heading on a course opposite to our original one, by which time I had the mainsail down. We then had time to observe the writhing pendant of cloud twisting down from the thundery cloud mass aloft and could watch it lose itself over the farthest shore and disappear.

FOG IN HEAVY WEATHER

Fog is not usually considered to be a phenomenon associated with heavy weather. However, the official limits of visibility for fog (i.e. below 1,000 metres or 1,100 yards) leads to fog limits being reached in rain, drizzle, and especially snow, even with Force 6–7 winds. The rain needs to be heavy and the drizzle thick, in association with low amorphous cloud. The latter is often due to the rain, which moistens the lower layers into which it evaporates as it falls, until they are sufficiently saturated to condense into cloud with no definable base. The most likely parts of depressions where such conditions can obtain is under active warm fronts and occlusions. Temporary fogs may occur under cold fronts, but they are of short duration—tens of minutes rather than hours. Snow with its high reflectance lowers visibility out of all proportion to the intensity of precipitation, and visibilities near or below fog limits will be the rule rather than the exception with snow showers if not more continuous snowfall. However, the showers pass and tend to conform to the idea that in high winds fog does not persist for very long. Only under the slow-moving parts of quasi-stationary fronts, and especially ones which were moving one way and have stopped and are now being pushed back the other way, as happens sometimes, will high wind and persistent fog be likely companions.

Poor visibility at mist limits (2,000 metres or 2,200 yards) still makes navigation by D.R. difficult and from this point of view mist might be said to define the limit below which a yacht's safety is impaired. These limits are likely in tropical maritime air (warm sector type air) whenever the cloud is thick enough to produce rain or drizzle and the air is routed over decreasing sea isotherms. This is usually the case with such air from the southern quadrants over the open sea or in the SW. quadrant when in more sheltered waters such as the English Channel.

FORECASTING

What has been said up to now is hindsight. What about the immediate forecasting of the bad stuff blowing in to harry the yacht at sea?

The most potent of the early-warning signs is the banner-like cirrus bands which stretch across the sky and appear to converge towards the horizon. They are usually orientated from the north-west. If moon, stars or sun give a reference point, they can be seen to be moving very fast across the sky. If the very high cirrus can actually be seen to be in motion, even from the moving platform of a yacht, then the winds aloft are 80–100 knots or more. Such winds—and this cloud form—tell of a jet-stream.

A jet-stream is a high-speed wind river, usually some 6–8 nautical miles aloft, which is part and parcel of the development of vigorous depressions. Of course, every one knows that most strong wind comes with the onset of the circulation of a depression, and weather lore tells that the jet-stream cirrus banners signify the impending arrival of a depression of the stronger kind. Jet-stream cirrus must be assumed to mean that a gale is a real possibility some six to ten hours later.

Cirrus of some kind will always appear ahead of active and advancing warm fronts. These need not be part of a vigorous depression, but when the cloud thickens into grey banks of altostratus through which the sun struggles vainly not to be obscured, then some sort of front is on its way. If the barometer tumbles as well, then its rate of fall is related to the strength of the wind and, coupled to the cloud signs, state of sea, etc., will tell something of the wind to come. However, the Met. Office will only issue a gale warning on a single reliable observation if there is a tendency of 10 millibars or more in three hours.

The barographs of the passage of the Santander Race gale of 7–8 August 1948 at Scilly, Calshot and at sea in *Golden Dragon* (Fig. 40) show the relation between tendency of the barometer and wind. A line of slope, *10 millibars in three hours*, has been drawn on this figure and steeper gradient than this usually means severe gales are inevitable, if only temporarily, while lesser tendencies can mean gales, but need not necessarily do so.

At Scilly, some 40 miles north of the line of passage of the centre, only once did the tendency come close to the magic 10 millibars in three hours and that was between 1700 and 1800 G.M.T. The wind at Scilly at this time was a mean

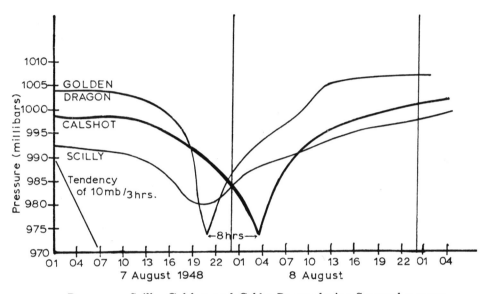

40   Barograms Scilly, Calshot and *Golden Dragon* during Santander storm.

of about 26 knots, gusting occasionally to 35–40, but by 1900 it had risen to a mean of 30 knots, with occasional gusts to 44 knots and one gust to 48 knots.

At Calshot (200 nautical miles westward and eight hours later "as the low flies") the barometer plummeted, at a gradient of 10–12 mb/3 hrs between 0200 and 0400 on the Sunday morning and rose more rapidly, at gradients between 20 and 10 mb/3 hrs from 0400 to 0600.

The barograph from *Golden Dragon* shows a quite phenomenal fall, whose gradient for ½ hour attained the astonishing rate of 45 mb/3 hrs, and a slower but none the less exceptionally rapid, rise. The position of *Golden Dragon* with reference to the passage of the low centre can be gauged from the account in Chapter 5. It seems inevitable that the report of Force 11 from the Clan liner was correct, even though the very abruptness of the barometric tendency meant that such wind strength could not be sustained for long. By contrast, the far more gentle barometric tendencies associated with the Channel Storm (Chapter 11) followed by winds of Force 10 and 11 for an extended period. The old adage of "short forecast soon past" still applies!

However, tendency is no help to a yacht at sea in foretelling what is going to happen, say, four hours ahead—you only know what the barometer has done, not what it will do. It may sink fairly steeply and look as if it will eventually knock its own bottom out, but then the fall is arrested as the trough goes through and nothing very bad occurs.

The barometer at sea is not a very reliable guide, because seeking shelter is a question of decision several hours ahead of the real blow. It must be the sky which commands the most attention.

The sky which goes rapidly through the well-known sequence of cirrus, and cirro-stratus (haloes about sun or moon) into alto-stratus (sun or moon as if seen through ground glass) presages a fairly short and not necessarily violent blow. The long build-up of these clouds signifies a bigger depression and so more prospect of a gale later. To which must be added the proviso that the ill-famed secondary depression can blow up shortly and sharply and give a real Force 7–8, or more even in the summer months, as evinced by the Santander Race gale already referred to.

The cloud sequence cirrus, cirro-stratus, alto-stratus then thickens into nimbo-stratus and with this cloud comes the rain. There will be pannus (scud) beneath it and a sight of the latter will tell of the immediate onset of rain and therefore when to reach for oilskins. Normal warm fronts (which the above cloud sequence accompanies) will rain gently, but persistently, and the rain will become moderate, but not normally heavy, before the cloud-line clears. It usually does so with a low ragged sweep of dirty cloud lying athwart the wind. The latter must be watched for, as a sharpish veer will come with the passage of a well-defined warm front, as well as some gustiness. Once the front has passed the cloud may be just as low as before, but rain will usually give way to drizzle. It becomes humid and muggy, for the warm tropical part of the depression has arrived. The wind will now be blowing at its strongest and nasty unpredictable eddies must be allowed for, especially at night in what would seem to be an otherwise homogenous and not very gusty airstream. These will be most severe with winds above Force 7–8, because the size of the eddies in warm sectors only increases to catastrophic proportions when winds are above this strength. What happens is that super-sized eddies bring very fast wind to the surface from much higher up and may deposit it with full fury on a yacht already hard pressed by the wind anyway.

The next hazard, after it is realized that the influence of the warm sector has been felt for a reasonable time—and that time may not be very many hours—is the arrival of the cold front. However, cold fronts have a habit of producing strongly ascending currents, and what goes up must come down somewhere else. Some currents often come down ahead of the front and this temporarily breaks the cloud, so that the cold front proper is presaged by a temporary clearance. Any real clearance in a cloud type should always be suspected. It may mean worse to come.

The "worse to come" of a cold front is the chance of very strong veers of wind, accompanied by equally vicious gusts. The veer may be 45 degrees or more and a craft beating on port tack might then be put in irons. If on the starboard tack

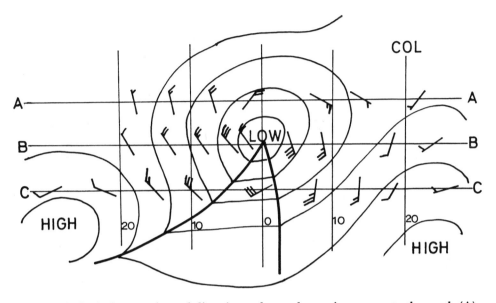

41 Typical wind strengths and directions when a depression moves to the south (A), passes directly over (B) or passes to the north (C) of the observer. A full barb = 10 knots mean speed; half barbs = 5 knots. Figures against vertical lines are typical times in hours ahead and behind the line of lowest pressure for a big depression moving at 30 knots from west to east.

there is a chance of being blown down as the gusts strike from the beam as the front goes through. Yet it is easier to make up to meet the veering wind on starboard than to bear away on port. With storm sails set this might not be important, but with less strong winds, when carrying as much canvas as practicable, it could be a useful point to bear in mind especially at night. There will also be the nasty cross-sea which comes when a sharply veering wind spreads across an already established seaway. However, careful observation of the longer, lower, faster-moving waves, running under the immediate seaway can foretell this wind change.

The sharp cold front can be recognized by the curious way in which the lower cloud elements cross one another. It may well look as if quite low clouds are

245

scudding in from the right of the existing wind. This is no illusion, as they show the new wind direction and give a warning of an impending veer.

The cold front usually brings a climb in the barometer. The stronger every aspect of a depression is, the more likely it is that the barometer will plumb down and shoot up again.

This rise should steady out after a couple of hours, and if it fails to do so, then any improvement is likely to be short-lived. The real clearance usually comes after a couple of days of gradually rising barometer, as the low moves away. During this post-cold-front stage the winds will normally be cool, squally north-westerlies, accompanied by frequent showers at first, but gradually moderating in all their aspects. Very strong and persistent winds accompanied by strong gusts and squalls can occur in this phase of the passage of a depression. The barometer may rise, but the wind increases. This is immediately interpreted as sure evidence that the invisible depression, which was thought to have passed, is sticking or has gathered some more strength and is deepening again. The incredible wind which sank parts of the East Coast of England and much of Holland and flattened four million trees in Scotland on the night of 31 January/1 February 1953, arose in the corridor between a deepening depression slow moving in the North Sea and a galloping tendency to high pressure over the eastern Atlantic.

A yacht alone on the ocean does not normally have the benefit of weather maps, so many prognosis based on such maps will find low priority in the list of gale-forecasting methods. It may, however, be worth noting that when the charts before the big gales are studied, then a particular pattern appears. It is typified by Fig. 38 of the Channel Storm sequence. Over the area ripe for the most trouble is a slack area of low pressure—a sort of bed into which a rogue low is about to tumble. This prepared position with a developing depression to fill it is the most suspect of situations and the sight of such a chart before putting to sea might make it worth thinking twice about going unless it were imperative. We find a somewhat less obvious example on page 124 in connection with the Cork Race. The low that caused the trouble ate its forebearer and used the energy to flay the life out of poor mariners sailing upon their lawful occasions.

It is almost the same again for the 1957 Fastnet. The Saturday-evening chart shows a low deepening into an already low pressure area. Again the chart (page 152) for 1800, 10 August 1960 is classical. The path of the depression to deepen is already laid. It can hardly help deepening.

WAVE LOWS AND TROUGHS

While great primary lows have secondaries in their circulations which provide sharp deteriorations, there are even smaller entities of the same general kind called "wave lows" or just plainly "waves". A "wave" is a small incursion of warm air into cold or cool air. It mostly occurs along a cold front where it produces local deteriorations, but not usually any very strong winds. Meteorologically "waves" are like very small depressions and the chart for 1200, 25 July 1954 (Fig. 42), which is reproduced here and precedes the ones shown in Chapter 9, p. 118 shows two waves within a relatively small distance of one another. As it requires something over 1,000 miles of undisturbed front between

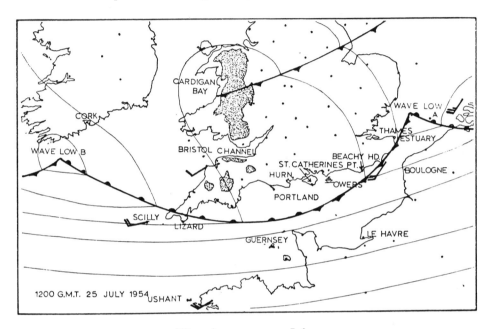

42   Wave lows 1200, 25 July 1954.

two such waves before they both have a chance to develop into proper depressions, one or both of these embryonic lows is due to die. Before that happens, they will prevent clearance of rain and low cloud along a cold front by pulling it up northward again, rather than letting it go through to the south. They can be understood by analogy with a rope secured to a stanchion and flicked into waves along its length. The frontal waves move along the front like those in the rope, sometimes at 60 knots.

A quick glance at the chart two hours later at 0600, 26 July, fig. 17, page 118, shows why neither of these waves developed. All the depression-forming energy was being imbibed by the bigger wave to the west of Ireland. Both A and B died out, leaving another, not normally mentioned, entity—the sympathetic trough—to hold the stage. The inquiring mind might legitimately ask how between 1800 and 0600 next morning the wave west of Ireland grew in occlusion towards the main low south of Iceland. Often, when a more than average-sized wave looks at a parent low like this, then it grows a great line of showers and heavy rain, with squalls of some severity, in sympathy with its parent and between the two centres. Such a line can only be described succinctly on the charts by the symbol for an occlusion, so one appears. The actual weather under such troughs is often of the foulest, with cold, driving showers of rain and hail, accompanied by much gustiness. The original tip of the wave may deepen considerably, as in this example and produce a crop of very close isobars over the areas to the south of it, also as in this case.

Then there are thundery troughs, mainly to be found in the sailing months and particularly in the worst of the summer months—August! The sooner we forget about August as a holiday month the better—everything meteorological gets worse in August—and better in September!

Perhaps the worst of thundery troughs is the damage they do to morale, especially at night. There, heaving down over the horizon, is a fine display of lightning which stretches across the wind—what there is of it—and you have to go through it. The wind begins to build in those fitful gusts which worry. Then it is arched over the white-flecked waters and the wind may whip up to 30 to 50 knots in the worst cases. The air becomes very cold and torrential rain roars on the coachroof and the thunder cracks and rolls while the lightning illuminates the details of the satanic clouds above. But once it's over, that's that. Normally the gusts and squall pass in half an hour to an hour and the general increase in wind is nothing more than to Force 4 or 5. It is not really a heavy weather phenomenon.

Yet at the same time there are old, extra-tropical cyclones who gain new leases of life on approaching the shores of the British Isles. Hurricane *Debbie* was one and the Wokingham storm of 9 July 1959 was another. In that storm people were washed out of their homes in more than one place, while hail the size of tennis balls fell elsewhere. Continuous lightning which keeps the cloud-tops illuminated is a sign of such storms and they are usually products of September. The line of the Caribbean hurricane jingle "September Remember" is also true on a lesser scale in Britain, especially in the South-west Approaches.

Other effects on the wind of thundery situations are to be found in my book *Wind and Sailing Boats*, including the curious fact that gusts due to thundery activity can occur tens and hundreds of miles from the actual thunderstorm area.

RAIN ON THE SEA

Finally a word about the effect of rain on the sea. There is no doubt that the meteorological conditions accompanying heavy rain calm the sea. We say the rain beats the sea down, Well, perhaps it does, but that is not all the story.

It is often noticeable that when rain starts fairly suddenly, then the wind also increases. This is easy to explain, because descending currents are pulled down with the falling rain, bringing stronger wind from higher up on to the surface. The more intense the rain the stronger the downdraughts. They are called precipitation downdraughts and they account for the very big gusts under thunderstorms and the still sizeable gusts under other less-violent shower clouds. Likewise on a lesser scale they explain why the rain and the wind come together.

They may also explain the efficiency with which heavy rain appears to beat down the sea, because not only have we the weight of water falling on to the surface but we also have the weight of air between—which is not inconsiderable, covering as it does a much larger area than that of the drops.

In the foregoing some of the meteorological aspects of heavy weather have been discussed. They are not exhaustive and no seaman worth his salt can get by without some knowledge of the face of the sky and what it portends. Knowledge coupled to experience is the recipe for keeping clear of trouble.

THE STORM OFF JERSEY

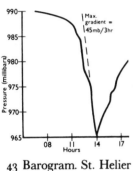

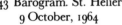

43 Barogram. St. Helier
9 October, 1964

The accompanying barogram of the storm off Jersey which brought tragedy to the motor yacht *Maricelia* in 1964 (see chapter 23) has been redrawn, by permission from *Motor Boat and Yachting*, to the same scale of pressure and time as used in the barographs for the Santander Race storm (page 243). The time (which is necessarily on smaller scale than on an ordinary barograph trace) has been adjusted to bring the trough to 1400. There is enough in this barometer trace to tell us all we want to know about the local severity of this disturbance.

The fall in pressure was 25 millibars in 3 hours to the trough, which gives a line of average slope over twice as steep as the fall of 10 millibars in three hours beyond which a severe gale may be expected. The final gradient for 40 minutes to the trough if extended would result in the remarkable fall of 45 millibars in 3 hours. The storm must inevitably have been as bad as Peter Haward has reported—or worse!

It is interesting to see that the disturbance off Jersey and the Minquiers, although localised, was as intense as the Santander Race storm. The average fall in the latter was 22 mb/3 hrs. as compared with 25 mb/3 hrs. in the former, and the maximum gradient near the trough was almost exactly the same at 45 mb/3 hrs. had it been maintained for that length of time.

22

MULTIHULLS IN HEAVY WEATHER

Contributed by Michael Henderson

The faintly jarring word 'Multihull' covers a very wide range of types, from the enormous spiderlike three-hulled creation where everything is subjugated to the concept of speed, through the less extreme examples of both the trimaran and the catamaran where the requirements of speed and habitability have been combined with varying degrees of success, to the unashamedly 'stodgy' comfortable family cruising type which gives the appearance—often deceptive—of almost being unable to get out of it's own way. It is interesting, if not *particularly* significant that examples of each of these extremes have recently carried out successful long-distance ocean voyages without undue incident.

Despite the many words written and spoken on the subject by the protagonists of the various types there is no real cause or justification for differentiating between either the trimaran or the catamaran basic form when discussing the multihull under these conditions. They both differ from the conventional yacht in obtaining their stability by the sideways displacement of buoyancy rather than by the attainment of a low centre of gravity through ballast, and therefore in general terms enjoy the same advantages of light displacement and high sail carrying power at small angles of heel and suffer the same disadvantages of rapidly decreasing stability with heel once a certain angle has been reached, and the consequent risk of capsize. Note that, contrary to some beliefs, displacement plays as important a part in the stability of a multihull as it does in that of the conventional boat. The main difference is that the total value of the righting moment is increased by the larger righting arm but since that righting moment is still the product of the righting arm and the displacement, the heavier the boat the higher the moment. Note also how the large righting arm, while granting great benefits at small angles of heel, confers equally great disadvantages as the capsize point is reached owing to the way in which the centre of gravity is raised far above the centre of buoyancy, causing a rapid tranference from righting to capsizing moment as the centre of gravity passes above the centre of buoyancy.

Accordingly, when considering these boats under heavy weather conditions their advantages and limitations must very much be born in mind and it must also be remembered that very little data exists compared with the vast amount

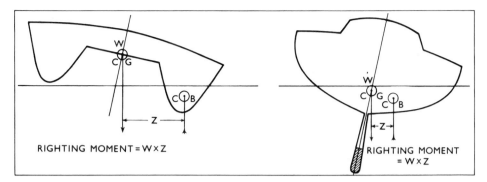

RIGHTING MOMENT = W × Z

RIGHTING MOMENT
= W × Z

44(a) Multihulls derive their stability by sideways displacement of buoyancy (left) rather than by the attainment of a low centre of gravity through ballast. (right)

that has been collected for the more conventional form; we are still very much breaking new ground, even though it is something like fourteen years since a multihull first took part in an ocean race in this country.

The problems connected with handling a multihull in heavy weather are precisely those of handling any other kind of vessel with the additional problems

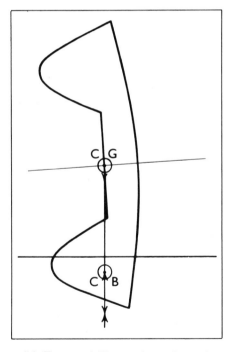

44(b) Zero stability point when the centre of gravity comes above the centre of buoyancy.

associated with the peculiar stability and drag characteristics peculiar to the type, and it is with these latter that I would propose to deal, the others being dealt with elsewhere in this book.

It would seem that the capsize risk is the most likely cause of difficulty and this can happen in one of two basic ways. The first is the more usual straightforward lateral capsize caused by carrying sail beyond the safe stability point of the boat. This usually happens when close hauled, or reaching fast. It needs little elaboration, being fairly obvious in its causes and effects. The second type is due to such a combination as could equally cause a serious broach in a conventional boat and results when the boat is being driven fast down wind and is overpowered longitudinally in such a way that one or all bows digs too heavily into a steep sea thus tripping the boat and causing capsize. An example of this is described in an Amateur Yacht Research Society Report No. C001.01A on the capsize of the catamaran *Haxted Argo II* where a well equipped and crewed 31 ft. catamaran was capsized when running under storm jib only at about 5 knots in a high wind and very steep seas off the Scharhorn Sands (shades of the *Dulcibella*). She was running under good control before a force 8 to 9 wind in shoal water when, as the report puts it "...... a high and steep wave passed underneath us. We went fast down the front of it but the bows rose on the other side. A second similar wave came along and I think that as we were going down the front of it we all realised that the bows were not going to rise". The bows were driven under water, the vessel capsizing to leeward with sufficient force to drive the masthead float well under the surface. The float then asserted itself and the boat finished up floating on her side well filled with water and therefore fairly deeply immersed; she eventually righted herself, probably because of the action of the steep seas on the masthead float and the lowering of the centre of gravity because of the flooding. The crew succeeded in cutting loose and inflating the emergency liferaft and this was kept alongside in case it was needed, but the crew were wisely and understandably reluctant to take to it until the last possible moment because of the fear of it being driven rapidly downwind upon the Scharhorn. They were, luckily, rescued fairly soon after the incident by a Dutch cargo vessel which had observed their plight. Writing after the event and after having discussed the incident with other experienced yachtsmen, the owner added, inter alia, ... "I think that from a wish not to appear to exaggerate I have not done justice to the conditions. I had never experienced waves anything like the two which I have described. The second must have been around 30 ft. high and so steep that it felt like going down a waterchute. It seems unlikely that a conventional yacht would have avoided a capsize."

It is interesting to note that this capsize happened when the vessel was not being driven unduly hard downwind, but was caused by the very steepness and shortness of the seas which did not give the vessel time to respond to them sufficiently. Clearly a similar risk will exist at any time where a boat is being driven downwind in waves of such a critical size that the boat's ability to respond can be overpowered; some of us will have heard of, and indeed been involved in, cases where even quite large ocean racers have had their bows driven under in such circumstances; this tendency to pitchpole can be and often is exaggerated by weakness in design, particularly by a lack of reserve buoyancy forward caused by an insufficient length of overhang, or insufficient flare. The problem, of course, is to maintain an adequately fine entry for good drag characteristics while still retaining the necessary reserve buoyancy, and one solution is to incorporate a chine at around half freeboard height so that the reserve buoyancy increases rapidly once this is immersed.

Notwithstanding all this the success of multihulls in such areas as the Single-handed Transatlantic Race will have done much to dispel early doubts about

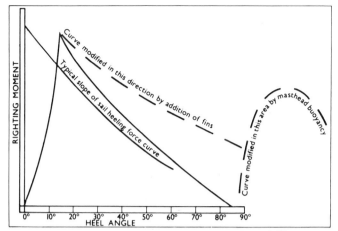

44(c) Typical Multihull stability curve showing increase in stability up to about 15° followed by a decrease to nil between 85° and 90°.

the seaworthiness of the type. It is significant perhaps that these successes have been attained with relatively large examples, and it is certainly true that with these boats more than with other types the laws of scale play a more significant part in their behaviour, the smaller boats being always much nearer to the knife edge of capsize than their larger brothers. Since stability varies as the fourth power of the scale, a boat twice the size of another will require roughly one and a half times the windspeed to take it to the same point on its stability curve, and it is this one characteristic above all others that distinguishes the multihull from the conventional sailing boat and introduces another consideration to its handling techniques.

It is in winds above force 5 or 6, depending on size, that these special considerations come into play. It is then that the multihull is likely to be being operated at the critical point of its stability curve, namely that just before which its stability starts to fall off rapidly with heel. It is precisely at this point that the most careful judgement is required and also most difficult to exercise. While the conventional boat can tolerate less and less supervision as the windspeed rises the multihull is in precisely the opposite state and needs more and more careful control in those circumstances, and it is not difficult to understand the conditions which caused the capsize of, for example, *Apache Sundance* in the Round Britain Race—strong winds, confused seas, heavy rain and the crew fatigue inevitable towards the closing stages of such a gruelling race. This is not to say that the multihull is an unsuitable vehicle in which to indulge in offshore racing, but to suggest at any rate that such a sport is one which is more athletic in the true sense of the word than conventional offshore racing, and demands more continuous operational attention on the part of the crew. This difficulty may be reduced somewhat by the expedient of adding ballasted fins (the more popular masthead buoyancy does not come into play until *after* the capsize has happened!) thus grafting some of the stability characteristics of the conventional boat on to the multihull. Obviously there must be an optimum point on this addition of weight where it's stability advantage will cease to pay, but very little work has been done in this respect and certainly no definite conclusions can be drawn. Obviously, as displacement increases, so does resistance; what few investigations *have* been made into this subject tend, however, to indicate the likelihood that resistance increases no more rapidly than does the sail carrying power conferred by the increased ballast, at any rate within reasonable ballast ratios—up to say 30%. It is conceivable that at least the really serious offshore racing multihull may develop along these lines. This may still be regarded as a faintly heretical suggestion in the eyes of most of today's multihull enthusiasts, but that is not to say that it is an unacceptable proposition. Certainly, if the kind of stability range of the conventional yacht could be given to the multihull, possibly by a combination of ballasted fins *and* a masthead float, without incurring any drag penalty, the best of both worlds could be attained.

The other problem can be that of excessive speed, caused by the excellent drag characteristics of the type. This may cause difficulties either in that they tend to lead to the capsize previously discussed, or to the equally embarrassing problem of running out of available sea room too quickly. In short, the problem is that of slowing the boat down sufficiently. Even under very reduced canvas or bare poles, any decent multihull will travel at a considerably higher speed than a conventional boat in similar wind strengths and special techniques of putting on the brake may well be necessary. If the distribution of windage is such as to allow the boat to lie a-hull successfully, this may be the answer. In other cases, towing warps or drags may be necessary.

Our experience in *Misty Miller* in the 1961 Fastnet may illustrate the point. *Misty* was a 24 ft. waterline experimental self righting catamaran equipped with ballasted fins and a masthead float, which piece of equipment I can fairly claim to have originated; I had designed her during the previous year, after a couple of seasons in a smaller J.O.G. sized cat, of similar design, *Golden Miller*, in order to see whether the type could be successfully developed for offshore racing. She had a typically Class III ocean racing crew for those days, with a pretty good standard of experience and competence, and those who took part in that race will remember that as the main body of the fleet arrived in the Lands End area a small and intense secondary arrived quickly from the Bay of Biscay, causing many hardluck stories amongst the fleet, especially those smaller boats that were caught between the Scillies and Lands End itself. Indeed, one friend of mine relates with heartrending precision the story of seeing his logline and spinner streaming out *in the wind* and rotating very rapidly indeed. The gale arrived with very little warning and in *Misty* we had been running under spinnaker from about noon that day, making the passage between the Scillies and Lands End with a light south easterly breeze, and it was not until, fortunately

29. *Golden Miller.* Michael Henderson's 21 ft. catamaran, designed and sailed to test the suitability of the type for ocean racing. *Photo: Beken, Cowes.*

30. *Misty Miller,* 30 ft. experimental self-righting catamaran, which was unofficially tried out against ocean racers in the severe Fastnet Race of 1961, see page 161. *Photo: Beken, Cowes.*

31. The 40 ft. catamaran *Apache Sundancer* capsized in the strong winds and confused seas in the closing stage of the gruelling Round Great Britain Race 1072. *Photo: Beken, Cowes.*

32. The 42 ft. trimaran *Toria*, an early design of Derek Kensall, first in the 1966 Round Great Britain Race and renamed *Gancia Girl* was 7th in Transatlantic Race 1068. *Photo: Beken, Cowes.*

perhaps, after supper that the wind began to rise. The cloud cover increased rapidly and we were running under spinnaker, no. 1 jib and full main. At about 7 o'clock the speed had built up to quite a respectable level—probably 15 knots—and it became obvious that we would soon have to shorten sail; I remember climbing onto the cabintop and making preparations to douse the spinnaker, and while this operation was being carried out the wind rose to such a pitch that it became depressingly obvious that the sooner we got every bit of canvas off her the better.

Accordingly we changed from virtually every inch of canvas we could set to a small storm jib in as short a time as was possible—and continued nevertheless to cream along at a very respectable speed indeed. The cloud cover descended, the rain started, and darkness fell, and by 9:30 P.M. we were encased in visibility of no more than 15 yards, and the navigation lights were casting such a halo in the heavy torrential rain that they had to be switched off to give us some kind of visibility at all. It very soon became clear that we were travelling at such a speed that it was unsafe in that one had seen a number of larger yachts ahead before the visibility closed down, who were probably travelling at a slower speed than us and the danger of overtaking and ramming them was great. Accordingly, at about 11 o'clock at night all sail was taken off and the boat was allowed to lie a-hull. This she did very successfully, lying beam onto the very short steep seas, rolling heavily—indeed rolling her weather hull out of the water at each wave—and moving forward at a speed of about 2 knots. Provided she was kept moving, it was possible to steer anywhere from dead down wind to just short of beam on; if she was allowed to luff beyond this point she stopped and lay absolutely a-hull, beam onto the wind, and making hardly any way at all. If I wanted to get her under way again, all that was necessary was to send a man to afford windage by the forestay, when her head fell off, her speed rose to the point where her rudders would take effect, and she was then steerable again. It was excessively uncomfortable, excessively cold and miserable, particularly as my oilskins leaked like sieves, and we were all of us very glad indeed when, by dawn, the wind had moderated to a more normal kind of force 6 northwesterly.

The lessons learnt from this experience were firstly that with a boat of such a large speed potential as a catamaran, its very speed in strong winds can be a disadvantage, particularly in bad visibility; that if all sail be taken off, the boat generally will behave as a conventional vessel and lie a-hull satisfactorily, although perhaps giving some cause for concern as to her ultimate stability as the rate of rolling in the seas increases. On the occasion I have just related, we were certainly very glad of *Misty Miller's* ballasted fin keels and her masthead float, and it is conceivable that a lighter, unballasted type of multihull could possibly find herself rolled beyond the point of recovery in seas of a particular height and wavelength under such conditions.

Since those days a fair number of lengthy ocean passages have been made in multihulls of varying types, all, as far as I know, being of the unballasted type; the most notable of which of course, being the successful entrants in the 1972 Singlehanded Transatlantic Race, outstanding amongst them being *Pen Duick* under Alain Colas, who before that race started had already some extremely good ocean passages under his belt. Not a lot has been published about the behaviour of these boats in really severe conditions.

Summing up it can be said that heavy weather, which may provide conditions likely to confuse the acquisition of control data by the helmsman, viz. heavy rain, strong winds, bad visibility and confusing motion, demands the kind of handling which does not press the boat too hard towards the extremes of its abilities. In extreme conditions, provided the sea characteristics are not such as to roll the boat too violently or to overwhelm her, it would appear that most multihulls will lie a-hull satisfactorily. If the worst happens and capsize occurs, it is probably better to stay with the boat rather than to abandon it in whatever kind of liferaft is carried. While not decrying the value of these in the last resort, it would be wrong to pretend that they offer an automatically better solution to the survival problem than a capsized but still floating boat, especially if due forethought has been given to the problem. Many things can be done to make a capsized multihull a more habitable proposition than merely a wave-swept raft. Handholds can be provided all over the underside of the bridge deck and on the inner sides of the hulls; access hatches into the accommodation from the underside of the bridge deck can be provided so that provisions and fresh water can be reached and, at the very least, there should be a locker, accessible from both above and below the bridge deck in which the liferaft and survival equipment should be stowed. One can develop this concept to the point where one can imagine a capsized crew, relaxed and happy on the underside of their boat, equipped with all the comforts including colour television, powering home under the emergency outboard motor, and this is by no means a farfetched concept. Certainly, provided adequate provision on the lines discussed has been made, the chances are very high that adequate survival activities can be carried out and there can be a fair chance of eventually recovering the boat.

There does not seem to be any overwhelming evidence that a properly designed and built multihull is any less capable of dealing with heavy weather than a more conventional boat provided the limitations of its stability and the technique of handling it are well and properly understood. The type will tend to be more demanding upon its crew in such conditions and this must always be born in mind; crew fatigue is therefore more likely to have a bearing upon the outcome on any heavy weather incident. However, as more and more experience is built up, the problems will be more fully understood and will be more successfully overcome.

23

MOTOR CRAFT IN HEAVY WEATHER

Contributed by Peter Haward

Let me explain at once that I am not a yacht designer, although when caught out in winter storms at sea I have sometimes wished that such was the case. My own work over the past 25 years has been in the delivery of yachts and other small vessels for their owners, agents or builders. In this period I have made 12 Transatlantic crossings and many hundred passages in Northern European and Mediterranean waters, at sea summer and winter alike. The following comments are based on these experiences.

Motor cruisers and even motor yachts—the latter expression by custom is accorded to craft of 45 ft. or more—seldom make extended ocean voyages like sailing yachts of comparable size. A basic reason is the difficulty of carrying the necessary fuel. Hence it is still no small achievement to cross the Atlantic in, say, a 70 ft. motor yacht. A second reason is that the average motor yacht is not so versatile as a good sailing yacht which, with a deep heavy ballast keel and comparatively low superstructure, can be expected to survive a complete knock down.

Nevertheless, fishing vessels of 60 ft. and upwards regularly encounter and survive great storms out at sea and it is probably correct to regard motor yachts built on trawler lines as among the most seaworthy. I recently delivered a new 63 ft. M.F.V. type yacht *Patrona* from the Mediterranean to Scotland.

In contrast to the hard chine hull of the modern fast cruiser these M.F.V. type vessels have less initial stability but possess basically "stiff" qualities. They commence to roll easily but demonstrate an emphatic righting moment from around a 20° list. It was not until near the end of the voyage that we experienced really bad weather with the wind backing SE and increasing to a genuine Force 10 or more. The performance of this M.F.V. type during the spell of heavy weather greatly impressed me and the experience left me with great confidence in this kind of motor yacht.

Good motor cruisers and yachts can take a great deal of punishment, but to face extreme conditions such as in a prolonged Force 10 storm they must be designed to provide exceptional stability and this is very difficult to incorporate unless a prospective owner makes it top priority and is willing to sacrifice some of the requirements so often demanded by other motor yachtsmen. It must be realised that stability is essential only for safety, not for performance: in fact its inclusion in a design may intrude on desirable accommodation, on speed, on price and even on that vanity more-and-more affecting yachts today—*styling*. Having said this, it is a credit to good motor yacht designers that so many of their products prove so seaworthy.

However, the last thing the average yachtsman desires to encounter is a Force 10 storm, nor unless he is very unlucky is he likely to meet one if he pays attention to weather forecasts and avoids taking unnecessary risks. Most motor cruisers are fast compared with sailing yachts and they will frequently be able to run a considerable distance for shelter, thus dodging the worst part of a rising gale. There is one exception to this, which is the storm which arrives unexpectedly or with little warning, often due to the development of an intense and fast moving secondary. Storms of this kind may be very localised and of short duration, but they can cause considerable damage to yachts in their track. Happily they occur very rarely, and the story of the loss of the *Maricelia* is one of the most tragic on record.

I knew the *Maricelia*, having had the experience of delivering this 52 ft. twin screw diesel yacht from Rosneath, Scotland, to the Solent. She is a thoroughly seaworthy '*Brown Owl*' class boat, a popular product of James Silver Ltd., built just before the war. In 1964 she was purchased by James Fraser and he was cruising the North Brittany coast late in the year with his wife, his niece Alison Mitchell and two friends. Having experienced a fire in the galley they had decided to terminate their holiday and were returning to their home port of St. Helier, Jersey, from St. Malo, when they ran into trouble. This is a short sea crossing of some 40 miles and though the forecast told of rough weather there had been no hint at the time of leaving that conditions would deteriorate into a real Force 10 storm. They left St. Malo at 8 a.m. on 9th October 1964 and the weather quickly deteriorated, a S.W. wind remorselessly rising to gale and beyond. The course involved having the sea nearly on the port beam and the cruiser rolled heavily on her way to weather the buoys on the western edge of the Minquiers reefs. The two women were thrown several times out of their berths.

Real trouble began as the yacht approached the S.W. end of Jersey. The storm was due to an intense but very small depression unexpectedly careering in from the Atlantic. From a barograph reading in Jersey we learn that atmospheric pressure fell over 25 millibars in 3 hours to a minimum reading, which occurred around 2 p.m., of 965 millibars. The wind must have reached storm conditions during the steep barometric fall and the R.N.L.I. still reported N.W. Force 10 at 6 p.m., in the evening. A highest gust of over 90 knots was recorded in Jersey.

A sudden veer with frightful squalls must have come through at about 2 p.m., just as the *Maricelia* was making her Jersey landfall, her look-outs scanning the thick weather anxiously, probably unable to see more than half a mile. Already the owner's wife had been thrown across the yacht and was suffering a broken arm. Then a heavy sea landed on the foredeck and smashed open the main saloon windows sending a great quantity of water into the ship. Efforts were made to plug the gap with a mattress and at about the same time a brief glimpse of land was reported, though there was no further sight of Jersey for another half hour. By then a very serious situation had developed. Land was very near but barely visible and not properly identified. Almost certainly the yacht was in an area of tidal overfalls that would be desperately dangerous in the Force 10 storm that had just veered suddenly through about 90°. On top of this she was already seriously damaged and a crew member badly injured. Perhaps the skipper thought that by standing on he would identify La Corbière and then gain shelter under the lee of the South Coast of Jersey. As it was, with the swell of the old South West wind still rampant, and the rapidly rising sea from the N.W. becoming ever more threatening, a very violent, completely confused, utterly lethal cauldron must have existed off South West Jersey.

Exactly what happened next probably cannot be known, except that soon one of the tide ridden, wind crazed seas broke onto the yacht and raised the sentry box type wheelhouse clean overboard and with it the whole of the upper saloon roof and coach coamings, the forward windows of which were already stove in. The owner and one other man in the wheelhouse were flung into the sea but how the others were washed from the yacht is unknown. With the whole of the ship's company in the water, miraculously together, the *Maricelia* motored on. Erroll Bruce, who is a cousin of Alison Mitchell, suggests the auto pilot was still working, but had this been so I suspect she would have run into the rocks near La Corbière at the extreme S.W. of Jersey. In fact she went away to the east, probably her logical course not under command, and must have gained some shelter. With her heart exposed bare to the sea another big breaker must certainly have finished her.

Two and a half hours later Capt. R. S. Taylor and R.N.L.I. coxswain Edward Labalestier, and another, putting out in the Pilot launch *La Rosière* in an attempt to render help, found her just outside St. Helier breakwater, motoring round in circles. Had the crew managed to avoid going overboard it is likely that they could have been saved or might even have brought their yacht into harbour.

Only Alison survived the ordeal. I cannot conceive how she endured clinging to wreckage through the next 20 hours in the bitter, black, wild, hopeless night, but that is forever her private, incredible feat. She was washed ashore at 11:30 the next morning on the N.W. side of Jersey. She climbed a 100 ft. cliff, reached Lower Egypt Farm unaided and then collapsed.

This disaster illustrates a weakness in many motor yachts. The hull may be capable of surviving very heavy weather but it is the top hamper and wheel-houses which may be a source of weakness. In this respect sailing yachts are stronger, but few, if any, could carry sail in winds gusting up to 90 knots, an occurence which is unlikely to be encountered in a lifetime of ordinary cruising. The real danger was due to being caught out in storm force winds with exceptionally bad visibility in narrow rock infested waters. Under such conditions any small vessel whatever her type might be in peril. For Alan Watt's meteorological comments see page 249.

For Alan Watt's meteorological comments see page 249.

MODERN MOTOR CRAFT

The majority of modern motor craft are now designed for speed in excess of the normal waterline length formula. Speed is a safety factor for motor craft within their normal cruising range as the faster the boat the less is the risk of getting caught out in an unheralded gale or storm such as brought disaster to *Maricelia*. High speed usually requires hard chine forms, with a basically flat bottom or with a degree of 'V' bottom, partially or completely along the whole length. Given sufficient power, now available from high speed diesels and, of course, more easily, if more dangerously, from petrol motors, and a not too heavily constructed vessel, dynamic forces can hoist her on top of the sea like a surf board. Once 'planing' she will have broken free of the speed waterline length law. The way is open to new, interesting factors.

The craft gains an important element of stability from the dynamic forces pressing on the sea and these augment her natural stability. She will tend to have excellent *initial* stability, because the chines represent good buoyancy in the 'wings' or turn of the bilges, the position at which it will give an immediate righting moment. However, should a hard chine vessel be thrown heavily on her beam ends this ability to come upright will be much less apparent, and it must be recognised that rule 1 for power craft seamanship is to avoid being knocked down by a wave.

Another credit factor derives from the requirements for planing—lightweight. The designer has to specify lightweight—and strength to cope with pounding into rough seas. Lightweight is an important factor towards good buoyancy, an excellent quality towards seaworthiness. Of course it must be remembered that if a hard chine craft has to be slowed down to below planing speeds—often a necessity in bad weather, the dynamic stability goes, just as stabilizers for heavy displacement vessels do not work if speed is reduced. However, reduction of speed is more likely when punching into a heavy headsea, and that is not when stability is the big worry.

However there are problems. The best speed for a given power will be obtained from a completely flat bottom. The trouble is that for such a boat the sea would have to be completely flat too—a more difficult thing to arrange!

33. The Fraserburgh lifeboat overturning on the face of a wave beyond the distressed fishing vessel *Opal*, seen heading towards the right of the picture. One end of the lifeboat can be seen just to the right of her forward mast, *see page 306*.

34. The 52 ft. twin screw diesel yacht *Maricelia*. The picture was taken 10 years before she was caught out in the intense local storm between St. Malo and Jersey. *Photo: Peter Howard.*

36. Bay of Biscay gale. Picture taken from the 75 ft. motor yacht *Parama*. Built 1933 by Miller of St. Monance to design of G. L. Watson.
Photo: Peter Havard.

35. Spey Class motor sailer in a winter gale off the Southern Spanish coast.
Photo: Peter Havard.

Driving into even a slight sea will quickly become like driving a horse-and-cart over a ploughed field, not sparing the horses. Thus even the early hardchine craft had a decent 'V' entry, diminishing as it ran aft, soon to be unrepentantly flat bottomed. Going at speed in rough weather they had to absorb dreadful punishment—and so did the crew. Wartime 'mosquito' craft, M.T.B's., and Air Sea Rescue boats warranted requirements where maximum speed for available power was the first consideration. I was told that some Air Sea Rescue boats which coped with U.K. waters had to be hastily strengthened when sent to operate in the vicious steep seas common in winter in the Mediterranean. Extra strength for an existing design will always mean extra weight—less speed for the same power—but that is what had to be.

Then came American designer Ray Hunt who introduced 'Deep V'—carrying a substantial 'V' entry form right the way aft. You can tell a 'Deep V' hull by looking at the transom where the chine makes not a right angle turn but an obtuse angle, extending relatively deeply into the water. This simple, perhaps obvious development—all good ideas appear obvious in retrospect—went a tremendous way to improving the seaworthiness of hard chine craft. Ray Hunt's designs were adopted by Bertram Boats and Dick Bertram spectacularly demonstrated their superiority in contemporary Off-Shore Power Boat Racing. To get on the plane requires a little more power, but few of the power boat boys are squeamish about using petrol so there was no particular problem and this was more than compensated by the new sea keeping qualities.

The advent of Deep V planing boats has developed the seaworthiness-at-speed, and even total seaworthiness, in the same way as light displacement sailing yachts may often be superior to their heavily built, take-any-punishment-we-hope predecessors. It does not mean that going to windward at speed has now become comfortable—windward work in any boat, sail or power, will always be the ultimate in seagoing discomfort—but size-for-size, and other things equal, Deep V power boats are likely to make to windward faster in worse weather than other types.

A human vanity called "styling" appears now to be having an effect on boat design, rather in the way that it holds sway in the car world. Whatever effects this whim may have on the motor trade, its influence on the boat industry has slipped in some charlatan shapes, perhaps from science fiction. Without becoming the old sailorman, I suggest that a logical shape for a projectile is not necessarily suitable for something that has to survive on the border line between two mediums, sometimes not clearly defined and neither of them always docile. Contemporary styles in boats today have complicated the problem of creating a good craft. Sensible designs are tending to be at loggerheads with salesmanship to an uninitiated public. The idea of a visor, sun or whatever, extending ahead of the wheelhouse windshield, now included in so many modern designs has the effect of being an efficient lever by which a sea striking below it will more easily wrench the roof upwards.

Several years ago I was required to take a 55 ft. fibreglass hulled semi-fast twin screw diesel yacht from England to Southern Portugal. The semi-fast side of the boat was scuppered before I joined because her owner appeared to wish his boat to be independent of mankind for a decade. On board were enough spares to construct two extra engines and iron rations for an expeditionary force. A feature of the yacht was her enormous storage space, which must have been a great sales point for the broker in this case. Every square inch had been used for the above-mentioned whim, mostly with heavy stuff, and I was told that the forward water and fuel tanks must be left empty because she tended to 'dip her bow'. The extra water we could do without but the fuel was necessary to promote the Biscay crossing.

In the event we enjoyed a calm trip across to North West Spain and it was not until we were south of Lisbon with the fuel forward used up that we began to punch just a force 4 headwind. The bow dipping business was no myth. Heavily laden the craft laboured ludicrously into the ensuing sea. I halved our speed to under five knots but we wallowed and lumbered. Thinking he was designing a cruiser with planing qualities, the designer had perpetrated further on his magnificent sun visor roof by giving a reverse sheer forward. This was now busily engaged in scooping up ever larger samples of sea and sloshing it around the foredeck. I was occasionally cutting the throttles to discourage the habit but suddenly all our weaknesses were laid bare. She dipped into a good one, steeply. Green it rolled lazily along the short foredeck to assail the wheelhouse. The complete lump of water seemed to fit the triangular area formed by the windshield and visor roof extension and, arrested and deflected by the sloping glass, its weight came to the visor. The roof was torn from its fastenings to the superstructure, lifted 4 inches and permitted a torrent to desecrate the wheelhouse/saloon, doing an immense amount of damage, particularly to electrical equipment and switches. We crept into Villa Real the next day without even a good sea story.

In order to emphasize some glaring examples of nonseaworthiness let me confide a yarn that similarly does not, you may think, warrant inclusion in a book on heavy weather, but it does offer a lesson for those who aim to design or sail in proper seagoing craft.

Excellently powered with twin well proven 255 H.P. Mercruiser petrol motors with 'Z' drive transmission, this particular motorcraft was 36 ft. long, fibreglass, deep 'V', narrow gutted, low freeboard, straight sheer—but with her cabin coach roof carried right to the bow in a curve she had a reverse sheer look. The 'modern styling' made it more likely that anybody standing on the high camber, forward sloping coach roof would be in great danger of falling overboard and if the bow were dipped at speed it would create a dynamic down-ward force to augment the weight of green water. As if obligatory, she had the standard visor style extension to the wheelhouse roof. Her sleek projectile effect forward seemed to have very little to do with floatation. I fear to state that she appeared not unlike some of the latest breed of off-shore powerboat racers but with a proportionally large and lightweight wheelhouse. Either there is some-thing I have overlooked or else the ensuing experience is a complete freak or else some ominous possibilities may be revealed in further rough sea racing.

She could cruise at well over 30 knots and on our first leg we made good 150 miles in 6 hours, then having to make port to replenish the fuel supply that vanished considerably more quickly than we had been given to understand would happen. For my purpose the tale of teething troubles can be dismissed; sufficient to say that after some difficulties we finally left Brest bound, I hoped, for Leixoes, Portugal, with the "standard long range" fuel tanks augmented by 44 5 gallon Jerry Cans and 17 empty non-returnable oil cans, 20 litres capacity. To save overall weight, we carried less than a quarter of the designed freshwater capacity; even so, for the first two hours, because of the burden of extra fuel, this lightweight, very powerful craft could not get fully on the plane. When it did however, it was almost immediately capable of approaching its normal cruising speed. However, having made our departure from the Ar Men buoy off the Saints rocks at the northern end of the Bay of Biscay, in the interest of fuel supply, we made about 22 knots throughout the night—except for various stationary periods while we manually transferred fuel. At first the wind was North Force 4, probably reaching 13 or 14 knots mean true velocity, and by dawn it had veered NE and slackened to about 10 knots. The long, barely per-ceptible swell from the North was crossed by the new slight sea from the exist-ing wind.

At eight in the morning I estimated we were making 25 knots and overtaking the seas at some 14 knots. There was no sign of trouble—until it all happened. My crew Tim Jackson was happily asleep in the wheelhouse/saloon berth, while I was at the helm. Suddenly we seemed to be in the middle of an ex-plosion. The boat overtook and fell over the leading edge of what must have been a rather steeper sea than usual, or than we had overtaken before. She dipped I suppose a little lower or a little steeper, though that was not obvious at the time. Then she was impaled too steeply into the gently upward sloping trailing edge of the wave ahead—and just went on at 25 knots. Remember the unbroken water of the sea is not moving; it is the undulations of the sea that move. Only when the waves or the crests break is there actually movement of water; thus it is that when the boat dug herself into the solid water, the impact with the wheelhouse was at her true speed.

Both windscreens went to smithereens and the two heavy beams carrying the windscreen wipers were hurled aft, luckily hitting nobody. The centre stainless steel tube supporting the roof let go and was buckled; the roof itself was lifted a foot. The aft window was bent backwards and broken, as if it had let some of the sea go straight on. One starboard glass panel disappeared. A torrent of water was pouring into the forecabin nearly to bunk height and holding the fibreglass floorboards down so tightly that it was slow to find its way into the bilge.

The wheelhouse/saloon was a complete wreck, much equipment damaged and all our personal gear soaked and much of it ruined. I estimated she was about an eighth full of water. Broken 'pebble' safety glass was everywhere. I blessed this invention because normal glass would have cut me to ribbons. With this stuff I got away with 15 minor cuts and somehow a small pebble was embedded in my chest.

At some stage after this instant shambles I cut the throttles and put the engines into neutral. The boat now lay broadside on to an unbelievably slight sea. Imperceptible she lifted to long swell, bobbing gently to the modest waves.

Having gone through the night at over 20 knots we had used up a great deal of our fuel and taking into account the deliberately small amount of freshwater aboard we were now within our design laden weight.

We shovelled out glass, lifted a floorboard under the water in the forecabin to let it run aft to the pumps more quickly, and we easily pumped her out with the hand and electric bilge pumps. Because of partially blocked limbers through a bulkhead very little water got into the engine compartment before we were getting rid of it at a good speed. Power units and batteries were unharmed but we had to deal with a few live wires in the circuits. We rigged the cockpit cover as a windshield, sorted out the general mess, estimated we were some 110 miles north of Coruña and set a course in that direction, first at a cautious 10 knots, later to around 12, but never again allowing us the luxury of overtaking the waves. We arrived at Coruña that evening.

The whole accident was related to the idea of cruising at speeds faster than the speed of the seas. This is a feature of motor boating that is coming more to the fore, now that people are demanding not just cruisers that will get on the plane, but really high powered craft, direct developments from off-shore power-boat racing.

There is also the problem of avoiding a broach before heavy following seas. One answer often suggested, is to give her the gun and go faster than the waves, but as a complete solution I think this is invalid because in so doing you will eventually risk a new set of troubles, and if the weather was particularly bad you could pay for it very heavily.

Consider a basic characteristic of the wind raised wave. Leave aside the fact that waves are seldom uniform in their overall array along the seascape, one of the main things about waves is that the leading edge is nearly always far steeper than the trailing edge. It follows therefore that when meeting a sea head-on a boat will immediately tend to lift, head upwards clear of the sea. Eventually of course she must crash down, but this will commence from a substantial bow upward position. Of course a boat punching a sea can sometimes bury herself into it but even as she does so the tendency, momentarily, will be to lift clear first. The opposite prevails when running faster than the seas. The boat will first run up the gentle slope of the trailing edge of the wave, then take off, or fall off the steep edge. The bow will depress downwards and be in danger of burying itself into the sea ahead at a great speed *pointing downwards*. I submit that in my opinion the worst type of bow available for a boat subjected to such a hazard is one shaped like a projectile, however beautiful it may be in the eye of its creator or owner, and I have to express surprise at the number of boats designed for off-shore power-boat racing that follow this cult.

I am reminded of another encounter that was disaster free, but at the time nerve racking, when I was delivering a new 31 ft. 'Futura' Chris Craft from the builders at Fiumicino, Italy to Sheppard's Marina, Gibraltar. There are differences to the story I have just told which warrant evaluation. The primary one is that we were not, overall, going faster than the seas, although these were propelled this time not by a moderate breeze but a substantial Force 6 wind with a fetch of probably 50 miles or more. There was another factor, a mistake due to laziness. We had used fuel up in the night and on replenishing the tanks I had taken the nearest jerry cans to hand instead of thinking of trim and getting rid of the 30 gallons stowed in the forepeak.

These 'Futuras' are practical built to-a-price plywood, hard chine, beamy, with a nice flair at the bow and modest sheer. With certain petrol installations they could reach over 25 knots; with twin Perkins 4 236 diesels they could just get on the plane and reach perhaps 14 knots. Ours was one of these latter and that morning off South East Spain the rising wind and sea were treating us to some exhilarating surf rides. Despite the unfair bow weight she was not difficult to steer. Then a good big one came up from astern, set her at the crucial angle on its leading edge and off she went, increasing her speed, maintaining her stance on the wave. Then faster, and she began to make ahead into the trough, where the bows struck the sea ahead and her speed was checked with a lurch. The same sea came up from astern and picked her up just as before, and again she was speeding along surf board style. Again in the trough and again the same wave caught her up and carried her along with precision. Now the sea had grown larger and more vigorous and steeper, and on this occasion she slewed to starboard as she careered down hill. Full port helm, but no result; away she went, faster, heeling, down into the trough. But no particular pause this time and the bow went under; then the forecabin coach roof began to disappear, her list to starboard steepening. I wrenched shut the throttles and she seemed to hang there immersed halfway up to the saloon coach roof, heeling sickly. Slowly she lifted her bow, heaved herself to an even keel and lay beam on to the seas. I went below and saw John Dick ruefully picking his bedding off the floor.

We brought the 30 gallons of fuel aft, secured it in the cockpit and started off again. The change in trim made a tremendous difference and there was never a hint of a repeat performance.

I have noticed several times that semi-fast hard chine craft keep out of trouble if they have a bluff bow or a big flair that will promote more buoyant lift as the stem is driven into the sea. The effect, however, is to stop the boat in her tracks and that by itself gives the bow a chance to lift. Perhaps a combination of a bluff, buoyant bow, plus a raked flare at the upper stem topside to give a dynamic lift, would be a good combination. This would be remote from projectile styling.

High speed problems do not of course mean a particular boat is unseaworthy if kept at a modest speed. Both traditional displacement motor cruisers and motor yachts and also some hard chine craft, given good stability, perhaps due to good beam or even a ballast keel, can survive rough weather. It may be necessary to avoid beam sea conditions—and experience will develop reliable judgment—and it will almost certainly be necessary at some stage in deteriorating weather to slow down when driving into a headsea. Many boats of 35 ft. and upward can safely struggle into a Force 7 to 8 wind at around 4 knots. Size will be a factor in acceptable performance. If the weather worsens to say Force 9 or more it is likely to be prudent to give up trying to make to windward. Slow right down, even stop one engine on a twin screw boat if fuel supply is a problem. Keep the seas a little on the bow, presenting a nice slab of buoyancy. Just holding her own, the vessel should be fairly happy and have steerage way in a gale or worse. Of course the smaller she is the worse the discomfort and the greater the danger. Lying-to like this she will not use much fuel.

Possibly like sailing yachts, ultimate safety for a motor cruiser lies in running before the seas, but the ultimate remains beyond my experience I am happy to say. I suspect that lying-to could be the better policy to the end. It is the known tactics of fishing vessels in storms—'dodge' is the expression—of keeping head to sea with the bow paid off a little to present good buoyancy, and maintaining speed sufficient only for adequate steerage way. I have heard a number of motor yacht skippers claim remarkable deviations from their course because severe weather had made it impossible even to turn round into the seas and reach a lie-to position. I suspect that in many cases inexperience may account for many of these detours rather than the prevailing weather, but nevertheless there are doubtless times when it will be imprudent to maintain a beam to sea course in many motor yachts. Nevertheless I have always succeeded in making some little progress to windward in gales. Lying-to has only been adopted by me for reasons of fuel supply.

Notes for the engineer do not go amiss since power cruisers are often in command of a skipper-cum-engineer. By far the most frequent breakdown at sea is due to fuel failing to reach the engine. The violent motion caused by bad weather increases the chance of the debris of dirty fuel tanks being swilled into suspension in the fuel and therefore being carried to the filters and blocking them or even blocking the fuel lines on the tank side of the filter. Be prepared for both these problems. Ensure you have spare fuel filter elements aboard and can clean existing felt type filter elements. Make sure you have a way of blowing through or clearing a pipe at the tank itself. Sometimes a wire reamed through a valve is the answer. Regular attention to filters can prevent trouble at awkward times.

Some fittings currently used in motor yachts and cruisers are unseaworthy. I once brought a handsome but heavily top-hampered 64 ft. boat from West Africa against a persistent headwind reaching Force 7 for a considerable time. At times we were slowed to 4 knots and three port hole fittings failed in the forepeak, owing to the fins in the hinges severing through impact with seas, which gave us fun trying to devise methods of keeping out cascading water, and a great deal of use of the efficient bilge pumping system.

In complete contrast to enforced speed reductions in face of tough headwinds, the mention of port hole troubles reminds me of the elegant and seaworthy Tarquin motor yachts of the Aquarius Boat Company. When delivering one of their earlier 60 footers to the Mediterranean I was urged to make all speed in order to reach Genoa in time for the December 1972 Boat Show. It involved keeping up full speed across the Gulf of Lions during a Force 8 mistral. Departing from Palma on the last leg, we made 16 knots with that wind 6 points off the port bow. We gradually shortened the initial fetch of more than 100 miles until reaching the pleasing lee of Porquerolle Island. The boat's steep 'V' hull form, generous beam, heavy engine and bilge tankage offered reliable stability, strength and power. The latter item in this case was by twin 575 HP 'V' 12 GM diesels. Alternative MTU power gives higher speeds which, had we been so equipped, I am sure could have been exploited to ride into that gale even more dramatically and just as safely. It remained for us to grit our teeth, hold tight our eyeballs, keep a tenacious lookout and adopt the handhold religion that commands you never let go of one strong point before grasping the next. Thus adjusted we watched the boat get on with it. On arrival at Genoa we discovered no damage other than a port hole fitting that had been knocked clean out and across the forward crews' quarters which, on this craft, was isolated from the rest of the boat and uninhabited during the delivery voyage. Bilgewater was handled by the automatic pump.

In conclusion it can be said that there are increasing numbers of well designed types of motor yachts which combine high speed and internal luxury with really rugged sea keeping qualities. But like light displacement sailing yachts, light displacement motor craft must be kept light if they are to give their best performance. The weight of improvements (whether at the instigation of an enthusiastic yacht chandler or gradually acquired over a period of time) can add up to a substantial total. If this is added without consultation after a good designer has finalised all his weight and displacement calculations, it may make a hash of the stability problem, to say nothing of robbing the owner of those coveted top knots in speed that he has demanded and paid for.

24

HEAVY WEATHER CONCLUSIONS

In heavy weather the two principal factors to contend with are the force of the wind and the state of the sea.

The wind dictates the amount of sail which can be carried and can cause the loss of sails, rigging or the mast of a yacht, but it is the seas that do the damage to hull and superstructure which can be the more dangerous.

The state of the sea is derived from the wind, but is not always in direct relationship with its average force. Confused, and therefore potentially dangerous seas, are aggravated by gustiness and shifts of the wind. There is thus a logical reason for yachtsmen judging the strength of the wind by the velocity of the gusts rather than by the mean force on the Beaufort Notation. A really gusty Force 6 may do as much damage as a relatively steady Force 8, and in a storm, with gusts of hurricane strength, the seas can become absolutely chaotic. Other influences on the seas are current (Gulf Stream, Chap. 7, 15, 18, 19 and 20), tidal disturbances (*Mary Aidan*, Chap. 3; *Cohoe*, Chap. 4; *Tilly Twin* and *Dancing Ledge*, Chap. 11; *Cohoe III*, Chap. 12, etc.), shoals and obstructions on the bottom (*Zara*, Chap. 2; *Cohoe II*, Chap. 9; *Aloa* and *Marie Galante II*, Chap. 16).

It is not the size of a wave that is necessarily dangerous, but its shape and steepness (which can be nearly vertical), and the angle at which it strikes the yacht. The most dangerous are the freak waves, of which several examples have been given in this book: *Zara*, Chap. 2; *Vertue XXXV*, Chap. 7; Channel Storm, Chap. 11; *Aloa*, Chap. 16; *Puffin*, Chap. 17; *Atom* and *Tzu Hang*, Chap. 20.

High waves following on a succession of low ones form a common pattern of the sea, but to merit the label of a "freak" the wave must be abnormal in height or shape, arising from the combination of intersection of wave trains as explained by Laurence Draper in Appendix 2. Such waves, attaining dangerous dimensions, are few and far between and their life is short. They are rarely encountered in home waters, but it is interesting to note that they can occur in winds as low as Force 6 (*Puffin*, Chap. 17). I even heard that an American yacht, near the end of the Transatlantic Race of 1966, encountered two immense seas in the North Sea when the wind was no more than Force 5.

Where freak waves can be most dangerous is in an ocean storm when the ordinary run of the seas is already very high and the "freak" is so gigantic that it can roll a yacht completely over or pitch-pole her stern over bow. Plates 25,

26, 27 and 28 show freak seas and freak formations, but what puzzles me is how any yacht can survive them.

The experiences of yachts in gales and storms described in this book lead to drawing a distinction between what I call the ordinary gale in home waters, with which any yacht may have to contend, and the ocean storm which is rarely encountered, as the number of yachts making ocean voyages is comparatively few, and for the most part their skippers avoid the worst seasons, such as the hurricane months.

In ordinary gales when depressions pass there seems no great element of risk to a well-found yacht provided she remains in deep water. This was shown in the Santander Race gale of 1948 and the Channel Storm of 1956. Both were exceptionally severe for the time of year and, although some quite small yachts were involved, there were no losses among the yachts in deep water.

When the wind rises to Force 10 or more and the grey beards ride over the ocean we arrive at totally different conditions, and for yachts it is battle for survival as, indeed, it sometimes may be for big ships.

I will now comment on some of the various aspects of heavy weather and summarize the conclusions arrived at in earlier chapters.

SAIL CARRYING

When cruising in the ordinary way and not racing, a yacht should be reefed down progressively as the weather worsens, always in advance of immediate necessity, despite a natural inclination to postpone the unpleasant task, hoping that the weather may show an improvement. It is obvious that the longer reefing is deferred the harder it is to do, and the greater the strain and risk of damage to the gear in the meantime. Most of this is avoided by reefing in time and carrying less than the maximum that the yacht can stand. A cruising yacht should be reefed down to canvas to suit the squalls and gusts rather than the mean force of the wind. Very little speed is sacrificed by precautionary reefing. Once the wind rises to Force 5 and over a yacht approaches her maximum speed. An extra roll or two on the mainsail reefing gear or the setting of a smaller headsail may reduce speed by only a quarter or half a knot, which does not matter much when passage-making. The extra sail required to achieve the last quarter-knot places a load on a yacht's sail, gear and crew which is out of all proportion to the gain.

When sailing close-hauled or beating to windward there is no temptation to drive a cruising yacht too hard on the wind, as the strain on the helmsman is considerable, for he is exposed to the full force of the wind and often half blinded by spray and rain driven in his face. In a fresh breeze there are no particular problems but, if this strengthens to strong winds of say a mean of 25 to 30 knots or more, there comes a time when the boat should be steered fuller to maintain enough speed to drive against the head seas. As she lifts to the crest of a big sea she should be luffed a little to the breaking crest, and then at the top the helm should be put hard up for a moment as she subsides into the trough. Luffing may also be necessary to meet squalls, but if a luff is carried too far the boat may ship heavy water and may even be brought up all standing; the sails will flog and there is a risk of tearing them. Bearing away on the crest of a sea helps the boat to come gently on the other side at an angle to the sea instead of her stem falling on it. It also helps the boat to recover some of the way lost in the impact when she broke over the head of the sea. When turning to windward in strong winds and gales the boat should be weaving in the seas, lively and laughing. A good helmsman will soon get the knack of it, but with an inexperienced man at the wheel it may be best to shorten sail further, as real damage can be sustained through bad steering.

The determination of the amount of sail to carry when close-hauled is not difficult, because a boat has a voice of her own, and will clamour for a reduction in canvas when it becomes necessary, but when *running* before strong winds or gales the amount of sail which should be carried is more of a problem. It is difficult to assess the strength of the wind when it is following, and the increases in wind and sea may be almost imperceptible until matters begin to get out of hand. In bad weather there is much to be said in favour of not running with more sail than could be carried if close-hauled. The boat will be fast, but she will be under better control and more comfortable than if hard pressed. Besides this, an emergency may arise in which the yacht must be able to round up and beat back. It may be an accident such as a man overboard, or, as happened to me in 1966, a bad landfall may be stupidly made in fog. The yacht was cornered on a lee shore between Chesil Beach and Portland. On that occasion the wind recorded at Portland, as we passed, was Force 6 gusting Force 8. It is possible to carry full sail in a wind of this strength, but luckily we had shortened down by taking two or three turns in the roller reefing gear of the mainsail and had set a staysail instead of a genoa. We would not have had room or time to reef, but, shortened down as we were, we were able to beat effortlessly back round Portland through the very rough overfalls west of the Bill.

I repeat that when cruising there is no point in being overcanvassed, with the boat hard pressed, steering difficult and everything miserably uncomfortable for the sake of an extra half-knot. When cruising the purpose is to make a smart, seamanlike passage with the minimum of wear and tear on ship and crew.

When ocean racing it is a different matter. The object is to make the fastest time regardless of the weather. The amount of sail to carry varies with the individual design of the boat and her length in relation to the length and height of the seas. For racing in heavy weather precisely the right sail area must be

271

found. If it is too much, some speed will be lost, there will be excessive leeway and risk of damage which may put a boat out of the race altogether. On the other hand, if too little sail is carried, the boat will be hours behind. What is sometimes forgotten is that when turning to windward in heavy weather you must have sail area to drive against all the forces of nature. Plate 14 shows the sort of seas the ocean racers had to beat against round Portland in the Fastnet Race of 1957. The picture was taken from *Cohoe II*, when returning from La Coruña, but in exactly the same conditions as at night in the Fastnet Race, with wind Force 7 to 8 and a lee-going tide, which explains why the sea is wall-like, rather than breaking. Damage may occur when driving at 6 knots against such seas, because of the risk of "falling off the wave" on the other side, especially if the tide or current is weather-going, when the seas are steeper and breaking—references *Carina, Bloodhound, Cohoe III, Elseli IV*, see Chapter 12.

Mast, sails and rigging should be designed so that a boat can be laid flat on her beam ends in extreme gusts and squalls without damage. Something is wrong if anybody is comfortable, other than the watch below held in their berths by canvas leeboards.

I hate to say this, because I dislike discomfort, but I am afraid that it is true. It will be disputed by some inshore racing men and cruising men, and by those who believe in the science of simulated waves in tank tests. Nevertheless, it has been tested by long experience at sea, experimenting with changes of sail against level competitors. I remember vividly, for example, one Channel Race in which we had shortened sail on a reach, but *Meon Maid* (or another of the *Belmore* class) set everything, including her big genoa. She was grossly over-canvassed, almost laid flat in the water at times, but she nevertheless gained until we responded by setting more sail. However, in the easily driven more modern ocean racers the aim must be to carry exactly the right amount of sail as determined by speedometer and instruments, with frequent sail changes to get the best out of them.

When gales occur during races it is now a matter of pressing on. Sheltering to avoid a foul tide round a headland may pay a small ocean racer in headwinds of gale force, when little progress can be made against the stream, (*Cohoe*, Chap. 4; *Cohoe III*, Chap. 12), but minutes can no longer be lost, as competition is getting hotter every year. For courses steered under storm canvas, see *Lutine, Bloodhound, Rondinella* and *Galloper*, Chap. 11. Heaving-to or other gale tactics are no longer resorted to except in quite exceptional weather. There are, of course, risks in the game, but they are calculated and accepted as in any other form of hard sport such as motor racing or mountaineering. The principal ones are those of dismasting, breaking the rudder, or other serious damage on a lee shore. In these respects the risks in R.O.R.C. races in the English Channel equal those in the longer open ocean events.

NAVIGATION IN HEAVY WEATHER

Although it is known by experienced yachtsmen, I think it is worth drawing attention to the fact that navigation, and particularly pilotage, is more difficult in gales than in ordinary weather. In the early stages of a gale the weather may be thick, with rain and fog reducing visibility to as little as half a mile. When the seas have had time to build up, distant objects can only be seen when on the crests of the waves, which makes identification of lights difficult. (References: Chap. 1 and 11.) Spray and dense rain reduces visibility (Chap. 7, 14 and 15, *Barlovento*), though it has the merit of smoothing the seas temporarily.

PREPARATIONS FOR A GALE

The following affords a list of things to be done if strong winds develop into a gale and one gets caught out in it. Some of these will have been done already, but the list may be useful as a reminder.

(1) Don safety harness or lifelines.

(2) Shut off or bung the exhaust pipe.

(3) Close petrol cocks, both if there are two.

(4) Open cockpit drain cocks.

(5) Close all other skin cocks.

(6) See that cockpit lockers are shut and watertight. If there is an engine hatch in the cockpit, see that it is screwed down.

(7) Put storm sails in a quickly accessible position, such as in a quarter berth, or, if necessary, set them. Stow spare headsails below, not on deck.

(8) Secure all deck gear and spinnaker poles. Rubber shock cord is not enough to hold the poles in their chocks and extra lashings are necessary.

(9) Secure dinghy or raft with extra lashings.

(10) Shut hatches. Turn ventilator cowls to leeward and if thought necessary screw down ventilator covers, or stuff the vents with cloth or socks. Scuttles on the lee side should be kept open as long as possible to give ventilation and only closed under extreme conditions.

(11) Check that slide fastenings (shackles or stainless steel wire) are in good order. This should have been done in harbour, but is sometimes overlooked. Also check that shackles are ready for the storm jib at the head and tack to secure to the stay in addition to hanks.

(12) See that no loose tools are left on deck or loose in the cockpit, and that winch handles are properly secured.

(13) Hoist radar reflector.

(14) Put stopper in hawse pipe if this has not already been done. Where this has an opening for the chain link, stop it with waste or cloth to prevent leakage round the chain.

(15) Place foghorn in accessible position from the cockpit.

Work Below

(a) Mark position on the chart, bring log up to date, note barometer reading.

(b) Distribute sea-sick pills (at least an hour before the gale is expected) to any members of the crew who are likely to need them. It is useless to leave pills until the emergency arises and they should be kept in a known and readily available position so that nobody has to ask for them.

(c) Stow everything securely, especially cooking utensils and provisions, so that they cannot be thrown about or rattle.

(d) Check that bilge pumps are not choked.

(e) Check that the crew knows the position of the storm screens or panels to go over windows and where the nails or screws to secure them are stored. Screens are only required in exceptional gales.

(f) Check that navigation lights and anchor or masthead light are in proper working order. If oil lights, see that they are full (but not too full) and check that there is enough paraffin or calor gas for the stove, as anything in the nature of filling lamps or changing a gas cylinder during a gale is unpleasant.

(g) See that warps are conveniently accessible for streaming if necessary, and that they are free to uncoil.

(h) Check that no member of the crew has forgotten the position of flares, fire extinguishers and first aid.

(i) Place dry biscuits, cake, sweets, sugar and snacks in a position where they are readily available. Prepare soup or hot food and put into thermos if time permits.

(j) Put boxes of matches in a dry place or polythene bag, as if these are left lying around they will become damp owing to condensation and will not strike.

(k) Put polythene sheeting or waterproof over quarter berths if spray can reach them when the campanion doors are opened, or on any berths over which deck leaks can develop.

(l) Before nightfall put white flares in a polythene bag in a position handy for exhibiting in event of a ship approaching close on a collision course and unable to identify the yacht's lights in the seas and spray. Red flares can be left in their usual place, provided the crew knows where they are in case of emergency.

In the very rare event of a gale developing into a survival storm the boat will be swept by seas. In this event storm screens must be screwed down in advance over windows. The cockpit should be criss-crossed with ropes, following Warren Brown's recommendation, Chapter 19. A rigid dinghy must have really strong lashings to bolts through the main deck beams, not merely to the coachroof. It may have to be cut adrift.

GALE TACTICS

The following notes provide a summing-up of the conclusions arrived at from experiences in gales and storms described in earlier chapters.

Heaving-to

Heaving-to is the traditional way of riding out a gale. The best examples of weathering gales by this means were afforded by the Bristol Channel pilot cutters, big heavy vessels who short-handed, customarily hove-to in gales, summer and winter. Most yachts can be made to heave-to satisfactorily as this depends largely on sail and hull balance, but the livelier the boat and the shorter her keel the more difficult it is to achieve. It is a matter of trial and error in the individual boat. References: *Annette II* for heaving-to under all sail, reefed, Chap. 1; *Zara*, Chap. 2; *Cohoe I*, Chap. 4; *Cohoe* off Belle Île under trysail only with helm up, Chap. 6; *Mokoia*, Chap. 7. Several yachts hove-to satisfactorily in the Santander gale, including *Mehalah*, Chap. 11, and likewise *Seehexe* in the Channel gale, sailing under mainsail only, Chap. 5. Many of the American yachts in the Bermuda Race of 1960 hove-to, (see Chap. 15). See also *Cohoe III*, under mainsail and staysail, Chap. 16; *Puffin* hove-to in the Mediterranean Mistral, Chap. 17, under trysail only, but with a man at the wheel. In some boats it is possible to heave-to under storm jib with the helm down. If a yacht will heave-to satisfactorily under reefed mainsail and staysail or storm jib it is surprising how well she will stand up to a gale and how comfortable she will be below. When heading close to the wind most of the pressure will be taken off the sails, and I sometimes wonder whether the alleged difficulties in heaving-to may be due to carrying too little sail rather than too much.

From the experiences in the Santander and Channel storms it is clear that heaving-to can be resorted to in winds up to Force 9 or Force 10, or whatever strength they may then have been. However, there may come a time, if the wind rises above gale force, when the seas run so high that the yacht will alternately be under the partial lee in the troughs and subject to the full blast on the crests, which may throw her out of control. Those who have experienced survival storms seem to agree that heaving-to would be out of the question in the gigantic seas which were experienced. There is also a limit to what slides, fastenings and sails will stand up to, so other gale tactics must be considered.

Lying a-hull

A sailing ship is said to be lying a-hull, or hulling, when all sail has been lowered and she is lying under bare poles, the vessel being left to take her own position in the seas. The hull will always be giving to, rather than resisting, the waves and sometimes the bows or stern will fall off before the seas, as she takes the natural drift to conform with them. In a small, light-displacement boat like *Cohoe I* the angle of heel will be considerable if the wind is Force 8 or more. This may be an advantage, for it heightens the weather side above the water and the hull heels away from the seas, so that they can break over and run off to leeward, meeting less resistance than they would from a stiff hull. Safety depends upon giving to the seas and not standing up against them. As the hull moves to leeward it is said to create a "slick" on the weather side which tends to reduce the severity of breaking seas. It is also said that loops of rope streamed on the windward side from stem to stern will help, but I have no experience of this. If the helm is left amidships the boat will gather way under bare pole if a sea knocks her bow off so that she is heading downwind, so at times she will make appreciable lee-way. I fancy this occurred with some of the yachts lying a-hull in the Channel Storm of 1956 (Chap. 11) and with *Varua* (Chap. 20). In my own boats I always lash the helm down, so that as she gathers way she begins to luff and lies broad-side to the seas most of the time. Excessive drift to leeward is then prevented by the keel, which acts in much the same way as when sailing on a reach. The boat will forereach slowly in the direction in which she is heading on account of the windage in the mast. For drift when hulling see *Cohoe* (Chap. 5) and *Maid of Malham* (Chap. 11), and for risk of a knockdown see next page.

The cockpit will often be partially filled by the breaking heads of seas and in really severe gales the hull itself will receive some hard knocks. Below decks the crew can take it easy, but there should always be at least one man in oilskins, wearing life-jacket and safety harness, ready to go on deck instantly to run the boat off before the wind and cast off the drag ropes. These should be coiled and ready for streaming, in case the seas become too heavy or to use in the event of emergency.

I have sucessfully adopted the tactic of hulling in several severe gales: *Mary Aidan* (Chap. 3), *Cohoe* (Chap. 5, and 7), *Cohoe III* (Chap. 16). *Maid of Malham* did this with warps streamed in the Channel Storm (Chap. 11), and *Theta* and many other boats also hulled. However, there is an element of risk of being knocked down by freak waves (*Tandala* and *Aloa*, (Chap. 16) or of being rolled over as was *Atom* (Chap. 20) in a storm. This reminds me of another example of damage while lying a-hull which was reported in the *Royal Cruising Club Journal* of 1961. The yacht was *Tom Bowling*, a J.O.G. type, reverse-sheered 21-footer of only about 2 tons of displacement. Her owner, Dr. W. W. Deane, was cruising with his wife when they were caught in a severe gale about 100 miles WSW. of Belle Île when bound for la Coruña. They were hove-to under bare pole for twenty-nine hours and, as Deane puts it, for a further twenty-eight hours "under no pole", for, after suffering a number of knockdowns, *Tom Bowling* was picked up by a sea and hurled down on her beam ends, more than 90 degrees over. The mast broke about 5 ft. above the deck, but, astonishingly, no damage was done to the hull. After the mast had been broken the yacht apparently rode out the rest of the gale without further trouble and, when it subsided, Deane cut the broken mast adrift and contrived a jury rig on the stump of the mast and a sweep set up in the hatchway. The two of them then sailed the boat 100 miles ENE. to Belle Île. They had no engine and refused assistance offered by a steamer and by a tunnyman. *Tom Bowling* eventually got back to England with the help of John Guillaume's *Melody A*, and the owners were awarded the R.C.C. Seamanship Medal, which was well merited, to say the least of it.

However, what we are concerned with here is whether hulling is safe. *Tom Bowling* is a very small yacht and she took the full impact of an Atlantic storm for which the midnight forecast on 12 July was "Severe gale, Force 9, increasing to storm, Force 10". For her it was a survival storm, but it is not certain that she would have survived better by any other means (to which I refer later) than by hulling.

What is more significant is the damage to the ocean racers in the Biscay races, when the weather forecasts were only Force 7, which is three grades lower in the Beaufort Scale. When *Tandala* was severely damaged the wind was no more than Force 8, although perhaps gusting 50 knots. The real danger seems often to come with the shift and increase of wind after a cold front has passed.

I think the best explanation of the risk of hulling comes from Mr. Nigel Warington Smyth in the *Royal Cruising Club Journal* of 1961, in which, as then Commodore of the Club, he commented on *Tom Bowling*'s dismasting. "One has to realize", he writes, "that a large breaking crest in a full gale may well be travelling at 15 or 20 knots, whereas the green water underneath it has virtually no horizontal motion. It follows that any vessel which is small enough or of shallow enough draft may be picked up and carried to leeward by the crest, at great speed until some part of her stabs into the motionless green water, and she will be smashed down, capsized or turned head over heels."

What it comes to is that the element of risk depends upon the size of the yacht in relation to the size of the breaking crests or the steepness of the seas. Thus you find small yachts lying a-hull safely in severe gales in the English Channel but getting into trouble in ocean gales, where the seas build up higher with much bigger crests. It is difficult to draw the line between what is safe and what is dangerous, but countless yachts have weathered ordinary gales by lying a-hull and I personally propose to continue the practice up to the point where I consider the situation is getting out of hand.

What, however, is clear is that hulling is dangerous, or impossible, in exceptional storms or hurricanes, owing to the risk of the boat being picked up by a sea and rolled over through 360 degrees, and even a large yacht must be regarded as small in relation to the seas which can build up in an ocean storm.

Sea anchors

An alternative to hulling is to use a sea anchor. Captain Voss was the famous exponent of sea anchors, and in his great voyages in *Tilikum* and *Sea Queen* he put his theories to the test. He showed that a small shallow-draught vessel will ride out ordinary gales (but I do not think all of them were Force 8), satisfactorily lying to a sea anchor with a riding sail to help keep her head to the wind. However, when *Sea Queen* was involved in or near to a typhoon, she capsized after her mizzen sheet parted, so that her riding sail was inoperative and at the same time she lost her sea anchor. After another sea had righted her she survived by lying a-hull. This particular experience does not reflect to the credit of sea anchors, but their value has been proved in many shallow-draught vessels such as ship's lifeboats. Valuable evidence has been given in the voyages to Norway and Iceland made by Frank Dye in his 16 ft. *Wayfarer* dinghy. It is stated that a number of gales were encountered during these adventures, but the dinghy rode through them safely lying to her sea anchor. It is difficult to believe that the boat would have survived without one.

What is in doubt, however, is whether a sea anchor is of much use to a modern deep-keeled yacht. I tried one in the severe gale in the Santander Race and so did Humphrey Barton in *Virtue XXXV* in the storm north of Bermuda. But both experiments proved unsatisfactory. What is clear is that if a sea anchor is used in a modern short-keeled yacht it is essential that sail should be set aft to keep the boat heading up to the sea anchor. This can be done in a yawl, and in a sloop much the same effect can be achieved by setting a storm jib on the back stay, but there is a limit to what a mizzen or storm jib on the backstay can stand up to, especially if it flogs, as at times it is bound to do. Other objections to the use of sea anchors are the tremendous strain thrown on the anchor and its gear, and the risk of breaking the rudder owing to the sternway of the yacht. The alternative is to ride to the sea anchor astern. The boat will then lie better and there will be no strain on the rudder, but if the sea anchor is big enough to be effective she will be tethered by the stern and not giving to the seas, so that she could be overwhelmed. Moreover, she will be presenting her weakest end with the open cockpit exposed to the breaking waves.

278

One great advantage which a sea anchor has over lying a-hull or running streaming warps is that it reduces drift to leeward more effectively, provided its dimensions are adequate for the purpose. This could be useful in seas such as the English Channel, where lee shores are never far away.

Most cruising men are against the use of sea anchors in severe gales. Dr. W. Deane is not dogmatic about it, but in his summing up of *Tom Bowling*'s knock-down he wrote that "had *Tom* been held by a sea anchor the breaking crests might have caused serious damage". When *Right Royal* was caught out in the Channel Storm of 1956 her experienced skipper commented: "It is my considered opinion that if the sea anchor had been used at the height of the gale the *ship would have been overwhelmed*." This opinion is emphatically endorsed by Robinson, Warren Brown and Moitessier, who have experienced the unbridled storms of the ocean.

On the other hand, some experienced authorities, including Nigel Warington Smyth (who has made considerable research into the behaviour of small craft in breaking seas), consider that lying to a sea anchor provides the best way of riding out a gale. Joe Byars, after being twice turned over in *Doubloon*, also believes that the best method of surviving a storm is by lying as near as possible head to wind, see Chap. 18.

My personal conclusion is not in favour of sea anchors, and some small boat world voyagers (including Robin Knox-Johnson) complain bitterly of the trouble caused by the tripping line getting entangled with the warp. I would rather run off, streaming warps (provided there is sea room), than lie to a sea anchor by the stern. However, as some experienced cruising men disagree, let us admit the matter remains controversial.

The use of oil

It has long been known that oil has a smoothing effect on heavy seas and tends to tranquillize or reduce breaking waves. The oil must be heavy. Tins of fish oil suitable for the purpose can be bought at some ship's chandlers. Proper oil-bags can also be obtained which allow the oil to seep out slowly. Voss used a canvas bag filled three parts full by loose oakum, rags and waste saturated in oil. The bag was tied up and holes were punched in it so the oil could seep away steadily. Voss had wide experience of the use of oil which he had acquired during five years of sailing in northern waters, but he rarely used oil in his canoe *Tilikum*. His most illuminating comments on oil in his classic *Venturesome Voyages* occur in his account of his experiences near a typhoon in his 19 ft. waterline yacht *Sea Queen*. He writes:

"Up to an hour previously the oil-bags did quite a lot of good in keeping the break off the large seas, but now the oil seemed to have little effect, and no trace could be detected on the water." However, the use of oil in any gale, as Voss puts it, "would not be harmful", except for its revolting smell and making the cockpit and deck dangerously slippery.

When Jean Gau was caught out in the path of a hurricane in the ketch *Atom* he lay a-hull and hung a storm oil-bag at the bottom of the weather shrouds, which he evidently considered was of value (Chap. 20).

The best testimonial for oil comes from William Albert Robinson, for it was of value in *Varua* when she was caught in what he describes as the "ultimate storm", page 223. Indeed, Robinson goes so far as to say that when *Varua* was swept by a gigantic wave, which buried the entire after part of the ship under solid water, this may have been due to a lull in the slick of oil when the men, pumping it through the forward lavatory, changed shifts.

Unfortunately, I have no personal experience in the use of oil. I carried the correct oil, together with oil-bags for thousands of miles and had it ready for use in the storm north of Bermuda, but I kept it intact as a reserve in case of an emergency that did not arise. Miles Smeeton had oil on board when *Tzu Hang* was pitch-poled in the Pacific, but likewise, as the boat was riding the seas well, did not use it. In his case the emergency did arise, but it was then too late to try oil. It is curious that oil seems to have been so little used in gales during recent years. The Committee of the Royal Ocean Racing Club in their report on the Channel storm of 1956 (Appendix 3) commented on the fact that oil had not been tried in a single yacht during the gale. Sir Francis Chichester was given special storm oil in Australia, but he never used it.

For further information of the merits of oil I wrote to an executive of the Royal National Life-boat Institution, who replied as follows:

"In general, all boats of above the 35′ 6″ class are equipped with wave subduing oil tanks. The 35′ 6″ class, which is the smallest boat now in use, is provided with oil bags. Our experts advise that storm oil may calm the water around the life-boat to the extent of preventing wave tops being whipped off by the wind, but it is doubtful whether it does anything for the wreck unless the life-boat lies to windward. The concensus of opinion is that to be effective oil has to be used in *very considerable quantities*, and since the average life-boat does not have the capacity to carry such quantities of oil little use of it is, in fact made during actual services."

This authoritative opinion confirms the practice in ships where, if oil is used at all, it is distributed in large quantities from the heavy fuel-oil tanks. It is clear that when Robinson used oil in *Varua* he also used a considerable quantity. This could be carried in his 70 ft. brigantine, but few modern small yachts would have the room to stow the necessary drums. The amount required would be dictated by the size of the seas and not by the size of the yacht. If anything, a smaller yacht would require more oil than a large one, for the need to subdue the seas would be greater. There seems little evidence to support the text book theory that a thin film of oil seeping slowly from an oil-bag will subdue really big breaking seas. Nevertheless, a 2-gallon drum of heavy oil pumped out through the heads might be useful as a temporary measure when running into a harbour in very rough weather or crossing a bar, though it would be far safer to remain at sea in deep water.

When oil is used it should be released in such a way that it will give a spread of oil between the yacht and the advancing seas. This is difficult to accomplish when hove-to, because the boat will be forereaching, and it is easiest when she is running slowly, towing warps. When lying to a sea anchor the oil-bags should be forward, as the boat will be making sternway, unless she is riding by the stern, in which case the bags should be aft. If lying a-hull, with the boat left to take her natural position in the seas, the position of the bags (whether at bows or stern or amidships) can only be determined by trial and error. If enough oil is available it may prove best to pump it out of the lavatory. The essential thing seems to be that the yacht must be making leeway so that the oil spreads to windward in the direction from which the seas are coming.

Streaming warps

There remains the tactic of running before gales streaming warps to keep the stern to the seas and to slow the boat down. The best example of this was *Samuel Pepys* in the storm north of Bermuda (Chap. 11). The method was also used by several yachts in the Channel Storm of 1956, but the results were inconclusive, as all the boats remaining in deep water came through safely, whatever tactics they adopted. *Marie Galante II* streamed warps effectively (Chap. 16) until she arrived off the Gironde, where she was lost. In the accounts of survival storms (Chap. 20) it will be noted that *Curlew* ran with warps streamed, but she broached-to several times despite them. *Varua* ran with warps streamed in the tremendous storm in the South Pacific, but *Tzu Hang* was pitch-poled while towing 60 fathoms of 3 in. hawser.

Streaming warps can only be resorted to where there is plenty of sea room to do it and in very bad storms it has the disadvantage of presenting the most vulnerable part of the boat, the cockpit and aft bulkhead, to the following seas. I heard of a 15-tonner which was pooped in this way in the Bay of Biscay, and had the coachroof bulkhead stove in. Dr. W. Deane did not stream warps when *Tom Bowling* was caught out, because it was obviously impossible in that small ship for him and his wife to steer on end for the fifty-seven hours which the gale lasted. He stresses that "to have been anywhere but inside the yacht, and well shut in, would have been suicidal". I am sure that he is right in this, because it has been reported from other yachts involved in storms on the ocean that the cockpit is often swept by breaking seas and that the only safe place is below decks.

Nevertheless, my conclusion is that most authorities have found that running with warps streamed is the best answer in gales, provided there is enough sea room to do so. In this connection Robin Knox-Johnson states that in his single-handed race round the world he usually lay a-hull in gales in his Bermudan 44 ft. ketch *Suhaili*. But in the Southern Ocean he judged the size of the waves was so great that there was considerable risk of hull damage when lying abeam to the seas in a Force 10 ocean storm, which confirms once again that there is a limit to hulling beyond which it can be dangerous. He then adopted the tactic of streaming a very long 2-inch polypropylene rope in a bight from either side of the boat (the length adjusted to suit the seas) and setting his 40 sq. ft. storm jib sheeted hard amidships with both sheets. This proved successful. Aided by the stretch in the rope *Suhaili* rode easily in the following seas and was never pooped. Although this is primarily an ocean tactic it could be applied anywhere given adequate sea room and with a short handed crew it offers the advantage of not requiring anybody at the helm. For details of Knox-Johnson's experiences in his circumnavigation see his book *A World of my Own*.

MULTIHULLS AND MOTOR CRAFT

Multihulls

In chapter 22 Michael Henderson points out that the characteristic of multi-hulls is the ease with which they attain high speeds in rough weather even under greatly reduced sail. Therefore the principal danger in handling them in gales lies in their sheer speed.

It is the speed and liveliness of multihulls that rules out two of the traditional methods of riding out gales, or at least makes them very experimental. Henderson has a poor opinion of the value of sea anchors even in ordinary yachts and an even lower opinion of them for riding out a gale in a multihull. Tethered to a sea anchor a multihull might be vulnerable to damage in really big seas and there would inevitably be a risk of damage to her rudder by stern way if lying head to wind. Nor are there good prospects of being able to heave-to satisfactorily in a multihull. Success in heaving-to depends upon being able to forereach *slowly* but steadily close to the wind. A multihull is likely to prove too fast and too lively to accomplish this in a gale, however closely reefed she may be. This leaves only two alternatives open for multihulls in gales.

The classic tactic of running off before a gale can be adopted, if there is sufficient sea room, but as the waves build up higher the time may come when there is a risk of the boat getting "overpowered *longitudinally* in such a way as one or all the bows dig too heavily into a steep sea thus tripping the boat and causing capsize." See *Haxted Argo II* (page 252) which when running at only about 5 knots was capsized by two exceptionally high "freak" waves in the North Sea. The course of action to be taken when running before a gale in a multihull is the same as would be applied in a conventional yacht in similar conditions, namely to stream warps and if necessary drags of one form or another to slow the boat down to what may be estimated as the best speed to suit the state of the sea.

The remaining tactic is to lie a-hull, which may provide the best answer in ordinary gales. Multihulls have great lateral stability at reasonable angles of keel and Henderson found in *Misty Miller* (page 254) that she could be made to lie a-hull satisfactorily beam to the wind, forereaching under bare pole at about ½ knot. Of course, there is a limit to this if the waves attain the height and characteristics to roll her to the point where righting moment is much reduced or lost. Beyond this there may be a capsize, but Henderson points out that a capsize may not necessarily spell disaster.

Motor Craft

The motor fishing type of motor yacht and those deliberately designed with ballast keels and the stability to enable them to make long passages in all weathers may be just as seaworthy as sailing yachts of similar size. If caught out in gales they can adopt any of the recognised tactics, but Peter Haward recommends lying-to, or "dodging." That is, heading into the seas at a small angle to them and "maintaining speed sufficient only for adequate steerage way," which is the motor craft equivalent of heaving-to under sail, and appears to be the best tactic for any kind of motor yacht or cruiser.

I asked Peter Haward for his opinion on other tactics such as lying to a sea anchor or lying a-hull, but he replied that he had never tried either in motor craft and had no intention of doing so. However, there remains the tactic of running off before a gale, reducing speed if necessary, but Haward tells me that he has never streamed warps in motor craft.

It appears difficult to lay down rules as there is such a wide variety of motor craft. Size contributes more to seaworthiness than it does with sailing yachts. Most good designs of motor craft are capable of making long passages and take their share of punishment in heavy weather, but the weakness of some lies in their big windscreens, wheel-houses, styling and top hamper. However, Haward points out that modern very fast motor yachts with deep "V" planing hulls can be good sea boats. Furthermore, many of them are so fast that they can adopt the best gale tactic of all, which is not to get caught out in one. Their sheer speed can be a safety factor, as for example in the English Channel they need never be beyond reach of shelter within an hour or two in the event of a sudden change in the weather.

THE THEORY OF RUNNING AT SPEED

Traditionally it has been the practice for generations to slow down a sailing ship when running before gales and dangerous seas and this tradition is still maintained.

It does not follow, however, that what was right for ships in the past remains right for yachts in the present, when, thanks largely to the experience gained over years of ocean racing, their design has improved in seaworthiness out of recognition.

The late Professor K. S. M. Davidson has commented that the deep forefoot of the earlier ships had a tendency to dig into the back of the wave ahead when the vessel was running before a heavy sea. He states that this could be dangerous, as the centre of lateral resistance could temporarily be moved a long way forward, and might lead to a loss of directional control of the rudder, which might result in a broach-to and throwing her on her beam ends.

He adds that a yacht's hull with its cut-away forefoot is much less susceptible to broaching-to. This leads me to wonder whether in the modern yacht it is necessary to follow the practice of past generations.

Referring to the pooping in the Atlantic of my first ocean racer, *Cohoe*, it will have been noted that the worse the seas became the more I shortened down, until eventually the yacht was under bare pole, so that she was partially blanketed in the troughs and the boat became "almost unmanageable" (Chap. 8). *Cohoe* should have been kept running at 5 or 6 knots, so that she would have remained lively and responsive, as was *Samuel Pepys* under two running sails set on booms. It would have been better in *Cohoe* to have increased sail rather than have reduced it. When the spinnaker was set a day later the wind was not much lower, but the seas were more regular (Erroll Bruce logged the waves at noon as height 18 ft., period $9\frac{1}{2}$ seconds, probable length 300 ft.). *Cohoe* was easier to steer at Force 6 under spinnaker than she had been the previous day under bare pole, but a broach-to might have been more significant when surfing at 12 knots.

From this minor incident in what was only Force 6 or 7 we can turn to the broader experience of ocean racing generally. Nowadays ocean racers carry unreefed mainsails and big spinnakers in winds which I have verified to be as high as 35 knots in the gusts, and it is the gusts which are the determining factor of how long spinnakers can remain set. In my early cruising years this strength of wind might have been regarded as a gale and indeed storm cones were hoisted at Force 7.

Hair-raising as it is, ocean racers continue to run in anything short of a strong gale, as John Illingworth demonstrated when he won the severe Fastnet Race of 1949. Likewise in the Fastnet Race of 1961 the wind was Force 9–10, gusting 50 to 60 knots, but I doubt whether any of the skippers of the boats which fared well in the race thought of running at less than maximum speed or of paying any attention to the seas. But the seas developed in the few hours, when a vigorous secondary passes over, are trifling compared with those which can build up in a prolonged ocean storm, or for that matter in the Bay of Biscay.

Ocean racers rarely come to any harm running in gales and I have witnessed spectacular broaching-to without damage to the yacht. Sail may be shortened to ease the strain on the rudder and helmsman, especially in quartering seas, but I would say that speed is rarely reduced below 6 knots in gales. Of recent years, even when cruising in winds verified at Force 8, gusting a great deal more, I have not reduced below this speed. A generation ago a yacht would have hove-to at this strength of wind.

The classic objection to running before a gale at speed is that the disturbance created by the quarter waves will cause the following seas to break dangerously. This is true of big ships, but I am not sure that it is equally applicable to the modern yacht leaving a relatively clean wake. I am not advocating maximum speed when running, but a reduction in speed in a small yacht, such as my own, to 5 or 6 knots. The quarter wave is then insignificant in relation to the big seas riding up astern, which are breaking anyway. What I have noticed when running in gales is that the real brutes of seas always seem to pass a cable to ¼ mile distant, and I have wondered what would happen if the boat were struck by one.

However, my experience is limited to ordinary gales, so let us turn our attention to the big game of ocean voyaging. The deep-sea cruising man may sail round the world meeting no worse seas than in the English Channel, but there is the chance of encountering storms in the ocean when the seas build up to such a gigantic size that there is a real risk of being rolled over through 360 degrees or of being pitch-poled. The vast Cape Horn greybeards are notorious but equally dangerous seas can occur in any of the oceans, as is shown in some of the photographs in this book, though it is difficult to imagine how any yacht can survive them. Immense seas, which can engulf a yacht, rule out the conventional methods of riding out gales, and the tactics adopted to weather them are not necessarily applicable to ordinary gales, though I cannot see why.

When Vito Dumas sailed round the world in the Roaring Forties he had no use for sea anchors. He simply ran before the gales at a speed of 5 knots or more, taking the seas, so I understand, slightly on the quarter. What is more, he states that on no occasion, whatever the storm, did he lower all sail and that there were no reef points in the mainsail. His only complaint was that when the seas ran very high *Lehg II* was blanketed in the troughs, where she showed a tendency to luff and was on one occasion thrown on her beam ends. This emphasizes on to the grand scale of the Roaring Forties the point which I made earlier that a boat can get out of control in the troughs of big seas if she is running too slowly. Her speed falls too low for quick response to the helm, just at the time when control is most needed as the next crest rides up astern.

Moitessier is more explicit. He states that in the big storms of the Southern Ocean it is essential to maintain speed in order to keep the yacht under control, and that the seas must be taken at an angle of 15–20 degrees to the stern. He goes further than this, stating that he does not believe *Joshua* could have survived the gigantic waves by any other means (Chap. 20). He believes that had she continued to tow warps she would have surfed at such a speed that she would have run under in the trough and been pitch-poled.

All this is endorsed by Warren Brown. His opinion is expressed in Chapter 19, "September Hurricane". He is equally emphatic. He is certain that *Force Seven* would not have survived either hove-to, riding to a sea anchor or running with warps streamed. As with *Joshua*, the danger lay in surfing downwind at 15 knots and being pitch-poled in the trough or back of the wave ahead. He took the seas on the quarter, as elaborated in his book *Cape Horn, the Logical route*.

Further evidence on running is provided by the 14-ton *Coimbra*, which was overtaken by very severe weather, with winds estimated in excess of Force 10 in the winter of 1951, in the South Atlantic. She ran safely before the storm, with a boom staysail sheeted amidships, until her steering broke down and she broached-to. Lying a-hull she was rolled over twice and it was only the strength of her construction and a completely watertight bulkhead that saved her from sinking. When an emergency tiller had been rigged, the yacht was run off dead before the storm and she survived. It appears that *Coimbra* was able to run satisfactorily in what was estimated at being a Force 10 storm, so long as she had steering control.

The subject of tactics in weathering gales and storms is one about which yachtsmen like to argue, but I cannot help believing that the men who actually survived the exceptional storms or hurricanes probably did the right thing and were the best judges of what could be done in the particular conditions and seas which they had to face. Moitessier describes yachtsmen believing in running at speed as belonging to the Dumas school. I am impressed by it myself, because I think the danger when running in gales is not due to speed alone, but to loss of control, which may be attributable to lack of speed as much as to excessive speed. However, I shrink from recommending the method of running at speed, because if it proves wrong it could lead to loss of life. For those who are in doubt, especially when caught out in ordinary gales, I recommend the well-tried expedient of streaming warps, following what Moitessier calls the Robinson school of thought. What I think is clear is that you must either run fast enough to give absolute control so that the boat will respond to a flick of the wheel or tiller, or else slow down, when warps will have to be streamed to steady the stern to the seas.

More recent information on running before an ocean storm is afforded by the experience of Ramon Carlin's Sparkman and Stephens designed standard glass-fibre 64 ft. ketch *Sayula II*, which was capsized in the Roaring Forties on the morning of November 24th, 1973, during the Whitbread Round the World Race. An account of this accident by Butch Dalrymple-Smith, one of her crew, appeared in *Yachts and Yachting* which, together with information which he gave me later, provides the basis for the following comments.

The wind had been blowing at a mean of about 50–55 knots (measured by Brookes and Gatehouse anenometer) for about $2\frac{1}{2}$ days. *Sayula II* was running under a tiny storm jib and a small storm staysail with the wind just north of west. These were set principally to steady the steering and afford control, but even so in a Force 10 storm would give her a speed of 7 to 9 knots. The waves were high and Butch when on watch earlier had seen one of a height which appeared about to equal the 64 foot length of the boat. As explained in Appendix 2, this is quite possible for an exceptional wave in an ocean storm, although actual heights are usually considerably less than visual estimates.

The seas at the time were chaotic, coming from astern and from the quarter and when on watch Butch had found that the most worrysome ones were not the biggest but those which "start off small and peak absolutely underneath you . . . It was this sort of wave that rolled *Sayula*." He goes on to say:

"*Sayula II* was on the face of the wave when the falling crest caught the stern first, forcing it down the wave faster than the bow. With the bow gripping the water and the stern in the falling water, the boat slewed around almost broadside on to the wave." In other words she broached to. "And then the wave broke. The boat literally fell—no one knows how far." Judged later by the trajectory of fallen articles and by other evidence the angle of the capsize must have been between 155 and 170 degrees from the horizontal, which is nearly upside down.

Both men on watch in the cockpit were thrown into the sea but retained a grip on something as well as being secured by life lines, but the stainless steel clip-hook on one of the harnesses was later found to be so badly distorted by the strain that it would not close.

Down below there was a shambles of displaced mattresses, clothes, bedding, bunkboards, floorboards, tins, and provisions liberally sprayed with chicken noodle soup and salad oil, so slippery as to make even standing hazardous. Everything that could move did move, and one crew member was temporarily buried under the lot. Out of the crew of 12 in this large yacht there were six casualties; two with broken ribs, one with a torn shoulder, one with concussion, one with an injured leg and one with aggravation of an old back injury.

The amazing thing about this incident is that *Sayula II* was not dismasted. Nevertheless, a considerable amount of water was shipped and two fresh water tanks broke their connections thus adding 140 gallons to the water in the bilges. A great deal of damage was done to the boat but, apart from a broken deck window through which the sea poured, none of it was structural or disabling, which is certainly a credit to her builders, Nautor Oy of Finland.

All sail was lowered as quickly as possible and *Sayula* continued to run before the storm under bare poles. The wind moderated later and within 24 hours most of the essential repairs had been done and a spinnaker had been set.

This near disaster follows the well established pattern of the freak wave. At one moment all is well despite the very heavy weather and high seas. The crew although tired is confident and everything is under control. Then totally unexpectedly the wave arrives and in a matter of seconds disaster may follow. *Sayula II* was running fast and as she was racing in a great international event she had no alternative such as streaming warps, nor is it certain that she would have suffered less had she done so. Captain Th. de Lange's photographs show how chaotic waves can become in ocean storms. Plate No. 28 for example shows a wave with a vertical edge. I have often wondered what happens if a yacht finds herself perched on the edge of a precipice of water like this, or indeed falls into a hole such as is described in Appendix 2.

It is interesting to note that the freak wave which caused the capsize struck *Sayula* towards the end of the storm, apparently after a front had gone through, with a veer in the wind which created dangerous cross seas over the swell built up over the previous two days. At least, this is my assumption, as there was no second freak wave and the weather improved rapidly, the wind falling to 10 knots within a few hours of the mishap.

At the end of his article Butch gives the conclusions he arrived at as a result of the accident. Among these he mentions that the bilge pumps were clogged by muck for thirty per cent of the time, that a piece of $2\frac{1}{2}$ inch rubber hose stuck down the toilet makes a good extra pump, but the best bilge pump of all is a bucket in the hands of a frightened man. He adds that all four radios had been put out of action by water and mechanical damage.

The principal difficulty in restoring order out of chaos after the capsize lay in the bottleneck at the main hatch between the cockpit and access below, where most of the work has to be done "in an area not much bigger than a telephone box." At one time in this confined space a party was trying to get a crewman with a suspected broken leg down through the main hatch at the same time as others were trying to work or clear the pumps or bail out with buckets, all doing their best to help in one way or another. Butch's observation about this is: "Conserve manpower. You become exhausted quickly. Extra hands are often inefficient, getting in each others way. Rotate hands at the pumps and keep a reserve to get the boat racing again as quickly as possible."

Eventually order was re-established. The four dry bunks had been allocated to the worst of the wounded, the cabin window repaired and most of the water had been pumped or bailed out. Yvonne van der Byl, who had joined in South Africa, then served a hot supper which must indeed have been a godsend at that time. The water temperature was down to 2 degrees centigrade, and the six exhausted watchkeepers spent two hours on and then one hour off (in full oilskins on the bare floor boards) for the rest of the bitterly cold night. When daylight came boiled eggs were served for breakfast. Although meals may not matter much in modern fast ocean racers in 200 mile races taking about 30 hours, I remain convinced that substantial and regular meals pay racing dividends in long events, where results depend on morale and endurance, especially in heavy weather. Anyway, fortified by the eggs *Sayula's* crew set the mainsail and boomed out No 3 jib, and drying out began. Rapidly improving weather enabled them to set the spinnaker within 24 hours of the capsize.

Butch, with his medical background, makes interesting observations on the psychological effects of a near disaster such as this even on a very strong crew, which is a subject I have not read about before. Although the spinnaker was set within 24 hours of the accident he says that the crew lost interest in getting the best out of the boat. At meal times they were so on edge that if the boat lurched unexpectedly all would stop talking and instinctively grab something to hold on to. The effect of shock, or delayed shock which may have been augmented by the cold conditions sailing at about 49° south and remote from help, lasted a week before all-out racing was resumed. It seems to me that the near disaster affords a clue to the sort of thing which may have happened in some of the rare disasters where yachts have actually been overwhelmed in the ocean without trace.

The whole story of the experiences of the individual competitors and lessons learnt will be covered in Peter Cook's forthcoming book *The Longest Race*. So far as *Sayula II* was concerned she made good her lost time due to the capsize and sailed on to achieve the honour of first place in the Whitbread Round the World Race.

In conclusion to this chapter and to the book, I think I cannot do better than give a quotation from John F. Wilson, Master, S.S. *Pioneer*, which appears in Appendix VII of Typhoon Doctrine in *Heavy Weather Guide*. "Whatever decision you may make," he writes, "if you get into trouble you may be sure that someone, who was *not* there will come up with something you *should* have done."

289

WAVE THEORY AND FACTS

DIMENSIONS OF A WAVE

There can be very few people who do not have some concept of a wave, but waves, like people, are of endless variety; to identify one in the turmoil of a stormy ocean is as difficult as to distinguish a face in a crowd. However, like people, waves have structure, dimensions and character; if these are appreciated, then some understanding and prediction of the subject's behaviour is possible.

Many books have been written on the research undertaken in recent and past years by scientists of many countries; here only some of the elementary facts of waves with mention of theory can be made. Mostly the references will be to "idealized" waves, that is to say, waves in their simplest forms, but often the elements of theory are clearly recognizable in nature; for example, the shape and regularity of swell waves experienced on windless days are close to that of the "ideal" wave.

Figure 45 shows the dimensions of a sea wave. The length "L" and height "H" are usually defined in feet, the period "T" in seconds, and the velocity (or celerity) "C" in feet per second or knots.

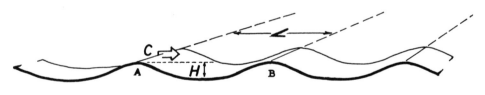

"T" (period) is the time it takes wave "A" to reach the position formerly occupied by "B".

45   The principal dimensions of a wave.

The shape of an "idealized" wave (Fig. 46) is variously described as sinusoidal, trochoidal or cycloidal (the term cylindrical, occasionally met with, means only that the cross-section of the wave is uniform throughout its width). Each shape has some virtue for theoretical purposes and a series or train of such waves is considered to have the crests of the waves parallel to each other. At sea the natural waves are, of course, of many different periods, heights and shapes, with perhaps two or three trains of waves crossing each other at some angle.

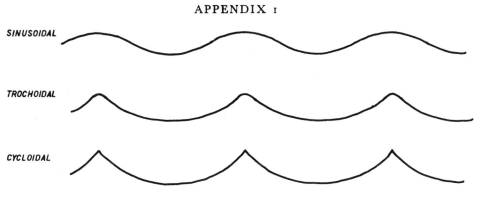

SINUSOIDAL

TROCHOIDAL

CYCLOIDAL

46   Three types of wave form.

Wave relationships—speed, length and period

In any form of wave motion there is a simple relationship between the speed of a wave, its length and its period. If C is the speed in feet per second, L the length in feet and T the period in seconds, then:

$$C = \frac{L}{T} \text{ or } T = \frac{L}{C} \text{ or } L = TC$$

In deep water, that is to say where the bottom has no influence on a wave:-

$$C = 5.12 \text{ T or equally } C = 2.26 \sqrt{L}, \text{ and therefore } L = 5.12 \text{ T}^2$$

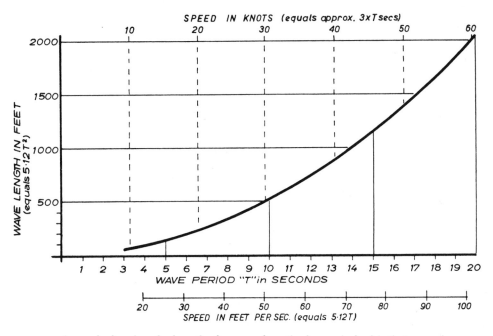

47   A graph showing the length of waves of particular period, also their speed.

Figure 47 is a graph showing the deep-water lengths of waves and their speed with respect to their period. (If the speed of a wave is required in knots, then, with but little error, C. knots = 3T secs).

A deep-water wave. A wave of any length is said to be a deep-water wave if the depth of water it is in is more than half its wave length. (Such a wave does not effectively "feel" the bottom.)

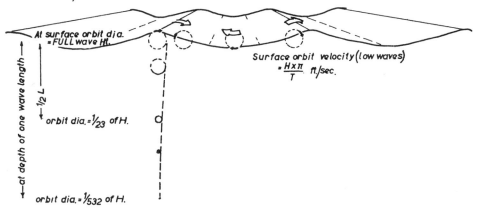

48   A diagrammatic representation of the movement of water particles in a wave in deep water.

A shallow-water wave. If the depth of water under a wave is about one twenty-fifth of its length, then a wave is in shallow water. (It "feels" the bottom; and, in fact, a wave is already starting to "feel" the bottom by the time the depth of water is half the wave's length.)

Transitional waves (or intermediate waves) come between the other two categories, and broadly speaking they might be said to be transitional when the depth of water is between half and one twenty-fifth of their wave length.

There is no definite line of demarcation between any of these three categories; each category merges into another. Occasionally the categories (of "deep", "transitional" and "shallow") are referred to as "deep water", "shallow water" and "very shallow water" respectively.

The *period* of a wave is *always the same,* no matter what depth of water it is in, but as a deep-water wave enters less deep water its velocity is reduced and its length is similarly shortened. In mathematical terms the length or speed of a wave is reduced by the amount:

$$\tanh \frac{2\pi d^{*}}{L}$$

* In fundamental mathematical terms, the velocity of a wave in *any depth of water* is correctly defined as:–

$$C^{2} = \frac{gL}{2\pi} \left(\tanh \frac{2\pi d}{L} \right)$$

where "g" is the acceleration due to gravity.

so in the transitional zone

$$L = 5.12 \ T^2 \times \tanh \frac{2\pi d}{L}$$

and

$$C = 2.26 \ \sqrt{L} \times \sqrt{\tanh \frac{2\pi d}{L}}$$

In (very) shallow water it can be shown that the speed of a wave may be quite simply expressed as:–

$$C = \sqrt{gd}$$

Note that the speed of a wave in shallow water is no longer dependent upon its length (or period) but only upon the depth of water "d" it is in.

THE STRUCTURE OF A WAVE BELOW THE SURFACE

Although the mariner is generally concerned only with the effect of waves on the surface of the sea, some understanding of its structure below the surface is of importance also.

It is generally realized that the sea surface is not progressing forward as the wave goes forward. If the path of a single particle of water in a low wave is observed—or more practically if a small cork floating is observed—it will be seen to move in a closed orbit which is in a vertical plane. The amount of rise and fall of the cork is the full height of the wave; its "to-and-fro" motion is also the same, although this is not so obvious. In fact the orbital path of the cork is circular or nearly so; in practice the orbit is usually not quite closed as there is a small "mass-transport" of water forward.

Figure 4 illustrates the movement of water particles both on the surface and below it, and it will be seen that the movement of water particles is with the wave's advance under the crest but against it in a trough, also the movement of the particles gets rapidly less the further below the surface they are. At a depth of one wave length (or even half a wave length) it is so small that it can be ignored—hence the criterion for a deep water wave.

An interesting phenomena of the to-and-fro movement of the water particles is that a small boat going with a wave can spend more time on a crest than in the trough and thus take advantage of the crest's forward movement of the particles. As Russell states in his book, it is theoretically possible for a small motor boat steaming at $9\frac{1}{2}$ knots with regular four-second waves 5 ft. high to stay on a crest and gain more than 2 knots over the ground. There is, of course, a decrease in speed over the ground when heading into a sea.[1]

THE GENERATION OF WAVES

The life cycle of a wave consists of its generation by a wind; its gradual growth to maximum size dependent upon certain limiting factors; its journey across the sea where, if there is no wind, the wave may gradually lose height, until finally, as a swell, it expends itself upon a distant shore.

A "swell" is usually distinguished from a "sea", as being a wave outside its own original area of generation. A swell is easily recognizable in an area of no wind, but it can be equally present running across a wind which is generating new waves, having itself been generated by winds elsewhere. The height of a swell wave decays as it moves away from its own area of generation, and can become almost undetectable until it reaches very shallow water close to the shore where it becomes apparent again as a "ground swell".

The curves or graphs (explained later) for forecasting wave characteristics, are not for swell but for waves generated by local winds. If the two simple waves of sinusoidal form combine together, their combined height is the addition of each, but under certain circumstances the combined height of two waves is more correctly given as the square root of the sum of their heights squared, i.e. their total height is $\sqrt{h_1{}^2+h_2{}^2}$.

The height and period of a wave generated in deep water by a wind depends on three things:

1. The mean speed (or strength) of the wind.
2. The duration (or time) for which the wind blows.
3. The fetch, i.e. the length (upwind of an observer) of the area over which the wind blows.

The fetch distance can, of course, be limited by the intervening presence of land, and it does not necessarily become nearly limitless if the wind is over an open ocean.

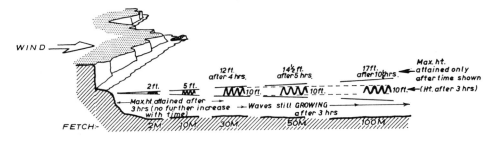

49 A diagram showing the growth and ultimate size of waves at different fetch distances. The figures quoted are for a mean wind speed of 30 knots (Force 7) and wind duration of three hours.

Figure 49 is a diagram illustrating the different heights of the waves that would exist (at any instant) in different parts of a sea over which a wind was blowing steadily.

The two particular features to notice are that the height of the waves near the beginning of the fetch (i.e. over the shorter fetch length) is less than the height to be found at the end where the wind has been able to blow over a greater distance; and that after a certain period of time (which is dependent upon the length of the fetch) the waves have attained their maximum height, whereas elsewhere downwind they are still growing. In the example, a mean wind speed of 30 knots is considered to have been blowing for three hours, and the waves have reached their maximum height in the area up to 33 miles from the land and will not increase however much longer the 30-knot wind may blow; but at greater distances the waves will continue to grow (if the same wind continues to blow) until such time that they also reach a maximum height.

In a similar manner the period of the wave lengthens and reaches a maximum.

The meaning of the term *maximum* wave-height (H_{max}) needs some clarification, because this height can on occasions be exceeded! The fact is that when the curves for forecasting maximum wave heights are used (see p. 299) the height obtained from these curves is the maximum which a wind of a certain strength can produce blowing over a certain fetch for a particular duration of time; however, during this time it is possible for component waves in a train to get into step, and thus together they will produce a much larger wave. The *most probable height* of the highest wave so formed increases with time; the problem is therefore a statistical one unrelated to the actual forecasting method, which is based upon the highest waves recorded in ten-minute records taken at regular intervals throughout a day.

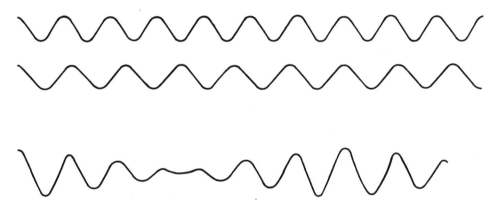

50   The profile of a wave train (bottom) caused by the combination of two wave trains of slightly different period.

Statistically speaking, then, in infinite time waves could occur which are infinitely large! But keeping within reasonable bounds of time and using the predicted "maximum wave heights" obtained from the curves, the most probable height of the highest waves which might occur, could be between about 20 per cent and 50 per cent higher than those shown;[2] for the two percentages just quoted the duration of the storms would be respectively one hour and forty-eight hours; for an increase of about 35 per cent, a storm of six hours' duration would be required. Statistical evaluation of "the most probable height of the highest waves" does not, of course, preclude the chances of even higher waves occurring!

A term "significant wave height" is sometimes encountered, and this simply means an average of high waves—actually the average height of the highest one-third of the waves. Similarly the "significant wave period" is the average period of the highest one third of the waves.

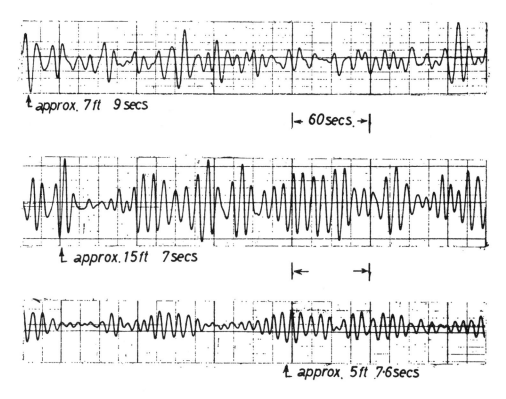

51 Traces from an actual wave record obtained in Weymouth Bay. (Reproduced by permission of the Hydraulics Research Station. (Ministry of Technology), Wallingford.)

The belief that every seventh or eleventh wave is the highest in a group or train of waves is not entirely without foundation. If two trains of waves of very slightly different periods exist, one (the longer) will advance with a slightly greater velocity through the other train, the result will be a "beating" phenomena similar to that audibly expressed when tuning a piano with a tuning fork, and waves of considerable height will be interdisposed between those of a very low height. Figure 50 illustrates the profile of such a train of waves, and Figure 51 shows actual traces of waves recorded (by pressure changes on the sea bed) in Weymouth Bay.

THE PREDICTION OF MAXIMUM WAVE HEIGHT AND SIGNIFICANT PERIOD

The curves for forecasting wave heights and periods[3] (Fig. 52 page 299) are derived from many years of wave records obtained by Ocean Weather Ships and analysed at the National Institute of Oceanography. (Similar curves have been produced by Bretschneider and others in the U.S.A.)[4]

To find the maximum wave height or significant period from these curves, refer to the appropriate diagram and follow the horizontal line for the mean wind speed along until it intersects with either the vertical fetch line or the duration curve; whichever is intersected first is the point for the correct prediction for maximum height or significant period.

Similar curves have been produced for coastal waters based upon wave recordings taken at lightvessels in the North and Irish Seas. There are differences between ocean and coastal waters, but not to a significant extent as far as a yachtsman's interest in prediction is concerned (see Table). But a tendency for the generation of shorter and higher waves in coastal waters than for a similar fetch over the oceans is noticeable; this seems to confirm the familiar steepness of waves of the "short seas" found in the more shallow waters of about 20 fathoms. As these waves in coastal waters travel over a gently shelving bed into water of even less depth, the bed will absorb some of the wave and its height will be slightly reduced; however, when sudden shelving takes place then the height will increase and, together with further shortening of the wave length, their steepness also.

TRANSIENT CHARACTERISTICS OF WAVES

Some maximum heights

As a very broad generalization it could be said that waves of 25 ft. in height are not unusual during severe Atlantic storms, heights of 40 ft. are not so uncommon and heights of 50 or 60 ft. not unknown—in fact, there is a reputedly reliable report of a wave 112 ft. high being sighted in the Pacific Ocean.[5] This latter record must help to give credence to the statistical chance of very high waves occurring occasionally due to the combination of two component waves, because to generate such a wave would probably necessitate a fetch of over 1,000 miles, and a mean wind velocity exceeding 100 knots blowing over the entire distance for 30 hours—a rather unlikely event.

Analysis, by the Institute of Oceanographic Sciences, of wave recordings taken by ocean weather ships in the Atlantic and by lightvessels around our coasts,[6] have yielded interesting and useful information. For instance, in the Atlantic the most common maximum summer wave height is around 12–17 ft., whilst in winter it is around 17–23 ft. and waves of 60 ft. in height are to be expected on odd occasions. In the Bristol Channel maximum heights of 30 ft. have been recorded, and in the Irish Sea (at the Morecambe Bay L.V.) there is a recorded height of 29 ft., whilst in the southern North Sea (at Smith's Knoll L.V.) the maximum height recorded has been only 25 ft. Further north, east of Peterhead, Scotland, a wave of 61 ft. high has been measured, and further north still there are even higher ones. However, the most common maximum heights in the Irish Sea and southern North Sea are relatively low.

An approximate formula[7] for calculating the maximum wave height that can be generated in the Atlantic over a *long* fetch is:

$$H = 1/50 \, W^2$$

where W is the surface wind velocity in knots, and H the maximum height in feet—for example, a 50-knot surface wind gives 50 ft.

The effect of currents and shoaling in wave height

Anyone who has sailed in coastal waters will be fully aware of the phenomenon of increased wave height when the tidal stream is running against the waves (or wind), and of a decrease in height when the tide and the waves are together. The primary cause of the phenomena is the change in the wave lengths of the waves as they come under the influence of the current or tidal stream.

When the direction of wave propagation is opposed to the stream, the wave length shortens with a resultant increase in the steepness of the wave; also because the period of the wave and consequently its energy remain the same, the height of the wave increases. Together these two effects result in high, short and steep waves, and the shorter the incoming wave (and stronger the currents) the more pronounced the effects.

The Scripps Institution of Oceanography, U.S.A., have made a study of the effect of current velocities upon wave heights and have shown that waves, entering an area of opposing currents, can quite easily have their heights raised by 50 to 100 per cent in currents as low as 2 to 3 knots.[8] Thus the breaking of waves may be a frequent occurrence even without much local wind.

When waves move into an area where they travel with the current, the result is an increase in their wave length and a reduction in their height.

In addition to the currents causing increases to existing wave height, it should be mentioned that waves, tide rips and general turmoil can be created by the hydraulic effects of strong currents meeting obstructions on the sea bed, even when there are no wind-generated waves present.

Shallow water also has a considerable effect upon the height of waves. In shallow water (i.e. where the depth is about one twenty-fifth of the deep water length of a wave) the height of an incoming wave has just started to increase; and when the depth to length ratio is about one one-hundredth, the increase in height will be about 50 per cent. For example, a low swell of ten-second period and 2 ft. high in deep water would become 3 ft. high in 5 ft. of water (and incidentally on the point of breaking). However, an unexpected decrease in the incoming wave height takes place shortly before the wave starts increasing; in depths between one-quarter and one-tenth of the wave the decrease amounts to nearly 10 per cent of the original deep-water height.

Breaking waves

There is usually a limit to the height of a wave of particular period, after which it breaks. Breaking in deep water theoretically takes place when the ratio of the wave's

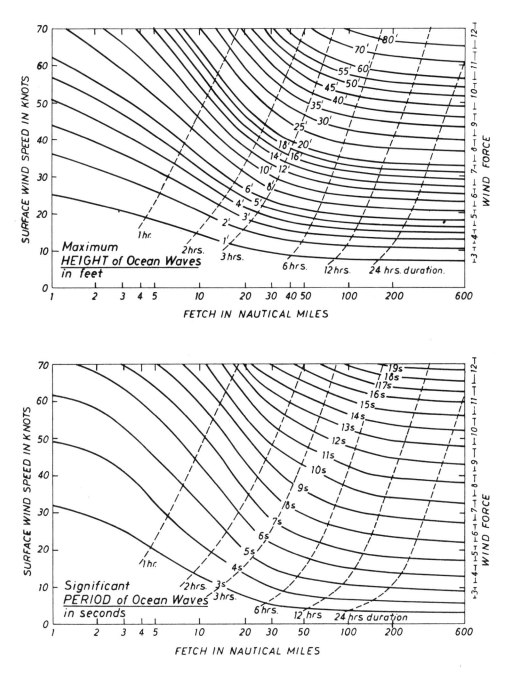

52 (a) and (b). Prediction curves for maximum wave height and significant period devised by M. Darbyshire and L. Draper. (Reproduced by permission of the Institute of Oceanographic Sciences, Wormley.)

height to its length is something just less than 1:7; in practice the ratio is more often about 1:14. (Note this ratio is not actually a measure of the steepest part of a wave.) At the crest of such a breaking wave—no longer a low idealized one—the water must be travelling momentarily faster than the wave itself; for a wave with a ten-second period this means a velocity in excess of 30 knots, which seems to confirm the reason why some yachtsmen prefer to run *before* a heavy sea with a warp over the stern.

In the shallow water of bays or on offshore shoals, the height to length ratio becomes less useful, and it is more a matter of the height to depth-of-water ratio which determines whether a wave will break or not. Theoretically this ratio is around 1:1¼— sometimes more, sometimes less. However, other variables or factors affect the breaking of a wave in shallow water, such as currents and the possible focussing effect of refraction.

Refraction

The refraction or bending of a wave front as it passes obliquely from one depth of water to another is reasonably easy to understand in that it is similar to light rays passing

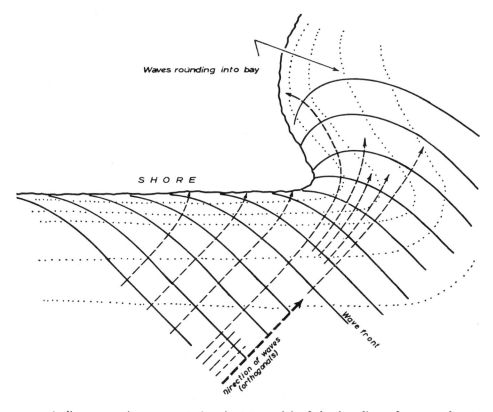

Waves rounding into bay

SHORE

Wave front

Direction of waves (orthogonals)

53a A diagrammatic representation (not to scale) of the bending of waves, due to refraction, as they obliquely approach a straight coastline or enter a bay.

obliquely through a more dense medium. For example, if waves from the open sea approach the coast at an angle, the wave front first entering shallow water is slowed down (because its wave length is shortened) but the rest of the wave front still in deep water retains its comparatively greater velocity until it in turn reaches shallower water (see Figs. 53a and 53b).

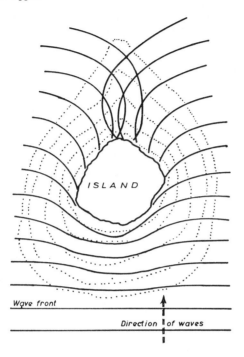

53b   A diagrammatic representation (not to scale) of the refraction of waves as they pass an island of circular shape. Note how the waves cross in the lee of the island—this effect would be emphasized by the shoal spit also.

Waves of longer length (i.e. longer period) start to be refracted sooner than those of shorter length. Therefore when waves from very deep water (which usually consist of a very wide variety of periods, that is, have a broad spectrum) round into a bay, there will be a tendency for the different parts of the bay to receive waves of different period. This effect is most noticeably felt in a sheltered anchorage where good protection is often obtained from the local gale and rough seas, but where the longer-period swell, which is more easily refracted around the headland, is still very much present. Cawsand Bay near Plymouth, or St. Ives Bay on the north coast of Cornwall, are examples of sheltered anchorages with noticeable ground swells.

Although refraction which spreads into a bay has a tendency to reduce wave height, it must be remembered that refraction over a ridge-type shoal can well cause "focusing" of the waves and thus an increased wave height.

Diffraction

Diffraction of waves is a phenomenon often confused with refraction because the radial spread of waves around a breakwater or steep-to headland appears similar to the phenomenon of refraction over a shoal or spit. Diffraction is independent of shoaling of the sea bed, it is merely the sideways spread of a wave crest into a zone protected from the direct effect of waves.

Figure 54 shows diagrammatically the spread of wave fronts after they are diffracted around a breakwater.

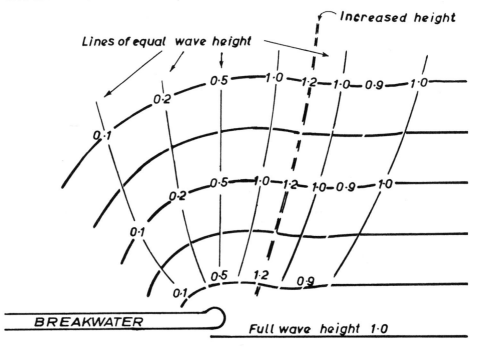

54   A diagram (not to scale) showing how waves are bent and lose (or gain) height due to diffraction, as they pass a breakwater.

An interesting feature to note is a line of increased wave height just clear and outside of the breakwater head, but a line of reduced wave height further out.

Reflections and standing waves

Although reflected or standing waves are not usually met with in the open oceans, it is as well to be aware of them if seeking shelter.

The average sea waves are mostly "absorbed" by slopes of about 1:3—the flatter the slope the better, but the longer the wave the more easily it is reflected back from a given slope. From a vertical, or near vertical wall, total reflection can take place and an area with a system of standing waves is set up. In this area there are bands of very high waves, nearly double their approaching (progressive) wave height, together with bands of very low wave height. The bands are the anti-nodes and nodes of the standing-wave system, with distances between the nodal points of half a wave length.

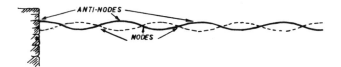

55   A "standing" wave pattern set up by reflections off a solid wall.

Figure 55 shows a standing-wave system caused by reflections off a sea wall. If the wall is not straight but curved towards the waves, it is possible that "focusing" of the reflected waves (as with a concave mirror and light waves) may take place and cause a very confused sea. Further, if the waves attack a breakwater obliquely then their reflection will give rise to a cross sea.

BIBLIOGRAPHY AND REFERENCES

The foregoing notes have of necessity been brief and omitted much, and perhaps been guilty of oversimplification of the complex phenomenon of waves. If the reader wishes to go more deeply into the subject, the references and books listed below may be helpful.

[1] Russell, R. C. H. "Waves and Tides." *Hutchinson's Sci. & Tech. Publication* (1952).

[2] Longuet-Higgins, M. S. "On the Statistical Distribution of the Heights of Sea Waves." *Jnl. Mar. Research.* Vol. 11 (1952).

[3] Darbyshire, Mollie, and Draper, L. "Forecasting Wind-Generated Sea Waves." *Engineering*, Apr. 1963.

[4] "Shore Protection Planning and Design." Beach Erosion Board U.S.A. Techn. Report 4 (1961).

[5] Whitemarsh, R. P. *Proc. Mav. Inst. U.S.A.* Vol. 60 (1934).

[6] Darbyshire, Mollie. "Wave Measurements made by the N.I.O." *Mar. Observer,* Jan. 1962.

[7] Darbyshire, J. "A further Investigation of Wind-Generated Waves." *Deutsche Hydrog. Zeitschrift.* Vol. 12 No. 1 (1959).

[8] "Wind Waves at Sea, Breakers and Surf." U.S.A. H.O. Pub. No. 602 (1947).

Tricker, R. A. R. *Bores, Breakers, Waves and Wakes.* Mills & Boon Ltd. (1964).

SEA AREA		DURATION OF BLOW IN HOURS			
		Fetch considered to be 120 miles (i.e. duration of more importance)			Fetch over 600 miles. Fully developed sea (i.e. duration great)
		1 hour	3 hours	6 hours	24 hours +
24 knots Force 6	Ocean	1¾ *(2)*	6 *(7¾)*	8¾ *(12)*	11 *(16)*
	Coastal	2 *(2¼)*	7 *(9)*	11 *(14½)*	14½ *(21)*
30 knots Force 7	Ocean	3 *(3½)*	10½ *(13½)*	14 *(19)*	17 *(25)*
	Coastal	3 *(3½)*	10½ *(13½)*	16 *(21)*	20 *(29)*
37 knots Force 8	Ocean	5¼ *(6¼)*	17 *(22)*	22 *(30)*	26½ *(39)*
	Coastal	4½ *(5¼)*	15½ *(20)*	23 *(30½)*	28 *(40)*
52 knots Force 10	Ocean	14 *(17)*	39 *(50)*	45 *(61)*	52 *(77)*
	Coastal	9 *(10½)*	30 *(38)*	39 *(52)*	47 *(68)*

MEAN WIND SPEEDS

WAVE HEIGHTS IN FEET

Bold figures = Maximum predicted wave-height.
Italic figures = The most probable height of the highest waves due to the combination of component waves. (A statistical evaluation.)

A table comparing predicted wave heights in Coastal Waters (Irish and North Sea) with those for the Atlantic Ocean. Heights for the English Channel would possibly lie somewhere between those of the two areas. (After M. Darbyshire, L. Draper and M. S. Longuet Higgins[2],[3].)

APPENDIX 2
*Contributed by Laurence Draper of the British Oceanographic Data Service,
Institute of Oceanographic Sciences*

FREAK WAVES

Whenever there are waves on the surface of the sea there is a small but finite possibility of the occurrence of one or more waves which are noticeably higher than the others, and when they occur they are often labelled "freak waves". Amongst sailors there are many stories of freak waves, usually concerning great waves maybe 100 ft. high (which may or may not have grown with the telling) and which overwhelmed or badly damaged many a vessel, but to a yachtsman a wave 15 ft. high occurring on a day when the highest he's seen had been perhaps 8 or 10 ft. high is in every sense a freak.

There is no need to invoke the supernatural to account for such oddities, because the occurrence of unusually high waves does seem to fit into established patterns. The explanation as to why, on a day when there is only a comfortable breeze and no storm within perhaps hundreds of miles, a nasty-looking wave arises out of an otherwise friendly sea is that no wave system consists of just one wave train; there are many wave components present, each with its own period and height, travelling along together at slightly different, but constant, speeds. As the components continually get into and out of step with each other they produce the groups of high waves followed by brief intervals of relatively quiet water which are characteristic of all sea waves. Every now and then, just by chance, it so happens that a large number of these components get into step at the same place and an exceptionally high wave ensues. The life of such a wave is only a transient one, being not much more than a minute or two in the deep ocean and even less in sheltered waters where the wave period is smaller. Because each wave component is travelling at its own characteristic speed, the faster ones will escape from the others and the monster wave will die just as surely as it was born. The energy it contains belongs to its component wave trains, which still exist and travel on, taking their energy with them. Somewhere else on the water surface at some other time some other wave trains will, again just by chance, coincide and produce another large wave which will have its brief moment of glory before disappearing for ever into the random jumble of the sea. Although we are never likely to be able to predict just where and when an exceptionally high wave will appear, because the instrumentation problems are immense, the probability of occurrence of of any such wave is finite and can be predicted; its calculation has the apparently contradictory title of Statistics of a Stationary Random Process. Using this theory, it has been shown that whilst one wave in twenty-three is over twice the height of the average wave, and one in 1,175 is over three times the average height, only one wave in over 300,000 exceeds four times the average height. The wave which *Puffin* experienced in the Mediterranean (Chap. 17) is an authenticated example of the effect of this phenomenon, and graphically illustrates the rule that a seaman must never relax his watch even though the worst of the storm appears to be over.

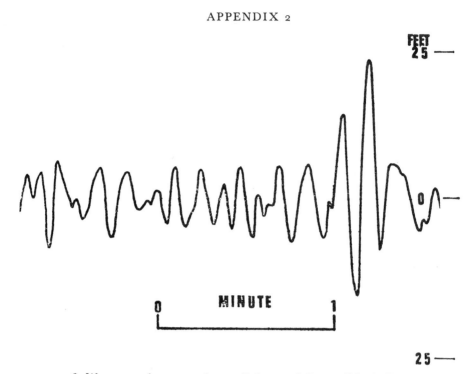

56. Wave recorder trace taken on light-vessel *Daunt* off Cork, Eire.

Because these rare events occur, almost by definition, only infrequently they are hardly ever photographed and virtually never measured by a wave recording instrument. However, such a rare event did present itself to the Daunt Light Vessel off Cork in 1969 during the time when its wave recorder was running. The instrument was installed for scientific purposes and was in use for two years, but during that time it was run systematically for only about a quarter of an hour every three hours, so it was quite remarkable that the unusual wave was recorded at all. The time was three o'clock in the morning, the Master was on his bunk but awake, and a gale was blowing outside. The sea was rather rough but not especially severe when the vessel shook violently, so much so that the Master raced to the bridge fearing that something catastrophic had happened, but by the time he had arrived the sea had reverted to its previous rough state, and nothing further untoward occurred. The Master described it as the most frightening experience in his sea-going life, and had it not been for the lucky fact that the wave recorder had been running, his story would probably have been put down to another bit of Irish Blarney. Nevertheless, the proof existed, and is shown in Fig. 56. The sea conditions at the time had a significant height of 16.5 feet, and that enormous wave was 42 feet from crest to trough.

An even more dramatic demonstration of the effects of this kind of wave behaviour occurred in 1970 when the Fraserburgh Lifeboat was overturned by a wave, apparently cartwheeled bow over stern. The conditions barely merited the title of gale and yet a high wave occurred, with tragic results. Plate facing page 260 was taken by an alert officer on a nearby Russian mother ship; it shows the vessel, the *Opal*, which had been in trouble and was under tow, sitting in the trough of a wave with the ill-fated lifeboat lying across the face of the high wave beyond her. From a knowledge of the dimensions of the *Opal* and of the lifeboat, that wave was subsequently estimated to have been about 37 feet in height.

Reports of freak waves usually concern waves with unexpectedly high crests, as in most of the instances described in previous chapters, but there is just as much chance of an unusually low trough occurring. The reason why they are not often reported must be that a high crest can be seen from a large distance, but a vessel would have to be on the very edge of a deep trough to notice it. Two reports of deep troughs (at least, that is what we believe them to have been) were described in the *Marine Observer* under the heading "The one from nowhere". The following is an extract from the report of Commodore W. S. Byles, R.D., master of the *Edinburgh Castle*, and a similar report of a wartime experience by Commander I. R. Johnston, R.N. (Retired), appearing in that article:

Ever since the *Waratah* was lost without trace, having sailed from Durban to Cape Town on 26th July 1909, Cape coastal waters have been suspect and especially in the vicinity of Port St. Johns. There was a report that she had been "spoken" and reported "all well" off Port Shepstone; she had a morse lamp but no wireless.

On 21st August 1964 in 31° 39′ S, 29° 46′ E the *Edinburgh Castle* was experiencing a strong south-west wind and a heavy south-west swell, but, being 750 ft. long and of 28,600 gross tonnage, these conditions presented no serious problem to her. As she dipped into the swell she was spraying forward a little, and (on the big ones) shovelling up a little water through the hawse pipes. The reputation of the coast, my previous experience and my desire to avoid damage of any sort, decided me to abandon the benefit of the Agulhas current, put up with a later arrival and close the coast. To further ensure that no untoward incident should occur, I took a knot off her speed and, to close the coast I had, of course, put the swell cosily on the bow instead of driving into it head-on. Under these conditions she was very comfortable for three-quarters of an hour or so. The distance from one wave top to the next was about 150 ft. and the ship was pitching and scending about 10–15 degrees to the horizontal. And then it happened. Suddenly, having scended normally, the wave length appeared to be double the normal, about 300 ft., so that when she pitched she charged, as it were, into a hole in the ocean at an angle of 30 degrees or more, shovelling the next wave on board to a height of 15 or 20 ft. before she could recover, as she was "out of step".

It was a hot night and so that the passenger accommodation might get some air, the steel doors at the after end of the foredeck had been left open, but, due to an oversight, this information was not passed to the bridge, so that not only was the foredeck swept with a wall of water which unseated the insurance wire reel which damaged a winch in its travel, and swept away the athwartship rails and the ladder to the well-deck, but a great quantity of water flooded into the passenger accommodation.

The lessons to be learned are twofold. Firstly, that whatever the weather prevailing the forward steel doors must always be shut and remain shut on passage from Durban to East London, because when this happens there will be no warning. The waves are no higher than their fellows, and in perspective the "hole" is not visible until the ship is about to fall into it! Secondly, that as this is out of keeping with the weather prevailing at the time, such a thing could happen in conditions of little or no wind at all.

Another question which poses itself is: why, after hundreds of voyages between Durban and East London, have I never experienced this before? I think the answer to that is that, in any event, it is very locally confined, and if it be a line as opposed to a spot, it is still easily possible to pass outside it, inside it, or to close or open the coast north or south of it. I have closed the coast before to get out of an awkward swell, but the decision to do this was taken at the time and my ship may well have been north or south of her position on this occasion, though, as far as I can recall, the action was always taken somewhere "off St. Johns". In this case the ship was just closing the hundred-fathom line on a true course of 260 degrees.

Commodore Byles's article was reported in the national Press and brought the following comments from Commander I. R. Johnston, R.N. (Retired):

When I was serving in the cruiser *Birmingham* during the Second World War we had a similar experience in those waters one night which I recall the more vividly for being on watch at the time. We were about 100 miles south-south-west of Durban on our way to Cape Town, steaming fast but quite comfortably into a moderate sea and swell when suddenly we hit the "hole" and went down like a plummet into the next sea which came green over A and B turrets and broke over our open bridge. I was knocked violently off my feet, only to recover and find myself wading around in 2 ft. of water at a height of 60 ft. above normal sea-level.

The ship was so jarred by the impact that many of the watch below thought we had been torpedoed and went to emergency stations. The Captain immediately reduced speed, but the precaution proved unnecessary, as the moderate conditions returned as before and no further "holes" appeared.

This experience, occurring as it did in pitch darkness in a blacked-out ship, was quite one of my most alarming at sea and I can well believe that a deeply laden ship might founder under similar circumstances.

In subsequent discussions we put the phenomenon down to the shelving of the Agulhas bank; this would account for the steepness of the swell, but not entirely for the sudden increase in swell length.

The conditions in which the "holes" appeared were those of a fairly heavy swell, the familiar characteristics of which are groups of large waves followed by an interval of relatively low waves. It seems possible that the holes were caused by the chance coincidence, already explained, of a large number of wave components in exactly the same way as high crests are formed. If the depth of the "hole" were, say, more than five times the average trough depth, the chance of it occurring to one vessel would require the time equivalent of scores of lifetimes at sea, so perhaps there is no wonder that such things are rarely seen.

The incidence of alarming waves off the South African coast has been highlighted recently by several occurrences. In one, the *Bencruachuan* was brought to a sudden halt by a large wave and the entire bow section was bent downwards until the bow was 20 feet lower than it should have been; the main beams become instantaneously white hot at the point of bending. The vessel stayed afloat, but had to be towed stern first into harbour. Another vessel, the container vessel *Neptune Sapphire*, had her bow section removed on her maiden voyage in a similar incident. It seems possible that the cause of these problems in this area is that the 60 to 100 mile wide Agulhas current sweeps south westward at a speed of 4 or 5 knots along the coast, often meeting a heavy swell coming up from the Antarctic. At the interface where the swell meets the current, the swell reacts by slowing down and by increasing its wave height. In extreme cases the wave heights may try to increase beyond the limits of steepness (ratio of height over length) within which a progressive wave can exist. The excess energy must then be dissipated almost instantly by wave breaking presenting a barrier which must be impenetrable by virtually any vessel. This could explain why a vessel travelling in moderate waves, either in or out of the Agulhas current, suddenly meets much more severe conditions in which, had she enough time, she would normally expect to reduce speed, but as the width of this interface is very small she receives virtually no warning, and by the time the increased severity has been appreciated she is through the interface and into somewhat quieter waters. It is only the unlucky vessels which, by mischance, arrive at the interface when the wave components are all in step, which suffer the severe damage. As the current meanders somewhat, and maybe even sheds eddies, the position of the interface changes from hour to hour, so no precise position for the dangerous areas can be given. This situation has been given prominence because it occurs on a busy shipping lane; if the explanation is correct the same cause, and effects, can occur in many waters of the world, and for small vessels the results can be just as drastic. For example, the race off Portland Bill is an example of the ferocity of the battle between waves and current, and few prudent small-boat sailors would venture near it with waves running into an opposing current.

On many occasions a freak wave is not just alone—sometimes two or three waves, all much bigger than the general run of large waves, are seen to occur together, and, of course, in such cases they have deep troughs between them. Many a vessel must have been lost when the first wave laid her over on her side and she did not have time to right herself before another and possibly larger wave crashed down on her exposed side. In those conditions no one survives to tell what happened. Recent figures from Lloyds show that over a ten-year period an average of 77 sea-going vessels, each of over 100 tons displacement, were lost every year due to overwhelming by the sea itself, without the aid of rocks, reefs or collision. One of these was a vessel of 20,000 tons displacement.

One of the most damaging features to a small yacht must be the breaking of waves, when the actual slope of the surface can reach the vertical. There is a theoretical limit to the height which a progressive wave can sustain for a given wave length; when the wave height reaches one-seventh of its length the accelerations required of the particles become too large for gravity to restrain, and the wave crest disintegrates. If the combined wave components reach this height, it needs little imagination to decide what will happen to any luckless vessel which finds itself at the crest. Of course, in a strong wind the higher waves can appear to break purely by having their tops blown off, giving the familiar "white horses", and the mass of water blown off on to a vessel temporarily in the lee can make life uncomfortable to say the least.

It is not only on the deep sea where frightening wave heights can occur in generally moderate conditions. If a wave runs over a shallow bank its speed is reduced and therefore the distance between one crest and the following one [the wavelength] is reduced, the energy is compressed into a smaller area and therefore the wave height has to increase. The result is that over shallow banks, and on a beach as well, the wave activity can be more dangerous than over deeper water.

We have already seen the effect of waves meeting a current in deep water; in shallower waters the current speeds can be even higher and the effect on the waves is much more dramatic. A wave will be stopped completely when it meets an opposing current travelling at a quarter of the speed of the wave, which will build up into a frightening wall of water. In both of these cases there will be an area of turbulent water which is continually being disturbed and which can be seen from a distance. Of course, waves in such places cannot truly be called freaks, but nevertheless it is always wise to give them a wide berth.

In waters around the British Isles away from the coasts, wave measuring instruments have shown that quite large waves can occur in normal conditions; this is without having to invoke any degree of improbability. Each year off Lands End the highest wave will be over 50 feet from crest to trough, and even in the eastern English Channel, southern North Sea and in the Irish Sea the highest waves are likely to exceed 30 feet in height. In the northern parts of the North Sea the highest waves are likely to be around 60 to 70 feet in height and out in the Atlantic around 70 to 80 feet high. These figures apply to an average year; in rougher ones the waves will be even higher.

Although freak waves have been illustrated by reference to observations from ocean-going vessels, the same mechanisms must apply to sea waves of all heights and periods, so that the skipper of a small yacht cruising for pleasure in coastal waters should keep as alert an eye for the unusual as the skipper of a racer in mid-ocean and the master of a liner in a storm. Although freak waves over deep water come in a vast assortment of shapes and sizes, they have the common characteristics that they appear with little or no warning, any one wave has a very short life, and they can all damage the unwary.

The extract from "The one from nowhere" is reproduced by kind permission of the Editors of the *British and Commonwealth Review*, house magazine of the British and Commonwealth Shipping Company, and the *Marine Observer*.

APPENDIX 3

REPORT OF THE SUB-COMMITTEE OF THE R.O.R.C.

The following are the principal findings after the Channel Storm
of 1956 which still hold good:

The basic lesson to be learned from this occasion is that in severe conditions it is far better to be out at sea in open water away from land influences, where, provided the vessel is well found and not hampered by the human element, she has the best chance of coming through without serious trouble. In general, the reports show the remarkable qualities of the modern sailing yacht in being able to look after herself, in spite of human error. Only three vessels, which struck the worst of the weather when in confined and most dangerous waters near the English coast, were in any real danger.

When nearing the finish of a race many a master would, no doubt, decide to take the risk of standing on rather than impair chances of success in the race by standing out to gain sea room, and this might, on occasion, prove unwise, but such decisions must be left to the master.

The main body of the fleet seem to have been situated between mid-Channel and a 12-mile-plus offing from the French coast. None of these vessels appear to have experienced any serious damage or to have been in real difficulties. The experience of these yachts does not help to show any preference for heaving to, lying to a sea anchor from the bow or stern, lying a-hull, or streaming warps ahead or astern.

In several cases storm gear and sail fastenings were of insufficient strength. Owners should be warned that all gear, and especially storm sails and their attachments, should be overhauled frequently to see that no deterioration has been suffered. Most damage to sails was caused by flogging causing the slides or hanks to carry away. Shackling the head and tack of headsails to the forestay would seem to be a sensible precaution.

Some vessels experienced trouble because a great deal of water got below through cockpit lockers, etc., even where self-draining cockpits were fitted.

It was found in one case that distress flares were ineffective in the prevailing conditions. Reliance should not be placed on flares which may have been exposed to the air or damp. The maker's directions should be studied carefully, and any suspect flares replaced.

The experience of *Right Royal* when dismasted illustrates the value of a serviceable pair of wire cutters.

One yacht had to anchor on a lee shore, and some of the crew received injuries which might have been serious when the cable took charge, because there was no chain stopper.

The yacht should carry a second pump and, most important, it should be possible to clear the strum box of the pump in any weather conditions.

THE YACHT: HER DESIGN AND CONSTRUCTION

In this and the following Appendix I will comment on the qualities of the yacht herself and of the equipment required in heavy weather. The subject is so wide that a whole book could be devoted to it, and I can only treat the subject broadly, mostly in the light of the experiences of yachts described in earlier chapters.

The ability of a yacht in heavy weather or a gale does not depend solely on wind and sea. It depends equally upon the yacht herself, taking her as a unit comprising design, sail plan, construction and in particular the condition of hull, mast, rigging and sails, and the strength and experience of her crew.

Size is not essential to survival in heavy weather, as has been proved time after time by the very small yachts which have safely crossed the Atlantic, such as the tiny *Nova Espero*, and by the increasing number of small boats which have accomplished long voyages, among them Bill Nance's 5-tonner *Cardinal Vertue* and the 20 ft. yawl *Trekka* in which John Guzzwell circumnavigated the world. Nevertheless, there is a lot of luck in the success or otherwise of long voyages, whether the yacht is large or small, and when it comes to meeting the greybeards in the Southern Ocean or round Cape Horn a large yacht stands a better chance than a small one.

In the ordinary way, by which I mean cruising and racing within a few hundred miles of one's home port, the best size of yacht for heavy weather is probably one of medium displacement of about 35 ft. overall, maybe a bit more or a little less in overall length, and round about 10 to 15 tons Thames measurement. I will call this medium sized, though in America the average size of a sea-going yacht is larger. In a boat such as this a great deal can be done by the sheer strength of one powerful man, and she can easily be handled in any weather by her normal crew.

When a yacht is much above this size the sail area in relation to the number of the crew will be greater. The individual sails (unless the area is split up into a number of small sails) are heavier and the pressure of the wind on them in bad weather will be incomparably higher. Individual beef in a big yacht will count for less, because however strong a man may be his strength is puny compared with the power exerted by big sails in strong winds. For this reason in a larger yacht it is teamwork, "know-how" and winches that count and, although I am a small-boat sailor, I readily concede that the bigger the yacht the higher the degree of seamanship that is called for in heavy weather. Reefing has to be done earlier and unreefing postponed until the weather has shown its hand, because it takes more time than in a smaller yacht, where it can be effected very quickly by an experienced crew. On the other hand, once snugged down, a bigger yacht will be more comfortable and with a bigger crew the spells at the helm will be shorter.

In a very small yacht of say 25 ft. overall the sail drill is lighter and can be done effortlessly by one man, except that the motion is livelier in a seaway, which makes it difficult to retain a footing on the foredeck. Reefing has to be done earlier than in a medium-sized boat. To sail hard on the wind in strong winds or a near gale requires weight and power to drive against the high breaking seas, which a small yacht usually lacks. On other points of sailing the small yacht is also at a disadvantage, expecially in strong tidal waters where, even at Force 6, when the wind is against the stream, the sea will be extremely rough in proportion to her size. A very small yacht seems happier on the oceans. It is in narrow waters that she has to be careful, partly because of the lack of power to get to windward, partly because her small crew of one or two has to cope with navigation and cooking as well as steering, seamanship and sail handling, and partly because the inshore seas, although lower than in the ocean, may well be more dangerous to her.

Seas in home waters should not be despised and, as marine underwriters will testify, casualties to shipping in the English Channel and North Sea are high. Many long-planned world voyages, have come to an early end at Falmouth, long before the ocean has been reached. H. G. Hasler, after crossing the Atlantic four times single-handed in his 5-ton folkboat *Jester*, told me that the only time his boat had suffered damage was in a severe gale (the tail end of a hurricane), not in the Atlantic but on the east coast of Scotland in '61, and this was caused by being in tidal waters with exceptionally steep seas.

While on the matter of size I must give a warning to those taking up yachting for the first time. Very small yachts, especially those with a big open cockpit like *Zara*, can be dangerous if caught out in gales, unless they have been deliberately designed for heavy weather sailing by an experienced designer. The lifeboats are kept busy during summer months rescuing small yachts which are unsuitable in design and in equipment. If a salesman at the Boat Show recommends some tiny yacht as "safe in Force 7" the chances are that his Force 7 is in reality a gusty Force 5, and this, after all, can be quite strong enough to cause trouble.

Turning now to the subject of design and construction, it can be said that there are good boats among all types of yacht, although it must be admitted that there are also some shockingly bad ones. The astonishing thing is that some of the great voyages in yachts have been made in what appear to have been woefully unsuitable craft. Their success must have been due to the seamanship of their crews aided perhaps by good luck.

Seaworthiness depends upon the skill of the designer, whatever the type. Light-displacement yachts can be good sea boats. They are easily driven by relatively small sail area, which sets up less strain on mast, rigging and hull. They are lively and give to the seas rather than fighting them. My first *Cohoe* was a good example, but she was designed in 1937 and there have been great developments in light-displacement yachts since then. The best example in this book is *Tilly Twin* (Chap. 11). Designed by Laurent Giles, she has the characteristics of strength combined with lightness, and her owner considers that she would not have weathered the Channel Storm of 1956 but for these qualities. Light-displacement yachts are not always tender, but I remember years ago the great designer, Charles E. Nicholson, told me that in his opinion a tender yacht was usually a good sea boat in the sense that she imposed less strain on her rigging and hull in heavy weather than a stiff one.

A good heavy-displacement yacht is at least as equally able as a light one at sea. I used to be a light-displacement fan, but I have been converted to heavier displacement by *Cohoe III*, which I have found to be a better sea boat. On the same length she has far more room, but the principal difference is the immeasurably improved windward performance in really heavy weather. She can stand up to much higher winds. Against this is the fact that she needs more sail area to drive her, which imposes much greater strain on mast, rigging, sails and hull. However, a heavy-displacement boat can have proportionately heavier scantlings, mast and rigging. I have had fewer breakages in the heavy boat than I had in the light, and, after ten years of hard racing, there is no movement in the hull and the topsides look as smooth as plastic. However, the strength is achieved at the expense of heavier weight, which is a disadvantage when ocean racing in light or moderate winds. My own preference, if building again, would be towards moderate displacement and a well-proportioned hull with no extreme features.

There are, however, two points for attention. The stern must be buoyant for running before gales, whether at speed or with warps streamed. The two examples of pooping, Chapters 2 and 8, illustrate the need for buoyancy aft, but one cannot lay down any rule for the shape of stern. *Lehg II* and *Joshua* had sharp ended sterns which proved satisfactory even in the storms of the Southern Ocean, but there is much to be said in favour of transom or short counter sterns. Transoms and all shapes of stern must be strong. Note damage to transoms: *Stormy Weather* (Chap. 15) and *Marie Galante II* (Chap. 16).

Likewise buoyancy is needed forward. I once owned a little straight-stemmed yacht that looked a picture of a sea boat, but her forward sections were so lean that I could run her bows under even in the Solent. A fine bow is not a good feature in gales and storms (*Pendragon*, Chap. 20), and adds to the risk of pitch poling.

High freeboard is an asset, as shown by *Tilly Twin*, *Petasus* and *Callisto* (Chap. 11), but I fancy that excessive sheer forward may cause the bows to blow off to leeward in very high winds, especially if the boat is under auxiliary power. Although straight or reverse sheer used to offend my conventional eyes, I am coming to the conclusion that they contribute to seaworthiness in small yachts, as they afford room below without resort to the high superstructures which are a common source of weakness. When the reverse-sheered *Tom Bowling* was knocked down and dismasted by a sea (Chap. 22) her hull was undamaged, whereas if she had been fitted with a high coachroof and doghouse these would undoubtedly have been split open on the lee side.

A moderately long keel contributes towards steadiness on the helm, whereas the excessive reduction in wetted surface of many ocean racers does the reverse. There is no objection to centreboards for weathering gales, but when it comes to meeting survival storms there seems to be an element of risk if the yacht is thrown down on her side so that the stability conferred by her beam is lost—*Doubloon* (Chap. 18) Edward Greeff's comment at conclusion of Chap. 17.

For ocean voyaging, where there is even a remote possibility of being rolled over, inside ballast is dangerous and any heavy objects such as batteries (*Doubloon*, Chap. 18) or ice box (*Marie Galante II*, Chap. 16) which can break loose may injure the crew. Dumas had no inside ballast in *Lehg II*, and Deane had removed 7 cwt. of inside ballast and substituted a lead keel in *Tom Bowling*, to which her survival when she was knocked down in the Bay of Biscay is possibly due (Chap. 22).

The matter of construction is also best left to the designer. Strength is essential for a boat which may have to weather storms, and should not be sacrificed for lightness in order to obtain higher racing speed. The desire to save weight can be carried to such extremes that some yachts are not really fit to go to sea. I know one such that was caught out in the open sea in a Force 6 in the Bay of Biscay and had to heave-to because she began to disintegrate under sail. I know others which after only a season's use leak like sieves, but I give no names. There is no need for such light scantlings in ocean racers, as the scantling allowance compensates for the extra weight required for strength. This is shown by the Sparkman & Stephens designed "One Tonners", which have relatively heavy scantlings, and by other designers.

For voyaging in dangerous waters, such as the high latitudes and round Cape Horn, Bernard Moitessier recommends a steel hull (Chap. 20) and he certainly ought to know. But the scantlings of steel hulls vary, and I fancy *Joshua*'s must be of fairly heavy gauge. I know of one steel-hulled ocean racer that bashed in one bow when she fell off a wave when thrashing to windward in a gale. She then went on the other tack and bashed in the other bow. After that she carried on with both sides bashed and won the race, which after all was the object of the exercise. The experience serves to illustrate that the scantlings in a steel hull are as important as in a timber one.

Superstructure

By this I mean cabin tops, coachroofs, deckhouses, doghouses, skylights and any excrescence above the deck. The lesson reiterated throughout this book is that when damage occurs it is due to the yacht being thrown down on her lee side so that the doghouse windows or the coachroof coaming are smashed. See references: *Vertue XXXV* (Chap. 7), *Tilly Twin* and *Dancing Ledge* (Chap. 11, *Tandala*, *Aloa* and *Marie Galante II* (Chap. 16), *Puffin* (Chap. 17), *Curlew* (skylight) and *Tzu Hang* (Chap. 20).

In a big yacht there is no need for high superstructures. She can even have sheer and flush decks while retaining plenty of headroom below. It is in medium-sized and particularly in small yachts that high coachroofs are required in order to provide reasonable comfort below. The height of these can be considerably reduced where the hull has reverse sheer, giving extra headroom just where it is wanted.

In fairness it must be said that few of the thousands of yachts with high superstructure have got into trouble by reason of them, because the average owner avoids getting caught out in severe gales if he can, and because these are rare in the summer months. Nevertheless, above-deck structures are an undoubted source of weakness, and certainly for ocean cruising some form of stiffening is required as suggested at the end of Chapter 17. Doghouse windows, and in fact any windows, should be fitted with panels which can be screwed over them in storms. It will have been noted that Joe

Byars had the four fixed windows in *Doubloon* replaced by smaller ports the year before she encountered a survival storm (Chap. 18). But for this foresight the yacht might have foundered. Deck fittings should not be skimped for the sake of saving weight, as all are vulnerable in heavy weather. For ocean voyaging Moitessier recommends steel deck and superstructures, or that if the deck is wood it should be flush.

Cockpits

The cockpit of a yacht is the most vulnerable part when running before gales, whether under bare poles, streaming warps or lying to a sea anchor astern. Heads of seas will constantly half fill it, and green water may fill it to the brim.

The cross-over drain pipes and their fittings are nearly always too small. See *Mary Aidan* (Chap. 3) (and it applies to all my boats), *Doubloon* (Chap. 18), *Force Seven* (Chap. 19), *Gypsy Moth IV* (Chap. 22). Cockpit cross-over drain pipes should be of wide diameter and in a large cockpit there should be four of them. I fancy the fittings are supplied by builders' merchants for domestic baths and sinks. Nearly half the effective area is lost in thick filters. Drainage is thus far too slow in the event of being pooped by a succession of seas.

The cockpit coamings should be strong, because in the event of a knockdown they are almost as liable to be carried away on the lee side as the coachroof or doghouse. Another weakness is leaking cockpit lockers, to which references is made in Chapter 11, and in the R.O.R.C. report in Appendix 3.

If a yacht is severely pooped and takes it green, the first impact will be at the forward end of the cockpit. Here a bridge-deck adds to the strength and the aft bulkhead of a coachroof should be strong. The cabin entrance should be closed by washboards and not by doors, which are always weak. Better still is to adopt Warren Brown's recommendation that there should be no direct access to the cabin from the cockpit. It should be through a hatch in the cabin top (Chap. 19).

The Modern Yacht

Let us first consider ocean racers. Yacht design over the past few years has been revolutionised, first by the influence of the One-Ton International events where yachts race level on rating with no handicaps and next by the introduction of the IOR (International Offshore Rule). The modern ocean racers are incomparably more efficient in sailing performance except perhaps in very heavy weather. Motion is livelier than in older boats and sail changes have to be more frequent as the area is critical and must be exactly right, neither too much and certainly not too little.

Cruising design tends to follow ocean racing fashion except in the smaller boats where the primary consideration may be the maximum number of berths within the minimum length. In some respects the older types with deeper bilges and with longer keels and rudders in the conventional position may be preferable to the short racing fin and skeg type. Some racing refinements such as internal halyards are not desirable for cruising and although sailing performance should be good there is no need to go to extremes.

RIG AND EQUIPMENT

The majority of modern yachts are sloops or cutters. The masthead sloop is a good rig for the small cruising yacht, as the absence of runners makes it easy to handle. It is also the fastest rig under R.O.R.C. rules, but there is a critical point, depending upon height and section, above which the mast cannot go without too much flexing, as it is unstayed fore and aft below the forestay and the backstay. *Cohoe III*'s mast used to flex considerably until I cut it down by 2 ft. to comply with the lower rating required for the One Ton races, which made an extraordinary improvement.

I have not sailed a cutter for many years, but experienced sailing men tell me that it is a better sea-going rig than a sloop, and it is adopted in many of the designs by John Illingworth. It is better stayed and allows a greater selection of headsails, which is useful in hard weather. In particular, a storm jib can be set to the inner stay to preserve a better balance when the mainsail is close-reefed, or a trysail is set, bringing the centre of effort forward.

I have a personal preference for a rig with two sticks independently stayed, because if one mast is lost it may be easier to contrive a jury rig aided by the one remaining. However, this line of thought may be prompted by the fact that yachts with any of the two-masted rigs are more satisfying to the eye than the conventional sloops. Schooners, ketches and yawls always look little ships.

The yawl rig is a good one (see references to *Cohoe II*, Chap. 9 and 10). In bad weather, with storm jib, reefed mainsail and mizzen, the sail area is split up over a number of small easily handled sails, set high so that they will not be struck by heavy seas. I had a sharp reminder of the danger of a low headsail in 1966, when we were carrying a masthead genoa in rough water south of Portland Bill. The reputedly "unbreakable" triple part tubular stainless steel bowsprit collapsed under the load when seas struck the low-cut genoa.

Another advantage of the yawl rig is that the mizzen provides a riding sail if it becomes necessary to lie to a sea anchor. On the other hand, a mizzen can be a bad sail if a boat is pooped by a freak wave (reference *Puffin*, Chap. 17). The advantages of sail area being divided over a number of sails are shared by ketches and schooners, the last-named being the prettiest rig of all.

Regarding sails, there is less trouble than there used to be, because terylene is incomparably stronger than canvas. What may give trouble is the stitching, which stands proud of the hard material and is easily chafed. There is much to be said in favour of extra lines of stitching and doubled patches where chafe is likely to occur. The latest terylene sail cloths are softer than the old, so the stitches sink deeper into the material, but after any hard blow sails require careful examination for broken stitches or signs of chafe. It is a matter of a stitch in time.

Storm sails (jib and trysail) need not be of very heavy material, because, although they have to stand up to gale or storm-force winds, their area is correspondingly small. They are not so cumbersome as the old canvas or flax storm sails, which were heavy to set, and worse to stow, when soaked through. A terylene mainsail is so strong that when reefed down it can be used instead of a trysail, but a storm trysail is a useful sail to have in the locker in case of damage to the mainsail and as a reserve sail for any yacht making long passages. Where a mainsail is roller reefed, and no trysail is carried, it should have cringles and a row of eyelets, so that a deep reef can be tied in if the roller reefing fails.

Many sails were torn in the Channel gale of 1956 (Chap. 11), but the principal troubles came from lifting of tracks, and breaking of hank attachments. Storm jibs should be shackled to the forestay at the head and tack. Slides on mainsail or trysail should be close spaced, and it is useful to have eyes in the luff of the trysail so that it can be laced to the mast as far up as the lower cross-tree—*Joliette* (Chap. 11).

The modern light-alloy mast is not an object of craftsmanship like a hollow spruce mast, but of its efficiency there is no doubt. Nevertheless, there is a tendency towards masts of too small a section in order to save weight and windage. This can be carried to absurd extremes, as exemplified by a yacht that lost three masts before entering her first serious race. Dismastings occur only too often in hard weather among ocean racers usually at about Force 5 or 6, when the maximum sail is being carried. There may be less risk of dismasting in gales when under storm canvas and the strains are reduced, unless the gales are very severe and the boat is knocked down or capsized by a sea—*Doubloon* (Chap. 18), *Tzu Hang* (Chap. 20), *Tom Bowling* (Chap. 22). Dismasting is a serious matter and, having regard to the frequency of the occurrence, it is surprising that there have not been more losses by reason of it. Despite having a strong mast and rigging in *Cohoe III*, I am always anxious when racing close to a lee shore in heavy weather.

For standing rigging I prefer galvanized steel and splices. It is more expensive than stainless, because it has to be replaced more often, but one can at least see when it deteriorates, whereas with stainless rigging fatigue is difficult to identify until the wire breaks. There is also an element of doubt about swaged ends. External halyards are preferable to windage-saving internal ones, because in the event of breakage they can be repaired or replaced. Sheaves should be of large diameter.

Dismasting is most often not due to the mast itself but to breakages of spreaders or tangs and to failure of rigging screws or shackles. These should therefore be of best quality, large enough to provide a good factor of safety. Stainless snap hooks break so often, despite their manufacturer's assertions to the contrary, that quantities of them are consumed in an ocean-racing season, or in a Transatlantic Race, but breakages are fewer when cruising as yachts are not usually driven so hard.

EQUIPMENT

It is useful to refer to the special regulations governing minimum equipment for yachts racing under the IOR (International Offshore Rule). These may be obtained from the national authorities in each country. They are divided into four categories ranging from long distance well offshore down to short inshore races in relatively warm or protected water, and the regulations are also useful as a guide for cruising yachts. The following comments are in no way outdated but the regulations go into greater detail such as improved navigation lights, and soft wood tapered plugs as emergency stoppers for broken pipework etc.

Radar reflector. In very heavy weather with big seas and spray the range of navigation lights is low, and the only light likely to be seen at a reasonable distance is an all-round masthead light. A radar reflector provides a better chance of the presence of a yacht being picked up by a ship.

Dinghy. Rigid dinghies can become a menace in very severe gales. They may be carried away (*Tandala*, Chap. 16) or crushed by seas (*Puffin*, Chap. 17), and if they break adrift they may injure the crew, which is what Warren Brown was anxious about (*Force Seven*, Chap. 19). Undoubtedly an inflatable rubber dinghy is better than a rigid one, because it can be stowed below uninflated, or on deck, upside down, if blown up, and cannot damage anybody even if it comes adrift.

Life-rafts. Circumstances may arise where a life-raft offers the only means of survival. The rafts should be capable of carrying the whole crew, and its pack should include drogue, bellows, signalling torch, hand and parachute flares, bailer, repair kit, paddles, knife and rescue Quoit. Biscuits and water are sometimes included in the pack, otherwise they must be added before the raft is cast off. A canopy is desirable, as the principal danger in a raft comes from exposure, but I imagine that a canopy would add considerable windage in a storm and add to the risk of capsize. Rafts should be overhauled every season, because, rather surprisingly, water gets into their covering and there is often deterioration, even after only one season. Stowage and positioning of a liferaft requires thought, because it must be available quickly if required at all. Note *Force Seven*'s experience, when it took twenty-five minutes to move the raft from forward to the cockpit in a hurricane (Chap. 19).

Fog horn. This obviously necessary in the rain and bad visibility of a warm front, but many fog horns would not be heard upwind in a gale.

Bow and stern pulpits and double lifelines. These fittings should be strong if they are to be of service, and stanchions should be through-bolted. They may break and often bend. See *Cohoe* (Chap. 5), *Tilly Twin*, *Theta*, Channel Storm (Chap. 11), *Puffin* (Chap. 17), *Doubloon* (Chap. 18). Lifelines are usually of the minimum 24 in. height to save windage and reduce interference with genoa sheeting, but this is low for a big man.

Rigid covers. Panels are required for screwing down over deckhouse windows exceeding 8 in. height; otherwise they nearly always break if a yacht is knocked down by a sea, of which many examples are given.

Bilge pumps. Two are the minimum, and it is best to have one operated from the cockpit and one from below. They must be fitted with strum boxes or wire mesh to prevent choking (see *Puffin*, Chap. 17). Two buckets should also be carried to bail out below in emergency, or assist in bailing the cockpit if the drains are inadequate.

Hatches and skylights. These must be secured to prevent loss overboard.

Life-jackets for each member of the crew, see pages 135, 143, Chap. 11, as to type.

Lifebuoys. Two, one of which should be rigged within reach of the helmsman and fitted with a self-igniting light. A brilliant electronic flare waterlight was invaluable to *Scylla* when one of her crew went overboard at night (Chap. 16). One lifebuoy should be heavy (see *Galloper*, Chap. 12). or equipped with a drogue. The horseshoe type is considered best. Lifebuoys may be carried away by seas when the cockpit is filled (see *Doubloon*, Chap. 18, and *Force Seven*, Chap. 19). Suitable stowage to prevent this, but leave them ready for instant casting off, presents a problem.

Personal safety belts or harness. There are many examples in this book of men being catapulted or swept overboard by seas. *Cohoe* and *Erivale* (Chap. 5), *Galloper* (Chap. 12), *Aloa* (three men) (Chap. 16), *Puffin* (Chap. 17), *Doubloon* (three men) (Chap. 17), and *Djinn* (six men), *Royono*, *Scylla* (see page 174), and others in the 1960 Bermuda Race (Chap. 15). The most dangerous position is on the foredeck, shifting jibs or setting or lowering spinnakers. Safety belts cannot always be worn, because they hamper movement, but lines or wire rope can be fitted to the deck, on which the safety lines can be hooked, to permit of freedom to move fore and aft. However, the danger is so apparent that crews endeavour to keep a hand for themselves. Where most accidents take place is in the comparatively safe position of the cockpit, when safety belts are temporarily detached when changing helmsman, or when a man emerges from below to empty a gash bucket, to be sick or to come on watch. In very heavy gales seas (especially unexpected freak waves) may break aboard and sweep men over the side, but in nearly every case they are saved by their safety belts. Time and again safety belts and safety harness (which is better) have proved life savers. They, and especially their fittings, must be really strong, and they require proper stowage and attention and greasing to keep them in good order. The helmsman's lifeline should be short to hold him in position (*Puffin*, page 190).

Distress signals and flares. A useful average might be: 4 red parachute flares, 4 red hand flares, 4 white hand flares (to warn ships where necessary of the presence of the yacht) and 2 orange smoke day signals. Distress signals should be stowed in a watertight container. Hand flares may deteriorate with time. When brought on deck in heavy weather with rain or spray they should be stowed temporarily in polythene bags with rubber bands.

Emergency steering. Breakages of wheels (*Curlew*, Chap. 20) and of tillers are by no means rare in rough weather, and some form of emergency steering from the rudder stock is required. A curved tubular steel tiller with a fitting to screw round the rudder stock is useful as a substitute for a broken tiller. Breakages of rudders are almost as common as breakages of masts (Chap. 15), but owners and crews have got their ships safely back to port either by sail balance or by contriving steering sweeps, or by both means. Very fine seamanship is often shown in such passages back to port, whether rudderless or under jury rig.

First aid. Obviously a comprehensive first-aid outfit is a necessity in any yacht, together with instructions on its use. Accidents are more likely to occur during gales and rough seas than in normal weather. Sprains are common and ribs are easily broken, this accident happening to Humphrey Barton in *Vertue XXXV*, and to Joe Byars in *Doubloon*.

When *Puffin* was knocked down Mrs. Greeff's nose was broken. Minor injuries and bruises are common. Provision for burns and scalds is important (Chap. 4), because, when all seems peaceful, kettles and saucepans can suddenly take off from a gimballed stove if the boat is struck by an unexpectedly high sea. Handholds help to prevent injuries. In *Cohoe III* I have strong handholds in the saloon the whole length of each cabin coaming, in the centre, and at galley and chart table and wherever they can be fitted, as well as on deck.

Tools. A set of tools at least sufficient to enable simple repairs to be done is necessary on any kind of yacht. Wire cutters are desirable, because in event of dismasting it enables the rigging to be cut away quickly (see *Right Royal*, Chap. 11). The list of tools should be as comprehensive as possible.

Provisions and water. When a long voyage or even a long passage such as across the Bay of Biscay is planned, provisioning is usually carefully calculated to include reserves in case of accident. However, when cruising in the ordinary way, making passages of only 100 miles or so, the matter of provisioning may not be given the same amount of thought, as stores can be replenished at the next port. When racing in an average off-shore event of about 200 miles, reserves of provisions usually provide only for an extra day in order to save weight.

My complacency in this matter received a rude shock when a friend related the following experience. His yacht was dismasted in the Little Russel and the tide carried her south of Guernsey. Here the wind took charge and she was carried round Ushant and off the Bay of Biscay, being unable to make any progress eastwards under jury rig. When eventually the yacht reached port the crew were nearly starving. That this could happen in what are virtually home waters seems incredible, having regard to the number of ships and fishing vessels using them, but it happens to be true. The distress signals were never seen.

The lesson drawn is that the sea can be a very empty place if one gets into trouble and most yachts (including my own) carry inadequate reserves of food and water. I have referred to minimum water consumption (Chap. 5). There should if possible be two or more independent water tanks which can be shut off from each other by cocks. It is essential also to have emergency water rations in a separate container. As regards provisions, I need only add that carbohydrates (biscuits, sugar, sweets, etc.) provide the most compact form of survival rations.

THE LOSS OF MORNING CLOUD

This account of the tragic disaster which befell Mr. Edward Heath's third *Morning Cloud* on the night of 2nd September, 1974, with the loss of two crewmen, has been added as a late Appendix because there is much to be learnt or relearnt from the mishap.

Morning Cloud was just under 45 ft. in overall length and like her predecessors was of Sparkman and Stephens design. She was the boat in which Mr. Heath sailed as a member of the British Admiral's Cup team of 1973 and was built by Lallows at Cowes, who also built the second *Morning Cloud*. The construction of cold moulded multi-layered Honduras mahogany planking is considered to be very strong and she was well equipped in all respects.

On completion of a successful week's racing at Burnham-on-Crouch, she was handed over as usual to an amateur crew numbering seven, with Don Blewett as skipper, to sail to Cowes. All except Christopher Chadd had been on similar deliveries of all three *Morning Clouds*. All the crew were experienced, although two were rather less so than the rest.

Casse Tete IV (a standard glass fibre Nautor built Sparkman and Stephens' Swan 41) was making the same passage and made a fast time taking the quickest course between the sands across the Thames Estuary. During the severe gale which was to follow she maintained a speed of 6 to 7 knots with 12 rolls in her mainsail and storm jib, which enabled her to reach the shelter of the Isle of Wight without mishap.

Morning Cloud made a good but slower passage as Don Blewett was in no hurry and doubtless felt the responsibility of skippering such a famous boat. He took the safest course east of the dangers of the Thames Estuary and always reefed earlier than perhaps he might otherwise have done.

The cause of the exceptionally heavy weather which developed towards the end of the passage was a deep depression which moved into the St. George's Channel, midway between the Isles of Scilly and Ireland, about 0400 British Summer Time (which I shall use throughout) on September 2nd. By 1900 the depression was centred off the coast of Wales. It was moving on a NE course across England toward the North Sea and had deepened to a central pressure of 972 millibars giving rise later to severe gale to storm force winds in parts of the eastern part of the English Channel, but the unstable conditions were marked by wide variations in wind values over relatively short distances. The worst was felt in the vicinity of Beachy Head and the Royal Sovereign light tower to the eastward of the two boats. This is shown in the accompanying synoptic chart at 2200, an hour before *Morning Cloud's* first knock down, which I will come to later, when she was somewhere about half way between the Royal Sovereign to the east where force 10 was reported at 2300 and St. Catherines Point in the Isle of Wight, where hourly meteorological records are kept which show that winds of no more than force 8 were recorded and then only for two hours.

Morning Cloud and *Casse Tete* reported winds of 45 to 50 knots and, allowing for differences between apparent and true wind, agree with the 43 to 47 knots, severe gale 9 on the synoptic chart.

The B.B.C. shipping forecasts given earlier that day for sea area Wight at 0630 were for winds "Southerly 6 to gale 8 veering SW *perhaps* severe gale 9 later," and at 1355 for winds "South 6 to gale 8, *locally* severe gale 9 veering SW. Periods of heavy rain." The forecasts were right but I have italicised the words "perhaps" and "locally" because they represent warnings of the highest probable winds rather than definite forecasts of them. Both Don Blewett in *Morning Cloud* and John Irving in *Casse Tete* independently took the same decision to carry on, as there was every prospect of reaching the shelter of the Isle of Wight encountering no more than the boats were well able to cope with.

Returning now to the passage of *Morning Cloud*, she was slightly west of Brighton at about 1830 steering on a course, after allowing for leeway, of west magnetic for the Owers Lanby (large automatic navigation buoy) which had recently replaced the light vessel, and the weather was worsening. Blewett gave the order for a second reduction in sail in advance of possible further deterioration. First the small genoa was lowered, but not replaced by the storm jib as it could not be found. This did not worry him as he did not want to risk men working on the narrow foredeck head-to-wind at night if it had to be lowered again in the weather that might come later. The mainsail was then reefed right down leaving only a third standing. The boat was then ready if necessary to face storm conditions. Under this reduced sail the speed fell to 4 or 5 knots but was much less over the bottom owing to a foul easterly running tide which would not slacken much before midnight.

It was well that he had drastically shortened sail because about half an hour later the wind rose to force 7–9 and the sea was becoming wild. The wave tops were being sheered off in the gusts and it became difficult to see or hear.

By nightfall the flash of the Owers buoy had been reported. The wind had risen to 40–50 knots giving an average of 45 knots, severe gale 9, accompanied by violent gusts. *Morning Cloud* continued to sail on in the turmoil of the seas, well balanced under her close reefed mainsail alone. The hatch over the companion way was closed but so little heavy water was coming aboard aft that the wash boards did not have to be positioned across the entrance.

At 2200 the watch was taken by the highly experienced Nigel Cumming with Gardner Sorum. Gerry Smith, mate of the other watch, returned on deck later and lay down wedged in the narrow space outside the top of the companion way where he soon dozed off. Towards 2300 three men including Christopher Chadd, the youngest in the crew, were below lying down in the saloon and Don Blewett was forward working amongst the sail bins.

All had continued well until about 2300, the fatal hour when *Morning Cloud* was suddenly struck by a gigantic wave on the port side, throwing her down so violently on the water that considerable damage was done, but the boat recovered quickly to even keel.

Gerry Smith who awoke immediately when submerged by water had seen Gardner Sorum trailing astern on his lifeline. He immediately shouted the alarm of "Man Overboard."

Two crewmen (Bob Taylor and Barry Kenilworth) rushed on deck. Don Blewett paused on the companion way to start the engine before joining the others. Working in the darkness in the rough seas it took the men nearly five minutes to pull Gardner Sorum out of the water over the transom and into the cockpit where he fell heavily. It was only then that it was realised that Nigel Cumming was missing. His lifeline had broken and by this time he was far astern.

The boat had remained on course and was still under control. Bob Taylor took the wheel and tacked (to gybe would probably have broken the boom) aided by the engine which soon stalled. *Morning Cloud* was then run off on a reciprocal course and the four men on deck searched for Nigel Cumming, who would be a small object at night in the breaking seas.

Don Blewett went below. He found several of the laminated deck beams had been split and there was about a foot of water above the cabin sole. He fetched the whip aerial from the forepeak and rigged it. He then attempted to transmit distress signals, but the switch on the handset would not activate the transmitter. Next he tried to send up parachute flares. The first and second failed to work and the third failed to gain altitude and was blown horizontally by the violent wind into the sea.

After over-running the position where *Morning Cloud* had been knocked down and Nigel Cumming might be found, the boat was tacked again bringing her back on her original westerly course while the search continued.

On arrival at about the position where the first wave had struck *Morning Cloud*, Christopher

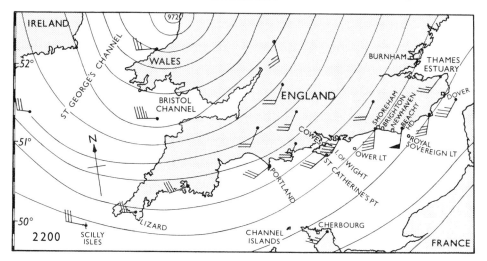

57   2200 Sept. 2, 1974, an hour before *Morning Cloud's* first knock down.

Chadd had just come up to the cockpit. He was wearing an inflated lifejacket but no harness. A warning was shouted to him but apparently not heard in the din of wind and sea.

At that critical moment *Morning Cloud* was struck by another huge wave. This time she was knocked right down bringing the masthead well below the sea. She lay capsized seemingly for many seconds with water from every sea cascading through the companion way and down the big forehatch, the cover of which had been carried away when the securing bolt broke. Then suddenly she righted.

The wave had swept Christopher Chadd overboard. He was seen in the sea only about twenty yards away. Bob tried to get one of the lifebuoys to throw, but the dan buoy lines were trapped under the helmsman's footrest which had been displaced by the sea. Every effort was then made to throw him a line but in seconds he was lost in the tumultuous seas.

The three other men on deck were safe, but the spreaders on the mast were twisted about 45° from their normal position athwartships and the forward compass had gone. The top of the port side cockpit locker was missing and with it the 6-man raft contained in it. The coaming bearing her name level with the main hatch on the lee side and a length of the toe rail had become de-tached. Down below more deck beams were found split or broken away from the deck completely and the water was nearly waist deep. This was more than could be accounted for by entry through the hatches alone.

Of the survivors Don Blewett had broken a shoulder blade and three ribs, one of which had perforated his lung. Gardner Sorum had also broken three ribs and his right arm was broken in three places. Gerry Smith had one cracked and three displaced vertebrae. Of the seven men who had sailed from Burnham the previous day, only two remained relatively unharmed.

The lives of the five men were at stake and Don Blewett feared that another wave like the first two must surely send *Morning Cloud* to the bottom. He gave the order to abandom ship.

The 4-man life raft remained intact and was inflated on deck and put over the side. Boarding it was not difficult because *Morning Cloud* was already so low in the water that the raft was level with the freeboard of the yacht. Gardner Sorum, crippled by his injuries, was helped into the raft and they cast off.

Five men drifting towards a lee shore in a 4-man raft through the night in a severe gale offered a grim prospect and Don told me later that he had little hope of survival at the time. The seas at first were as alarming as he had feared, but strangely enough it proved fortunate that they were in the 4-man instead of the 6-man life raft because the concentrated weight of the 5 men in the middle within it acted as ballast. They streamed the drogue which checked the speed and steadied it to the following seas and the canopy acted as a drag sail. After a while the seas moderated somewhat but the motion of the raft caused seasickness.

Under the influences of wind and tide (which was about to turn to the west) the raft drifted towards Shoreham. At 0500 before it got light a handflare was lit, but further attempts tried later including the parachute flares failed as they were too wet from spray and water within the raft.

There had been a growing threat of being carried against Shoreham breakwater, but at about this time the wind veered and the early inshore easterly running stream commenced so that the raft was carried quite quickly eastward along the coast. It passed Hove and about half way between Brighton Palace Pier and the Marina works it entered surf about a quarter mile offshore.

The first breaker capsized the raft and its crew were thrown through the canopy into the sea but they hung to the lifelines of the raft. The next wave in the surf righted it and two of the injured men were helped back inside. Don Blewett (despite his injuries) and the other two remained in the water holding onto its lifelines and swimming to guide the raft on its way through the surf to the shore. Finally it was dragged in until it grounded on the sand where willing helpers waded out to their assistance. The survivors landed at 0733 and the ambulance arrived to take them quickly to hospital.

Immediately after the survivors had been landed and the alarm given an intensive search for *Morning Cloud* was put into operation by the Shoreham Lifeboat, a rescue helicopter and the light cruiser *Glamorgan*. Apart from the piece of the coaming bearing her name which was washed ashore at Shoreham the same morning not a sign of her could be found.

It was not until a week later (10th September) that it was reported in the press that two small trawlers had fouled their nets on an obstruction about two miles off Shoreham (5 miles west of Brighton where the raft landed,) in about forty feet of water. The skipper of a fishing boat who was also a diver was called in to investigate and discovered they were foul of the damaged hull of a yacht. He attached ropes to the hull and it was towed in, lifted and moored on buoys outside the harbour. This was *Morning Cloud*, (Plate 23) with nearly half her starboard side broken away, dismasted and with her keel and engine gone. Little remained of her except for the planking on the port side but her bows were intact forward of the position of the missing forehatch cover. It is thought that an air pocket had formed here which, with the timber in the remaining planking, gave the neutral buoyancy which enabled the wreck to be towed to Shoreham.

There are many theories of how the drastic damage might have occurred. My own is that after abandonment she probably drifted shoreward gradually filling until finally she went down in the surf somewhere near where the wreck was found. The surge on the sea bed could have been enough to account for the damage if she were lying on her side bumping on the bottom for over a week which included another severe SW gale the following weekend.

I now come back to the position of *Morning Cloud* at the time when she was struck by the first big wave reported as 9 to 10 miles eastward of the Owers buoy.

The visibility was good between rain squalls and Don tells me that he had identified the Owers Lanby light buoy with certainty as it gives very short brilliant flashes which are absolutely unmistakeable. The set of the tidal streams had set *Morning Cloud* slightly northwards as it had *Casse Tete* and the light buoy was bearing fine on the port bow. This is corroborated by two crewmen, who were on deck and are both highly experienced men.

Looking at the Admiralty chart covering the Owers to Beachy Head I see that the position of *Morning Cloud* as reported was in about 12 fathoms allowing for rise of tide. When I consulted Laurence Draper he said he considered at that depth the waves at the time would not have been severely affected by the sea bed and therefore any unusually high wave, or group of waves, would be caused by the chance super-position of wave components. He added that at a depth of 5 fathoms there would have been the occasional plunging breaker similar to those which can be seen when storm waves or swell approach a beach. This is a significant point which the reader should bear in mind for the future. However, quite unpredictably high waves can occur in deeper water as was shown by the 42 ft. wave at the *Daunt* light-vessel, referred to in Laurence Draper's Appendix 2. This was in 18 fathoms and other examples have been known.

The two waves which struck *Morning Cloud* must have been very abnormal both in height and steepness. They follow the pattern of freak waves traced throughout this book where a yacht may be picked up under a breaking crest and thrown bodily down against the water below, damaging her on the *lee* side as she strikes the water. That is what happened to Humphrey Barton's *Vertue XXXV* in 1950 and has happened to other boats since, but the damage done in earlier examples to boats of older type has usually been limited to smashing the doghouse windows and splitting the coamings of the coach roof. In the case of *Morning Cloud* the damage caused by the two waves was far more serious as it was structural.

Conclusions. At the Inquest a full enquiry was made into the disaster and the Coroner exonerated Mr. Blewett from any responsibility for the loss of *Morning Cloud* and the two members of her crew. As there had been premature and unreasonable criticism in circulation I welcomed this verdict.

Lee Shores. Granted that *Casse Tete* made the same passage without mishap, I think both boats would have been safer had they tacked to seaward immediately as the Owers light buoy opened on the port bow. The disaster underlines the R.O.R.C. recommendation given after the Channel Storm of 1956, page 311, that "it is better to be out at sea in open water away from land influences where . . . she has the best chance of coming through without serious trouble."

Life Rafts. The safe passage in a 4-man raft to a lee shore through very rough seas and finally through surf affords remarkable proof of the value of life rafts carried in yachts. Five men owe their lives to it. The Velcro fastening of the canopy and draw cord was not entirely adequate and the canopy had frequently to be held closed by hand; even so considerable amount of spray and water entered.

Safety Harness. The breakage of the line of a safety harness in *Morning Cloud* cost the life of one member of the crew and other failures of safety harnesses, lifelines and clip-on hooks have been reported. Maybe the shock loading in extreme cases can be greater than anticipated. Nothing can be more dangerous than safety equipment that is relied upon with absolute confidence and then fails at the critical moment. There seems to be a strong case for the testing of safety harnesses and their fittings and safety lines as there are now many makes on the market.

Distress Flares. Some of the flares and parachute flares proved useless both in *Morning Cloud* and in the life raft, owing to the exceptionally severe wind and weather conditions in the former and getting wet in the latter. These failures of flares did not cause loss of life but they prevented distress signals being made just when they were most wanted.

Fore Hatches. In modern ocean racers fore hatches have to be large to facilitate rapid changes of sail. During the severe gale one screw broke and three had worked loose in *Casse Tete's* fore hatch, simple to repair in normal conditions but risky in a severe gale, involving men having to work on the fore deck. In *Morning Cloud* the cover was washed away by the second wave and left about 9 sq. feet open to every sea which cascaded below. The strengthening of fore hatches and fittings certainly merits consideration.

Pumps. In a boat lacking bilges it is difficult to rid her of any accumulation of water in very rough seas because the pumps can only operate momentarily when the strum box is immersed as the water rushes across from one side to the other. (I found the same thing in *Cohoe V*, a Sparkman and Stevens 31.) As Butch Dalrymble-Smith remarked on the *Sayula II* capsize, "The best bilge pump of all is a bucket in the hands of a frightened man."

Final Point. It has been argued that extra high waves from the synchronisation of wave trains should not be called freaks as they arise from natural causes, but as all seas come from natural causes this appears somewhat pedantic. It is the shape and steepness of occasional freak (abnormal) waves as well as their size which can do the damage. The addition of the *Morning Cloud* disaster to other mishaps described in this book may cause anxiety but I must emphasize that such occurrences are extremely rare and their number is infinitesimal compared with the countless safe passages made by yachts all over the world.

BEAUFORT WIND SCALE

Force 5 to Force 12

Beaufort number	* Limits of wind speed in knots	Descriptive terms	Sea criterion
5	17–21	Fresh breeze	Moderate waves, taking a more pronounced long form; many white horses are formed. (Chance of some spray.)
6	22–27	Strong breeze	Large waves begin to form; the white foam crests are more extensive everywhere. (Probably some spray.)
7	28–33	Near gale	Sea heaps up and white foam from breaking waves begins to be blown in streaks along the direction of the wind.
8	34–40	Gale	Moderately high waves of greater length; edges of crests begin to break into spindrift. The foam is blown in well-marked streaks along the direction of the wind.
9	41–47	Strong gale	High waves. Dense streaks of foam along the direction of the wind. Crests of waves begin to topple, tumble and roll over. Spray may affect visibility.
10	48–55	Storm	Very high waves with long overhanging crests. The resulting foam in great patches is blown in dense white streaks along the direction of the wind. On the whole the surface of the sea takes a white appearance. The tumbling of the sea becomes heavy and shocklike. Visibility affected.
11	56–63	Violent storm	Exceptionally high waves. (Small and medium-sized ships might be for a time lost to view behind the waves.) The sea is completely covered with long white patches of foam lying along the direction of the wind. Everywhere the edges of the wave crests are blown into froth. Visibility affected.
12	64+	Hurricane	The air is filled with foam and spray. Sea completely white with driving spray; visibility very seriously affected.

* Measured at a height of 33 ft. above sea-level.

WIND SYMBOLS

The direction of the wind is indicated by arrows which fly with its direction. On the Beaufort Scale each long feather represents two figures and each half feather one figure on the notation. Thus three and a half feathers represents Force 7, which is 28–33 knots.

However, on the symbols printed below, which are now generally used by international meteorological organizations, and appear on weather charts, an arrow with no feather represents 1–2 knots, above which the symbols alter at intervals of 5 knots. Each half feather indicates a maximum of an extra 5 knots, and each feather 10 knots.

This can be confusing, because, for example, a symbol with three and a half feathers indicates 33–37 knots, but 34–37 knots would be Force 8 on the Beaufort Notation, which would have been indicated by four feathers had the older convention been used.

symbol	knots	symbol	knots
	1 – 2		43 – 47
	3 – 7		48 – 52
	8 – 12		53 – 57
	13 – 17		58 – 62
	18 – 22		63 – 67
	23 – 27		68 – 72
	28 – 32		73 – 77
	33 – 37		103 – 107
	38 – 42		

CONVERSION TABLE
Inches to millibars

Inches	Millibars	Inches	Millibars	Inches	Millibars
28.35	960	29.09	985	29.83	1,010
28.50	965	29.23	990	29.97	1,015
28.64	970	29.38	995	30.12	1,020
28.79	975	29.53	1,000	30.27	1,025
28.94	980	29.68	1,005	30.42	1,030

INDEX

Page numbers in italics indicate figures

INDEX